FEB 1 3 2014

VARIORUM COLLECTED STUDIES SERIES

Approaches to Monteverdi

Jeffrey Kurtzman

Jeffrey Kurtzman

Approaches to Monteverdi

Aesthetic, Psychological, Analytical and
Historical Studies

ASHGATE
VARIORUM

Jeffrey Kurtzman has asserted his moral right under the Copyright, Designs and Patents
Act, 1988, to be identified as the author of this work.

Published in the Variorum Collected Studies Series by

Ashgate Publishing Limited
Wey Court East
Union Road
Farnham, Surrey
GU9 7PT
England

Ashgate Publishing Company
Suite 3–1
110 Cherry Street
Burlington, VT 05401–3818
USA

www.ashgate.com

ISBN 9781409463337

British Library Cataloguing in Publication Data
A catalogue record for this book is available from the British Library.

The Library of Congress has cataloged the printed edition as follows: 2013932248

VARIORUM COLLECTED STUDIES SERIES CS1031

The paper used in this publication meets the minimum requirements of the American
National Standard for Information Sciences – Permanence of Paper for Printed Library
Materials, ANSI Z39.48–1984. ∞™

MIX
Paper from
responsible sources
FSC
www.fsc.org   FSC® C013056

Printed and bound in Great Britain by
TJ International Ltd, Padstow, Cornwall

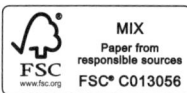

CONTENTS

This volume contains xviii + 288 pages

PUBLISHER'S NOTE

*The articles in this volume, as in all others in the Variorum Collected Studies
Series, have not been given a new, continuous pagination. In order to avoid
confusion, and to facilitate their use where these same studies have been
referred to elsewhere, the original pagination has been maintained wherever
possible. Article IV has necessarily been reset with a new pagination, and with
the original page numbers given in square brackets within the text. Article XII
appears here for the first time.*

*Each article has been given a Roman number in order of appearance, as
listed in the Contents. This number is repeated on each page and is quoted in
the index entries.*

*For bibliographical details of the articles included here, please see the
Bibliography that follows the Introduction.*

INTRODUCTION

I am grateful to Ashgate Publishing for undertaking the publication of several of my essays on Claudio Monteverdi as well as a second book, soon forthcoming, of essays on sixteenth and seventeenth-century Italian music. Selecting the Monteverdi essays required a retrospective look at my studies in this area, which became, in a sense, an autobiographical review of my interest in this remarkable composer. I first became aware of Monteverdi's music through a graduate seminar on rhythmic and tempo issues in Monteverdi's madrigals under the direction of Charles Hamm at the University of Illinois at Urbana-Champaign. When I later had to consider a dissertation topic, the fact that Monteverdi's sacred music had been the subject of only limited attention by musicologists steered me toward the 1610 Vespers, even though among his sacred music, the Vespers had received by far the most attention. It was already apparent to me that this collection of compositions could not have sprung full-grown from the head of one of the muses and that there must be an unknown musical context out of which it grew and from which it could be determined what aspects of this music were a normal part of its environment and what aspects were unique to Monteverdi.

More than forty years later, investigation of Monteverdi's music, including his sacred music, has become the focus of numerous scholars, including some of the best in the entire field of historical musicology. My own contributions have included two books on the 1610 publication in which the now famous Vespers are found, critical editions of both the Mass and Vespers from that print, editions of other Monteverdi mass music, and a variety of articles. In deciding what articles to republish, or in one case, to publish for the first time, I was influenced especially by the fact that many of them had originally appeared in conference reports and Festschriften not readily accessible to most readers. But in addition, after reviewing my own bibliography, I was reminded of the variety of approaches I had taken to Monteverdi's music and that the articles selected for re-publication should represent this variety. My thoughts and interests have always been broad and eclectic, and I have been consequently led to the examination of Monteverdi's repertoire from different standpoints on the supposition that music of this calibre cannot be understood from one or two perspectives alone; rather, it touches on so many aspects of human experience and its representation in sound that only a variety of investigations from diverse angles could help me obtain a deeper and more coherent understanding of it. As a result, many of these articles may be considered open-ended – establishing ways of thinking about and analyzing Monteverdi's music without the assumption that what I have written is either definitive or closes the matter even on the specific compositions studied.

The book is divided into three general categories. The first represents the kinds of philosophical and psychological approaches that have always interested me in all the music to which I listen. Apart from a variety of aesthetic writings from Plato and Aristotle to Descartes, Kant, Schopenhauer, Hegel, Nietzsche and Suzanne Langer, I was especially stimulated by Michel Foucault's *The Order of Things: An Archeology of the Human Sciences* and its broad contrast between "resemblances" and "identities and differences," two divergent ways of thinking about and organizing the world in the sixteenth and seventeenth centuries, amply demonstrated by Monteverdi's own writings and music and investigated in the first article in terms of metaphor vs. icon.

The very notions of metaphor and icon conjure up the field of semiotics, the subject of an article omitted from the present volume because of its overlap with the first essay, though pursued in some additional ways.[1] These aesthetic investigations also had their practical side, resulting in application of their theories to a new kind of analysis of the most famous madrigal from Monteverdi's Eighth Book of Madrigals, a setting of Petrarch's sonnet, *Hor che'l ciel e la terra*. Here the seventeenth-century interest in taxonomy and the representative icon, combined with the emphasis on contrasts described in Monteverdi's Eighth Book preface serve as the basis of a structural analysis which also reveals underlying dynamic and proportional aspects of the musical structure.

The psychological approach, represented in the last three articles in the first section of this volume, is especially relevant to music of Monteverdi's era as well as to his own compositions, for the program of the musicians and patrons that led to the development of monody and opera at the end of the sixteenth century was itself inherently psychological – the attempt to affect the emotional state of listeners by means of poetic concepts set to music by composers and brought to life phenomenologically by performers. Monteverdi himself stressed what we can call today the psychological function of his music (though the terminology didn't exist in his own time) in some of his most famous letters as well as in the aforementioned preface to his Eighth Book of Madrigals.

The three psychologically oriented articles begin with "Intimations of chaos in Monteverdi's *L'Orfeo*," which was originally published in Italian under the

---

[1] See "Monteverdi's changing aesthetics: a semiotic perspective," in the bibliography at the end of this introduction.

title "Intrusioni del caos nell'*Orfeo* di Monteverdi" (see the bibliographical notes at the end of this Introduction) and has been returned to English with a few minor modifications. This essay examines the mental disintegration of Orfeo as the opera proceeds, and the increasingly chaotic musical means by which Monteverdi expresses that disintegration. As with the essay on *Hor che'l ciel e la terra*, a supra-musical orientation is bolstered by detailed musical analysis.

At about the same time as I originally wrote the Orfeo essay, I had begun for quite other reasons to study the psychology of Carl Jung, where I found numerous concepts that helped explain fundamental features of Monteverdi's music, including basic aspects not only of *L'Orfeo*, but also of his Eighth Book of Madrigals, aspects of which other scholars had been quite critical. I have only scratched the surface in considering Monteverdi's music from the perspective of Jungian psychology, but the final two psychologically oriented essays in the first section are rooted in what I have gleaned from Jung.

The first of these, "A Jungian perspective on Monteverdi's late madrigals," takes its point of departure from Jung's typology of extraversion and introversion and the dialectic and dilemma of opposing forces and choices, which Monteverdi, in the preface to his Eighth Book of Madrigals (1638), frames as three musical typologies, the *stili concitato, molle* and *temperato*, and as contrasts: "knowing that contrasts are what greatly move our souls" (*sapendo che gli contrarij sono quellli che movono grandemente l'animo nostro*). The psychological emphasis on the emotional force of contrasts is the basic aesthetic principle informing the madrigals of the Eighth Book, with these contrasts musically reified in the different musical typologies. Thinking of these late madrigals from this perspective offers a different way of understanding these works, exemplified in this article by an analysis of the madrigal *Perche t'en fuggi Fillide*. An important aspect of Jung's theory of oppositions is the possibility of resolving them through a "third way," which I see in Monteverdi's madrigals as the underlying organizational principles uniting musical opposites in coherent structural plans. In this particular madrigal that structural plan is based on Golden Section proportions combined with generally symmetrical organizational patterns.

My Jungian studies also led me to a fully Jungian interpretation of *L'Orfeo* in "The psychic disintegration of a demi-god: conscious and unconscious in Striggio and Monteverdi's *L'Orfeo*," though a rather different interpretation from the one presented by Robert Donington in 1967.[2] My approach examines Orfeo's failure at individuation, analyzed in terms of text, music and action. This essay explores the conscious and unconscious aspects of Orfeo's and

---

[2]   Robert Donington, "Monteverdi's first opera," in *The Monteverdi Companion*, eds Denis Arnold and Nigel Fortune (London: Faber and Faber, 1967), 257–76.

other characters' behavior, the roles of Euridice, Persephone and Pluto, and suggests a new meaning for the final act based on Jung's concept of a "third way" as a resolution of an otherwise irresolvable dilemma. As in the earlier essays, perspectives from outside of music itself are supported by detailed analysis of the music.

Another essay on *L'Orfeo* has been omitted from this volume because of its ready accessibility online in the *Journal of Seventeenth-Century Music*.[3] In this article I argued against Susan McClary's interpretation of *Orfeo* in her well-known article, "Constructions of gender in Monteverdi's dramatic music." My quarrel with McClary is that her analysis of the text and music in her *L'Orfeo* analysis is both inaccurate and distorted to fit her overall theory (much of which is valid in her comments on other Monteverdi dramatic works). My response redresses the problem with a different analysis based on the text and music as they actually appear and function, leading to quite different conclusions from McClary's.

The second section of the present book reprints a number of essays focused specifically on Monteverdi's sacred music, organized in chronological order. The first, "What makes Claudio divine?" attempts to explain one aspect of his compositional process that contributes to the high level of his music's quality – the organization of time. Analysis of the first *Dixit Dominus* from Monteverdi's *Selva Morale et Spirituale* reveals that durational balances and Golden Section proportions, often overlapping in different musical parameters, combine with both *varietà* and similarity in musical materials to create a complex, sophisticated musical structure. Another analytical essay is the third one in this section, *Laetatus sum* from the 1610 Vespers, which explores the use of the psalm tone in the piece as well as a unique set of repetitive bass patterns constituting the underlying structure of the composition.

The second essay in this section is a survey of the evidence regarding Monteverdi's composition of and participation in sacred music while employed at Mantua. Though only the *Missa in illo Tempore* and *Vespro della Beata Vergine* of 1610 survive from this period in his career, there is considerable evidence of substantial composition of sacred music by Monteverdi, especially after his appointment by Duke Vincenzo Gonzaga in late 1601 or early 1602 as *maestro e della camera e della chiesa* ("music director of both the chamber and the church"), as Monteverdi described the position in his letter of application.[4]

    [3] See "Deconstructing gender in Monteverdi's *Orfeo*" in the bibliography at the end of this introduction.

    [4] November 28, 1601. See Eva Lax, ed., *Claudio Monteverdi: Lettere* (Florence: Leo S. Olschki Editore, 1994), 2. English translation in Denis Stevens, *The Letters of Claudio Monteverdi* (revised ed. Oxford: Clarendon Press, 1995), 30.

Della chiesa probably meant for all sacred music sponsored by the duke in the cathedral of San Pietro, in the church of Sant'Andrea, and in all other churches and sacred venues outside of the palace church of Santa Barbara, which had its own *maestro di capella.* Unfortunately, there is no direct evidence of any other specific sacred compositions by Monteverdi in Mantua except for a letter briefly describing a vesper service composed by Monteverdi for Ascension Day in 1611, first brought to my attention by Licia Mari, Vice-Director of the Archivio Diocesano in Mantua, who is co-author of the article "A Monteverdi Vespers in 1611" reprinted here.

The final two articles in this section discuss sacred music by Monteverdi that doesn't survive. Over the years, a story had been built up by a number of different scholars over the mass that Monteverdi composed and performed in St Mark's, Venice on November 21, 1631 to celebrate the end of the plague of 1630/31. While there is no doubt that Monteverdi performed (and presumably composed) a mass on that occasion, the *Mass in F* from the *Selva morale et spirituale*, with the *Gloria a 7* and substitute concertato sections for the Credo had been variously declared to be the mass performed during the elaborate ceremonies, based primarily on a description of brass instruments (*trombe squarciate*) used in the *Gloria* and *Credo*. James H. Moore had even argued that nearly half the music in the *Selva morale* was composed for ceremonies in connection with various stages of the plague and its conclusion.[5] In an article first published in 1994 entitled "Monteverdi's 'Mass of Thanksgiving' revisited," already reprinted by Ashgate in a volume edited by Richard Wistreich, entitled simply *Monteverdi*, I first questioned many of the assumptions and conclusions that had accumulated regarding the Thanksgiving Mass and then tackled the question of how the trumpets might have been used. At that time I was still willing to accept that the *Mass in F*, with substitution of the *Gloria a 7* and the concertato Credo segments for the four-voice settings of those texts in the *Mass in F*, constituted the "Mass of Thanksgiving." However, subsequent re-examination of the history of arguments regarding the Mass as well as investigation of the *trombe squarciate* mentioned in the brief contemporary accounts of the *Gloria* and *Credo* brought me to the conclusion, maintained in "Monteverdi's Mass of Thanksgiving: Da Capo" that we have no evidence whatsoever to associate any of the music in the *Selva morale* with the Mass of Thanksgiving or any other aspect of the thanksgiving ceremonies. Moreover, I now think that my suggestions in "Monteverdi's 'Mass of Thanksgiving'

---

[5]   James H. Moore, "*Venezia favorita da Maria*: Music for the Madonna Nicopeia and Santa Maria della Salute," *Journal of the American Musicological Society* 37/2 (Summer 1984), 299–355, esp. 351–4.

revisited" for what the *trombe squarciate* might have played in the *Gloria* and *Credo* were overly ambitious and that the suggestions given in Moore's article are more plausible.

In the course of my re-examination of theories regarding the "Mass of Thanksgiving" I came to the realization that the vast majority of Monteverdi's sacred production must be lost. For example, while only three masses by Monteverdi survive (one by chance alone), at least thirty masses are known to be missing and the total may be significantly higher. Likewise, there are only two psalms remaining to us in the *coro spezzato* style required for most major feasts at St Mark's. All others are in the *concertato* style favored by other churches and the major confraternities in Venice as well as the imperial court in Vienna. The final essay in this section, "Monteverdi's missing sacred music: evidence and conjectures," explores all the references and information relevant to this question known to me, distinguishing specific compositions that are mentioned in letters, annual obligations that Monteverdi had for liturgical music, annual obligations that he likely had, vague references in letters and other documents to unnamed sacred works, commissions from patrons, and occasions on which it was likely he would have provided the music. Although there is no accurate way to assess what percentage of Monteverdi's sacred compositions survives, I am doubtful that it is more than 10–15%.

The final section of this volume represents another long-standing interest of mine, the editing of music of this period. This section comprises a single essay – a comparison of the Malipiero and Cremona editions of Monteverdi's complete works. Both editions are fascinating with respect to their very different editorial procedures and significant flaws. Both make apparent the great difficulties inherent in producing scholarly critical editions of this music stemming from a period when performers were expected tacitly to understand many aspects of the notation that are problematic or puzzling to us today and to play a much larger role in interpreting that notation through improvised or *ad hoc* performance practices.

I owe debts of gratitude to a number of people in connection with this volume: to Geoffrey Chew for organizing the session on seventeenth-century music at the 1991 British Music Analysis Conference in London and inviting me to take part and ultimately editing the papers of that session for publication; to Gregory Johnston of the University of Toronto for inviting me to give a public lecture in 2003 which ultimately became the article on psychic disintegration in *L'Orfeo*; to David Clarke and Eric Clarke for asking me to include the paper on psychic disintegration in *L'Orfeo* in their volume of selected papers from the 2006 Sheffield conference on "Music and consciousness;" to John Whenham and Richard Wistreich for inviting me to provide chapters for their *Cambridge Companion to Monteverdi*; to Licia Mari for bringing the 1611 letter to my attention and agreeing to work with me as co-author on "A Monteverdi Vespers in 1611;" to Claire Fontijn and Piotr Wilk for inviting me to contribute articles for their Festschriften for Lex Silbiger and Piotr Poźniak; to Reinmar Emans for inviting me to compose the essay on the Malipiero and Cremona editions of Monteverdi's works; and most of all, to Maurizio Padoan, who invited me repeatedly to present papers at the biennial conferences organized by Antiquae Musicae Italicae Studiosi (A.M.I.S.) of Como, some of which are reproduced in this volume. Thanks are also due to Reinmar Emans and Maurizio Padoan for permission to publish here the aforementioned articles, and to Claire Jarvis and Lindsay Farthing of Ashgate Publishing for their exceptional helpfulness and diligence in the production of this volume.

JEFFREY KURTZMAN

St Louis, Missouri
January 2013

ACKNOWLEDGEMENTS

Grateful acknowledgement is made to the following persons, institutions, journals and publishers for their kind permission to reproduce the papers included in this volume: Antiquae Musicae Italicae Studiosi, Bologna (A.M.I.S.) (for articles I, III, IV and VI); Blackwell Publishing, Oxford (II); Oxford University Press (V, IX); Cambridge University Press (VII, VIII); Harmonie Park Press, Sterling Heights, MI (X); Musica Iagellonica, Kraków (XI); and Dr Reinmar Emans, editor of *Musik-Editionen als Spiegel der Editionsgeschichte* (XII).

Every effort has been made to trace all the copyright holders, but if any have been inadvertently overlooked the publishers will be pleased to make the necessary arrangement at the first opportunity.

BIBLIOGRAPHY

Original presentations of papers and publications from which articles are derived

"Monteverdi and early Baroque aesthetics: the view from Foucault," in *Il madrigale oltre il madrigale. Dal Barocco al Novecento: destino di una forma e problemi di analisi: Atti del IV Convegno internazionale sulla musica italiana nel secolo XVII. Lenno-Como, 28–30 giugno 1991*, eds Alberto Colzani, Andrea Luppi, Maurizio Padoan (Como, Italy: A.M.I.S. [Antiquae Musicae Italicae Studiosi], 1994), 107–19.

"A taxonomic and affective analysis of Monteverdi's *Hor che 'l ciel e la terra*," British Music Analysis Conference, London, September 1991. Published in *Music Analysis* 12/2 (July 1993), 169–95.

"A Jungian perspective on Monteverdi's late madrigals," in *Relazioni musicali tra Italia e Germania nell'età barocca. Atti del VI Convegno internazionale sulla musica italiana nei secoli XVII–XVIII. Loveno di Menaggio (Como), 11–13 luglio 1995*, eds Alberto Colzani, Norbert Dubowy, Andrea Luppi, Maurizio Padoan (Como, Italy: A.M.I.S. [Antiquae Musicae Italicae Studiosi], 1997), 123–36.

"Intimations of chaos in Monteverdi's *L'Orfeo*," originally "Intrusioni del Caos nell'*Orfeo* di Monteverdi," in *Il melodramma italiano in Italia e in Germania nell'età barocca. Atti del V Convegno internazionale sulla musica italiana nel secolo XVII. Loveno di Menaggio (Como), 28–30 giugno 1993*, eds Alberto Colzani, Andrea Luppi, Maurizio Padoan (Como, Italy: A.M.I.S. [Antiquae Musicae Italicae Studiosi], 1995), 181–204.

"The psychic disintegration of a demi-god: conscious and unconscious in Striggio and Monteverdi's *L'Orfeo*," in *Music and Consciousness: Philosophical, Psychological, and Cultural Perspectives*, eds David Clarke and Eric Clarke (Oxford: Oxford University Press, 2011), 343–74. First presented as a paper at the University of Toronto, February 2003.

"What makes Claudio divine? Criteria for analysis of Monteverdi's large-scale concertato style," in *Seicento inesplorato: L'evento musicale tra prassi e stile: un modello di interdipendenza. Atti del II Convegno internazionale sulla musica in area lombardo-padana nel secolo XVII. Lenno-Como, 23–25 giugno 1989*, eds Alberto Colzani, Andrea Luppi, Maurizio Padoan (Como, Italy: A.M.I.S. [Antiquae Musicae Italicae Studiosi], 1993), 257–302.

"The Mantuan sacred music," in *The Cambridge Companion to Monteverdi*, eds John Whenham and Richard Wistreich (Cambridge: Cambridge University Press, 2007), 141–54.

"'Laetatus sum' (1610)," in *The Cambridge Companion to Monteverdi*, eds John Whenham and Richard Wistreich (Cambridge: Cambridge University Press, 2007), 155–61.

With Licia Mari: "A Monteverdi Vespers in 1611," *Early Music* 36 (November 2008), 1–9

"Monteverdi's Mass of Thanksgiving: Da Capo," in *Fiori Musicali: Liber amicorum Alexander Silbiger*, eds Claire Fontijn with Susan Parisi (Sterling Heights, Michigan: Harmonie Park Press, 2010), 95–128.

"Monteverdi's missing sacred music: evidence and conjectures," in *Muzykolog Wobec Świadectw Źródłowych i Dokumentów: Księga Pamiątkowa Dedykowana Profesorowi Piotrowi Poźniakowi w 70. Rocznicę Urodzin. The Musicologist and Source Documentary Evidence: A Book of Essays in Honour of Professor Piotr Poźniak on his 70th Birthday*, eds Zofia Fabiańska, Jakub Kubieniec, Andrzej Sitarz, Piotr Wilk (Karków: Musica Iagellonica, 2009), 187–208.

"Collected works of Claudio Monteverdi: the Malipiero and Cremona editions" to be published in *Musik-Editionen als Spiegel der Editionsgeschichte* (Tübingen: Max Niemeyer Verlag).

Other Monteverdi bibliography

"The Monteverdi Vespers of 1610 and their relationship with Italian sacred music of the early seventeenth century" (Ph.D. dissertation, University of Illinois at Urbana-Champaign, 1972).

"Some historical perspectives on the Monteverdi Vespers," *Analecta Musicologica* 15 (1975), 29–86.

Essays on the Monteverdi Mass and Vespers of 1610 (Houston: Rice University Studies, 1978).

"An aberration amplified," *Early Music* 13/1 (February 1985), 73–6.

"Why would Monteverdi publish a Vespers in 1610? Lifting the shadows on the development of a repertoire," in *De Musica et Cantu: Studien zur Geschichte der Kirchenmusik und der Oper. Helmut Hucke zum 60. Geburtstag*, eds Peter Cahn und Ann-Katrin Heimer (Hildesheim, Zürich, New York: Georg Olms Verlag, 1993), 419–55; revised as "A brief history of vespers in the sixteenth century" in Kurtzman, *The Monteverdi Vespers of 1610: Music, Context, Performance* (Oxford: Oxford University Press, 1999), 79–98.

"Monteverdi's sacred music: the state of research," in *Claudio Monteverdi: Studi e prospettive. Atti del Convegno Mantova, 21–24 ottobre 1993*, eds Paola Besutti, Teresa M. Gialdroni, Rodolfo Baroncini (Florence: Leo S. Olschki Editore, 1997).

"Il Vespro della Beata Vergine di Claudio Monteverdi ed il repertorio italiano dei vespri dal 1610 al 1650: un quadro riassuntivo," *Barocco padano 2: Atti del X Convegno internazionale sulla musica sacra nei secoli XVII–XVIII, Como, 16–18 luglio 1999*, eds Alberto Colzani, Andrea Luppi, Maurizio Padoan (Como, Italy: A.M.I.S. [Antiquae Musicae Italicae Studiosi], 2002), 7–39.

"Write to reply," *The Musical Times* 142 (Winter 2001), 52–60.

"Monteverdi's 'Mass of Thanksgiving' revisited," *Early Music* 22/1 (February 1994), 63–84; reprinted in *Monteverdi*, ed. Richard Wistreich (Farnham and Burlington, Vermont: Ashgate Publishing, 2011), 507–27.

"Monteverdi's changing aesthetics: a semiotic perspective," in *Festa Musicologica: Essays in Honor of George J. Buelow*, eds Thomas J. Mathiesen and Benito V. Rivera (Stuyvesant, New York: Pendragon Press, 1995), 233–55.

The Monteverdi Vespers of 1610: Music, Context, Performance (Oxford: Oxford University Press, 1999).

With Linda Koldau: "*Trombe, trombe d'argento, trombe squarciate, tromboni*, and *pifferi* in Venetian processions and ceremonies of the sixteenth and seventeenth centuries," *Journal of Seventeenth-Century Music* (sscm-jscm. org) 8 (2002).

"Deconstructing gender in Monteverdi's *Orfeo*," *Journal of Seventeenth-Century Music* (sscm-jscm.org) 9/1 (2003).

"Monteverdi's Mass and Vespers of 1610: the social and economic context," forthcoming in the *Journal of Seventeenth-Century Music: Selected Papers of the Frankfurt Monteverdi Conference, May 2009*.

"Neo-platonic Readings of Rinuccini's and Monteverdi's *Il ballo delle ingrate* and *Arianna* of 1608," forthcoming.

Editions

Claudio Monteverdi: Gloria a 7 from *Selva morale et spirituale* (Stuttgart: Carus-Verlag, 1991).

Claudio Monteverdi: Missa in F from *Selva morale et spirituale* (Stuttgart: Carus-Verlag, 1992).

Claudio Monteverdi: Missa in illo tempore (Stuttgart: Carus-Verlag, 1994).

Claudio Monteverdi: Vespro della Beata Vergine (1610), 2 vols (Oxford: Oxford University Press, 1999).

Reviews

Music of Claudio Monteverdi: a Discography, comp. Gunnar Westerlund and
  Eric Hughes (British Institute of Recorded Sound, 1972), *Music Library
  Association Notes* 30/3 (March 1974), 532–3.
Claudio Monteverdi: Il Primo Libro dei Madrigali, ed. Bernard de Surcy, and
  same title, ed. Raffaello Monterosso, *Journal of the American Musicological
  Society* 27/2 (Summer 1974), 343–8.
Claudio Monteverdi: Vespro della Beata Vergine, ed. Jürgen Jürgens. *Music
  Library Association Notes* 36/4 (June 1980), 981–3.
The New Monteverdi Companion, eds Denis Arnold and Nigel Fortune. *The
  Musical Quarterly* 72/3 (1986), 418–21.
*Claudio Monteverdi: Vespers of St John the Baptist and Second Vespers of
  Santa Barbara*, eds Fritz Noske, Graham Dixon. Record reviews in *Early
  Music* 72/3 (August 1989), 429–38.
Claudio Monteverdi: A Guide to Research. K. Gary Adams and Dyke Kiel
  (New York: Garland Publishing, 1989). *Music & Letters* 71/4 (November
  1990), 545–50.
Claudio Monteverdi: L'incoronazione di Poppea, ed. Alan Curtis (London
  and Sevenoaks: Novello, 1989). *Music Library Association Notes* 48/1
  (September 1991), 276–9.
Monteverdi. Denis Arnold, Third ed. revised by Tim Carter (London: Dent,
  1990*). Music& Letters* 73/3 (August 1992), 438–40.
Monteverdi Vespers of 1610. Jeanette Sorel and Apollo's Fire, *Journal of
  Seventeenth-Century Music*, 11/1 (2005).

I

MONTEVERDI AND EARLY BAROQUE AESTHETICS:
THE VIEW FROM FOUCAULT

The uniqueness of Monteverdi's life and career has always been viewed in terms of the aesthetic and stylistic duality he represents in spanning the great watershed of the early 17th century. Monteverdi's genius is revealed first in his role as a madrigalist in the traditions of the fading Renaissance at the court of Mantua, and secondly, as the most important figure in defining early 17th-century Baroque style through opera, *concertato* madrigal and *concertato* sacred music. This paper will attempt to understand Monteverdi's role in this aesthetic and stylistic watershed in terms argued by Michel Foucault in *Les Mots et les Choses: Une Archéologie des Sciences Humaines*, where quite distinctive thought processes are claimed to represent the respective cultures of the 16th and the 17th centuries[1].

Historical watersheds are complicated affairs, and as historians we tend to look at them in diverse manners. The very concept of a watershed suggests that things are different on either side of the great divide - indeed, early opera and the *concertato* style are quite different from late 16th-century polyphony, whether expressed in madrigal, motet or mass. But from another angle historians are always on the hunt for continuity, for connections and transitions between seemingly radical divergences. Manfred Bukofzer, writing in 1947, stressed the dichotomies which divided Baroque from Renaissance music[2]. Claude Palisca and other recent writers have tended to draw attention to the continuities between the late 16th and early 17th centuries[3]. An evolutionary view, illustrating how the early Baroque developed out of the late Renaissance, has been the predominant modern trend. Foucault, on the other hand, while not writing specifically about music, has once again emphasized dichotomies in his olympian historical perspective.

---

[1] Originally published in France by Editions Gallimard in 1966. Translated into English as *The Order of Things: An Archaeology of the Human Sciences*, New York Pantheon Books, 1971. Quotations in this paper are taken from the Vintage Books Edition, New York, 1973.

[2] MANFRED BUKOFZER, *Music in the Baroque Era*, New York, W. W. Norton & Co., 1947, pp. 9-19.

[3] CLAUDE PALISCA, *Baroque Music*, Englewood Cliffs, Prentice-Hall, Inc., 1968, pp. 8-26. Vol. IV of *The New Oxford History of Music*, London, Oxford University Press, 1968, is entitled «The Age of Humanism, 1540-1630,» thereby encompassing under one cover the same time frame that served to highlight dichotomies for Bukofzer. Similarly, MARIA RIKA MANIATES stresses an underlying continuity of thought between Renaissance and early Baroque in her *Mannerism in Italian Music and Culture, 1530-1630*, Chapel Hill, The University of North Carolina Press, 1979. LORENZO BIANCONI also is concerned to show continuities between the late 16th and early 17th centuries in *Il Seicento*, Torino, Edizioni di Torino, 1982.

In periods of rapid change, such as the late 16th and early 17th-centuries, the dynamics and threads of historical development are complex, convoluted and difficult to untangle. This is true not only for contemporary historians, but was equally so for those living through such times. And those figures who are the objects of our studies were often beset with the same psychological needs as modern historians - the necessity of finding ways to define and shape the seemingly chaotic flux in which they lived. Such needs are undoubtedly a significant factor behind the theoretical treatises, manifestos, polemics and exegeses of new styles and techniques that proliferated in the early 17th century.

Monteverdi was drawn into the fray in his early thirties by Giovanni Maria Artusi, and two of Monteverdi's prefaces, as well as a number of his letters, subsequently provide us with important glimpses into his aesthetic thinking as it evolved from early in the century to near the time of his death. But Monteverdi was primarily a composer, not a theoretician or polemicist, and he felt himself compelled to articulate his theoretical and aesthetic ideas mainly in response to attacks, in deflecting uncomfortable pressures from patrons, or when he felt threatened in some way.

The most extensive such statement, of course, is his brother Giulio Cesare's *Dichiaratione* of 1607 in reply to the published attacks of Artusi[4]. This *Dichiaratione* is the most frequently cited evidence of Monteverdi's transition over the watershed of early 17th-century style in its definition of what the Monteverdi brothers call the *prima prattica* and the *seconda prattica*. By the mid-17th century music theorists-*cum*-historians had seized upon these two terms as alternative designations for *stile antico* and *stile moderno,* and modern historians have followed suit[5]. But that is a somewhat skewed historical hindsight and not what Monteverdi originally had in mind, even if he did modify his viewpoint on the *seconda prattica* later in his life[6].

---

[4]   The first blow in the Artusi-Monteverdi polemic was struck in Artusi's *L'Artusi overo Delle imperfettioni della moderna musica*, printed in Venice in 1600. An English translation is found in OLIVER STRUNK, *Source Readings in Music History*, New York, W. W. Norton & Co., 1950, pp. 393-404. Monteverdi first responded in the preface to his Fifth Book of Madrigals in 1605, which was subsequently reprinted and substantially glossed by his brother Giulio Cesare in the *Scherzi Musicali* of 1607. Both prefaces are printed in DOMENICO DE PAOLI, *Claudio Monteverdi: Lettere, dediche e prefazioni*, Roma, Edizioni de Santis, 1973, pp. 391-404. English translations in STRUNK, *Source Readings*, cit., pp. 405-412. For a thorough discussion of the controversy, see CLAUDE PALISCA, *The Artusi-Monteverdi Controversy*, in *The New Monteverdi Companion*, ed. Denis Arnold and Nigel Fortune, London, Faber and Faber, 1985, pp. 127-158.

[5]   Marco Scacchi is one of the first writers to identify the «first practice» with old style and the «second practice» with modern style. See CLAUDE PALISCA, *Marco Scacchi's Defense of Modern Music (1649)*, in *Words and Music: The Scholar's View*, ed. Laurence Berman, Cambridge, Harvard University Press, 1971, pp.189-235.

[6]   In a recent unpublished paper entitled *Claudio Monteverdi's Seconda Pratica: Poetics and Practice*, Massimo Ossi has dealt with two letters of Monteverdi to Giambattista Doni, dated October 22, 1633 and February 2, 1634 in which Claudio describes his plans for the theoretical treatise on the *seconda*

In fact, the *seconda prattica,* as defined in 1607, is nothing more than an attempt to justify irregular dissonance treatment in the polyphonic madrigal on the basis of the conceptions embodied in individual words of the text. Giulio Cesare is at pains to trace Claudio's lineage in this process all the way back to Cipriano de Rore. The *seconda prattica* is not the Monteverdi brothers' manifesto of the new Baroque style; it is a justification of the modern freely dissonant approach to the compositional methods and textures of the old style. The *Dichiaratione* makes no direct mention of *concertato* techniques, and its only references to accompanied monody and to musical drama are quite oblique: Giulio Cesare remarks on the *canto alla francese* and the *Scherzi musicali* only to claim his brother's priority in introducing this *«modo moderno»*, and Peri and Caccini are simply listed at the end of a group of *seconda prattica* composers that begins with Rore and Ingegnieri. Giovanni Bardi and Emilio Cavaliere are also named in a list of composers from the *«Eroica scola»* which also includes Rore and Gesualdo. Claude Palisca has likewise noted that Giulio Cesare refers to polyphony rather than monody: «He is not saying, as has sometimes been inferred, that melody in the sense of tune or monody should now take precedence over counterpoint or harmony. Melody in this sense is not even in question»[7].

Aside from its basis in the tradition of polyphony, the *Dichiaratione* reflects an underlying perspective on musical composition and thought processes that permeates Renaissance music as far back as Dufay. This perspective is characterized by Foucault as the organization of reality through the search for resemblance. As summarized by the cultural critic Hayden White, «Foucault argues, in the sixteenth century the dominant mode of discourse was informed by a desire to find the Same in the Different, to determine the extent to which any given object *resembled* another; the sciences of the sixteenth century were obsessed, in short, by the notion of similitude»[8]. Foucault's formulation is intended to demonstrate that the search for resemblances serves as the foundation, or very condition, of thought processes and employment of language in the 16th century. Resemblances are the means by which perceptions, knowledge and creative activities were organized, classified and discussed. Although Foucault bases his analysis on a study of economics, natural history and language, the manifestations of this type of thought process are evident

---

prattica, originally promised in the preface to the Fifth Book of Madrigals. Ossi demonstrates that Monteverdi's own view of the *seconda prattica* had evolved considerably since 1605-1607, and that by the 1630's he too saw the second practice as defining modern style. The letters in question are published in DOMENICO DE' PAOLI, *Claudio Monteverdi: Lettere, dediche e prefazioni,* cit., pp. 320-322 and 325-328 (where the date 4 ottobre is erroneously given). English translations in DENIS STEVENS, *The Letters of Claudio Monteverdi,* Cambridge, Cambridge University Press, 1980, pp. 409-411 and 414-416.

[7] PALISCA, *The Artusi-Monteverdi Controversy,* cit., p. 155.
[8] HAYDEN WHITE, *Tropics of Discourse: Essays in Cultural Criticism,* Baltimore, The John Hopkins University Press, 1978, p. 241.

in music as well. The cyclic mass, homogenous textures, pervasive imitation, the evenly flowing tactus, and the easy interchangeability of voices and instruments are all products or characteristics of Renaissance music traceable to the creative force of resemblance. Resemblances of these types are integrative - they tend to create a perceptible unity, all or most of the parts of which contribute to that sense of integration or wholeness.

Another type of resemblance that comes to the fore in the 16th century, especially in connection with the madrigal, comprises the relationship between music and poetry, and owes its development to humanistic concerns for texts and their interpretation. Its manifestation in the madrigal and later the motet is in the form of musical metaphors for textual concepts. This wonderfully diverse and imaginative process consists of the search for musical means by which a composer may draw resemblances between the semantic meaning or rhetorical significance of one or more words of text and the immediate, localized compositional setting of those words.

The process is a classic case of metaphor, only it is the metaphor between two different media. Metaphor requires that there be some overlap, some connection between the two elements that are drawn into relationship with one another, thereby creating an expanded meaning beyond and different from the separate meanings of the two terms brought together in the metaphor[9]. One of the facets of these musical/poetic metaphors is that they tended to be highly localized events, and usually had very little significance beyond the immediate situation in which they are found. Composers in the 16th century sought musical metaphors for words as the words occurred, and the significance of such metaphors was often completed once the music and text moved on to the next phrase and set of words.

In the *prima prattica* as one finds it in the music of Arcadelt, Willaert and the early Cipriano de Rore, musical metaphors are limited in number and scope and are not normally disruptive of the balanced High Renaissance polyphonic style. But shortly after mid-century, beginning with later works of Rore and continuing on through Giaches de Wert, Marenzio, Luzzaschi and Monteverdi, the metaphorical process became increasingly important, leading to the invention of ever bolder musical metaphors, and finally resulting in the disregard for the contrapuntal rules of Zarlino we find in Monteverdi's fourth and fifth books of madrigals. This is where the conservative Artusi entered and Giulio Cesare defended his brother with the declaration of the *seconda prattica*. The *prima* and *seconda prattica* are different from one another, therefore, only in terms of degree, not of substance. The *seconda prattica* is no more than a shift in emphasis in the types of resemblance. Whereas

---

[9]   Perhaps the most complete recent examination and critique of theories of metaphor is PAUL RICOEUR, *La métaphore vive*, Paris, Editions du Seuil, 1975. Engl. version, *The Rule of Metaphor*, Trans. Robert Czerny, Toronto, University of Toronto Press, 1977.

the musical resemblances of imitative contrapuntal technique and homogeneous textures, inherent in the polyphonic style, had held sway in the first half of the 16th century, the resemblances between text and music in the second half of the century tended to disrupt the balance and harmony of the earlier style, leading to frequent interruptions in the homogeneity and continuity of the polyphonic texture. Integration of style in the early part of the century was gradually displaced by integration between word and music in the second half[10]. The surface result is different, but the underlying, what Foucault would call the archeological, significance of resemblance or similitude still prevails. Monteverdi's *prima* and *seconda prattica* reflect the surface differences, not a difference in fundamental aesthetic and creative processes.

When we reach the other side of the watershed, however, the underlying aesthetic and creative processes have changed dramatically. While the transition from one side to the other is fascinating, it is the radical differences in comparing the earlier with the later aesthetic that is of interest to me at the moment, and here again Foucault may be able to help us understand the dichotomies that have emerged. Foucault is not interested in transitions, and without suggesting any rationale as to how or why things might have changed, he describes a new set of conditions of thought for the 17th century, characterized as the search for taxonomies. According to Foucault, «What has become important is no longer resemblances, but identities and differences»[11]. He states further that:

> «The activity of the mind [...] will therefore no longer consist in *drawing things together,* in setting out on a quest for everything that might reveal some sort of kinship attraction, or secretly shared nature within them, but, on the contrary, in *discriminating*, that is, establishing their identities, then the inevitability of the connections with all the successive degrees of a series. In this sense, discrimination imposes upon comparison the primary and fundamental investigation of difference: providing oneself by intuition with a distinct representation of things, and apprehending clearly the inevitable connection between one element in a series and that which immediately follows it»[12].

It is, of course, identities and differences that fueled the empirical investigations of the 17th century, whether represented by Galileo, Descartes, or Mersenne, and allowed for new forms of conceptualization and taxonomic classification. In order to organize thought empirically, the investigator has to be most interested in what *is*, not in its relationship to something else, its utility for humans, or its divine

---

[10]   This process is highlighted especially in MANIATES, *op. cit.*
[11]   FOUCAULT, *op. cit.*,.p. 50.
[12]   *Op. cit.*, p. 55.

significance. That is why Descartes began his odyssey by establishing the one, fundamental empirical truth of being. Empirical reality is conceived as inherent in the characteristics of an object, event or experience as an independent entity.

Taxonomy requires not only classification, but also the appropriate naming of the separate categories established by the classifying process. Foucault claims that the «fundamental task» of this period «is to ascribe a name to things, and in that name to name their being»[13]. Taxonomy also demands organization of the separate categories into larger series. These series result from some underlying principle of connection, not necessarily because of any resemblances or direct relationships. The criteria for connecting a series in a particular way can be quite diverse, even somewhat arbitrary, since the emphasis in the 17th century is on the individual taxonomic units rather than on sophisticated underlying structural schemes. Consequently, the larger structures of this period often appear as concatenations of taxonomic categories.

This looseness of structure, of seeming arbitrariness in the succession of items or events, is difficult for modern culture to grasp, even in some of the more coherently ordered products of the 17th century. We moderns have inherited the aesthetics and thought processes of the 19th century which emphasized the functional integration of all parts of a construction, the so-called «organic» model, and we live in a century that has evolved this emphasis into the complete structural integration of works of art, whether in terms of Bartokian motivic and structural symmetries or the rigors of total serialism. The separate categories of 17th-century taxonomic processes and their less-than-tightly ordered organizatio-nal schemes are difficult for us to understand and to value.

This difficulty can be seen in the judgements of Gary Tomlinson, who says of madrigals from Monteverdi's Eight Book of 1638, «their martial images, mainly furious melismas and fanfare melodies over repetitive harmonies, are simple pictorial madrigalisms - and tedious ones, at that. Such bellicose bluster [...] mars even the otherwise deeply felt setting of Petrarch's sonnet 'Or che'l ciel'»[14]. Tomlinson then refers to Monteverdi's large *concertato* madrigals as «sonorous, grandiloquent, but after all hollow works»[15]. But Tomlinson isn't the only one to take a negative stance toward the Eighth Book. The brief biographical introduction to Oliver Strunk's English translations of Monteverdi's 1607 *Dichiaratione* and the preface to the Eighth Madrigal Book says «In the Eighth Book [...]., the pieces no longer have anything in common with the tradition. That Monteverdi should call

---

[13]   *Op. cit.*, p. 120.
[14]   GARY TOMLINSON, *Monteverdi and the End of the Renaissance*, Berkeley, University of California Press, 1987, p. 209.
[15]   TOMLINSON, p. 210.

such pieces 'Madrigali' is an indication of the level to which the madrigal had sunk by the third decade of the seventeenth century»[16].

It is the difficulty in evaluating this music on its own aesthetic turf that compromises Tomlinson's *Monteverdi and the End of the Renaissance*. Tomlinson sees the integrative aspects of Monteverdi's 16th-century search for metaphorical and stylistic resemblance in absolute terms, as an absolute value, while Monteverdi's shift to the taxonomic processes of the 17th century represents for Tomlinson a decline or degeneration. Modern historiography, anthropology and aesthetics have taught us, however, that different cultures must be viewed in relative terms, not according to absolutist criteria. Without having to succumb to a radical relativism, it is our responsibility as scholars to try to understand other cultures on their own terms, to understand their criteria of value from the perspective of those cultures. It is only on the basis of this kind of understanding that cross-cultural comparisons and comparisons between musics of different historical periods in the same culture can claim any validity. To understand Monteverdi's later works, we must attempt to understand them on the ground of 17th-century Venice, not 16th-century Mantua, or 19th-century Germany. We can compare his later works to his earlier ones to illuminate the differences between them, but not to say that one set of aesthetic goals and values is inherently superior to the other.

With that *caveat* and Foucault's formulation of 17th-century thought processes in mind, it is instructive to compare the preface to Monteverdi's Eighth Book with the *Dichiaratione* of 1607, a comparison previously highlighted by Barbara Hanning[17]. In the *Dichiaratione* Giulio Cesare justified the extreme methods Monteverdi employed in dealing with individual words or passions of the text. In the preface to the Eighth Book, Claudio sets about establishing taxonomies of the passions, of the voice and of music. Monteverdi begins, «*Havendo io considerato le nostre passioni, od d'affettioni del animo, essere tre le principali, cioè Ira, Temperanza, et Humilità o supplicatione [...]*»[18]. Similarly the nature of the voice is threefold: «*la natura stessa de la voce nostra in ritrovarsi, alta, bassa e mezzana: et come l'Arte Musica lo notifica chiaramente in questi tre termini, di concitato, molle, et temperato*»[19]. The main thrust of Monteverdi's preface is to claim his

---

[16] STRUNK, p. 405. It is not clear if these words are by Strunk, or by Dragan Plamenac, who wrote many of the biographical introductions to Strunk's translations.

[17] Review of TOMLINSON, *Monteverdi and the End of the Renaissance* in «Opera Quarterly» VI (1988), n. 1, pp. 87-89.

[18] Monteverdi's preface is translated into English in STRUNK, *op. cit.*, pp. 413-415. This passage in Strunk's translation reads as follows: «I have reflected that the principal passions or affections of our mind are three, namely, anger, moderation, and humility or supplication».

[19] Strunk: «the very nature of our voice indicates this in having high, low, and middle registers. The art of music also points clearly to these three in its terms 'agitated', 'soft', and 'moderate' (*concitato*, *molle*, and *temperato*)».

priority in the invention of the *concitato* genre, first used in the *Combattimento di Tancredi et Clorinda* in 1624, but he sees his invention in terms of completing the musical taxonomy which «*è stata, si può dire con ragione, sino ad hora imperfetta, non havendo hauto che gli duoi generi, molle et temperato*»[20]. At the end of the preface, Monteverdi indulges in yet another taxonomy, remarking that «*la Musica de Gran Prencipi viene adoperata nelle loro Regie Camere in tre modi per loro delicati gusti; da Teatro, da camera et da ballo; perciò nella presente mia opera ho accennato gli detti tre generi con la intitulatione Guerriera, Amorosa, et Rapresentativa*»[21].

Other theorists of the period also engaged in taxonomic classification. In 1640, Giambattista Doni classified dramatic monody into three categories: narrative, recitational, and expressive[22]. In 1648 and 1649 Marco Scacchi classified modern music into three styles: church, chamber and theater. Church music itself he divided into four types, Chamber music into three types and Theatrical music into two types[23].

Monteverdi, in describing his *concitato* or agitated style, admits that «*l'oratione non seguitasse co piedi la velocità del Istromento* [...]»[24]. He also calls attention to the necessity for rapid strumming of the *basso continuo* in order for the music to resemble agitated speech. Note that resemblance creeps in again here, but with an entirely different meaning from its significance for the 16th century. Resemblance here is not the discovered or invented relationship between a word and a particular, localized musical setting; it is, rather, the relationship between a generalized passion, that is, agitation, and a generalized way of setting it. What characterizes the warlike passion, according to Monteverdi, is «*oratione contenente ira et sdegno,*» and what characterizes the music is the reduction of one spondaic beat to «*sedici semicrome, et ripercosse ad una per una* [...]»[25].

The resemblance of which Monteverdi speaks in the Eighth Book preface can no longer be considered metaphorical, it has become iconic or emblematic, as Tomlinson has noted in his criticism of this feature of Monteverdi's late style. The difference between an icon and a metaphor is significant. The metaphor is particularized and wholly bound to the relationship established between the two

---

[20]   Strunk: «It may be said with reason that until present music has been imperfect, having had only the two general - 'soft' and 'moderate'». Strunk has mistranslated Monteverdi's *generi* as «general».

[21]   Strunk: «And since the music played before great princes at their courts to please their delicate taste is of three kinds, according to the method of performance - theater music, chamber music, and dance music - I have indicated these in my present work with the titles *Guerriera*, *Amorosa*, and *Rapresentativa*».

[22]   PALISCA, *Baroque Music*, 3rd edition, p. 36.

[23]   PALISCA, *Marco Scacchi's Defense of Modern Music (1649)*, pp.189-235; *Baroque Music*, 3rd edition, p. 60.

[24]   Strunk: «the words did not follow metrically the rapidity of the instrument».

[25]   Strunk: «words expressing anger and disdain» [...] «sixteen semiquavers, struck one after the other».

individual terms that comprise the metaphor. That is why the musical metaphor is localized in the musical texture, even though certain metaphorical conventions do develop in the 16th century in response to the conventional nature of poetic and sacred texts of the Renaissance. The icon on the other hand, creates a longer lasting association between a type of musical setting and a more generalized textual conception, and constitutes a symbol in the sense given the word by Ferdinand Saussure[26]. The musical icon is a symbol for the significance of the text, and that significance is expressed by Monteverdi in general terms, such as *concitato, molle* or *temperato* rather than in terms of specific words from the text. Once it has been established as a convention, the icon, as a symbol, is capable of conveying its significance in the absence of the words that generated it in the first place. The *concitato* genre can be used not only for a wide variety of texts signifying emotional agitation, it can be recognized as symbolizing agitation *in the absence* of texts, i.e. in instrumental music. In Foucault's terms, signs in the 16th century were «part of the things themselves, whereas in the seventeenth century they become modes of representation»[27].

The establishment of icons according to a systematic taxonomy created new kinds of compositional possibilities for composers of the 17th century. These possibilities are principally structural. Apart from the mass, 16th-century music was confined to small-scale organization by the nature of overlapping polyphony, and in the mass, three of the movements are small-scale structures; even *Glorias* and *Credos* are often no longer than many of the larger motets of the period. In the 17th century, the creative process of the concatenation of taxonomies allowed for the building of large-scale structures around the differences between taxonomic categories and opened up the possibility of the repetition of one or more taxonomic units to extend sections of a composition or to act as anchoring blocks dispersed throughout a composition, as in the *ritornello* or *ripieno*.

Thus, any attempt to understand and to analyze the music of Monteverdi's late Venetian period must proceed from a grasp of the taxonomic impetus and its aesthetics. A valid critique of this music must come to grips with the challenges posed by taxonomic structures and their ordering processes, which do not readily fit the mold of either Renaissance resemblances or more modern concepts of «organic» unity or structural integration.

---

[26]   The words «icon» and «symbol» have different meanings for different writers. I am using them as synonymous here, with both terms referring to the special case in which a signifier bears an analogical relationship to the signified. C.S. Peirce used the word «icon» in this sense, while Saussure used the word «symbol» for the same kind of relationship. For a comparison of differing definitions of «symbolic function» and «symbol» by different authors, see JEAN-JACQUES NATTIEZ, *Music and Discourse: Toward a Semiology of Music*, trans. by Carolyn Abbate, Princeton, Princeton University Press, 1990, pp. 35-37.
[27]   FOUCAULT, *op. cit.*, p. 129.

There is no time in a paper of this length to discuss individual works from Monteverdi's Eighth Book of Madrigals to illustrate how these compositions divide into taxonomic categories built out of the iconic musical materials generated by the text. And if we rely on Monteverdi's threefold taxonomy of musical icons, we will run into difficulty in explaining the music of these late madrigals. In actual deed Monteverdi's musical iconography is much more complicated than in his theory. Only the *concitato* genre stands as an immediately recognizable entity. While there are segments of pieces that may also easily be described as *molle* or *temperato*, these two taxonomies are too general to be of much analytical use. Many sections with clearly defined musical character seem ill-served by either the term *molle* or *temperato*. Moreover, the monodic passages in some Eighth Book madrigals, especially those in recitative style, have virtually nothing to do with Monteverdi's soft and moderate categories. I would suggest that a more complicated taxonomy needs to be developed to deal successfully with the music Monteverdi presents us.

In constructing a series of musical icons to form a multi-sectioned madrigal, the ordering process must be governed in some way. Monteverdi hints at one in his preface when he comments «*et sapendo che gli contrarij sono quelli che movono grandemente l'animo nostro, fine del movere che deve havere la bona Musica, come afferma Boetio* [...]»[28]. In other words, contrasts are a generating feature of the ordering process. This is easily enough said, but where do we go from here?

The problem is highlighted by a comparison with the way we deal with resemblance and relationships built on resemblance. The very structures of our most basic analytical and descriptive tools, discursive language and mathematics, are relational in character. The mathematical system that has been invented for analyzing functional harmony is relational at its core and the graphs that have been devised for Schenkerian analysis highlight both hierarchical and long-term linear relationships. Most language structures are likewise built on a relationship-the relationship between subject and predicate. The subject is linked to a predicate either through an action or some level of identity, depending on the character of the verb. Language structures describing objects, including musical objects, join the subject with the predicate through the identification of resemblance between the two. In descriptive and analytical language a predicate *is* identical to the subject or *is like* the subject in some way. Language not only establishes the resemblance between the two, but has a virtually infinite capacity to ferret out and describe the most subtle and remote relationships or resemblances. Language is a marvellously effective medium for the discussion of Renaissance resemblances, of 19th-century «organic» unities, and of 20th-century integrative processes.

---

[28]   Strunk: «And since I was aware that it is contraries which greatly move our mind, and that this is the purpose which all good music should have - as Boethius asserts [...]»

But the music that concerns us at this moment is music structured around the *contrast* between successive taxonomic categories. Such contrasts are much more problematic for language than resemblances. It is a simple matter to denote a contrast in language, to point out that something is *not* something else or *is not like* something else, but the discursive linguistic process comes to a halt at that point. Instead of the myriad ways we can describe resemblances in language, contrasts often leave us linguistically paralyzed beyond the initial observation that the contrasting items are different from one another. This is especially true if they are quite opposite in character.

This problem suggests that in order to understand more fully the music of the 17th century, we need to develop some different methods for coping with it. First of all, we should not be baffled or frightened by the prospect of having to deal with an issue that is linguistically problematic. Contrasts are, in fact, fundamental to our existence, especially binary oppositions. Up and down, male and female, good and evil, right and left, forwards and backwards, earth and water, earth and sky, hot and cold, are binary contrasts that govern our daily lives and are fundamental to our sensory and affective experience. Moreover, these binary contrasts are obviously linked together in meaningful relationships based on their very opposition. Up is meaningless without down; male is meaningless without female, etc. Yet we can recognize immediately that the meanings of these contrasts of opposites are very complex, and perhaps impossible to articulate in discursive language.

These basic binary contrasts, called archetypes by Carl Jung, can be understood, according to his theory, as involving relationships between the conscious and the unconscious. The principal oppositions illuminated by Jung are male/female and good/evil. One of the two elements in each binary opposition, or antimony, stems from the conscious, the other from the unconscious. Because one originates in the unconscious, it cannot be directly known to the intellect. Cognition and analysis of that element of the duality arising from the unconscious is impossible; it makes itself evident, rather, through symbols, and mankind's symbolic expressions often reveal the workings of the unconscious and the interaction of the binary opposites on the psyche and personality.

A basic tenet of Jung's theory is that the personality or «self» is made complete or whole by the healthy integration of the antimony derived from the unconscious. Suppression of the binary opposite, on the other hand, produces one-sidedness or distortion of personality and eventual psychological problems[29]. In this light it is interesting to note that Monteverdi conceives of his *genere concitato* as completing the emotional taxonomy, thereby making whole the possibilities of emotional expression available to the composer.

---

[29]   These ideas are scattered throughout many of Jung's writings. A late, representative example is *Aion: Untersuchungen zur Symbolgeschichte*, Zürich, Rascher Verlag, 1951.

I

118

Jung's contention that these antimonies cannot be analyzed by the conscious intellect underscores our inability to deal effectively with Monteverdi's psychological oppositions and their symbolic manifestation in musical contrasts. Instead, we must understand them as essential elements in the completeness, or wholeness, of psychological expression, attempt to grasp this wholeness, and if we wish to explain it, to use other symbolic or metaphorical forms of speech than discursive, analytical language.

Let me now summarize where we stand with regard to Monteverdi's late music: if we can understand his aesthetic objectives; if we can understand his iconic approach to the interpretation of his texts; if we can understand his taxonomic approach to large-scale musical organization; and if we can recognize the structural and psychological significance of contrasts in his music, then we can view his late madrigals and other late works from a different perspective from Tomlinson and from Monteverdi's own earlier *prima prattica* and *seconda prattica* aesthetic as revealed in the 1607 *Dichiaratione*. By 1638, Monteverdi has taken a somewhat different compositional approach, reflecting early Baroque aesthetics and creative processes, similar to those described by Foucault. His goal has been first of all to identify clearly the emotions and situations described by the text. This is the beginning of the taxonomic process. Secondly, he has invented musical icons to interpret the conceptions embodied in the text. Subsequently he has created homogenous musical segments - musical taxonomies - as the structural building blocks of his compositions. Finally he has built his compositions by arranging these musical taxonomic units in particular series, based on repetition and contrast. In these late madrigals Monteverdi's purpose is no longer to make the listener feel the passions of the performer as the aesthetics of early opera had demanded in accordance with Greek theories and legends of the transference of affect. His purpose, rather, is to convey in music knowledge about affective states - first to identify their character, then to present them for our understanding in an appropriate musical garb. This knowledge is principally of separate affects, but in the more sophisticated Eighth Book madrigals, such as *Hor che'l ciel e la terra*, there are passages where the simultaneous combination of separate ideas creates a more complicated psychological affect, which is also clearly expressed musically. Monteverdi's approach is more empirical than passionate, more interested in conveying concepts of emotion than in inducing emotion. To illustrate with a specific example, the opening quiet, static segment of *Hor che'l ciel e la terra* is not so much about the silence of nature as described by Petrarch, but rather about the nature of tranquility in general. The *concitato* passage further on in the madrigal is not so much about the poet's warlike state in this particular instance as it is about the general character of warlike agitation. And these two archetypes, together with the archetypical contrast between the male warrior and the female giver of peace, help bind these taxonomic units into a psychological whole.

This is a more objective view than in his Mantuan works or even than in many pieces from the Seventh Book of Madrigals, and it is fully consonant with the efforts of contemporary thinkers to understand their world in more objective and concrete terms - the basis of the new empirical science of the 17th century - as well as the basis of life as theater and psychological drama, aptly characterized by Shakespeare's remark, «all the world's a stage.»

II

A TAXONOMIC AND AFFECTIVE ANALYSIS OF MONTEVERDI'S 'HOR CHE'L CIEL E LA TERRA'

The madrigals of Monteverdi's Eighth Book of 1638, the *Madrigali guerrieri, et amorosi*, have often proved problematic for scholars attempting to explain their coherence, aesthetic impact and significance. Indeed, the difficulty of doing so has in some instances led to claims against the aesthetic worth of these compositions. According to Gary Tomlinson, 'Hor che'l ciel' and other madrigals of the Eighth Book 'are *madrigali senza gesto*, and their martial images, mainly furious melismas and fanfare melodies over repetitive harmonies, are simple pictorial madrigalisms – and tedious ones, at that. Such bellicose bluster . . . mars even the otherwise deeply felt setting of Petrarch's sonnet "Or che'l ciel."' Tomlinson then refers to Monteverdi's large *concertato* madrigals as 'sonorous, grandiloquent, but after all hollow works'.[1] But Tomlinson is not the only one to look askance at the Eighth Book. The brief biographical introduction to Oliver Strunk's translations of both (Giulio Cesare) Monteverdi's 1607 *Dichiaratione* and the Eighth Madrigal Book preface declares: 'In the Eighth Book . . . , the pieces no longer have anything in common with the tradition. That Monteverdi should call such pieces "Madrigali" is an indication of the level to which the madrigal had sunk by the third decade of the seventeenth-century'.[2] Even Alfred Einstein and Denis Arnold held perjorative views of Monteverdi's late madrigals.[3]

These judgements all begin from the perspective of the integrated polyphonic style of the sixteenth century and find Monteverdi's late madrigals wanting in the fulfilment of the aesthetic goals of the Renaissance madrigal. But by 1638, Monteverdi had developed a new aesthetics of the madrigal, resulting in quite different compositional objectives from his Madrigal Books I-VI (1587-1614). In order to understand better Monteverdi's compositional style in his Eighth Book, it is necessary to see more clearly his new aesthetic aims and to apply analytical perspectives that will help to unravel how these aesthetic aims are fulfilled in individual compositions. My starting point will be a brief examination of the famous preface to the *Madrigali guerrieri, et amorosi* and

II

an assessment of its significance.[4] This assessment will then provide criteria for a study of one of the best-known madrigals from the Eighth Book, 'Hor che'l ciel e la terra'.

The preface to the Eighth Book is devoted throughout to the establishment of emotional and musical taxonomies. Monteverdi declares that the 'principal passions or affections of our mind are three, namely anger, moderation, and humility or supplication'.[5] Similarly the nature of the voice is threefold, 'having high, low, and middle registers. The art of music also points clearly to these three in its terms *concitato* (agitated), *molle* (soft), and *temperato* (moderate)'.[6] Although the main thrust of Monteverdi's preface is to claim his priority in the invention of the *concitato* genus, first used in the *Combattimento di Tancredi e Clorinda* (1624), he sees his invention in terms of completing the taxonomy of musical categories which 'until present . . . has been imperfect, having had only the two genera – soft and moderate'.[7] At the end of the preface, Monteverdi indulges in yet another taxonomy, remarking that 'the music played before great princes at their courts . . . is of three kinds, according to the method of performance – theater music, chamber music, and dance music – I have indicated these in my present work with the titles *Guerriera, Amorosa,* and *Rapresentativa*'.[8]

Monteverdi, in describing his *concitato* or agitated genus, admits that 'the words did not follow metrically the rapidity of the instrument'.[9] He also calls attention to the necessity for rapid strumming of the *basso continuo* in order for the music to resemble agitated speech. The resemblance of which Monteverdi speaks is not the close resemblance between musical setting and specific words or phrases of text that we find in sixteenth-century madrigals and in Monteverdi's own madrigals up to and including Book VI. The resemblance is, rather, the relationship between a generalized passion, that is, agitation, and a generalized way of setting it. What characterises the warlike passion, according to Monteverdi, are 'words expressing anger and disdain' and what characterises the music is the reduction of one spondaic beat to 'sixteen semiquavers, struck one after the other'.[10]

The resemblances between music and text which characterise the sixteenth-century madrigal and which serve as the justification for Monteverdi's irregular dissonance practice in the well-known *Dichiaratione* of his *Scherzi musicali* of 1607, can be considered metaphorical in nature, whereby the composer finds an appropriate musical metaphor for individual words and phrases of text as they occur. Such metaphors tend to be ephemeral, their significance having been completed once the composer moves on to the next word or phrase and searches for a new musical metaphor. But the resemblances of which Monteverdi speaks in the Eighth Book preface have become iconic or emblematic, as Tomlinson himself has noted in his criticism of this feature of Monteverdi's late style.[11] The difference between an icon and a metaphor is significant. The metaphor is particularized and wholly bound to the relationship established between the two individual terms that comprise the metaphor. Thus the musical metaphor is normally localised in the musical texture, even though certain general types of metaphors do develop in the sixteenth century in response to the conventional nature of poetic and sacred texts. The icon, on the other hand, is more generalised, and thereby becomes a symbol for the significance of the text, and that significance is expressed in general terms, such as *concitato*, *molle* or *temperato* rather than in terms of specific words from the text. Once it has been established as a convention, the icon, as a symbol, has durability and is capable of carrying its significance in the absence of the words that generated it in the first place. The *concitato* genus can be used not only for a wide variety of texts signifying emotional agitation, it can be recognized as symbolizing agitation *in the absence* of texts, i.e. in instrumental music. Monteverdi's Eighth Book preface identifies these musical icons and classifies them taxonomically, that is, in distinct categories. It should be noted that while most metaphors disintegrate when one of the two terms is removed, some metaphors, if there is sufficient analogy between the two terms and the metaphor is capable of sufficient generalisation, can become icons through repeated use leading to acceptance as conventions.

The establishment of icons according to a systematic taxonomy creates new kinds of compositional possibilities for composers of the seventeenth century. These possibilities are both structural and psychological, enabling composers to build large-scale works around the differences between taxonomic categories as well as to utilise the differences between one or more taxonomic units as the vehicle for dramatic effects and the exploration of human psychology. Monteverdi's own emphasis on the *genere concitato*, on agitation, is an indication of his interest in the expression of psychological stress and excited states of emotion.

Michel Foucault has contrasted seventeenth-century thought processes with those of the Renaissance in terms of the contrast between the Renaissance search for resemblances in all things (an example of which is the search for metaphors) and the seventeenth-century impulse towards taxonomic classification (an example of which is the production of icons):

What has become important is no longer resemblances, but identities and differences. ... The activity of the mind ... will therefore no longer consist in *drawing things together*, in setting out on a quest for everything that might reveal some sort of kinship attraction, or secretly shared nature within them, but, on the contrary, in *discriminating*, that is, establishing their identities, then the inevitability of the connections with all the successive degrees of a series. In this sense, discrimination imposes upon comparison the primary and fundamental investigation of difference: providing oneself by intuition with a distinct representation of things, and apprehending clearly the inevitable connection

II

between one element in a series and that which immediately
follows it.[12]

It is identities and differences that fuelled the empirical investigations of
the seventeenth century, whether represented by Galileo, Descartes or
Mersenne, and allowed for new forms of conceptualization and classification. In order to organize thought empirically, the investigator has to be
most interested in what *is*, not in its relationship to something else, its
utility for humans or its divine significance – interests so often articulated
by sixteenth-century writers in almost any discipline.

The process of discovering what *is*, in searching for the empirical mode
of being, requires grasping simultaneously both identities *and* differences
between things that are not identical. Thus differences have replaced
resemblances as the driving force behind thought processes, the organization of knowledge, and creative activity. But differences, from the very
outset, require some kind of coherent grouping; otherwise, every item and
every experience in the world is different from every other, and the mind
cannot manage so much singularity in any fashion at all. Therefore
taxonomy develops as the means for organizing identities or near identities
as well as understanding the difference between separate categories of
coherent things.

Taxonomy requires not only classification, but also the appropriate
naming of the separate categories established by the classifying process.
Foucault declares that the 'fundamental task [of this period] is to ascribe a
name to things, and in that name to name their being'.[13] In Foucault's
terms, signs in the sixteenth century were 'part of the things themselves,
whereas in the seventeenth century they become modes of representation'.[14] Taxonomy also demands organization of the separate categories
into larger groupings. In the seventeenth century, the creative process of
stringing together taxonomic units allowed for the building of large-scale
structures around the differences between taxonomic categories. The
immediate repetition of a taxonomic unit, or some slightly varied or
expanded form of such a unit, led to the enlargement of structure. The
repetition of one or more taxonomic units dispersed throughout a structure
created anchoring building blocks, such as the *ritornello* or *ripieno*. The
distinct character of each taxonomic unit in a structure also allowed for the
juxtaposition of these units in dramatically contrasting successions.
Monteverdi hints in his preface at an ordering process for the construction
of multi-section madrigals out of distinct taxonomic categories when he
comments that 'it is contraries which greatly move our mind, and that this
is the purpose which all good music should have, as Boethius affirms'.[15] In
other words, contrasts are a governing principle of his musical
organization.

Thus, any attempt to understand and analyse the music of Monteverdi's
late period must proceed from a grasp of the taxonomic impulse and its

aesthetics. A valid critique of this music must begin with the challenges posed by taxonomic structures and their ordering processes, which do not readily fit the mould of either Renaissance resemblances or modern concepts of structural integration. However, if we rely on Monteverdi's threefold taxonomy of musical icons, we shall find ourselves limited in explaining the music of the late madrigals. In actual deed Monteverdi's musical iconography is much more complicated than his theory. Only the *concitato* genus stands as an immediately recognizable entity. While there are segments of pieces that may also easily be described as *molle* or *temperato*, these two taxonomies are too general to be of much analytical use. And many sections with clearly defined musical character seem ill-served by either of these terms. I would suggest that ultimately a more complicated taxonomy needs to be developed to cope successfully with the actual music with which Monteverdi presents us.

The recognition of a compositional process arising out of an aesthetic of taxonomic categories of text-derived passions or affects, on the one hand, and a structural ordering based on contrasts, on the other, allows us to examine Monteverdi's Eighth Book madrigals from a perspective appropriate to the materials themselves rather than attempting to apply criteria developed for study of the sixteenth-century madrigal. What follows is an attempt to understand 'Hor che'l ciel e la terra' in the taxonomic and affective terms described here.

'Hor che'l ciel' sets, in two parts, the entirety of Francesco Petrarca's sonnet 164 from *Le Rime* (the text and its translation are given in an Appendix below). Monteverdi's *prima parte* sets the two quatrains, and the *seconda parte* the two terzets. This is a poem replete with typically Petrarchan contrasts and oxymorons. But Petrarch's emotionally charged contrasts are brought into harmony and smoothed over by the mellifluous sounds and varied, rolling rhythms of his refined poetic style, as described by Pietro Bembo in the *Prose della volgar lingua*.[16] This is easily seen in Petrarch's fifth and sixth lines, where the most abrupt semantic juxtapositions are couched in an elegantly structured and alliterative sentence that draws attention away from the contrasts towards their union in a highly stylised and carefully crafted poetic conception. Resemblances of rhyme, rhythm, line lengths, stanzaic structure and, especially, sonority all serve to mitigate the semantic contrasts. In contrast to Petrarch's moderating of the opposing elements, Monteverdi seizes upon the oppositions as the means for creating rhetorical statements and musical icons which serve as the affective and constructive basis for his composition.

Contrasts in Petrarch's sonnet occur on several levels. First there are the obvious, immediate contrasts between successive words or concepts in the second quatrain. 'Dolce pena' (sweet pain) at the end of the sixth line is an oxymoron; 'guerra' (war) and 'pace' (peace) are contrasted in the seventh and eighth lines. In the first terzet, 'dolce' and 'amaro' (bitterness) are contrasted in the middle line, while the final line opposes 'risana' (heals)

II

and 'punge' (wounds). In the middle line of the final terzet 'moro' (I die) is contrasted with 'nasco' (I am born).

On a lower structural level there is dramatic contrast between the first quatrain and the second. The first quatrain unites in silence and motionlessness a series of natural elements and living creatures. This quatrain is an evocation of nature at rest, and the rocking rhythm of all four lines is reminiscent of a lullaby. The second quatrain, in which the speaker awakens, contrasts his individual experience with the backdrop of quiescent nature. This quatrain also commences with a series, but rather than different elements being united in a smooth, rocking rhythm, 'Vegghio, penso, ardo, piango' (I awake, I think, I burn, I weep) constitute an abrupt sequence of disjunct activities whose enumeration is characterised by both qualitative and quantitative accents on the first syllable of each two-syllable word and by double consonants – what Bembo calls *gravità* (seriousness), in Petrarch's style.[17] The beginning of this line is an effective characterisation of the intense psychological state in which a troubled spirit may abruptly awaken in the middle of the night.

This startled series is then followed by a rational attempt to explain the psychological state: 'she who undoes me is always before me for my sweet pain', though the rationality of the thought is undermined by the affective oxymoron at the end. The next sentence compounds the emotional contradiction. The speaker's state is now warlike, full of anger and sorrow, but in the fourth line, 'and only in thinking of her do I have some peace', the cause of the warlike state turns out also to be the only source of tranquillity. In this quatrain emotional contradictions and confusions are articulated in utter contrast to the stability and quietude of nature described in the opening quatrain.

The sestet generates yet more contrast. The description and experience of the octave are given additional meaning through the metaphor of the 'clear, living fountain'. The fount is the source of nourishment from which the speaker drinks both sweetness and bitterness, and the hand of the beloved, like the fount, both heals and wounds. The speaker is like the waters of the fount in that his martyrdom never reaches its end, so that a thousand times a day he dies and is reborn as the waters cycle forth. This is how far he is from regaining his mental health, which could only be achieved through resolving the emotional contradictions engendered by his lady. While nature and the speaker had been completely separate in the octave, the sestet brings the two into relationship. Through the metaphor of the fountain, the speaker and nature are reunited in thought, but this is an active, seething nature, not the sleeping nature of the first quatrain. As a consequence, the emotional conflict is left open and unresolved at the end, as if the speaker's salvation must always remain distant as long as the fountain of life continues to flow.

Monteverdi's setting of this text, following the programme set out in the Eighth Book preface, is organized both taxonomically and iconographically in distinctly separate sections focusing on specific categories of affect. Although the following analysis could be presented in the vocabulary of seventeenth-century modes, finals, diapente motions and so on, I prefer to use modern harmonic and tonal terminology whose significance is not anachronistic, that is, whose commonly understood meanings are applicable to the seventeenth-century functions they identify: this will adequately serve for the points I wish to make.

The opening of the madrigal, which sets the entire first quatrain, consists of static chords, organized rhythmically around the rhythms of the text, although the concluding trochees of 'terra', 'tace', 'affrena', 'mena' and 'giace' are all set as spondees rather than trochees, thereby increasing even further the sense of stasis. The only pitch motion in this entire section is a slow moving I-V-I-VI-V-I chord progression, obviously stimulated by the phrase 'in giro mena' (leads in a circle) in the third line; the first return to the tonic chord occurs precisely with this phrase (Ex. 1).[18] The homogeneous opening section of the piece is thus a single icon for the tranquillity described in the first quatrain of Petrarch's sonnet.

Petrarch's second quatrain, as shown above, not only contrasts with the first but is less internally unified (Ex. 2). Monteverdi begins with a graphic representation of the startled awakening of the sleeper, then proceeds immediately to a typically Renaissance metaphor for 'piango' (I weep) in suspended figures of falling tones or semitones. In contrast to the opening quatrain, each word is now on a new chord and at a higher pitch level than the last, proceeding around the circle of fifths (Ex. 2, bs 24-8). The continuation of the thought with 'e chi mi sface' (and she who undoes me) is cast in a descending lament in two voices in parallel thirds, the descent an obvious metaphor for depressed emotional states (bs 30-1).

Already Monteverdi is at work dealing with the psychological contrasts and contradictions in these two lines by superimposing a restatement of 'veglio, penso, ardo, piango' over the completion of the thought (Ex. 2, bs 31-41). The restatement proceeds with wider gaps between 'veglio', 'penso', 'ardo' and 'piango', thereby giving them the effect of a psychological background to the more immediate thought about the beloved who undoes the speaker. And Monteverdi artfully times these background superimpositions so that the final one, 'piango', occurs simultaneously with the final word of the second line, 'pena' (pain) (bs 40-1).

Monteverdi has by now not only generated three musical metaphors, but turned them into structural icons, in order to expand the section as well as make the psychological connection between the sudden awakening and the cause of that awakening. In so doing, he has built a larger structural metaphor for the confused, contradictory state expressed by the speaker. The sudden awakening comprises six bars, followed by twelve bars in which the awakening is combined with the vision of the undoer in front of the speaker's face and the weeping it brings. Having used the original metaphors in this way, Monteverdi repeats them in varied form –

Ex. 1

what I would call iconic repetition – through seventeen bars of gradually increasing textures until all six voices are involved, leading to a full-textured cadence in A major (Ex. 3). This allows him to bring the section to a close, culminating a structural dynamic of varied repetition in increasingly thicker textures, a dynamic found over and over again in Monteverdi's large-scale *concertato* works. Superimposed on the dynamic of increasing textures is another dynamic of arithmetically increasing lengths, from six bars to twelve to seventeen, although the final section falls one bar short of a perfect additive sequence at the end.

Since our analytic concerns are not only with the separate taxonomic categories, but also with the ordering of these categories, we may look back at the piece up to this point in terms of a dynamic of arsis and thesis. In Petrarch's sonnet, the arsis is the first quatrain with its description of tranquil nature, followed by the thesis of the startled awakening. In Monteverdi's madrigal, the first taxonomic unit similarly serves as an arsis,

Ex. 2

with the musical awakening functioning as thesis. Monteverdi's choice of
tonalities helps establish this relationship. The entire first section is in the
tonic of the madrigal, A.* But because of its static quality, the first section
serves as introduction (arsis) to the subsequent awakening, and the tonic of
A proves to have been the dominant of the awakening, which begins on a
D major triad. The artic-thetic quality of dominant and tonic are then
immediately expanded through the circle of fifths: each successive chord of
the awakening becomes the dominant of the next. At 'piango', B♭ has been
reached, and Monteverdi then slides back down a musical sigh to the
original A tonic (see Ex. 2, bs 28-9). The iconic repetition and expansion
of the next twelve bars follows the same harmonic process at a slower pace,
although, beginning on A rather than D, it logically concludes on E instead

* Cf. Geoffrey Chew's discussion of this section above, pp.150-2. *Ed.*

Ex. 2 cont.

of A. The E then conveniently serves as the principal tonic of the seventeen-bar expanded repetition, returning to A at the end in yet another artic-thetic movement. One might say that the artic-thetic character of Petrarch's octave has been transformed by Monteverdi into an artic-thetic structural use of dominant and tonic relations. This is not to say that dominant-tonic relations serve as an icon, but rather as a means for differentiating and ordering the taxonomic units of the composition.

The next two lines of Petrarch's second quatrain contrast 'guerra' with 'pace'. As we would expect, 'guerra' is represented by the *genere concitato*, in G major, which is Monteverdi's usual key for the *concitato* affect (see Ex. 4). This passage, whose beginning is clearly a principal structural point in the piece, commences just one tactus short of the large golden section of the *prima parte*. While the *genere concitato* clearly contrasts with the

Ex. 2 cont.

preceding two sections, the two earlier sections have also proceeded dynamically towards the *concitato*, that is, from tranquillity, through the more active but confused awakening, to the most active but rigidly circumscribed condition of 'guerra è il mio stato' (war is my state). This latter *concitato* passage occupies nine bars before being interrupted by its affective opposite, setting the line 'E sol di lei pensando ò qualche pace' (And only in thinking of her do I have some peace) (Ex. 5). The state of peace induced by thoughts of the lady contrasts with the previous passage by means of a homophonic and homorhythmic style in slow tempo, an obvious icon for 'pace'. Moreover, Monteverdi drops out the lower two voices, since the thought is focused on the feminine 'lei' (her). The contrast between the two passages highlights Monteverdi's conception of gender roles in this composition, for the musical statement of peace in the

II

Ex. 3

higher voices, ultimately cadencing in the relatively remote key of B major
after emphasizing the B minor triad, characterises Monteverdi's portrayal
of feminine traits just as the warlike section does of masculine traits. The
peaceful feminine section nearly balances the warlike masculine one (eight
bars as compared to nine). The tonal relationship between the two,
however, is unlike the tonal movement found earlier in the madrigal. Here
there is no artic-thetic sequence between the taxonomic categories, only
the bald contrast of war and peace, masculine and feminine. Consequently
Monteverdi directly juxtaposes two keys that in seventeenth-century terms
were radically opposed, G major and B minor/ major. Moreover, there is
no change of key within each of these two stable taxonomic categories.

These two musical icons are then repeated structurally, expanding to
twelve bars for the 'guerra' segment and nine bars for the 'pace' segment.

Ex. 3 cont.

The expansion is accompanied in the 'pace' segment by a full-textured setting so that the entire two-segment passage provides a weighty cadential close to the *prima parte*. In order to conclude the *prima parte* in E major, the dominant of the entire madrigal, the feminine section is reset with the bass a fifth lower. While I would not characterise the two feminine sections, the first in B and the second in E, as being in an artic-thetic relationship, the movement by a fifth downwards is part of Monteverdi's large-scale tonal planning, since the conclusion of the *prima parte* in the dominant key sets the stage for the ultimate drop of a fifth to the tonic at the final close of the *seconda parte*. It is also important to the overall poetic conception of the madrigal that there is an inconclusive close in the dominant at the end of the *prima parte*, in order to leave the way open for the sestet to bring the speaker and nature together. Thus tonal organ-

Ex. 3 cont.

ization once again serves the affective dynamic of the poem.

The *seconda parte* opens with a descending figure reminiscent of 'e chi mi sface' (Ex. 6). This resemblance serves a structural purpose in linking the two parts of the madrigal, but also performs an affective role in relating the image of the living fountain to the beloved who undoes the speaker. One might say that the descent from e^1 at the beginning of the *seconda parte* has a musical function similar to the linking function of the word 'Così' (thus) at the beginning of Petrarch's sestet. But the most important part of the opening is the overlapping of the phrase 'Così sol d'una chiara fonte viva' (thus only from a clear, living fountain) with 'Move'l dolce e l'amaro, ond'io mi pasco' (moves the sweetness and the bitterness, whence I nourish myself) (Ex. 7). The latter is set to a chromatically rising motive treated in imitation, a typical icon for situations of anguish in Monteverdi,

Ex. 4

the most famous of which is 'non morir, Seneca' from *L'Incoronazione di Poppea*. This particular version abjures dissonance almost altogether in recognition of the sweetness that is also imbibed from the fountain. The combination of these two motives brings together in simultaneity the source of the water and its effects on him who drinks it; the source is strictly diatonic and objective in character, while the human effect is chromatic and filled with increasing tension. Monteverdi's texture gradually expands through the imitation, reaching his typical full-textured climax, which is immediately followed by a more extended structural repetition of the chromatic motive. But there is a third line to the terzet, and Monteverdi cleverly introduces it into the texture by simply varying the descent from e^1 and substituting the final line 'Una man sola mi risana e punge' (A single hand heals and wounds me) (Ex. 8, Tenor II). Thus,

Ex. 4 cont.

when Monteverdi once again reaches his textural climax, the section *and* the terzet can come to a close, and the passage has once more been built upon varied structural repetition of a musical icon.

The final terzet revolves mostly around the second line, one of the most common textual conceits of the Petrarchan sixteenth century, set over and over again by composers from Arcadelt through Rore to Monteverdi in multiple imitations. This second line is briefly introduced by a simple, declamatory statement of the first line. Monteverdi's treatment of the second line is in some respects antiphonal; only the final word, 'moro', cast in longer notes in stepwise descent, overlaps. At the end of the passage, Monteverdi dovetails the words 'nasco' and 'moro', bringing them into even closer oppositional relationship to one another than Petrarch could do in the linear medium of language (Ex. 9, bs 42-3). Structural repetition,

Ex. 5

transposed by a fifth, then serves to expand the section, just as in earlier portions of the piece.

Petrarch's concluding line is somewhat separate from the rest of the sonnet in making a final statement about the poet's circumstances. Monteverdi likewise sets this line apart, with a single voice in static repetition, preparing for its musical opposite on the word 'lunge' (far, distant), whose significance is emphasized by a long leap and an even longer slow, melismatic descent (Ex. 10, bs 65-73). A transposed, full-textured structural repeat then serves to close out the entire madrigal, returning to the opening key (Ex. 11). The melisma now not only travels a long distance, but the texture expands from a close triad to the longest conceivable distance between bass and treble.[19] Massimo Ossi has observed that the soprano moves stepwise towards the highest pitch of the piece, a^2,

II

Ex. 6

Seconda parte

which has heretofore appeared only in the violins. The passage is clearly climactic and summarizes in concentrated fashion the gradually expanding pitch movement of the *prima parte*.[20] In its long stepwise motion in asymmetrical rhythms (and in contrary polyphony in the second statement), this melisma stretches the musical tension to the limit through the contrasting extremes of high and low registers. It is the most powerful single moment in the composition. It lacks the specific import of Petrarch's final line, where the continuing problem of the poet is clearly delineated, but, more powerfully than Petrarch, it captures the emotional anguish of the speaker whose psyche is pulled in opposite directions by the unresolved, conflicting passions induced by his lady.

The sestet (Monteverdi's *seconda parte*) comprises a reflection by Petrarch on the significance of the contrasting emotions exposed in the

Ex. 7

octave (Monteverdi's *prima parte*). From a dynamic and structural point of view, the first terzet of the *seconda parte* displays two overlapping motives which are treated imitatively in an ever-thickening texture. The first segment occupies twelve and a half bars, culminating in a full-textured, largely homophonic and homorhythmic close as in several passages in the *prima parte*. From a harmonic standpoint, however, there is no functional closure at all; the segment ends on a C major chord approached contrapuntally by a sixth expanding to an octave. The subsequent iconic repetition of the two motives results in an expanded segment of eighteen and a half bars, larger by half than the first segment. This time there is a clear-cut cadence in A.

The final terzet begins precisely at the small golden section of the *seconda parte*, with the first line serving only as a brief introduction to the

Ex. 8

main event, the multifold repetitions of 'mille volte il dí' (a thousand times a day). These two lines occupy twelve bars, whereupon they are repeated, as in the first portion of the *seconda parte*, for eighteen and a half bars, creating a near-perfect structural symmetry between the first two portions of the *seconda parte*. But there is one line left, and this comprises a structural coda, singling out the word 'lunge' for the lengthy melisma. This motive is also heard twice, once for solo tenor, and again accompanied by the full ensemble, both statements occupying eleven bars. Thus the coda has a twofold structural repetition like the preceding segments, but with the repeat expanded in texture rather than in length. The *seconda parte*, therefore, like the *prima parte*, consists of three main segments, though it is a bit shorter because of the briefer text.

On the whole, the *seconda parte* is less concerned with the psychological

Ex. 9

contrasts of the *prima parte* and more interested in the objective description of the fountain as metaphor for the poet's lady. In composing a more objective *seconda parte*, Monteverdi was following Petrarch, whose concrete language in the sestet helps the speaker to conceptualize his emotions, thereby exerting a form of intellectual control over them. Petrarch ends with a declarative statement providing the logical reason for the thousand deaths per day. Monteverdi, by contrast, summarizes the poet's anguish with his dramatic final cadence.

What is apparent from this analysis of the dynamic movement and structure of the composition is that Monteverdi's successive sections are not merely a concatenation of separate taxonomic categories; there is a rationale to his ordering process. In the *prima parte* that rationale is based on the psychological dynamic of the poem, leading from stasis through

Ex. 10

startled mental activity to the contrast between two clearly conceived, gender-oriented emotional states. Nevertheless, the lengths of the various segments reveal concern for mathematical proportions. In the *seconda parte* the rationale seems less semantically and psychologically based and more purely structural, where the first two segments each have a dynamic of repetition expanded by half, but balance each other symmetrically, and the third segment comprises a briefer, mathematically symmetrical coda. This emphasis on structural balances suggests the musician's attempt to bring the passions of the octave under some kind of control, just as the poet did through the concrete language of the fountain metaphor.

Monteverdi's overall organization is not unified through motivic similarity, nor is it an 'organic' structure, in which all of the parts interact functionally with one another. Neither is it a wholly integrated structure

Ex. 11

where the smallest and largest parts all reflect a single structural concept. It does, however, consist of a coherent, comprehensible ordering of taxonomic segments, an ordering which in some of its features leans heavily on the text and in others relies more on formal musical considerations. And the elements upon which this structure is based are the musical icons derived from general concepts named in Petrarch's poem.

An exegetical analysis such as this is by definition incomplete, as is, of course, any analysis. It presents one perspective on the work, and other excgeses could present other, complementary or even conflicting, explanations. The depth of any important work of art extends ultimately beyond analysis, and the most we can hope for is a constantly deepening understanding through a series of analyses made from differing perspectives and with differing focuses of attention. I have taken as the basis

Ex. 11 cont.

of my analysis the impulse toward taxonomic categories that characterises early seventeenth-century thought processes as well as the interest in psychological contrasts expressed by Monteverdi himself. As with any such exegesis, the question is not, 'Is this analysis true in an absolute sense?' but 'Can it be supported by the work itself, and is it persuasive?' I hope I have demonstrated the former; only my readers can judge the latter.

APPENDIX

Francesco Petrarca: 'Or che'l ciel e la terra'*

1   Or che'l ciel, e la terra, e'l vento tace,
E le fere, e gli augelli il sonno affrena,
Notte il carro stellato in giro mena
E nel suo letto il mar senz'onda giace;

5   Vegghio, penso, ardo, piango; e chi mi sface
Sempre m'è inanzi per mia dolce pena:
Guerra è'l mio stato d'ira e di duol piena;
E sol di lei pensando ò qualche pace.

     Cosí sol d'una chiara fonte viva,
10   Move'l dolce e l'amaro, ond'io mi pasco;
Una man sola mi risana e punge.

     E perché'l mio martir non giunga a riva,
Mille volte il dí moro, e mille nasco:
Tanto da la salute mia son lunge.

1   Now that heaven and earth and the wind are silent,
And sleep restrains the beasts and the birds,
Night leads its starry chariot in a circle,
And the sea without waves lies in its bed,

5   I awake, I think, I burn, I weep; and she who undoes me
Is always before me for my sweet pain.
War is my state, full of anger and of sorrow,
And only in thinking of her do I have some peace.

     Thus only from a clear, living fountain
10   Moves the sweetness and the bitterness, whence I nourish myself;
A single hand heals and wounds me.

     And so that my martyrdom does not arrive at shore,
A thousand times a day I die, and a thousand [times] am born;
So far am I from my salvation.

* Petrarch's text is taken from *Le Rime di Francesco Petrarca*, ed. Nicola Zingarelli (Bologna: Zanichelli, 1963), pp.881-3. The English translation is my own.

II

NOTES

1. *Monteverdi and the End of the Renaissance* (Berkeley: University of California Press, 1987), pp.209-10.
2. *Source Readings in Music History* (New York: Norton, 1950), p.405. It is not clear whether these words are by Strunk, or by Dragan Plamenac, who wrote many of the biographical introductions to Strunk's translations.
3. Einstein begins to find fault with Monteverdi's later madrigals as soon as the *basso continuo* is introduced in Book V of 1605. Book VII is already so far beyond the polyphonic madrigal of the Renaissance that it does not merit detailed discussion. Book VIII 'has almost nothing to do with the madrigal'. See *The Italian Madrigal* (Princeton: Princeton University Press, 1949), Vol. 2, pp.854, 863-4. Denis Arnold comments that 'perhaps the best that can be said is that these battle pieces are not quite as dull as Jannequin's "La Bataille de Marignan"'. See Denis Arnold, *Monteverdi Madrigals*, BBC Music Guides (London: Billing, 1967), p.57.
4. A more detailed account of the significance of the Eighth Book preface in comparison with the preface to the *Scherzi musicali* of 1607 will appear in my forthcoming article 'Monteverdi's Changing Aesthetics: A Semiotic Perspective'. A number of recent studies have examined Monteverdi's aesthetics, including the Eighth Book preface, from various angles. See Mathias Bielitz, 'Zum Verhältnis von Form und Semantik in der Musik von Monteverdi', in *Claudio Monteverdi: Festschrift Reinhold Hammerstein zum 70. Geburtstag*, ed. Ludwig Finscher (Laaber: Laaber, 1986), pp.53-121; Sabine Ehrmann, *Claudio Monteverdi: Die Grundbegriffe seines musiktheoretischen Denkens* (Pfaffenweiler: Centaurus-Verlagsgesellschaft, 1989); Gerald Drebes, 'Monteverdi's "Kontrastprinzip", die Vorrede zu seinem 8. Madrigalbuch und das "Genre concitato"', *Musiktheorie*, Vol. 6, No. 1 (1991), pp.29-42; and Barbara Russano Hanning, 'Monteverdi's Three Genera: A Study in Terminology', in *Musical Humanism and Its Legacy: Essays in Honor of Claude V. Palisca*, ed. Barbara R. Hanning and Nancy K. Baker (Stuyvesant, NY: Pendragon Press, 1992), pp.145-70. I am indebted to Barbara Hanning for an advance copy of this article.
5. 'Havendo io considerato le nostre passioni, od d'affettioni del animo, essere tre le principali, cioè Ira, Temperanza, et Humilità o supplicatione ... ' The translation and those that follow are from Strunk, *Source Readings*, pp.413-15.
6. '... la natura stessa de la voce nostra in ritrovarsi, alta, bassa e mezzana: et come l'Arte Musica lo notifica chiaramente in questi tre termini, di concitato, molle, et temperato'. [Cf. Geoffrey Chew's article above, pp.155-6. *Ed.*]
7. '... è stata, si può dire con ragione, sino ad hora imperfetta, non havendo hauto che gli duoi generi, molle et temperato'. Strunk has mistranslated Monteverdi's 'generi' as 'general'.
8. '... la Musica de Gran Prencipi viene adoperata nelle loro Regie Camere in tre modi per loro delicati gusti; da Teatro, da camera et da ballo; perciò nella presente mia opera ho accennato gli detti tre generi con la intitulatione

Guerriera, Amorosa, et rapresentativa'.

9. '... l'oratione non seguitasse co piedi la velocità del Istromento ...'
10. '... oratione contenente ira et sdegno' ... 'sedici semicrome, et ripercosse ad una per una ...' [Cf. Geoffrey Chew's Plate 1 above, p.158. *Ed.*]
11. *Monteverdi*, pp.202, 205, 210.
12. Michel Foucault, *The Order of Things: An Archaeology of the Human Sciences* (New York: Vintage Books, 1973), pp.50, 55. This book was originally published in France as *Les Mots et les choses* (Editions Gallimard) in 1966.
13. *Ibid.*, p.120.
14. *Ibid.*, p.129.
15. '... et sapendo che gli contrarij sono quelli che movono grandemente l'animo nostro, fine del movere che deve havere la bona Musica, come afferma Boetio ...'
16. The *Prose della volgar lingua* was first published in 1525 by Tacuino in Venice.
17. See the discussion of Bembo's concepts of *piacevolezza* and *gravità* in Dean T. Mace, 'Pietro Bembo and the Literary Origins of the Italian Madrigal', *The Musical Quarterly*, Vol. 55, No. 1 (January 1969), pp.65-86.
18. This and all of the following examples are taken from G. Francesco Malipiero, *Tutte le opere di Claudio Monteverdi*, Vol. 8, No. 1, rev. edn (Vienna: Universal, 1967). Malipiero's dynamics and phrase marks have been omitted.
19. I am grateful to Craig Monson for this observation.
20. Massimo Michele Ossi, 'Claudio Monteverdi's *Concertato* Technique and Its Role in the Development of his Musical Thought' (Diss., Harvard University, 1989), pp.185-93.

III

A JUNGIAN PERSPECTIVE
ON MONTEVERDI'S LATE MADRIGALS

Although my paper focuses its attention on Claudio Monteverdi, it serves the theme of this conference on relations between Italian and German music in the Baroque Era since Monteverdi's music spread so widely north of the Alps, as Peter Wollny has shown, and had such obvious influence on northern composers[1]. Anything that assists us in understanding the aesthetics and style of Monteverdi helps us understand the aesthetics and style of Baroque music in German-speaking lands as well.

The relationship between Monteverdi's Venetian music and the North is also evidenced by the dedication of Monteverdi's Eighth Book of Madrigals of 1638 to the Hapsburg Emperor Ferdinand III (changed at the last minute from his recently deceased father Ferdinand II), and the dedication of the *Selva morale et spirituale* of 1641 to Eleanora Gonzaga, widow of Ferdinand II and stepmother of Ferdinand III.

Monteverdi's Eighth Book of Madrigals has proved something of an aesthetic puzzle to musicologists. Its preface outlines three genera of music, which have been demonstrated by Barbara Hanning to be based on a long tradition of classification[2]. Monteverdi's description of the *genere concitato* is clear and unequivocal; however, he is by no means as clear about what determines the *genere temperato* and the *genere molle*. He simply relies on the contemporary reader's general knowledge of musical style and aesthetic theory to understand what he is talking about[3].

---

[1]   P. WOLLNY, *The Distribution and Reception of Monteverdi's Music in Seventeenth-Century Germany*, Paper delivered at 1994 annual meeting of American Musicological Society, Minneapolis.

[2]   B. R. HANNING, *Monteverdi's Three Genera: A Study in Terminology*, in *Musical Humanism and its Legacy: Essays in Honor of Claude V. Palisca*, ed. Nancy Kovaleff Baker and Barbara Russano Hanning, Stuyvesant, New York, Pendragon Press, 1992, pp. 145-70. Hanning for the first time illustrates clearly the complicated relationship among the various categories Monteverdi mentions.

[3]   See Hanning's tracing of some of these concepts in Vicentino, Zarlino and Galilei, pp. 161-62, and in Girolamo Mei, p. 167. See also notes 19 and 20 below.

The preface also mentions Plato's *Rhetoric*, which Massimo Ossi has recently convincingly argued is not only a mistake for Plato's *Republic*, but also for Aristotle's *Rhetoric*, which lies behind much of Monteverdi's argument[4]. At the end, the preface names three types of music performed at the courts of great princes: theater music, chamber music, and dance music. Monteverdi goes on to say that in his Eighth Book of Madrigals he has entitled these three genera: *Guerriera, Amorosa* and *Rapresentativa*. This latter classification has given rise to some confusion, since these three categories are not analogous to the categories of theater, chamber and dance music, but map onto these in complicated, overlapping ways[5].

Aside from the confusions arising from some of Monteverdi's pronouncements in the preface, scholars have traditionally had difficulty understanding the music of Book Eight. Gary Tomlinson has dismissed much of it out of hand[6]; Denis Arnold declared the battle pieces as «not quite as dull as Jannequin's 'la battaille de Marignan'»[7]; and Oliver Strunk declared that «the pieces no longer have anything in common with the tradition. That Monteverdi should call such pieces 'Madrigali' is an indication of the level to which the madrigal had sunk by the third decade of the seventeenth century»[8]. Alfred Einstein also declared that «this many-sided work of the composer's old age has almost nothing to do with the madrigal», though he refrained from an outright negative judgment[9]. In all of these comments, the authors seem to be reacting to the simplicity and one-dimensional character of passages in the *genere concitato* alone, taking the part for the whole. The obvious difficulty in understanding and appreciating these madrigals aesthetically is in my view related to difficulties scholars have had in approaching them analytically. I have myself in the past few years attempted some new approaches to understanding and analyzing these works on the basis of a

---

[4]   M. OSSI, *Monteverdi's miglior filosofo*, Paper delivered at 1993 annual meeting of American Musicological Society, Montreal.

[5]   See HANNING, *op. cit.*, pp. 147-149.

[6]   See G. TOMLINSON, *Monteverdi and the End of the Renaissance*, Berkeley, University of California Press, 1987, pp. 209-210.

[7]   D. ARNOLD, *Monteverdi Madrigals*, B. B. C. Music Guides, London, Billing & Sons, 1967, p. 57. Also quoted in HANNING, *op. cit.*, p. 150.

[8]   O. STRUNK, *Source Readings in Music History*, New York, W. W. Norton & Co., 1950, p. 405. It is not clear whether these words were written by Strunk himself, or by Dragan Plamenač, who wrote a number of the introductions to Strunk's translations.

[9]   A. EINSTEIN, *The Italian Madrigal*, Princeton, Princeton University Press, 1949, II, p. 864.

semiotic, iconographical approach to composition and an examination of musical structure based on separate, repeatable taxonomic categories[10].

What is the source of the difficulty scholars have had in understanding and analyzing these works? The key lies in another pronouncement in Monteverdi's preface that has often been overlooked because it is so obvious: «*et sapendo che gli contrarij sono quelli che movono grandemente l'animo nostro fine del movere che deve havere la bona Musica, come afferma Boetio* [...]», or, as Oliver Strunk translates it: «And since I was aware that it is contraries which greatly move our mind, and that this is the purpose which all good music should have - as Boethius asserts [...]»[11]. Our difficulty, I would argue, lies in the fact that this music is based on the juxtaposition of contrasts. Such contrasts may move our spirit (*l'animo nostro*), but they are devilishly difficult to discuss or analyze.

The problem lies in our very means of discussion and analysis. All western languages are based on predicative structures designed to facilitate the articulation of relationships between a subject and a predicate, mediated by the verb. Adjectives and adverbs, adjectival and adverbial phrases, independent and dependent clauses, all serve to qualify and refine the set of relationships established in the principal predicative structure. Languages are very good at dealing with relationships of the most sophisticated and subtle kinds.

But what about contrasts, especially direct oppositions? What does discursive language do for us in helping us understand contrasts and oppositions? Unfortunately, very little. What more can we say other than that one thing is *not* like another or is different from another? We can say what is different about the two elements in opposition, but even that kind of description merely places two sets of characteristics in juxtaposition with one another and doesn't explain at all what that juxtaposition means.

The fact is, many of the most basic experiences of life are based on oppositions: up and down, night and day, male and female, good and evil, cold and hot, sleeping and waking, etc. These oppositions are obviously extraordinarily

---

[10] See J. G. KURTZMAN, *What Makes Claudio 'Divine'? Criteria for Analysis of Monteverdi's Large-scale Concertato Style*, in *Seicento inesplorato. Atti del III convegno internazionale sulla musica in area lombardo-padana del secolo XVII*, ed. A. Colzani, A. Luppi, M. Padoan, A.M.I.S., Como, 1993, pp. 259-302; ID., *A Taxonomic and Affective Analysis of Monteverdi's Hor che'l ciel e la terra*, «Music Analysis» XII (1993), 2, pp. 169-195; ID., *Monteverdi and Early Baroque Aesthetics: The View from Foucault*, in *Il madrigale oltre il madrigale. Atti del IV convegno internazionale sulla musica italiana nel secolo XVII*, ed. A. Colzani, A. Luppi, M. Padoan, A.M.I.S., Como, 1994, pp. 107-119; ID., *Monteverdi's Changing Aesthetics: A Semiotic Perspective*, in *Festa Musicologica, Essays in Honor of George Buelow*, Stuyvesant, Pendragon Press, 1994, pp. 233-255.

[11] STRUNK, *op. cit.*, p. 413.

meaningful to us, but how do we explain that meaning? In some cases, such as night and day, we can focus on the transition between the two. In others, such as male and female or good and evil, we can discuss what they have in common apart from their opposition. But as far as the oppositions go, aside from describing the differences in characteristics between them, discursive language often fails us; it can help us wonderfully with the meaning of relationships and resemblances, but assists far less in understanding the meaning of oppositions and differences. If we want to understand something about the meaning of contrasts through language, we must have recourse to poets: to Petrarch, to Tasso, to Shakespeare.

The same thing I have asserted about discursive languages also applies to analytical systems. Our analytical techniques, like discursive language, are designed to explain the meaning of relationships, not differences. Whether our analysis is based on modal theory, on functional harmonic theories, or on theories of melodic direction and structural tones in melodic descents, the character of relationships is what is illuminated. These relationships imply differences as well, but it is the resemblances that we are able to understand through the analytical systems, not the differences of direct opposition. Analysis, too, offers us little help in understanding the meaning of contrasts. Little wonder that scholars have had such a difficult time grasping these late works of Monteverdi.

Monteverdi's phrase, *che gli contrarij sono quelli che movono grandemente l'animo nostro,* does not imply that we should be able to understand the meaning of his contrasts intellectually, the way we can understand his detailed description of the *genere concitato* or even the vaguer *genere temperato* and *genere molle.* What he says is that it is contrasts that move us, that cause an emotional response in us. This is not a descriptive or taxonomic statement, like the other pronouncements in the preface, it is a psychological declaration. In the preface, Monteverdi is not only telling us of what elements his music consists and how it is categorized, he is also telling us that its purpose is a psychological one: to move our spirit through its contrasts. Therefore, in order to understand this music, we need to approach it from a psychological standpoint, and our use of language and analysis needs to have psychological understanding as its ultimate goal.

It is for this reason that I have found the psychology of Carl Jung to contain useful ideas for grasping Monteverdi's late music, since a fundamental premise of Jung's psychology, permeating all of his multitudinous writings, is the recognition of oppositions and their role in shaping the human psyche. Jung's most concentrated study of oppositions is found in his *Psychologische Typen,* written largely between 1913 and 1917 and published in Zurich in 1921[12]. This large

---

[12] C. G. JUNG, *Psychologische Typen*, Zürich, Rascher Verlag, 1921. English transl. by H. G. Baynes, revised by R. F. C. Hull, Princeton, Princeton University Press, 1971.

book is a dense work which is to me as a layman confusing and convoluted in some of its details; nevertheless, its main concepts and their significance are clear enough and form an adequate basis for the present investigation.

The focus of Jung's study is the division of psychological types into two basic categories, the extroverted and the introverted. Jung discusses a number of other schemes for categorizing psychological types, but ultimately finds them all subsumable under his extroverted and introverted types. What Jung means by these two terms overlaps, but is not identical with, their significance in common parlance. According to Jung, the extroverted type shows an outward movement of interest, away from his own psychological processes, towards an external object. The extrovert subordinates the subject, i. e. , himself, to the external object, so that the external object has a higher value than himself. The object works like a magnet upon the tendencies of the subject; it determines the subject to a large extent and even alienates him from himself. His qualities may become so transformed by assimilation to the object that one might think it possessed some higher and decisive significance for him[13]. The extrovert, one might say, attempts to approach the external world on the terms the world presents to him, through an interest in the objects of that external world that supersedes the subject's interest in himself. We tend to refer to such a personality type as objective, as having a realistic notion of objects in their own right.

The introverted type, by contrast, shows a «movement of interest away from the object to the subject and his own psychological processes [...]. The introverted standpoint is one which sets the ego and the subjective psychological process above the object and the objective process [...]. This attitude, therefore, gives the subject a higher value than the object, and the object accordingly has a lower value. It is of secondary importance; indeed, sometimes the object represents no more than an outward token of a subjective content, the embodiment of an idea, the idea being the essential thing. If it is the embodiment of a feeling, then again the feeling is the main thing and not the object in its own right»[14]. The introverted type, therefore, is «subjective»; «as though all the life-energy were ultimately seeking the subject, and thus continually prevented the object from exercising any overpowering influence. It is as though the energy were flowing away from the object, and the subject were a magnet drawing the object to itself»[15]. Objects are assimilated by the introverted type into that person's own psychology and transformed into internal experience that may ultimately make the original object unrecognizable by anyone else. The personal psychological experience and feeling

---

[13] *Ibid.*, pp. 4-5.
[14] *Ibid.*
[15] *Ibid.*, p. 5.

become the most important thing, not the realistic nature of the object itself. Introverted types, therefore, often have an unrealistic assessment of the objects of the external world.

According to Jung, everyone «possesses both mechanisms, extroversion as well as introversion, and only the relative predominance of one or the other determines the type»[16]. Jung also considers both types to be successful adaptations to the world, one based on an external approach to the world, the other based on an internalizing approach.

It is not difficult to associate two of Monteverdi's genera with these two psychological types. The *genere concitato* and its associated *guerriero* style are clearly extroverted[17]. The *guerriero* style does not always require the rapid semiquavers Monteverdi describes in his preface as the essence of the *genere concitato*. The more broadly generalized *guerriero* style employs simple triadic outlines, simple cadential basses, sequential melodic patterns and unequivocal metrical organization articulated by clear, repetitive rhythms. These elements result in a uni-dimensional music that articulates a single, clear psychological state: the state of anger or agitation of some kind, unmitigated by any internal psychology. The nature of the *guerriero* style is constant; its individual manifestation may vary somewhat, emphasizing certain of the musical features that define the style, but the essence of the style does not change from one composition to the next. This music is objective in the fullest sense of the word and is therefore just as readily recognizable in instrumental music as it is music with text.

The *genere molle* is a bit more problematic in Monteverdi's formulation. He defines it as *umiltà o supplicatione*. However, in the Eighth Book of Madrigals there is little in the way of *umiltà o supplicatione*, but quite a number of inward-looking reactions to the anxieties and agonies of love. Since these passages can hardly be considered the *genere temperato*, they must belong to the *genere molle*. Monteverdi seems to have relied for his preface more on the traditional theoretical subdivisions of three types of music, where the systaltic genus was associated with humility, restraint and submissiveness, than on his own practice in the Eighth

---

[16]   *Ibid.*, p. 4.

[17]   Monteverdi uses the term *guerrieri* to refer to a group of madrigals in Book 8, which can exhibit any of the three genera: *concitato, temperato* or *molle*. However, it is also clear from Book 8 as well as Monteverdi's later sacred publications, that he conceived of a warlike style, what I have called the *guerriero* style, which shares many of the features of the *genere concitato*, but does not necessarily contain the rapid repeated notes Monteverdi considered integral to the *genere concitato*. Silke Leopold also refers to a *genere guerriero* resulting from the combination of the *genere concitato* with the basic elements of the traditional *battaglia* style. See Silke Leopold, *Claudio Monteverdi und seine Zeit*, Laaber, Laaber-Verlag, 1982, p. 90.

Book of madrigals[18]. The *genere molle* in practice clearly embraces what I would call the *genere amoroso*, or the affective music of love[19]. This is music characterized by irregularity and unpredictability in rhythm, meter, bass motion, and harmonic goals. It shifts direction and character constantly, and often employs chromatic melodic or harmonic motion[20]. The *genere amoroso* represents Jung's introverted psychological type. In this style the speaker is internalizing the love experience and expressing his or her feelings about that experience in a personal, subjective manner. Unlike the *genere guerriero*, this *genere amoroso* can take any number of forms, each particular form shaped by the nuances of the individual, internalized love experience.

These two styles are as easily recognizable in aural terms as they are easy to describe in verbal terms. [Brief excerpts of *Perchè t'en fuggi, o Fillide* were played].

While Monteverdi is most vague about the *genere temperato*, I have taken it to refer to those passages in the Eighth Book of Madrigals that are basically emotionally neutral, largely comprising narrative recitative, or perhaps the quiet opening of *Hor che'l ciel e la terra*[21]. The direct address to Emperor Ferdinand III in *Altri canti d'Amor* is a case in point. [A brief excerpt from *Altri canti d'Amor* was played].

However, the *genere temperato* is of limited significance in these works and of little interest for the present discussion.

Although Jung finds both the extroverted and introverted psychological types equally successful in adapting to the world, he also finds them so contrasting, especially in their more extreme forms, as to be unable to communicate with or understand one another. Because the extroverted type sees the world in one way,

---

18 See HANNING, *op. cit.*, pp. 157-164.

19 As with *madrigali guerrieri*, Monteverdi uses the term *amorosi* to refer to a specific group of madrigals in Book 8, any of which may feature the *genere concitato, genere temperato* or *genere molle*. But the madrigals of Book 8 also argue for a *genere amoroso*, subsumable as I have suggested, under the *genere molle*, defined by the musical characteristics listed in the text above. See also note 20 below.

20 See Galilei's association of the ancient chromatic genus with «soft and effeminate affections» and Monteverdi's natural association of the *genere molle* «with small intervals and with intervals that were chromatically altered» in HANNING, *op. cit.*, p. 165. Hanning goes on to say «And since this genus was appropriate for imitating the affections of humility and supplication, it was also suitable for the expression of amorous and erotic feelings [...]. For Monteverdi, then, the connection between the [...] *genere molle* and chromaticism must have been sufficiently evident in sixteenth-century theory and practice that he saw no reason to define or rationalize it in his preface of 1638».

21 HANNING, *op. cit.*, pp. 169-170, associates the *genere temperato* with the *prima prattica* as well as with music «suitable for the expression of serene thoughts and peaceful feelings».

and the introverted type in exactly the opposite way, they cannot grasp one another's viewpoints and cannot interact with one another in such a way as to modify each other's mechanism or type.

If we return to Monteverdi's *genere guerriero* and *genere amoroso*, we see the same phenomenon. The two styles remain completely apart from one another in separate sections of the same composition. The *genere amoroso* never invades the *genere guerriero*, gradually mollifying it. The *genere guerriero* doesn't infiltrate the *genere amoroso*, causing it to become more clearly and predictably defined, even though, given the «love and war» poetic conceit, love may be expressed by the *genere guerriero*. Monteverdi simply sets the two styles side by side, as juxtaposed contrasts, and claims in his preface that these contrasts move our spirits. While we might now understand better the psychological basis for Monteverdi's comment, we are at this point still no closer to understanding how or why our spirits are moved, or why these compositions may be thought good, bad, or mediocre, whether in comparison to Monteverdi's own music or to the music of his contemporaries.

Once again, Jung may help us to move forward. The fact that the extroverted and introverted types cannot communicate with or understand one another does not mean that there is no form of resolution to their opposition. It is not reason, however, which effects this resolution. According to Jung: «opposites are not to be united rationally: *tertium non datur* - that is precisely why they are called opposites. [...] In practice, opposites can be united only in the form of a compromise, or *irrationally,* some new thing arising between them». That new thing is a symbol of some kind, «a symbol in which the opposites are united; 'a concept that serves to denote all aesthetic qualities of phenomena and, in a word, what we call *Beauty* in the widest sense of the term'. But the symbol presupposes a function that creates symbols [i. e., the creative faculty of a composer such as Monteverdi], and in addition a function that understands them [i. e., the knowledgeable listener] [...]. The essence of the symbol consists in the fact that it represents in itself something that is not wholly understandable, and that it hints only intuitively at its possible meaning. The creation of a symbol is not a rational process, for a rational process could never produce an image that represents a content which is at bottom incomprehensible. To understand a symbol we need a certain amount of intuition which apprehends, if only approximately, the meaning of the symbol that has been created, and then incorporates it into consciousness [...]. The third element, in which the opposites merge, is fantasy activity, which is creative and receptive at once»[22].

---

[22] *Ibid.*, pp. 105-107.

I alluded earlier when discussing the limitations of discursive language to poets as a source for understanding the meaning of contrasts. Poetic language is of an entirely different sort from discursive language, often de-emphasizing or eschewing altogether the predicative structure of discursive language in favor of association, allusion, disjunction, metaphor, rhetorical gestures and other non-linear linguistic forms to generate meaning where discursive language fails. Poetic language is the outcome of fantasy, the creation of a symbol, that produces, as Jung says, «an image that represents a content which is at bottom incomprehensible». Likewise a musical composition, such as a madrigal from Monteverdi's Eighth Book, is the creation of a symbol, «an image that represents a content which is at bottom incomprehensible».

Monteverdi's *Madrigali guerrieri et amorosi*, therefore are symbols generated out of his fantasy of the rationally incomprehensible juxtaposition of the *genere guerriero* and the *genere amoroso*, the opposition between extrovert and introvert. But as rationally incomprehensible symbols, we cannot hope to understand their meaning in rational terms. What we can hope to achieve is some grasp of the psychological meaning of bringing these two contrasts into side-by-side opposition with one another.

What helps in this regard is the symbol itself, the musical composition. The juxtaposition of contrasts alone is not sufficient to create an effective symbol. The symbol must have some intuitively sensed order and form that allows us to perceive it as a symbol rather than as a mere succession of events. It is this form that underlies and helps generate the sense of *beauty*, or, in even more general terms, the aesthetically satisfying character of the work. Thus it is to the form that we should look for the manner in which Monteverdi has resolved the intractable opposition between the extroverted *genere guerriero* and the introverted *genere molle*.

It is no revelation to say that Monteverdi was a master of musical structure. More and more studies of his works, whether secular or sacred, have revealed not only the coherence of individual passages of his music, but also the intricate, sophisticated and remarkably varied approaches to musical form that infuse everything from dance music to recitative. The question in regard to the issues raised above is «How does Monteverdi in the Eighth Book of Madrigals create musical forms that resolve the contrasts between musical styles in an aesthetically satisfying manner?». The answer to this question varies for each madrigal in Book Eight, but those madrigals that rely on contrasts all depend on the same basic method: the generation of convincing formal structures out of the oppositions, structures whose proportions are carefully organized and balanced, often either through repetition and symmetry, or asymmetrically according to the Golden Section proportion. In most instances, Monteverdi combines repetition, symmetry and Golden Section proportions in complicated, interlocking arrangements, but never so complicated that an underlying order is not readily perceptible to the listener.

I can only take a single case study for purposes of demonstration here, and I have selected the *madrigale amoroso, Perchè t'en fuggi, o Fillide*, excerpts of which you've already heard as examples of the extroverted and introverted styles. I have chosen this madrigal both because it is relatively brief and because its structure illustrates well the kind of sophisticated, interlocking organization that constitutes Monteverdi's resolution of oppositions. Figure 1 is a diagram of the structure of this piece, showing the contrasting styles and the manner in which they are organized according to both symmetries and Golden Section proportions. The contrasting styles are delineated by the mensuration signs - triple meter denotes the extroverted style, duple meter the introverted. The mapping of this structure onto the text, requiring repetition of several lines or sets of lines, is shown at the bottom. The Arabic numerals refer to the number of tactus, or measures in Malipiero's edition.

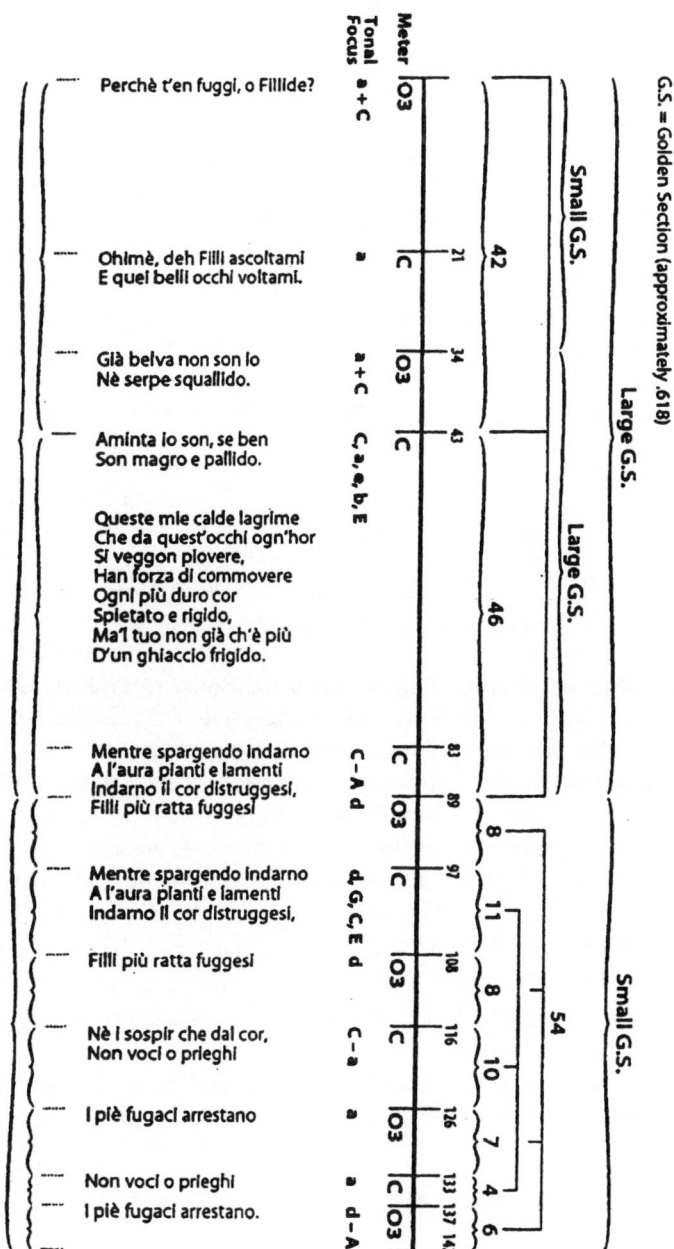

A Jungian Perspective on Monteverdi's Late Madrigals

Figure 1

Claudio Monteverdi, *Perchè t'en fuggi Fillide*, 1638

G.S. = Golden Section (approximately .618)

Text	Tonal Focus	Meter			
Perchè t'en fuggi, o Fillide?	a + C	O3		42	Small G.S.
Ohimè, deh Filli ascoltami E quel belli occhi voltami.	a	C	21		
Già belva non son io Nè serpe squallido.	a + C	O3	34		Large G.S.
Aminta io son, se ben Son magro e pallido.	C, a, e, b, E	C	43		
Queste mie calde lagrime Che da quest'occhi ogn'hor Si veggon piovere, Han forza di commovere Ogni più duro cor Spietato e rigido, Ma'l tuo non già ch'è più D'un ghiaccio frigido.				46	Large G.S.
Mentre spargendo indarno A l'aura pianti e lamenti Indarno il cor distruggesi, Filli più ratta fuggesi	C – A d	C / O3	83 / 89	8	
Mentre spargendo indarno A l'aura pianti e lamenti Indarno il cor distruggesi,	d, G, C, E d	C	97	11	Small G.S.
Filli più ratta fuggesi	d	O3	108	8	54
Nè i sospir che dal cor, Non voci o prieghi	C – a	C	116	10	
I piè fugaci arrestano	a	O3	126	7	
Non voci o prieghi I piè fugaci arrestano.	a d – A	C O3	133 137 142	4 6	

It is important to understand, in studying Monteverdi's structures, that mathematical precision is of less interest to him than the general balance or proportion. Thus, in structural repetitions, if the slightly varied figure requires a tactus or two more to come to a satisfactory conclusion, Monteverdi will add those extra tactus, since they do not change the general perception of the piece and its proportions for the listener - the aural perception of time is not that precise[23]. The same is true of Golden Section proportions. In some instances, as in *Perchè t'en fuggi Fillide,* Monteverdi's structural subdivisions are at precisely the mathematical point of the Golden Section, but on other occasions they are off by a tactus or more. Nevertheless, it is obvious that the Golden Section ratio is behind the structure; local circumstances have simply altered the proportion slightly and imperceptibly. That such slightly out-of-proportion structures still reflect the thinking of Golden Section proportions is obvious when we examine other Monteverdi compositions that show no hint of Golden Section structuring at all.

We can see this lack of interest in mathematical precision in Figure 1 in the durations of the triple and duple meter sections of the second part of the piece. The triple meter sections are 8, 8, 7 and a truncated 6 bars respectively. Since the piece concludes abruptly on an observation that leaves the opening question unanswered, the final musical statement is shortened for rhetorical reasons. The duple meter sections consist of 11, 10 and 4 bars, again with the final statement truncated. A certain symmetry obtains in both sets of sections, but Monteverdi foreshortens both at the end, especially the duple meter passage, for dramatic effect.

Nevertheless, the overall patterning of the composition is evident. On the largest scale, its 142 bars are divided precisely at the point of the Golden Section, between bars 88 and 89. Not only is there a structural subdivision, returning from the introverted duple meter to the extroverted triple meter at the beginning of bar 89, the tonal focus changes as well, from the *a-C* axis of the first part to *d*.

In looking at the organization of the first part of the piece, we see a significant structural division between bars 33 and 34: the shift from duple meter back to triple takes place at this juncture. This point of division marks a reverse Golden Section, i. e., a Golden Section proportion in which the smaller segment comes first and the larger segment follows. Thus the first section, the large segment of the Golden Section of the entire piece, is itself divided according to a reverse Golden Section.

The first part of the madrigal, through bar 88, has another, overlapping structure. After the return of triple meter in bars 34-42, the lengthiest passage in

---

[23] See the discussion of the perception of durations in J. D. KRAMER, *The Time of Music*, New York, Schirmer Books, 1988, pp. 55-56 and 322-333.

the piece occurs in duple meter, bars 43-82, where Aminta describes his miserable condition, followed by a solo recitation of 6 bars. These 46 bars in duple meter approximately balance the opening three segments alternating triple and duple time, comprising 42 bars. I would maintain that the listener is aware of the approximate balance, especially since the 46-bar segment is in a freer rhythmic style, even though the two segments are not exactly equal in terms of tactus.

The second part of the piece is structured differently, with the approximately equal alternation of triple and duple segments I described earlier, concluding with the dramatically truncated duple and triple passages at the end. In this second part, the psychological contrast between Aminta's laments and Phyllis's obdurate flight is heightened through text repetition and much more frequent juxtapositions between the stylistic dichotomies in duple and triple time. At the conclusion, the contrast between the extroverted flight of Phyllis and the introverted musings of Aminta is left structurally unresolved, just as the issue of Phyllis' flight remains unanswered and unresolved as a dramatic and rhetorical gesture.

Perchè t'en fuggi, o Fillide represents just one example of many different approaches to organizing music that we find in the Eighth Book of Madrigals. But many of these compositions rely on various combinations of Golden Section proportions, exact or approximate repetitions, symmetries based on alternation, and symmetries based on structural divisions at mid-points.

Thus the creation of convincing form out of the contrasting elements that comprise each piece is the method by which Monteverdi reconciles his psychological opposites and moves the spirit of his listeners. This process is first a method of composition, i. e., it gives the composer a framework and set of goals as he begins his work. But when the composer's work is finished, this process serves the aesthetic and psychological needs of the listener, for it is only on the basis of convincing form that this music becomes aesthetically satisfying and fulfills its stated psychological intention of moving *l'animo nostro*. Since my analysis is fundamentally rational in its approach, it still does not explain the psychological mechanism that causes Monteverdi's convincing form to move our spirits, but it does, I believe, identify a pre-condition for that mechanism. We may never be able to understand the mystery of how our spirits are moved by the music, but we can understand what the conditions must be for that mysterious interaction to take place. This is ultimately the purpose of all analysis and aesthetic judgment. In my view, it is only through grasping the psychological purposes of this music and understanding how these purposes are furthered not only on the structural level of individual passages but in the structural organization of contrasting sections at the scale of the entire composition that we can accomplish meaningful analyses and critiques of the Eighth Book of Madrigals.

Monteverdi's aesthetic concepts, as expressed in his prefaces, were often unclear and ambiguous, but his insights were true to the mark, and the more closely we examine these insights and their implications, the closer we will come to penetrating the secrets of his art.

APPENDIX A

Text of *Perchè t'en fuggi, o Fillide?*

1	Perchè t'en fuggi, o Fillide?	O3
21	Ohimè, deh Filli ascoltami	C
	E quei belli occhi voltami.	
34	Già belva non son io	O3
	Nè serpe squallido.	
43	Aminta io son, se ben	C
	Son magro e pallido.	
	Queste mie calde lagrime	
	Che da quest'occhi ogn'hor	
	Si veggon piovere,	
	Han forza di commovere	
	Ogni più duro cor	
	Spietato e rigido,	
	Ma'l tuo non già ch'è più	
	D'un ghiaccio frigido.	
84	Mentre spargendo indarno	
	A l'aura pianti e lamenti	
	Indarno il cor distruggesi,	
89	Filli più ratta fuggesi	O3
97	Mentre spargendo indarno	C
	A l'aura pianti e lamenti	
	Indarno il cor distruggesi,	
108	Filli più ratta fuggesi	O3
116	Nè i sospir che dal cor,	C
	Non voci o prieghi	
126	I piè fugaci arrestano	O3
133	Non voci o prieghi	C
137	I piè fugaci arrestano.	O3

IV

Intimations of Chaos in Monteverdi's *L'Orfeo*

In response to the Monteverdi anniversary year of 1967, Denis Arnold and Nigel Fortune edited a volume of essays entitled *The Monteverdi Companion*.[1] Several of these essays were reprinted in 1985 in *The New Monteverdi Companion*,[2] but one of the more provocative articles was unfortunately omitted: Robert Donington's "Monteverdi's First Opera," in which the author proposed a Jungian interpretation of Striggio's and Monteverdi's version of the myth.[3] A related interpretation was more recently taken up by Eric Chafe in his new book *Monteverdi's Tonal Language*.[4] I take my point of departure for the present essay from a key observation of Donington's: that Euridice, in her first and only "number" in the opera, responds to Orfeo's *Rosa del ciel* with "happy words . . . *contradicted* [italics original] by the music to which she sings them: a melodically outlined tritone (D descending to G sharp), which is the very interval (and on the very notes) subsequently most prominent in the sad scene of Act II where Euridice's death is tragically announced. The tragedy is already implicit in the happiness."[5] Donington then gives a series of examples where the tritone occurs at moments of grief in connection with the loss of Euridice.[6]

Now, it is well known that the Prologue and Act I of *L'Orfeo*, as well as much of Act II, up to the point of the announcement of Euridice's death by the messenger, are given over to lively, stable, pastoral music. This music is characterized by diatonicism, clear cadences, symmetrical or balanced phrases, dance rhythms and large-scale, symmetrical structures. Even the recitatives are consistent with these features – in other words, all those elements of musical style that contribute to a sense of order, stability and simplicity are

---

[1]   Denis Arnold and Nigel Fortune, eds, *The Monteverdi Companion* (London: Faber and Faber, 1968).

[2]   Denis Arnold and Nigel Fortune, eds, *The New Monteverdi Companion* (London: Faber and Faber, 1985).

[3]   *The Monteverdi Companion*, pp. 257–76.

[4]   Eric T. Chafe, *Monteverdi's Tonal Language* (New York: Schirmer Books, 1992), pp. 126–58

[5]   Donington, "Monteverdi's First Opera," *The Monteverdi Companion*, p. 263.

[6]   Donington, p. 265

IV

exploited by Monteverdi to create an idyllic pastoral atmosphere against which the personal tragedy of Orfeo will unfold.

In a famous letter of December 9, 1616, Monteverdi criticized the libretto of the maritime fable *Le Nozze di Tetide*, which he had been asked to compose, and at the same time commented briefly on what he thought had made his operas *L'Orfeo* and *Arianna* successful. In complaining about winds as potential characters, Monteverdi declared:

> How, dear Sir, can I imitate the speech of the winds, if they do not speak? And how can I, by such means, move the passions? Ariadne moved us because she was a woman, and similarly Orpheus because he was a man, not a wind. . . . Nor do I feel that it [the libretto] moves me at all . . . nor do I feel that it carries me in a natural manner to an end that moves me. *Arianna* led me to a just lament, and *Orfeo* to a righteous prayer, but this fable leads me I don't know to what end.[7]

It was the personal, human nature of Orfeo's feelings that allowed Monteverdi to succeed in designing a recitative that would move his listeners. As Donington, Chafe, and Apollo himself in Monteverdi's last act point out, the tragedy of Orfeo is his very excess of feeling – his inability to respond to love and the loss of love with some degree of moderation. Monteverdi, who was fond of quoting Plato, would likely have been quite sensitive to Plato's own philosophy of moderation, of balancing the extremes by the middle ground.[8]

Throughout the opera, Orfeo falters, both in his practical actions and in his understanding of those actions by failing to grasp their implications and their limitations. For example, Orfeo attributes his success in securing the release of Euridice from Hades to his lyre, when all it did was put Charon to sleep. It is actually the pity for Orfeo of Pluto's wife Persephone, not induced by his virtuosity, but by his heartfelt plea, that moves her to persuade her husband Pluto to let Euridice go.[9] And, of course, it is Orfeo's inability to control his fears that cause him to turn to see Euridice on the way out of Hades, resulting in her loss forever. Orfeo overestimates the power of his music and underestimates his slavery to his feelings.

---

[7]   Domenico de' Paoli, ed., *Claudio Monteverdi: Lettere, dediche e prefazioni* (Rome: Edizioni de Santis, 1973), p. 87; and Eva Lax, ed., *Claudio Monteverdi: Lettere* (Florence: Leo S. Olschki Editore, 1994), pp. 48–51. English translation in Denis Stevens, *The Letters of Claudio Monteverdi*, rev. ed. (Cambridge: Cambridge University Press, 1995), p. 110.

[8]   Plato is cited as authority in all three of Monteverdi's important prefaces: *Il quinto libro de' madrigali* (1605), *Scherzi musicali* (1607) and *Madrigali guerrieri ed amorosi* (1638) as well as in the letter of 9 December, 1616.

[9]   See Chafe, pp. 149–51

While these might be character flaws that define Orfeo as a tragic figure, they are also the basis for some of the most intense musical expression Monteverdi was ever to create. Orfeo's faith in his virtuosity leads to the astonishing display of *Possente spirto*, and the excess of Orfeo's feeling leads to a remarkable musical evocation of psychological disintegration as Orfeo is thwarted twice in his effort to achieve perfect happiness.

The tritone Donington observed is the first step in Orfeo's process of disintegration – of movement from the pastoral landscape of idyllic stability and happiness to the interior psychological realm of torment and disassociation. It is this psychological movement that I would like to explore in order to focus more specifically on the musical process by which Orfeo's mental disintegration is accomplished. The tritone, of course, has from medieval times been recognized as a disruptive force in music, the *diabolus in musica*. As such, it is a force capable of initiating musical movement toward chaos, the chaos of Orfeo's final incomprehension and mental dissolution. The tritone, however, is only one aspect of musical chaos – dissonance, chromaticism, abrupt and confusing tonal shifts, irregular and disrupted phrases, and irregularity of rhythm are all part of the process of musical disintegration, to which I would like to turn in some detail.

In the prologue of *L'Orfeo*, the figure of music speaks in the first verse of coming from her beloved Permessus (a river on Mount Helicon sacred to Apollo and the muses in Greek mythology) to sing the praises of the Gonzagas, sponsors of *L'Orfeo*, but cannot adequately succeed because the goal is too lofty (*Ne giunge al ver perch'è tropp'alto il segno*). The excessively lofty goal is also a thinly veiled reference to the perfect happiness Orfeo seeks in the course of the opera but cannot achieve because it too is beyond reach. The phrase in which music sings of her inability to succeed, as Chafe notes, emphasizes the tritone $Bb-E$ though a shift from *d mollis* with its Bb to *A durus* with $B\natural$.[10] While the climactic *e"* on the words *tropp'alto* ("too lofty") is approached and resolved by a perfect fifth *a'*, the negative beginning of this final sentence, *ne*, is set to the bb' before the shift to *A durus* and the climb to *e"* (see **Example 1**).

In the third verse, the strophically varied melodic, harmonic and rhythmic shape presents more directly the $bb'-e"$ melodic tritone accompanying a reference to music's celestial lyre as the encourager of souls – the instrument, of course, which is represented in the opera by Orfeo's lyre. In the fourth verse, the parallel passage refers to the immortal glory of Pindo and Helicon (two different mountains cited as the seat of the muses in Greek mythology),

[10]   Chafe, pp. 126–7.

Example 1

but with the bb' and the e'' further apart and even separated by an intervening rest. The second and fifth verses omit melodic motion from $bb'-e''$ altogether, so that the tritone relationship between the two is between the vocal line and the later dominant harmony at the end of the verse. It is thus only the verses where the elements of Orfeo's tragedy are referenced in which the tritone is prominent.

Other $Bb-E$ tritones occur as the Act I recitatives unfold. For example, at the very beginning of the act, the first shepherd sings a rhythmically accented bb, dissonant against the underlying D minor harmony. The resolution of the shepherd's bb to a is then supported by an A minor chord, producing the $bb-e$ tritone between the voice and the continuo. The juxtaposition is ironic since the text celebrates the *lieto e fortunato giorno* ("joyful and fortunate day") of Orfeo's wedding (see **Example 2**).

The chorus *Vieni Imeneo* emphasizes an indirect E to bb as a consequence of harmonies based on C and on Bb as well as a chromatic shift from $b\natural$ to bb (in harmonies of G major and Bb major) where the text reads "*E lunge homai disgombre de gl'affanni e del duol gl'orrori e l'ombre*" ("And far away now drive the horrors and shadows of worry and sorrow") (see **Example 3**).

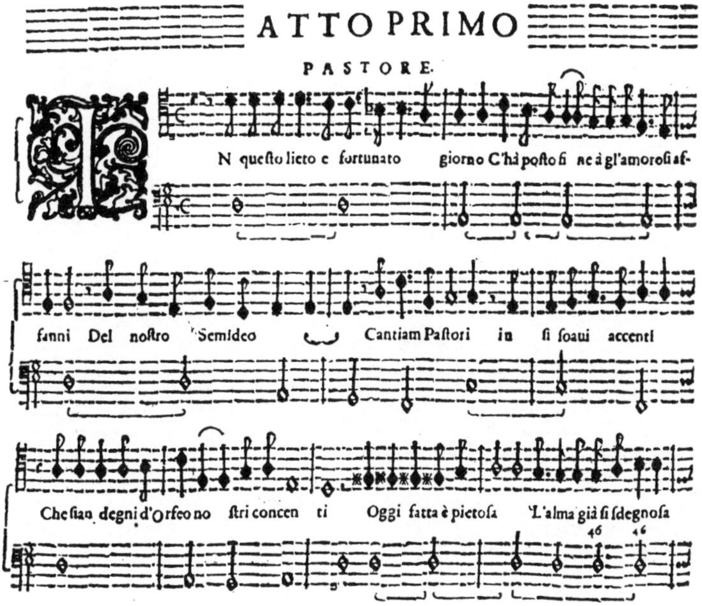

Example 2

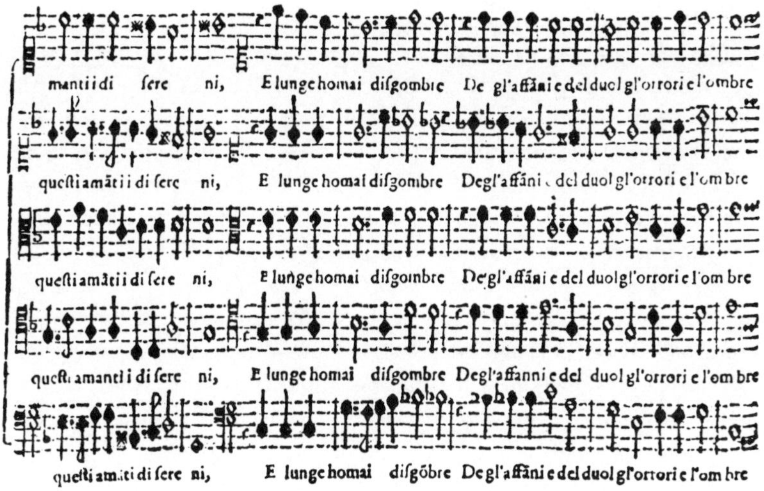

Example 3

Example 4

The second, triple-meter part of the chorus *Lasciate i monti* begins with the diminished eleventh *b*–*e♭"* between tenor and soprano (resulting from the juxtaposition of *G* major and *C* minor harmonies) as the text addresses the sun: *Qui miri il sole vostre carole più vaghe assai di quelle* ("Let the sun look upon your rounds, so much more charming than those"), but introduces the tritone *b♭–E* when the moon and the dark night enter into the comparison: *ond'à la luna la notte bruna danzano in ciel le stelle* ("in the dusky night the stars dance in heaven for the moon"). In the second verse the text for this same passage shifts from adorning the locks of the lovers with flowers to referencing the former torments of their desires which now are at an end (*Poi di bei fiori per voi s'honori di questi amanti il crine, c'hor dei martiri de i lor desiri, godon beati al fine*). Once again the tritone underscores the irony embedded in the text, since these resolved torments are about to be renewed on a much deeper level.

When Orfeo finally gets to sing, his entrance is impressive, defined by both seriousness and stability. G minor and an almost eternally sustained bass establish not only a sense of solemnity at the beginning of *Rosa del ciel*, but also of musical mastery, as Orfeo wends his way according to his own volition, unhampered and unfettered by a bass and harmony that can only wait for him to complete his initial thought before finally changing at Orfeo's command: *Dimmi* ("Tell me"). Orfeo's rhythms, his harmony, his range of

Example 5

melody and his phrase structure are all freer and more sophisticated than
the prologue or the shepherds who have preceded him (see **Example 5**).

IV

Intimations of Chaos in Monteverdi's L'Orfeo

One aspect of the sophisticated harmony comprises chromatic melodic shifts accompanied by cadences moving in close proximity or even directly juxtaposed from B♭ major to D major and back, or from F major to D major. These shifts occasionally produce indirect tritones in Orfeo's melody, such as in the phrase where he refers to his sighs after having first seen Euridice: *E più felice l'hora che per te sospirai* ("and even happier the hour in which I sighed for you"), or at the end, when he expresses his present happiness: *di quel piacer ch'oggi mi fà contento* ("of that pleasure that today makes me happy"). The latter exhibits once again the irony of incommensurability between text and music. Monteverdi doesn't quite place the b♭ and the e on the words *mi–fà*, but comes close. After all, his objective is not musical puns but musical expression.

Example 6

It is at this point that Euridice makes her only entrance as a human character, foreshadowing the tragedy to follow, as Donington demonstrated. Orfeo's concluding D major changes to D minor and Euridice commences with an indirect, but distinctly emphasized tritone, *d"–g♯'*. This is the first prominent G♯ in any vocal part other than the first shepherd's reference to Euridice and Orfeo's previous lamenting over her in the opening recitative of Act I. As the concluding note of the tritone, *g♯'* serves to announce from the outset of Euridice's response that perfect harmony is not to be expected in the relationship between these two lovers (see **Example 6**). In fact, the instability of the relationship announced by Euridice's change of mode from major to minor and the tritone is furthered by Euridice's vocal line and its supporting harmony. Her melody has more frequent and larger leaps than Orfeo's, and the harmony is constantly shifting. Even the final cadence is unstable in its too-rapid change from *F* to *D* major and Euridice's close on the fifth of the chord. Note also the *e'–bb'* tritone in Euridice's vocal line in the final two bars, and between Euridice's *bb'* and the continuo's fifth of the *A* chord in the final bar. Throughout her short speech, the listener senses that something is not quite right.

It is significant that from this point forward there are no tritones and very little chromaticism until the messenger's dramatic entrance at *Ahi, caso acerbo* ("Oh, bitter accident!") in Act II. Once the musical suggestion has been made that the love of Orfeo and Euridice is headed for trouble, Orfeo is allowed in the remainder of Act I and the first part of Act II to celebrate with his woodland friends unhampered by any thoughts of future problems. This pure joy, at its highest level in *Vi ricorda bosch'ombrosi*, is epitomized in the last verse of this strophic song where Orfeo blesses his former torment for the sake of Euridice, proclaiming that after his sorrow and misfortune his contentment and happiness are greater by far. Noteworthy is that the contrast between sorrow and happiness is no longer underlined here by references to *e* and *bb* as similar contrasts were in Act I; the song instead is utterly diatonic and energetic, never wavering from its positive, almost ecstatic sentiment. Such stability makes the shock value of the messenger's announcement all the more striking when it occurs as an abrupt interruption to a brief diatonic shepherd's recitative immediately following *Vi ricorda.*

Not only does Silvia, the messenger, bring a sudden change of tonality, of continuo instruments, of rhythm and meter as well as an almost shrieking entrance on a high *e''*, her first dissonance is the result of her *g#'* on the word *acerbo*, and her second phrase outlines the same *d–g# tritone* Euridice sang at the beginning of her own entrance. Even the third shepherd's uncomprehending question of the messenger emphasizes the *bb–e'* tritone between its first and last notes (see **Example 7**). Silvia's response commences with a *g#'–d'* tritone (Example 7, last line), and after Orfeo finally summons the presence of mind to question the messenger, her answer is based around the *d''–g#'* and *g#'–d''* tritone (see **Example 8**).

When Silvia finally narrates the account of Euridice's death, the world of musical chaos has intruded on the idyllic diatonicism prevalent up to the crucial turning point of the story. The narration includes more tritones, chromatic shifts between *f'* and *f#'*, *g'* and *g#'*, *e'* and *eb'*, and *b'* and *bb'*, dissonant melodic intervals, such as diminished fourths and diminished fifths, remote pitches, such as *ab*, and a mostly low register for the voice.

It is only after the narration that Orfeo finally responds to what has happened to him and the way his world has turned upside-down. This is where we begin to see both his emotional disintegration and his heroic resolve.

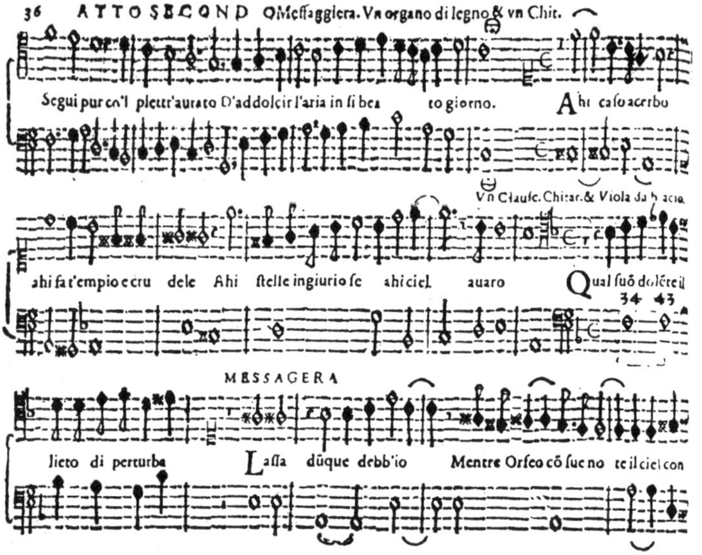

Example 7

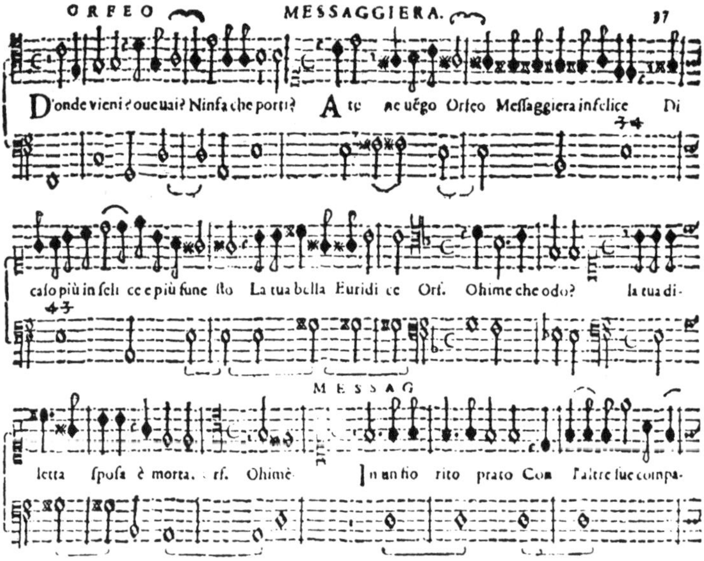

Example 8

Example 9

Tu se' morta is a masterpiece of psychological interpretation, tracing both Orfeo's bewilderment and his determination to regain what he has lost, despite the dangers (see **Example 9**).

Tu se' morta begins with the same sustained G minor chord as *Rosa del ciel*. On the one hand, this is an unambiguous reference to Euridice in both capacities, as Orfeo's delight and as his deceased consort. But the chord is sustained only a brief time and we no longer find Orfeo freely and confidently rhapsodizing in balanced phrases. Instead, a gasp of realization interrupts his very first note, and his extremely short initial phrase requires a long pause for him to recover. As he progresses, chromaticism is much in evidence, shifting from *b♭* to *b♮* (bars 3–5) and from *g* to *g♯* and back again (bars 2–4, 6–7). Dissonant *f♯*'s clash against bass G's and *g♯*'s against A's (bars 2–4, 6–7). G minor changes abruptly to A minor and its dominant (bars 2–3), then just as abruptly back to G minor (bars 4–5) before repeating the process (bars 6–8). All of these factors are elements in musical disassociation – a breakdown in the stability and predictable teleology of the prologue, Act I and the first part of Act II. Even Orfeo's chromatic melodic and harmonic sophistication in *Rosa del ciel* did not dispel the sense of order – it only enhanced it by its excursions into new territory. But in *Tu se' morta*, Orfeo's territory is no longer in his command. Instead, he is disrupted by external forces and driven forward by internal pressures reflected in his increasing emotional intensity. While *Tu se' morta* displays Orfeo's stunned bewilderment, leaving him virtually breathless, there is nevertheless an internal emotional dynamic that drives the piece forward in a clearly defined direction.

This direction is evident in the first phrases. While the drop in pitch at the very beginning, as in the messenger's *Ahi, caso acerbo*, coincides with the deflation of Orfeo's spirit, the phrase rises again from its low point of *f♯*. *Se' morta mia vita* ("You are dead, my life") continues chromatically upward, and *ed io respiro?* ("and I breathe?") (bars 4–5), while reverting back to *g♮*, rises again to *b♭* for Orfeo's question. This upward dynamic then continues sequentially with *Tu se' da me partita* ("You have left me"), which, despite a longer drop from the initial *d'* to *f♯* (bars 5–6), rises gradually, first to *c'* (bar 7), then to *d'* (bar 8) and finally to a high, sustained *e'* for the question *ed io rimango?* ("and I remain?") (bar 9). In this pitch ascent we hear the steadily increasing emotional tension, leading to the strained question on the highest note at the end of the passage.

The response to the question does the only thing it can – it descends, not only into the *più profondi abissi* ("the deepest abysses") (bar 11), but also into the realm of firm resolve. Similar to the sequential melodic ascents, the descent is echoed in shorter form, this time with the *g♯–d* tritone, accompanied by descending chromatic bass motion, as the vehicle for making tender the heart of the King of Shades: *e intenerito il cor del Rè de l'ombre* (bar 12). Once this rising and falling motion has been established, it is reiterated in shorter phrases (bars 14–18) for Orfeo's determination to bring Euridice back to the light again (rising) or to remain with her among the dead (descending). Monteverdi's command of emotional psychology is astute, since Orfeo's posing of the alternatives is both naive and facile. It neither requires nor contains deep emotional intensity, for it is not the product of a psychological wrestling with difficult circumstances and choices. The Orfeo we see in this moment is almost childlike in his decision. It is the same personality who had shortly before sung *Vi ricorda bosch'ombrosi*, and he seems not to have progressed to any more profound state through the experience of Euridice's death.

Monteverdi's conclusion to *Tu se' morta* encapsulates the teleological direction of the entire number, for there is a sequential rise in short phrases as the farewells ascend from earth to sky to sun, followed by a precipitous drop as he departs for the Underworld (bars 19–22).[11] While the low notes on *terra* and the high notes on *cielo* and *sole* may resemble simple madrigalisms, Monteverdi has turned them to his dramatic purpose by revisiting in abbreviated form the emotional and melodic direction of the whole piece, thereby creating a convincing cadence to the entire number and confirming Orfeo's resolve for the listener.

These events, of course, affect the musical language of the remainder of Act II, with its repetitions of *Ahi, caso acerbo* and a heavy emphasis on dissonance, tritones and abrupt changes of harmony and tonality. Orfeo himself doesn't reappear until the beginning of Act III, where he is escorted by Speranza (Hope) into Hades. His accustomed *G* minor has now turned even more to the flat side with an unusual *C* minor (see **Example 10**).[12] *C* minor gives us not only *e♭*, but also *a♭*, which has been heard only once before in the opera, at the point where the messenger, in describing Euridice's death, had said *scolorissi il bel viso* ("her lovely face paled"). In fact, that very phrase cadences briefly in *C* minor before moving to *D* minor and beyond. The tonality of *C* minor, therefore, is itself a disruption, an intrusion of abnormal and unstable elements into the normal scope of tonalities of *L'Orfeo*. In his interchange with Hope, Orfeo seeks her support, and his own mind seems reasonably in control, as we can tell from the relative stability

---

[11]   George Buelow, in personal conversation, noted that Orfeo reaches only as high as *d'* in bidding farewell to the sun, since he is unable at this point to attain the *e♭'* that is associated with the sun (and therefore with Apollo, the sun god and father of Orfeo) in the second part of the chorus *Lasciate i monti* in Act I. Both Orfeo and Apollo sing *e♭'* as their highest pitch in their Act V duet as they sing of their ascent into heaven.

[12]   See Chafe, p. 131, where he notes the infrequent use of *cantus mollis C* in the opera.

48
ATTO TERZO
ORFEO.
Corto da te mio Nume Speraнza Speranza vnico bene De gl'afflitti mor
ta li Omai ſon giunto a queſti meſti e tenebroſi regni Oue raggio di Sol gia mai nō
giōſe Tu mia cōpagna duce In coſi ſtra ne e ſconoſciute vie Regeſti il paſſo debole e treman-
te Ond'og gi ancora ſpero Di riueder quelle beate luci Che ſo l'a gl'ochi mei portā'il giorno
SPERANZA.
Ecco l'atra palu de ecco il nochiero Che trahe l'ignudi ſpir tia l'altra riua Doue hà Plu

Example 10

Example 11

of sustained harmonies on *C* minor, *F* minor and *G* minor in the first two systems of **Example 10**. Despite a few short phrases interrupted by rests when he first addresses Hope and later exclaims *homai*, his phrases appear balanced, repeated notes are frequent, the rhythms are carefully controlled according to syllable accents, and every phrase except for the final cadence concludes with the reassurance of a slow repeated note. Only toward the end, as Orfeo expresses his own hope of retrieving Euridice does he employ more upward leaps and frequent changes of harmony, the majority involving major triads.

Once Hope departs and leaves Orfeo alone, however, his composure breaks down. His middle and low registers are replaced by the high register, dissonances and diminished fourths encompassing *f'–c#'* are placed in relief, phrases are more breathless than controlled (see **Example 11**). Yet Orfeo

IV

Example 12

can't lose complete control or he would be in no position to sing *Possente spirto*, so his anxious questions unfold over a sustained *A* major harmony and most of his phrases still end with slower repeated notes, though in a high register and often in the form of questions.

The most famous number of the opera, *Possente spirto*, need not detain us long, both because it is so well known and because it so obviously displays Orfeo's virtuosic mastery of his profession (whether the singer follows Monteverdi's ornamentation, or generates his own based on the alternative simpler version Monteverdi supplies). Only in the last two verses does Orfeo depart from his rigid strophic structure and the emphasis on vocal virtuosity for a more direct, emotional appeal to Charon. The last verse is an almost breathless, whining and shrill complaint, with the *terza rima* stanzas run together in exceptionally long phrases, the longest of which lasts ten full semibreves without even a short rest to gasp for air (see **Example 12**). The final plea, *rendetemi il mio ben* ("return my love to me") comprises a chromatically rising sequence with rapidly changing harmony from *B♭* to *G* major, *C* major, *A* major and *D* minor before finally cadencing in *G*.

As mentioned before, the singing of Orfeo, capable of taming wild beasts, moving stones to tears and winning the originally reluctant Euridice, is largely ineffectual in the Underworld. Charon merely falls asleep at the end of Act III and Pluto in Act IV is unmoved. Only Persephone, Pluto's wife, herself ravished from the world above, is responsive to Orfeo and through her own plaints softens the heart of Pluto to win the conditional release of Euridice.

Orfeo's reaction to this eventual (but only temporary) success is indicative of his immaturity. He sings a song of praise to his "omnipotent lyre" quite in the style of the pastoral scenes of Acts I and II (see **Example 13**). The walking bass serves as the underpinning for a set of strophic variations interspersed by a lively ritornello. Having survived the most terrible forces of Hades and been granted an exception by Pluto to its immutable law (not through the direct power of his music, but through the sympathetic intervention of Persephone), there is no humility in Orfeo's response, no recognition of the solemnity of such an event – merely a childlike rejoicing in the illusion of his lyre's power and its eternal place in the heavens.[13] Orfeo has not changed in the slightest through the experience of his tragedy; he has not grown in depth and sophistication of feeling; he has not grown in wisdom. He knows

---

[13]   Joseph Kerman comments that Orfeo's reaction to the release of Euridice is "neither gratitude nor real affection, but a hymn of praise to himself and to his lyre." Joseph Kerman, "Orpheus: the Neo-classic Vision," in John Whenham, ed., *Claudio Monteverdi: Orfeo* (Cambridge: Cambridge University Press, 1986), p. 132.

Example 13 (beginning)

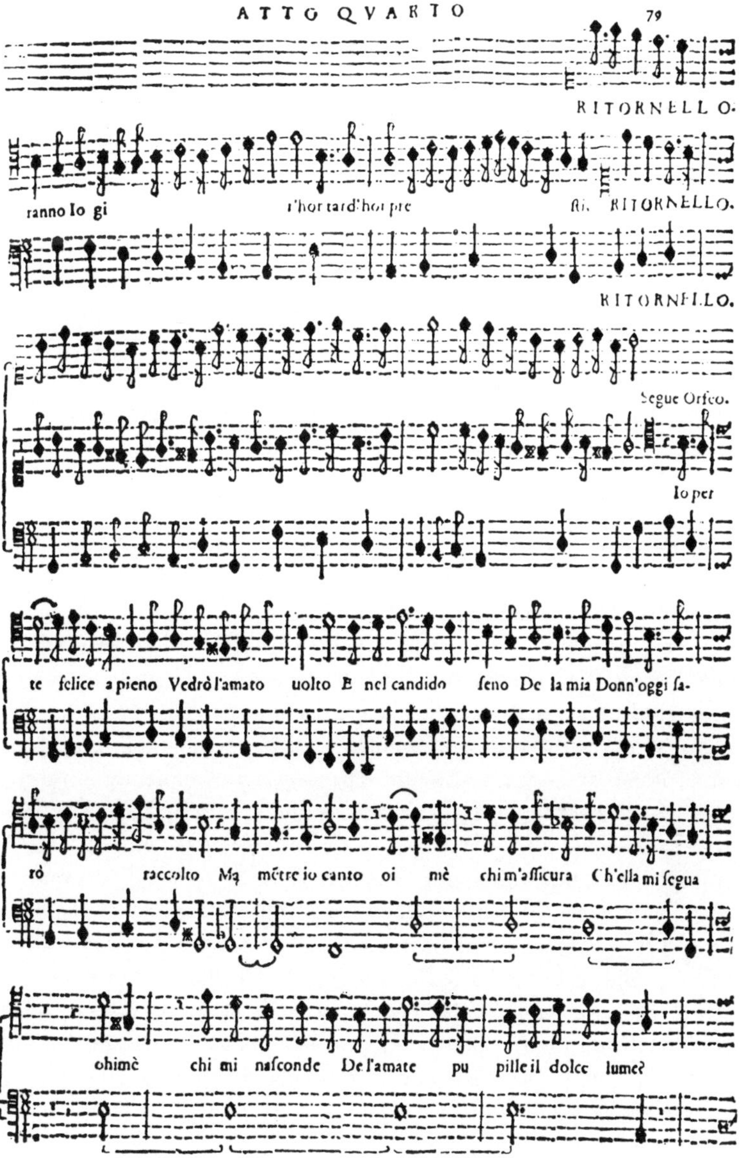

Example 13 (continued)

only the simplistic emotions of unmitigated joy, inconsolable grief and incautious determination.[14] Only after three stanzas does it dawn on him that he might possibly have been deceived. Naturally, his confident mood quickly dissolves and the energetic walking bass is replaced by sustained chords, while prominent tritones appear once again along with abrupt shifts of tonality.

Orfeo is unable to restrain his anxiety, to master his immediate emotions in favor of a wiser course of action, and turns to look for Euridice, thereby losing her forever, as Pluto must have known he would. As Orfeo sees Euridice fade into obscurity, the $g\sharp$–d'–$g\sharp$ tritone sequence returns (see **Example 14**, second bar) and Euridice responds with the same descending d''–$g\sharp'$ tritone we heard in her initial entrance in Act I, only this time harmonized more dissonantly (see **Example 14**, second system). Indeed, she laments her loss with some of the most disorienting music yet heard in the opera, involving chromatic bass motion and another d''–$g\sharp'$ tritone at *Et io misera* ("And I wretched one") (see **Example 14**, third system). As she takes her leave, an Underworld spirit orders her to return to Hades with an echo of *Ahi, caso acerbo* (see **Example 14**, fifth system, first bar).

This second, permanent loss of Euridice, not through the fate of a snakebite, but through Orfeo's own weakness, results in a complete disintegration of his mind. He has lost all power, whether of his will or of his lyre, and his mental state is chaotic. This psychological chaos yields some of the most radically chaotic music of the seventeenth century – even more psychologically chaotic than Gesualdo's most chromatic madrigals.

Orfeo's speech becomes discontinuous, his pitches outline diminished fourths, tritones and sevenths, and the harmony shifts frequently and abruptly. The sequence of triads beginning in the second system of **Example 15** runs *D* major – *D* minor – *B*♭ major – *E* major – *D* major – *C* minor – *G* minor – *A* minor – *E* major – *D* minor. Such a harmonic sequence, accompanying the voice with sevenths, tritones, diminished thirds, diminished fourths and minor seconds, is quite simply incoherent. As Orfeo attempts to follow the vanishing Euridice but is barred by one of the Shades, his question *chi me'l neg'ohime* ("who prevents me, alas") is sung to the descending d'–$g\sharp$ tritone that has become the motive of his separation from Euridice, and his final question, appropriately, is left open-ended on a dominant chord. This is psychological chaos, induced by Orfeo's inability to come to grips with his loss. It is fitting that the chaos occurs in Hades, the Underworld, which in the Christianity of Monteverdi's audience, as well as in Greek mythology, is the seat of chaos.

---

[14]   Kerman makes similar observations about Orfeo learning nothing, failing to grow, and failing to transcend his fate. See Kerman, "Orpheus," pp. 134–5.

Qui canta Orfeo al ſuono del Clauic. Viola da braccio baſſo, & un chitar.
pur'vi ueggio io pur
Ma qual Ecliſſi ohime u'oſcura? un Spir.
Rott'hai la legge E ſe di
EVRIDICE
gratia indegno
Ahi uiſta troppo dolce e troppo amara
Coſi per troppo a-
mor dūque mi perdi? Et io miſera perdo Il poter più go dere E di luce e di
uiſta e perdo inſieme Te d'ogni ben più caro ò mio conſorte.
Vn Spirto de Coro canta.
Torn'a l'ombre di morte Infe lice Euridice Ne più ſperar di riue der le ſtelle
ORFEO
Ch'omai ſia ſordo à preghi tuoi l'inferno.
Doue ten uai mia uita Ec-
L'Orfeo del Monte verde.
M

Example 14

Example 15

The denouement of the story reveals again Orfeo's inability to grow and to learn. We next see him in sorrow on the fields of Thrace seeking comfort in the woods, not in his lyre (see **Example 16**). It is as if Orfeo himself has lost confidence in his music and has abandoned it in his greatest need. For his greatest psychological need was not to recover Euridice, but rather to recover a wiser self from the experience of his tragedy. Music will not serve this end because Orfeo's soul, his inner being, is insufficiently mature. What is required instead, in the final, altered version of Act V, is a *Deus ex Machina* intervention in the form of his father, Apollo.

Orfeo's lament is indicative of his helpless state. The almost interminable recitative is conventional in character; even its dissonances and occasional tritones sound ordinary and have much less impact than in his earlier utterances. The harmony is unremarkable and frequently, though not always, cadences as expected. The only radical shifts of tonality are reserved for changes of topic or of the character or characters addressed, such as *monti e sassi* ("mountains and stones") and *anima mia* ("my beloved"). But most of all, Orfeo's melodic lines lack the kind of coherent structural direction that characterized *Rosa del ciel* and *Tu se' morta*. Monteverdi has given us in this lament a personality at

Example 16

loose ends, devoid of direction, and sorrowing prosaically over his loss. There is no new understanding, no new feeling, no sense of personal growth.

Our own aesthetic responses probably tend to agree with those of Eco, who mimics the ends of several words in the lament, responding partway through Orfeo's plaint to *Non ho pianto però che basti* ("I don't have, however, a sufficient lament") with a simple *basti* ("enough"). But Orfeo doesn't get the hint and goes on for almost twice as long as he's already sung up to that point. Since he is incapable of coping with his grief himself and concludes by condemning all other women as vile in comparison with the peerless Euridice, the intervention of Apollo is required, who brings the moral of the tale home to Orfeo: *"Troppo giosti di tua lieta ventura, hor troppo piangi tua sorte acerba e dura"* ("Too much you rejoiced in your happy fortune, now you weep too much at your bitter and hard fate"). And although Apollo takes Orfeo with him into heaven to see Euridice configured in the stars, their virtuoso duet is in no way transforming or transfiguring.

We have seen Orfeo reach the nadir of psychological disintegration and chaos during his visit to Hades, but his ascent to heaven does not even suggest that Hades and its effects have been conquered by better, more powerful forces. Monteverdi here remains true to the spirit of the myth, whether in its traditional form where Orfeo is torn apart by the Thracian women, or in its recast ending with Orfeo and Apollo ascending heavenward. Monteverdi's version is also in the spirit of the *intermedii*, out of which *L'Orfeo* grows, in its limited dramatic progress. Indeed, the heavenly ascent takes Orfeo back in a spiral to the idyllic pastoral paradise of Acts I and II, only raised to a higher level: *la 've ben non mai vien meno, la 've mai non fu dolore* ("there where the good never declines, there where there is never sorrow") as declared by the final chorus. In the opera, the counterpart to chaos is not a hard-won stability and order born of difficulties met and overcome; it is a pre-established, simplistic order that has itself never been challenged but merely offered as a reward for Orfeo's courage in descending into Hades. In this respect I part company with Donington's interpretation.[15]

In summary, the adventures of Orfeo through the course of the opera result in an increasing psychological disintegration that is mirrored and expressed by appropriate degrees of musical disintegration in all musical parameters. Orfeo's growing mental chaos is transformed by Monteverdi into intimations of musical chaos. Monteverdi says that "Ariadne moved us because she was a woman, and similarly Orpheus because he was a man, not a

---

[15]   Donington sees Orfeo's ascent into Heaven as "moving forward into a maturer state." See Donington, "Monteverdi's First Opera," p. 274.

wind," but we must remember that Orfeo, as the son of Apollo, was a demigod and not fully human. While he suffers like humans, he, like the ancient gods from whom he descends, does not undergo a growth process in the face of destiny, for psychological growth is reserved to mortals alone.

V

The psychic disintegration of a demi-god: conscious and unconscious in Striggio and Monteverdi's *L'Orfeo*

'Consciousness' is a word used casually in everyday parlance, suggesting that, in the Western world at least, we have an unproblematic understanding of the term, however problematic it may be when examined more closely. Its opposite, 'unconscious', however, is far more vague and manifold in its usage and significance. Both concepts may be studied from many different angles, according to the criteria and practices of many different disciplines. My objective in this chapter is to examine the methods of poetic and musical expression employed by the librettist Alessandro Striggio and the composer Claudio Monteverdi in their first opera, *L'Orfeo* (1607), from a psychological standpoint. Such an approach is particularly fruitful, for the premise of opera from its incipient stages was psychological, leading to a rich musico-dramatic portrayal of both the conscious and unconscious levels of its protagonist's mind.

Monteverdi and the birth of opera

The origins of opera in the late sixteenth century through the efforts of the Florentine Camerata are too well known to require review here. What is worth emphasizing, however, are psychological aspects of the theoretical foundations of opera. Vincenzo Galilei, the principal theorist of the Camerata, argued that the purpose of music was to convey the significance of a textual idea (*concetto*) and to affect an audience emotionally for their moral benefit and improvement, as he believed the Greeks had done in their tragedies. The Camerata had the same objective as contemporaneous oratory: to move an audience the same way a singer had been moved by the ideas contained in the text (Strunk 1950: 302–22).[1] This was an age in which the importance of rhetoric was at its apogee in education, in the Church, in politics and diplomacy, and in poetry (the literature on rhetoric in the Renaissance is vast). Famous preachers, such as San Filippo Neri, had brought untold numbers back into the Church and prayer houses (*oratorii*) by the emotional impact of their rhetoric.

In opera, musical rhetoric combined the magical effects of the word with the magical effects of music.[2] First a *concetto* and its attendant passion were embodied in words

V

by the poet, then realized in music for solo voice and accompaniment by the composer, then projected by the singer functioning as orator, and ultimately received by the listener who was emotionally moved and morally improved. Following Plato, Galilei believed that music had ethical effects upon its listeners, but the more practical musicians of the Camerata, the singer–composers Jacopo Peri and Giulio Caccini, quickly abandoned the moralistic aspect of the recitative and other monodic vocal forms and stressed only the passions—the ability of the singer to move the passions of the listener in accord with the significance of the text and its musical setting. Opera was born as an ideal medium for carrying out this programme.

The Florentine project was profoundly psychological, for its aim was to influence the way people experienced and thought about the world through stimulating their feelings, their affections. This entailed something more than one individual striving to induce a particular psychological state in another; it meant a chain of persons involved in the creation, production, and performance of an opera seeking to affect psychologically a large number of people in an audience.[3]

The first Florentine opera was *La Dafne* of 1598, only fragments of which survive. The tale of Orpheus and Eurydice was the second myth to which these Florentines applied their theories and their practice in the first surviving opera, Peri's and Caccini's *Euridice* of 1600.[4] The story was commissioned again from the Mantuan court poet Alessandro Striggio and court composer Claudio Monteverdi in 1607 by Prince Francesco Gonzaga. Their first effort at the new genre was in obvious emulation of and competition with the Florentines. There had been long-standing Gonzaga interest in this myth, which had previously been dramatized by the Mantuan poet Angelo Poliziano in a court play of 1480 and depicted by the Mantuan painter, Andrea Mantegna, in a series of frescoes in the bridal chamber of the ducal palace in the same period (Scavizzi 1985: 117). Striggio's and Monteverdi's opera, entitled *L'Orfeo*, was first performed in the Gonzaga palace on 24 February 1607 and received another performance on 1 March (Fenlon 1986). Also in emulation and competition with the Florentines, the libretto and music were published: the libretto first in 1607 and the music in 1609, with a second, corrected edition issued in 1615.[5]

The story of Orpheus has long been considered an ideal subject for opera, not just because of its tragic aspects, but because of Orpheus's identity and role as the master musician, the one who could tame wild beasts, make stones weep, stop streams from flowing, and ultimately win the reluctant Eurydice as bride with his music. Orpheus represents the magical power of music, its power to penetrate directly to the soul, as so many sixteenth- and seventeenth-century writers declared.[6] And no one succeeded so well in the early seventeenth century as Monteverdi in accomplishing precisely that: grasping intuitively the psychology of Orpheus as a human-like character and penetrating with his music to the emotional depths of listeners.

Trying to understand just how Monteverdi achieved this is what leads me to an examination of the expression of both consciousness and the unconscious in *L'Orfeo*. Clearly, a psychological approach is required in keeping with the psychological power of the music, but there are many psychological avenues for exploring this matter. I take my point of departure from the writings of Carl Gustav Jung, whose approach I find the richest and most useful in explanatory potential, allowing insight not only into the psychology of Striggio's and Monteverdi's protagonist, but also into their own psychological knowledge and instincts in finding convincing means to express his tragedy. Jung's psychology might be deployed on hermeneutic grounds, but it is also a fact that there are aspects of Jung's psychology that have been widely accepted as valid by the psychological profession, which suggests that these may serve as guides to Striggio's and Monteverdi's own understanding of the psychology of Orpheus. These aspects include Jung's definition of the unconscious in much broader and more inclusive terms than Freud, the idea of psychological growth through self-knowledge (previously emphasized by Friedrich Nietzsche), the identification of psychological types, and the concepts of the 'anima' and 'animus' (the feminine and masculine sides) in men and women.

Jung's conception of consciousness and the unconscious

Jung provided a definition of consciousness in his seminal work *Psychological Types* (1921), whose last chapter constitutes a series of definitions of terms used throughout the book. Jung's definition of consciousness is not easy to grasp apart from the entire complex of ideas contained in this volume. Basing his conception on Paul Natorp's *Einleitung in die Psychologie nach kritischer Methode*, published in Freiburg im Breisgau (1888), Jung begins:

> By consciousness I understand the relation of psychic contents to the *ego*, in so far as this relation is perceived as such by the ego. . . . Relations to the ego that are not perceived as such are *unconscious*. Consciousness is the function or activity which maintains the relation of psychic contents to the ego. (1971: 421–2)[7]

Having grown up with the dialectical intellectual model of Platonic and nineteenth-century German philosophy, Jung defined and understood many of these terms in relation to their opposites. In this case consciousness is understood in relation to the unconscious—and vice versa. Jung's definition of the unconscious begins:

> The concept of the *unconscious* is for me an *exclusively psychological* concept, and not a philosophical concept of a metaphysical nature. In my view the unconscious is a psychological borderline concept, which covers all psychic contents or processes that are not conscious, i.e., not related to the *ego* in any perceptible way. (1971: 483)

Jung later defined the unconscious more concretely:

> Everything of which I know but of which I am not at the moment thinking; everything of which I was once conscious but have now forgotten; everything perceived by my senses but not noted by my conscious mind; everything which involuntarily and without paying attention to it I feel, think, remember, want and do; all future things that are taking shape in me and will sometime come to consciousness—all this is the content of the unconscious. (Segaller 1989)

Key to the definitions of both consciousness and the unconscious in *Psychological Types* are the terms 'psychic contents' and 'ego'. Although Jung offers no definition explicitly of 'psychic contents', it is clear from his definition of the psyche as 'the totality of all psychic processes, conscious as well as unconscious' (C.G. Jung 1971: 463), as well as his use of this term in other discussions, that 'psychic contents' comprehends all mental processes of any kind. Jung's concept of the ego, on the other hand, is specifically dependent on consciousness:

> By ego I understand a complex of ideas which constitutes the centre of my field of consciousness and appears to possess a high degree of continuity and identity. Hence I also speak of an *ego-complex*. The ego-complex is as much a content as a condition of *consciousness*, for a psychic element is conscious to me only in so far as it is related to my ego-complex. (1971: 425)

What Jung means by ego-complex is clearly the individual aware of him or herself, that sense of self-identity that maintains continuity transcending time. 'Psychic contents', or mental processes, therefore, are conscious when the ego, the individual, is aware of them, and unconscious when the ego is unaware of them.

Another way to put this is that consciousness entails the focus of attention on external perceptions or internal thoughts and feelings. As long as we focus sufficient attention on something, we are aware or conscious of it. Those functionings of the mind that go on beneath our level of consciousness, therefore allowing us to focus our conscious attention selectively on just a few things at a time, occupy the realm of the unconscious, that substratum of the mind on which consciousness rests. Jung considered the term unconscious to be a metaphor for all kinds of mental activities that take place without our being aware of them, without entering into consciousness.

Jung divided the unconscious itself into two strata: an underlying *collective* unconscious and a *personal* unconscious. He describes the collective unconscious in this manner:

> in addition to these personal unconscious contents, there are other contents which do not originate in personal acquisitions but in the inherited possibility of psychic functioning in general, i.e., in the inherited structure of the brain. These are the mythological associations, the motifs and images that can spring up anew anytime anywhere, independently of historical tradition or migration. (1971: 485)

The collective unconscious, Jung claimed, is the substratum of the mind whose psychic contents are universal to all humanity. On Jung's view the collective unconscious is the origin of such mythological figures as Orpheus, whose counterpart appears in a number of other mythologies around the globe, resulting from the tendency of the collective unconscious to produce images (archetypes) that embody basic apprehensions and ideas significant to all humankind.

The personal unconscious rests on the collective unconscious and may include the personal aspects of underlying psychic contents from the collective unconscious. The contents of the personal unconscious range from the vast storehouses of memory to the symbolic content of dreams, from the neural networks that generate feeling to suppressed complexes that impinge on behaviour, from instinctive value judgements to imagination and the mysterious ruminations that result in sudden ideas or artistic inspiration. Jung also describes the contents of the unconscious as often in dialectical opposition to the contents of consciousness or as representing the complement or opposite of incomplete or indistinctly focused conscious thoughts, feelings, and experiences. One of

V

the facets of this dialectic Jung explores most deeply is the concept of the *anima* and the *animus*, the gender opposites of the conscious individual—gender images and gender-associated characteristics and behaviours that in their universality originate archetypally in the collective unconscious, but are distinctively shaped in every individual's personal unconscious. These unconscious gender images have profound effects on our attitudes, thinking, feelings, and behaviour, whether positively or negatively. According to Jung, an 'impassioned relationship' between the sexes results from the projection of the unconscious gender opposite, the *anima* or *animus*, onto a real individual. The difficulties in love relationships often result from the failure of that real individual to conform to the unconscious, projected gender image. In Jung's definitions in *Psychological Types*, the concepts of anima and animus—among the most complex and difficult of his ideas to grasp fully—are explained under, and in fact identified with, the term *soul-image*. I give here only part of his explanation:

> The soul-image is a specific *image* among those produced by the unconscious. Just as the *persona*, or outer attitude is represented in dreams by images of definite persons who possess the outstanding qualities of the persona in especially marked form, so in a man the soul, i.e., anima, or inner attitude, is represented in the unconscious by definite persons with the corresponding qualities. Such an image is called a 'soul-image'. . . . With men the anima is usually personified by the unconscious as a woman; with women the animus is personified as a man. . . . In all cases where there is an *identity* with the persona, and the soul accordingly is unconscious, the soul-image is transferred to a real person. This person is the object of intense love or equally intense hate (or fear). The influence of such a person is immediate and absolutely compelling, because it always provokes an affective response. The *affect* is due to the fact that a real, conscious adaptation to the person representing the soul-image is impossible. . . . Affects always occur where there is a failure of adaptation. Conscious adaptation to the person representing the soul-image is impossible precisely because the subject is unconscious of the soul. Were he conscious of it, it could be distinguished from the object, whose immediate effects might then be mitigated, since the potency of the object depends on the *projection* of the soul-image. For a man, a woman is best fitted to be the real bearer of his soul-image, because of the feminine quality of his soul; for a woman it will be a man. Wherever an impassioned, almost magical, relationship exists between the sexes, it is invariably a question of a projected soul-image. (C.G. Jung 1971: 470–1)[8]

As we will see, the projection of Orfeo's *anima* upon Euridice (I will use the Italian forms of Orpheus and Eurydice to refer to the characters in the opera) is a critical factor in a psychological understanding of Striggio's and Monteverdi's work.

The unconscious and its workings are beyond cognition. As Jung wryly observed very late in his life, 'The research comes to the question of the unconscious—there things become necessarily blurred, because the unconscious is something which is *really* unconscious. So you have no object, you see nothing, you only can make inferences'.[9] Nevertheless, it is possible to understand something about the unconscious and its 'psychic contents' through inductive reasoning and other indirect methods, such as dream analysis, hypnosis, or the study of mythology.[10]

In Jung's psychology, the unconscious inevitably holds vastly more 'psychic contents' than does consciousness and is infinitely more complex; indeed, Jung declares,

V

348

'The range of what *could* be an unconscious content is simply illimitable' (1971: 485). The unconscious is like an endless sea, ill-formed, deep, unpredictable, uncontrollable and unknowable. But even though the contents of the unconscious are beyond cognition, the boundary between the unconscious and the conscious is permeable. In his definition of the unconscious in *Psychological Types* Jung describes the movement of psychic contents from consciousness to the unconscious through a loss of psychic energy:

> Conscious contents can become unconscious through loss of their energic value. This is the normal process of 'forgetting'. That these contents do not simply get lost below the threshold of consciousness we know from the experience that occasionally, under suitable conditions, they can emerge from their submersion decades later, for instance in dreams, or under hypnosis, or in the form of cryptomnesia, or through the revival of associations with the forgotten content. We also know that conscious contents can fall below the threshold of consciousness through 'intentional forgetting,' or what Freud calls the *repression* of a painful content, with no appreciable loss of value. (1971: 484)[11]

Even more commonly, whenever we change the focus of our attention, whatever had been its previous focus slips into the unconscious. Just as conscious contents may lose sufficient 'energic value' and recede into the unconscious, these and other contents, such as sense perceptions, associations, and judgements whose intensity was originally inadequate to reach the level of consciousness, may gather enough 'psychic energy' to appear in dreams, under hypnosis, or in consciousness under the stimulus of some associated conscious thought, perception, or experience. When a thought, image, or memory suddenly appears in our minds, it has, in Jung's terms, accumulated enough 'energic value' to cross the boundary; it has attained enough psychic energy to bring the 'psychic content' out of the murky and chaotic unconscious into the light and concreteness of consciousness where it can be perceived, subjected to thought, and selectively acted on.

It is through this process of accumulating 'energic value' that the vast contents of the unconscious are productive of contents that reach consciousness. The one such activity Jung cites in his definition of the unconscious is the production of mythological images from the collective unconscious, whereby the image gathers enough psychic energy to become conscious, but its associations and significance remain unconscious. However, Jung's concept of the unconscious, as he describes it in *Psychological Types*, *Two Essays on Analytical Psychology* and in so many other writings, is productive of much more: it is the source of instincts, habits, spontaneous actions, intuitions, creativity, and all new ideas that so often appear abruptly and unexpectedly in consciousness. In Jung's theory, any unconscious contents may at some point be infused with enough psychic energy to come to the surface as conscious thoughts, associations, ideas, images, feelings, judgements, and reactions.

It is fundamental to Jung's psychology and generally accepted in the psychological profession that the unconscious also regularly influences behaviour without its psychic contents gathering enough 'psychic energy' to come to consciousness. Instinctive behaviours, habitual behaviours, emotional reactions that suddenly surface without a known specific cause, most judgements about experiences, people, objects, and situations, come about through the workings of the unconscious, often in response to an external stimulus or some inner rumination. Consciousness too, of course, affects behaviour, for we can deliberately choose to react to something and behave accordingly. On the other hand, many of our reactions and behaviours are unconscious, without our being aware of the relationship between our underlying psychic contents and our response to external stimuli, persons, or events. In such instances, our reaction or behaviour occurs spontaneously, without our thinking about it. Frequently we only become aware of our behaviour or reaction through some outward manifestation commanding attention, or through someone else calling attention to it, while its underlying motivation remains obscure. Indeed, far more of our daily activity and behaviour is governed by the unconscious than by conscious, deliberative planning or judgement.

Beyond this type of interaction between consciousness and the unconscious, Jung considered their overall relationship to be critical to the mental health and well-being of any individual. According to Jung, mental health depends on keeping the conscious and the unconscious in some kind of balance. This requires consciousness to recognize that much of the mind's activity—and much of what motivates our behaviour—is located in the unconscious. Psychic health requires that the individual ego not only rely on the awareness and functions of consciousness, which are quite limited, but also seek to understand something about the unconscious in order to find assistance from that psychic realm in responding to and coping with life. Only by delving indirectly into the unconscious, by descending into its uncharted darkness and chaotic contents, can individuals become aware of their underlying motivations, discover the gender-opposite aspects of their personality, find solutions to the more intractable of life's problems, and grow towards the fullest possible realization of their potential. All broadening of personality, all creative approaches to problems, all wisdom and psychic health depend on a lifelong effort to learn and grow from the unconscious, to bring aspects of the unconscious out of darkness into the light of consciousness where the ego can grapple with them and make effective choices in governing the individual's actions as well as coming to grips with the inevitable frustrations, traumas, and suffering of life.

Jung called this process of learning and growing from the encounter with the unconscious 'individuation'. It is a process not only of defining oneself more specifically by bringing unconscious psychic contents to the light of consciousness, but also of differentiating oneself from others:

> The concept of individuation . . . is the process by which individual beings are formed and differentiated; in particular, it is the development of the psychological *individual* as a being distinct from the general collective psychology. Individuation, therefore is a process of *differentiation*, having for its goal the development of the individual personality. . . . Individuation is practically the same as the development of consciousness out of the original state of *identity*. It is thus an extension of the sphere of consciousness, an enriching of conscious psychological life. (1971: 448–50)

The connection between the process of individuation and the unconscious becomes explicit in Jung's definition of identity—not the unique characteristics of the individual, as the word is often understood in English, but rather the identification of the individual with others, such as the identification of an infant with its parents, or a person with the group of which he or she is a part:

> I use the term *identity* to denote a psychological conformity. It is always an unconscious phenomenon since a conscious conformity would necessarily involve a consciousness of two dissimilar things, and consequently, a separation of subject and object, in which case the identity would already have been abolished. Psychological identity presupposes that it is unconscious. It is a characteristic of the primitive mentality and the real foundation of *participation mystique*, which is nothing but a relic of the original non-differentiation of subject and object, and hence of the primordial unconscious state. (C.G. Jung 1971: 441)

But Jung's definition of individuation in the last chapter of *Psychological Types* only scratches the surface of the process and its importance for the individual in his psychology. The discussions of the subject in this and his subsequent writings repeatedly emphasize not only the separation of the individual from the collective, but the significance of awareness and understanding of the contents of the unconscious, of the individual's underlying attitudes, motivations, feelings, and behaviours, in order to expand consciousness of oneself and bring these matters under the critique and control of consciousness, that is, to integrate the conscious and unconscious. To be unknowingly motivated and moved by the unconscious is to fail to understand or have authority over oneself. Bringing unconscious psychic contents increasingly into consciousness not only achieves greater self-understanding and increased command over one's reactions to life's experiences, but also increasingly differentiates the individual from the collective.

Individuation is a difficult, lifelong effort, resulting in ever-developing maturity and psychological health. Without the aid of the unconscious, ego consciousness is so limited that at times it cannot deal adequately or productively with the hardships and tragedies of life. But because the unconscious contains the potential for everything, not every exploration of the unconscious, every influence of the unconscious, or everything that emerges from the unconscious into consciousness is positive. The unconscious indiscriminately contains the potential for both positive and negative—for both good and evil, creation and destruction—so that delving into and encountering the unconscious can be not only fruitful and energizing but also dangerous and destructive. If the conscious ego becomes confused or overwhelmed by the unconscious, then conscious intentions can fail and psychological chaos can ensue, for the very nature of the unconscious is that it is undifferentiated, untamed, disorganized, fragmented, and beyond conscious control. Such a serious psychic disturbance can, in turn, culminate in psychic disintegration, whereby the conscious ego itself fragments under the pressure of overwhelming unconscious forces or of experiences in a world with which consciousness cannot cope and from which exploration of the unconscious provides no positive relief.

Thus, individuation is a serious matter for the personality, especially in those times of life when the efforts of consciousness to construct one's individuality, orient oneself in the world, and pursue one's goals encounter unexpected difficulties, or fail. That is when it is most crucial to turn one's attention to the unconscious, to seek new understandings, new solutions, and new ways of approaching a world that is no longer manageable by the old conscious means.

V

These concepts, definitions, and explanations form the investigative and hermeneutic basis for my study and discussion of the psychological aspects of Striggio's and
Monteverdi's *L'Orfeo*. What I wish to demonstrate is not that either Striggio or
Monteverdi thought about the psychology of their characters and the expression of
that psychology in the same terms as Jung, but rather that their own experiential
and instinctive knowledge of human psychology and emotions led them to forms of
expression which Jung's concepts and formulations can assist in interpreting and
explaining. If Jung's understanding and explanation of human psychology is valid
irrespective of the fluctuations of history (which Jung himself clearly believed), then
this type of investigation should be able to bring to conscious awareness what the
librettist and composer understood in many respects only intuitively and instinctively,
that is, unconsciously. Such an investigation should also be capable of illuminating
how the true-to-life representation of Orfeo's psychology is fundamental to the
attraction and power of the opera.

Conscious and unconscious in *L'Orfeo*

The myth of the demi-god Orpheus has proved one of the most popular and enduring
tales of ancient Greece. Among several facets of the myth, the one that has fired the
imagination of the Western world for well over two thousand years is the story of
Orpheus the poet-musician, given his talent by his father, the god Apollo, enabling
him to perform the kind of magic typically associated by the Greeks with music. For
Orpheus himself, the highest of his musical achievements is to win as wife the nymph
Eurydice. In Virgil's and Ovid's versions of the myth, the two principal sources for
Striggio's libretto, Orpheus's winning of Eurydice does not last long,[12] for she is soon
bitten by a snake, whether in the act of fleeing the unwanted advances of the beekeeper
Aristea in Virgil's *Georgics*, or while celebrating her wedding in Ovid's *Metamorphoses*.
Orpheus is beside himself with grief and resolves to descend into the Underworld to
test the magic of his music in a novel way: to win Eurydice a second time by softening
the heart of Pluto. Pluto seems to relent, but he is no fool. He allows Eurydice to follow
Orpheus back out of Hades on the condition that Orpheus have complete trust in his
word and not look back to be certain. But on the way out of Hades, Orpheus suc-
cumbs, according to Ovid, to the fear that Eurydice might not be well; impelled by
love, he does turn and look back, thereby losing Eurydice for a second, final time.
Emerging from the Underworld, he travels to the plains of Thrace, where he bewails
his fate and forswears the company of women forever. In Ovid's story, after a period
of mourning, he takes up with young boys. But whether he simply abjures women, as
in Virgil, or turns his attention to boys, he meets the same fate. Because he has rejected
female company, a savage group of Maenads, female followers of Bacchus, tears him
limb from limb and scatters his body parts. There is more to the story, but it goes
beyond what Striggio included in his libretto and Monteverdi set to music and need
not concern us here.

The psychological picture of Orfeo presented by Striggio and Monteverdi is entirely human and individualistic, even though the myth of Orpheus may itself have
been a product of what Jung called the collective unconscious. That Monteverdi

V

understood his version of the protagonist as revealing a human psychology imposed on the mythical figure of the demi-god is implicit in a letter to Striggio, dated 9 December 1616. In reference to a proposal for an opera in which the four winds were to be principal characters, the composer writes: 'Ariadne [the heroine of his opera *Arianna* of 1608] moved us because she was a woman, and similarly Orpheus because he was a man, not a wind' (Stevens 1995: 110).[13] Striggio cast the tale in its language and structure in a manner that stimulated and enabled the composer to play upon the human psychological aspects of Orfeo, aspects which may be subsumed under Jung's definitions of the conscious and unconscious, in terms of both dramatic situations and the actions and reactions of the hero. The world in which Orfeo wins Euridice is representative of consciousness itself, for it is a place of light where things can be seen, understood, and enjoyed. The Underworld, on the other hand, is dark, mysterious, frightening, and dangerous—representative of the unconscious, the realm of the unknown and unbounded potential, both positive and negative. Thus, in the myth, the Underworld manifests not only the possibility for Euridice's return to the light of day and the conferral of eternal happiness on Orfeo, as happens in the libretto of Peri's and Caccini's *Euridice* of 1600, mentioned above; but also the potential for the eternal loss of Euridice, as described in Virgil's and Ovid's versions of the myth, in Angelo Poliziano's Mantuan play of 1480, and in Striggio's libretto.

The first act-and-a-half of *L'Orfeo* is all festivity, happiness, and delight. Orfeo and his shepherd companions are celebrating his wedding and his successful wooing of the formerly reluctant Euridice through his music. Dances and closed, strophic musical numbers of the type inherited from the *intermedio* tradition of court entertainment are prominent in this part of the opera. Monteverdi also creates rounded or symmetrical structures on a larger scale by means of repetition of certain numbers, such as the five-part madrigal *Lasciate i monti*, which both precedes and follows the first appearance of Orfeo and Euridice. As is well known, Monteverdi organizes these numbers in a palindromic symmetry in the first act, with the initial appearances of Orfeo and Euridice in the centre. These closed, repetitive, and symmetrical structures are representative of the conscious, rational world of the protagonists themselves and their pastoral companions. The music, whether in the form of recitative, arioso, strophic variations, or strophic song, is an expression of a consistency of feeling of which everyone on stage is fully aware and in which they all share. Moreover, we might assume that these feelings were as clear to Monteverdi's audience as they are to today's.

Yet even in the midst of this conscious revelry, Orfeo's unconscious becomes manifest—in the character of Euridice. Euridice is a shadowy figure in the ancient forms of the myth, in Poliziano's play, in Striggio's libretto, and in Monteverdi's music. She never appears in any of the poetic versions nor in the opera as a well-defined character. Euridice has only one substantive moment in the opera, and even that is brief and indecisively formed.[14] Indeed, in Striggio's libretto, she identifies herself entirely with Orfeo's heart rather than in terms of her own personal affection:

Io non dirò qual sia
Nel tuo gioire Orfeo la gioia mia,

V

Che non ho meco il core,
Ma seco stassi in compagnia d'Amore;
Chiedilo dunque à lui s'intender brami
Quanto lieta gioisca, e quanto t'ami.

I will not say what is
In your joy, Orfeo, my joy,
Since I do not have my heart with me,
But it remains with you in the company of Love;
Ask then of it if you wish to know
How happy it rejoices, and how much I love you.[15]

While this is a typical conceit in sixteenth- and seventeenth-century Italian love poetry, it is nevertheless indicative of the psychological fact that the woman whom Orfeo loves is not, in Jungian terms, an individual separate from himself, but rather his own *anima* projected from his unconscious onto the shadowy figure of Euridice. Monteverdi depicts the insubstantiality of Euridice by giving her music that itself is insubstantial and uncommitted, even ominous. She begins by outlining a dissonant tritone, and the entire brief passage is unstable harmonically, shifting rapidly from cadences on one pitch to another (see Example 20.1).[16] The passage begins on the fourth degree of A, whose cadence in bar 3 is reached melodically through the tritone D–G♮. But motion through F major and C major harmonies (bars 4 and 6) leads hastily to a cadence on G major (bar 7), thence to D minor (bars 10–11), and A minor (bar 13). Once again F major and C major harmonies intervene (bars 14–15) before Euridice concludes on D, whose dominant is preceded by a dissonant melodic B♭ resolved by the supporting G minor harmony (bars 15–16).

The atmosphere of celebration and revelry that characterizes Act I continues at the beginning of Act II; but upon the entrance of Sylvia, the messenger who bears the terrible news of Euridice's death, the musical style shifts radically to a powerful,

Example 20.1 Euridice, *Io non so dirò.*

anguished recitative. Sylvia is barely able to articulate her message because of the oppressive tragedy that overwhelms her:

> [Ahi, las]sa,
> Ch'ella i languidi lumi alquanto aprendo,
> E te chiamando Orfeo, Orfeo,
> Dopo un grave sospiro,
> Spirò' fra queste braccia, ed io rimansi
> Piena il cor di pietade e di spavento.

> *Ah, alas,*
> *That her languishing eyes [still] somewhat perceiving*
> *And calling you, 'Orfeo, Orfeo',*
> *After a heavy sigh,*
> *She expired in these arms, and I remained*
> *With a heart full of pity and terror.*

Her recitative is music of the unconscious, of outpourings of feeling that well up from the depths of the psyche, bursting forth with little sense of control or order (see Example 20.2). Impelled by the powerful emotions underlying the words, the music changes melodic direction and rhythmic configuration abruptly and is infused with dissonance and unexpected shifts of harmony. The excerpt, beginning on a D major triad, the dominant of G major, finally cadences in D, but not before passing through

Example 20.2 Excerpt from messenger's report.

chords or implied chords shifting with erratic and unpredictable chromaticism, a truly irrational succession.[17]

Striggio and Monteverdi's representation of this terrible news, and of Orfeo's reaction to it, is psychologically masterful. It takes some time, after an introduction of anguished lamenting, for Sylvia finally to say unequivocally that Euridice is dead. Orfeo is struck dumb by these words, and can only utter an inarticulate *Ohime, che odo? . . . ohime!* ('Alas, what do I hear? . . . alas'). Sylvia then proceeds to describe at length the circumstances surrounding Euridice's death before reaching the conclusion quoted above. This prolonged passage gives Orfeo time to collect his thoughts, to shape his reaction, both emotionally and intellectually. Even when the messenger has finished, it is a shepherd who first responds with his own anguished outcry, echoing the first outcry of Sylvia herself. When Orfeo finally does react, it is not in the form of an instinctive, unconscious emotional outburst, but rather with emotions couched in the terms of a reasoned, dialectical argument.

> Tu sei morta, mia vita, ed io respiro?
> Tu sei da me partita
> Per mai più non tornare, ed io rimango?
> No, che se i versi alcuna cosa ponno,
> N'andrò sicuro a'più profondi abissi,
> E, intenerito il cor del re de l'ombre,
> Meco trarrotti a riveder le stelle;
> O, se ciò negherammi empio destino,
> Rimarrò teco in compagnia di morte.
> Addio terra, addio cielo e sole, addio.[18]

> *You are dead, my life, and I still breathe?*
> *You have departed from me*
> *Never to return, and I remain?*
> *No, if my verses can do anything at all,*
> *I shall surely descend into the deepest abysses,*
> *And, having softened the heart of the King of Shades,*
> *Lead you back with me to see again the stars;*
> *Or, if cruel destiny will deny me this,*
> *I shall remain with you in the company of death.*
> *Goodbye earth, goodbye sky and sun, goodbye.*

While the text begins with an expression of disbelief that Euridice is dead and Orfeo still alive, this dichotomy serves as the launching point for an emotional, but still rational, dialectical discussion of how to proceed. The opposing conditions of Euridice and Orfeo quickly become a dialectic of spatial separation: Euridice is below in the Underworld and Orfeo remains above in the land of the living. This spatial opposition leads to a decision to act to eliminate the separation by one of two means: Orfeo will descend into the Underworld to retrieve Euridice by softening the heart of Pluto, the King of the Shades, and bring her back to see the stars; or, if that fails, he will remain with her in the Underworld. Once the decision to act is made, Orfeo closes the argument by bidding farewell to the cosmic objects of the space he currently enjoys above in order to descend

Example 20.3 Orfeo, *Tu sei morta.*

below. In contrast to the outpourings of grief by the messenger Sylvia, Orfeo, in a moment of great emotional stress, is composed and capable of conscious deliberation.

Monteverdi's musical representation (Example 20.3) takes its point of departure from Striggio's verbal cues. It is the beginning of the text that is most emotionally charged. Orfeo waits almost two bars before responding with an opening drop of a diminished fourth in *cantus mollis* in G, from B♭ to a very dissonant F♮ followed by an

V

upward resolution (bars 3–4).[19] A chromatic ascent from the G ending Orfeo's first phrase through a dissonant G♮ at the beginning of the second, to A and B♮ at the dissonant high point of the phrase, leads to a half-cadence on an E major triad, remote from the opening G minor (bars 4–8). The dissonance and the remote harmonic juxtaposition underscore the psychological disruption Orfeo has experienced by the sudden loss of his wife. This opening gambit establishes a musical dichotomy paralleling the opposed terms by which Euridice is described: the first phrase ends with *morta* on G, while the second, referring to her as Orfeo's *vita*, concludes on G♮, each representing a radically contrasting harmony and tonality. The expression of dichotomies continues as Orfeo again contrasts his condition to that of Euridice with the words *ed io respiro* (bars 8–10). He begins on G, the pitch of Euridice's death, and moves to B♭, supported by a V–I progression, which sets him, still alive, apart in a different tonality and a different mode from the opening G minor of the deceased Euridice.

The next phrase (bars 11–17) represents an intensification of the first. The bass is repeated, but the opening vocal pitch is a third higher, on D, making the leap down to the dissonant F♮ (also sustained longer) even more striking; and the chromatically inflected ascent, previously to B, is now extended to D and settles on B♮ in contrast to G♮. Whereas the second phrase paused on a dominant E major chord, this variant version continues pressing upward (bars 17–18) to the highest pitch in the piece, E4, on the word *rimango*—musically representing the spatial distance between the living Orfeo, who remains above, and the dead Euridice, whose note of death is the *g* below.

This opening passage is Striggio's and Monteverdi's way of expressing the anguish of Orfeo, but it is not the anguish of a spontaneous, unconscious outburst of pain. Rather, it is a carefully constructed expression of sorrow by someone who has already grasped his circumstance and decided what to do. That decision comes immediately on the heels of the high E4 (bars 19–21) with the word *no*, first on C then repeated and intensified on D, before beginning a stepwise descent. This motion (bars 20–3) articulates Orfeo's intention to descend into the Underworld to return Euridice to life, and the music follows him into the abyss (*più profondi abissi*) to the lowest pitch of the piece, C3. The entire phrase (bars 14–23), beginning with *se' da me partita*, has been one long ascent and descent, with only a couple of momentary pauses for breath, reaching its apogee in citing Orfeo's spatial position and its depth in citing Euridice's. The harmony throughout is much more stable, and far less dissonant, than in the opening phrases, for these are the words not of the distraught Orfeo, but of the Orfeo of decision and action.

Orfeo's purpose in his descent into the abyss is to soften the heart of Pluto (*e intenerito il cor*), and the tritone leap in the bass from F to B♮ is softened by the chromatic descent to B♭, then A (bars 24–6). Similarly, Orfeo's melodic line, which begins with a consonant A, becoming dissonant as the bass moves, is softened by its own resolution to G♮, which itself becomes dissonant in its repetition when the bass moves again, and is in turn softened by its tritone leap down to D and resolution upward to F. But as the phrase continues with the bass descending, the F too becomes dissonant before resolving downwards to the consonant *e* as part of the cadence on D minor (bars 25–8). Thus the entire phrase comprises a succession of consonances and dissonances that concludes on the as-yet-unheard chord of A major as dominant to the new tonic of D, for Orfeo is seeking to change the state of affairs.

By softening the heart of the King of Shades with his verses, he will carry Euridice up again to see the stars, reversing her spatial position. Monteverdi's melodic line (bars 28–30) likewise changes position, from a low tonic D reaching up for a second time to its high point of E4 before settling back to a cadential D an octave above its starting point. But recognizing the possibility of failure, Orfeo presents an alternative solution to his dilemma: he will remain with Euridice in the company of death, that is, he will exchange his spatial position for hers. Once again Monteverdi expresses and reinforces the dialectic with a descent reaching the lowest pitch of the piece, C3, on the word *morte* (bars 31–7). At this point the argument is concluded, and all that remains is for Orfeo to bid farewell to the world and sky above before commencing his descent into the Underworld. As he names earth, sky, and sun, Monteverdi gives him an ascending and intensifying sequence, reaching D4 again as he names the sun (his father Apollo, whom he had already addressed as *Rosa del ciel* in his first musical appearance at the centre of Act I). The final *addio* (bars 38–45) then suddenly drops an octave to D3, as if he had already begun his descent.

Orfeo's decision to descend into the Underworld hinges on his hope that his verses and song can soften the heart of Pluto, repeating with the lord of the Underworld the same kind of success he had previously had with Euridice. When Orfeo reaches the river dividing the living from the dead, he must persuade the ferryman Caronte to carry him across. Here he sings the most famous number in the opera, *Possente spirto*, in which he summons up the most astonishing virtuosity, even verbally and musically thumping his chest in the climactic fourth stanza (see Example 20.4) with Striggio's words, *Orfeo son io*, 'I am Orpheus':

Orfeo son io che d'Euridice i passi
Seguo per queste tenebrose arene
Ove già mai per huom mortal non vassi.

Orpheus am I who the steps of Euridice
Follow through these dark sands
Where never mortal man has gone.

An expression of conscious thought, this *tour de force* is cast by Striggio in the poetic form of a *capitolo* of six stanzas and a *commiato*, all in *terza rima*,[20] and by Monteverdi in the closed musical form of strophic variations on a *passamezzo antico* bass (Pryer 2007: 12–14), with each stanza separated by a ritornello. The structure is therefore similar to that of the dance songs of Act I and the first part of Act II before the interruption of the messenger. What is most different about *Possente spirto* is its extraordinary virtuosity. Monteverdi actually published two versions of the vocal line, a simple one and the highly ornamented one illustrated in Example 20.4. It is possible that the embellished version may represent what the first Orfeo, Francesco Rasi, sang at Mantua (Carter 2002: 130–1).[21] In any event, the precisely notated embellishments offer the performer one method of singing the piece, while the simple version furnishes the skeleton on which a skilled singer could improvise his own ornamentation.

But this magnificent vocal display is in vain, and for the first time in his experience, Orfeo utterly fails to achieve his goal by singing. His musical mastery and virtuosity cause a flutter in Caronte's heart but otherwise do not move him. This most forceful possible expression of Orfeo's conscious ego is inadequate to deal with a catastrophe of a kind he has never encountered before, which has completely upset the pattern of his life, and which has taken him to regions beyond his ken. On a musical level, even the most remarkable virtuosity is without power to move the passions, to stir Caronte. Virtuosity may cause one to marvel, but it has no effect on the passions of the soul.[22]

Orfeo recognizes that his virtuosity is ineffectual, and at this point Monteverdi breaks off the regular cycle of ritornellos and stanzas he has pursued up to now. Striggio has not deviated from his *terza rima*, but Monteverdi, recognizing that failure

Example 20.4 Orfeo, *Possente spirto*, verse 4.

Example 20.4 (continued).

has affected Orfeo psychologically, skips the expected ritornello, proceeds directly to the fifth stanza, and turns to recitative, with a more active bass and agitated harmony than before (see Example 20.5).

> O de le luci mie luci serene,
> S'un vostro sguardo può tornarmi in vita,
> Ahi chi niega il conforto a le mie pene?
>
> *O of my eyes the serene light,*
> *If a glance of yours can return me to life,*
> *Ah, who denies me comfort for my pain?*

At first Orfeo praises the light of Euridice's eyes, which could restore him to light, all in major tonalities; but then, turning to G minor, asks who could deny him comfort for his pain (bars 9–14). This recitative represents the beginning of an important psychological turning point for Orfeo, when, in the face of the unresponsive ferryman, he abandons the conscious pride of his ego-driven virtuosity and begins to pour out his heart in a more spontaneous, intense manner, expressing himself less predictably than the carefully structured preceding stanzas. The fifth stanza turns toward a more unconscious form of utterance, which is given added emotional urgency by repetition

Example 20.5 Orfeo, *Possente spirto*, stanza 5.

of the last line (the first time Monteverdi makes such a gesture in *Possente spirto*). This repetition (bars 15–20) is identical melodically (though slightly altered rhythmically), but its accompaniment is chromatically inflected with more first inversion chords that generate more dissonances with the vocal line.

The final stanza follows directly upon the fifth, again without any intervening ritornello, but with its own harmony and vocal line. This is Orfeo's final plea to Caronte, and even though still in recitative, it assumes a somewhat more formal character than the fifth verse, with more structured melody and harmony. Orfeo tries to win his way across with a conscious argument, still trusting in his familiar ally, the power of his lyre:

> Sol tu nobil Dio puoi darmi aita,
> Ne temer dei che sopra'un'aurea cetra,
> Sol di corde soavi armo le ditta,
> Contra cui rigid'alma in van s'impetra.[23]

> *Only you, noble God, can help me,*
> *Nor need you fear, since upon a golden lyre,*
> *Only with sweet strings arm I my fingers,*
> *Against which a rigid soul in vain hardens itself.*

In these fifth and sixth stanzas we hear the authentic voice of Orfeo's emotions, unencumbered by the ego-driven virtuosity and formal structure of the first four strophes, but in the end still controlled enough to make the kind of argument he hopes will persuade the ferryman to transport him across the river.[24] But despite being delighted with Orfeo's singing, Caronte, who is devoid of pity, remains true to character.

In response, Striggio abandons the lengthy 11-syllable lines of *terza rima* of the previous strophes, dissolving into a pair of terzets with 7- and 11-syllable lines followed

V

by a set of 7-syllable lines in paired rhymes. The vocabulary, too, loses its elevated style in favour of simpler words with fewer syllables:

Ahi sventurato amante
Sperar dunque non lice
Ch'odan miei preghi cittadin d'Averno?
Onde qual ombra errante
D'insepolto cadavero e infelice
Privo sarò del Cielo e de l'Inferno?
Cosi vuol empia sorte
Ch'in questi orror di morte
Da te cor mio lontano
Chiami tuo nome invano,
E pregando, e piangendo mi consumi?
Rendetemi il mio ben Tartarei Numi.

Ah, unfortunate lover
To hope is then denied
That the citizens of Averno will hear my prayers?
Whereby as a wandering shade
Of an unburied and unhappy corpse
Deprived will I be of both Heaven and Hell?
Thus does cruel fate wish
That in this horror of death
Far from you, my heart
I call your name in vain,
And pleading and weeping I consume myself?
Return to me my love, Tartarean gods.

This is a very significant shift in tone, for now Orfeo is gushing out his frustration in short words and rapid lines that tumble one after another. Rather than the language of deliberate, conscious planning and argument, this is the spontaneous, instinctive outpouring of despair that comes unpremeditated and unfettered from deep within the heart: the speech of the unconscious.

But even more important and obvious than the poetic change is the musical shift, for now not only virtuosity, but even any sense of melodic shape and harmonic structure have vanished (see Example 20.6). Orfeo, in desperation, spills out his anxiety in declamatory recitative with dissonances at several points of harmonic change (bars 2, 16, 17, 19), no longer singing with the structure of the conscious ego, but in an unconscious, instinctive, nearly staccato effusion of unbridled torment forced to the surface by the strength of its psychic energy. At the end (bars 23–30) his emotional outburst reaches its climax with his demand that Euridice be returned to him, repeated insistently three times in an ascending sequence of chromatic half-steps.[25]

But Caronte has no soul and remains untouched; instead, he is lulled to sleep by Orfeo's music, and Orfeo is able to seize the ferryman's boat and propel himself across the river. When he reaches the opposite shore, he finds that it is Persephone, Pluto's wife, who has been moved—not, I would argue, by his conscious egoistic virtuosity, but by his concluding spontaneous, anguished plea. Significantly, it is Persephone who is

Example 20.6 Orfeo, *Ahi sventurato amante.*

responsive to Orfeo, for she too came from the world above, from the light. She had been kidnapped by Pluto and brought down into Hades to be his wife, but to keep her he had to accede to the condition that she return once a year to the upper world and the light of day. Persephone comes from Orfeo's world, but she has also fallen in love with her kidnapper and instinctively feels the pain of Orfeo in his plea. It is Persephone, the feminine aspect of the Underworld, rather than Orfeo, who persuades Pluto to let Euridice go, not without some seductive musical gestures of her own. But as in Virgil,

V

Ovid, and Poliziano, Pluto is clever enough to fool both Persephone and Orfeo by setting a condition for Euridice's return that he knows Orfeo cannot fulfil.

This is the crucial moment for Orfeo. He has descended into the Underworld, that realm which in mythologies all over the world represents the unconscious; and by finally letting his heart, his spontaneous feelings, speak instead of his head and lyre, he has gained a measure of success in this dark and dangerous realm. But—and this is the key point—he learns nothing from his encounter with the unconscious. For as soon as Pluto agrees to let Euridice go and states his admonition, Orfeo begins his ascent out of the Underworld, out of the unconscious, singing a rather silly ditty in praise of the lyre he foolishly thinks has won the day (see Example 20.7). In fact, his song in praise of his lyre recalls the strophic celebratory music of Act I and the beginning of Act II. It reflects no change in Orfeo's personality or understanding as a result of his traumatic

Example 20.7 Orfeo, *Qual honor*, stanza 1.

V

experience and his descent into the Underworld.[26] The unconscious has made no impact on his consciousness:

Qual honor di te sia degno
Mia cetra onnipotente,
S'hai nel Tartareo Regno
Piegar potuto ogn'indurate mente?
Luogo havrai fra le più belle
Imagini celesti,
Ond'al tuo suon le stelle
Danzeranno [con] gir'hor tard'hor presti.[27]
Io per te felice à pieno
Vedrò l'amato volto,
E nel candido seno
De la mia Donna oggi sarò raccolto.

What honour could be worthy of you
My omnipotent lyre
If you, in the Tartarean Realm
Were able to bend every hardened mind?
You will have a place among the most beautiful
Celestial images
Where to your sound the stars
Will dance with turns now slow, now fast.
I, through you, am filled with happiness
I will see her beloved face,
And in the white bosom
Of my lady, today I will be received.

Orfeo thinks it was the magic of his lyre, the result of his conscious virtuosity in the first four stanzas of *Possente spirto*, that won Euridice's release rather than the subsequent spontaneous outpourings of his heart following the failure of his virtuosity. He does not realize that it was Persephone, rather than Pluto, who was the source of his apparent good fortune. He does not appreciate the seriousness of Pluto's warning and the need to constrain his instincts and impulses. He understands nothing about the falsity of appearances and the danger he still faces, nor of the profundity of restoring the dead to life. He perceives nothing new about the world he inhabits, nor about fate and the numinous forces of Hades. Orfeo has gained no new perspective, no new wisdom from his experience in the Underworld, from his plunge into the darkness of the unconscious, and most of all, he understands no more about himself and his unbridled passions than he did before he lost Euridice in the first place.[28]

It is this simple-minded, foolish Orfeo, the singer of the silly ditty to his lyre, who is so easily induced to turn around and look for Euridice by a few noises and taunting from the denizens of Hades. He claims that the god of love is more powerful than the admonition of the god of the Underworld.[29] But he is wrong, because he is unable to place love in a larger context, unable to grasp that conscious understanding of circumstances must hold love within its proper bounds, unable to understand when something else must command his attention in order for love to survive. He is wrong because his love is wholly a manifestation of his unconscious: the love of his own *anima* projection, not the woman Euridice herself.

Orfeo has failed to achieve any growth of consciousness from his experience in the Underworld, any integration of the unconscious with the conscious that would allow him to view himself and respond to his passions differently. In the face of catastrophe followed by an apparently successful outcome to his daring act, he remains the same as he was before, and his failure to achieve any individuation results in a double catastrophe: the permanent loss of both his *anima* and Euridice. The effect of his ineffectual encounter with the Underworld, the unconscious, is immediately devastating, as his psyche, with a crucial part now excised, chaotically disintegrates before our eyes and ears.

Monteverdi's musical interpretation of this disintegration begins already at the moment of Orfeo's uncertainty and fearfulness prompted by the loud noise he hears as he leads Euridice toward the light; it then continues with the shade Euridice herself (see Example 20.8).

Ahi vista troppo dolce e troppo amara:
Cosi per troppo amor dunque mi perdi?
Et io misera perdo
Il poter più godere
E di luce e di vita, e perdo insieme
Te d'ogni ben più caro, o mio consorte.

Ah, sight too sweet and too bitter:
Thus for too much love then you lose me?
And I, wretched, lose
The ability to enjoy again
Both light and life, and I lose at the same time
You, more dear than anything, oh my husband.

Example 20.8 Euridice, *Ahi vista troppo.*

V

Euridice begins with the same tritone outline with which she had first responded to Orfeo, dissolving into further dissonance (bars 4 and 7) and the tritone again (bars 9–10), as she departs for good. The G minor tonal implication of the opening chord is refuted by the E major triad of the third bar, and the passage remains tonally ambiguous and harmonically unstable, never truly resolving to any tonality until the final cadence on G.[30]

After a spirit orders Euridice back to Hades, Orfeo, bereft of the *anima* part of his psyche, now disintegrates altogether with a series of confused questions accompanied by jolting chromaticism and utter dissolution of harmonic stability and direction (see Example 20.9).

Dove te'n vai mia vita? Ecco i' ti seguo.
Ma chi me'l niegh'ohime: sogno, o vaneggio?
Qual occulto poter di questi orrori,
Da questi amati orrori
Mal mio grado mi tragge e mi conduce
A l'odiosa luce?[31]

Where are you going my love? Here, I'll follow you.
But who denies me, alas: do I dream or rave?
What dark power of these horrid realms,
From these beloved shades,
Despite my wish, drags me and leads me
To the hateful light?

Monteverdi's opening suggests an orientation toward G major (bars 1–4), but this is negated by the B♭ in the bass (bar 5), which in turn suggests a possible D minor (bars 5–6), only to be followed by a tritone leap in the bass to a sudden E major triad

Example 20.9 Orfeo, *Dove te'n vai?*

succeeded by a D major chord implying a dominant of G in keeping with the unanswered question it accompanies. However, not only is resolution to the G minor triad postponed by the C minor triad in bars 8–9, but the ensuing G bass of the minor triad itself immediately thereafter supports an ambiguous major sixth (bars 9–10). At this point the bass suggests A Aeolian for a substantial period, but the melodic line belies it with both sustained and brief dissonances (bars 10–14), and a particularly pungent one in bar 15 at the word *odiosa* ('hateful'). The entire passage then concludes on an unresolved dominant of A, as if suspending Orfeo's entire psyche in mid-air.

The next time we see Orfeo is in Act V on the plains of Thrace lamenting his bitter fate. I find this lament, however brilliantly composed, overly long and therefore ultimately tedious, but I also think that is exactly what Striggio and Monteverdi were trying to achieve psychologically. We witness this poor wretch who no longer seeks solace in the power of his lyre, who pours out his grief to the trees and rocks around him—those entities he used to be able to charm—which now simply echo his words back to him in truncated form. His words and music have no effect but to return amputated with only the final syllables remaining. Such echoes are a clever musical conceit found frequently in Italian music of the late sixteenth and early seventeenth centuries, but Striggio and Monteverdi turn this device to their dramatic ends, for Orfeo's lament is not merely ineffectual; Echo expresses his own frustration with Orfeo by responding in what appears to be a deliberately mocking tone. To Orfeo's *ahi pianto* ('oh tears'), Echo replies *hai pianto* ('you have wept'), in the perfect tense. But Orfeo keeps weeping, to the point of declaring *non ho pianto però tanto che basti* ('I do not have sufficient tears'), to which Echo responds simply *basti*, or, to render the meaning in modern colloquial terms, 'enough, already'. But Orfeo doesn't cease. He continues bewailing his fate for even more time than he had spent lamenting up to this point. A lament, like other forms of weeping, can have a positive psychological effect, discharging a large amount of emotional energy so that the lamenter can redirect his or her energies towards moving onwards, but in Orfeo's case the lament discharges nothing, leading only to more weeping and finally to the rejection of all women, to the denial of any possibility of his *anima* ever returning. To quote the Jungian analyst and scholar James Hollis, 'A reactive depression is . . . pathological when it profoundly disrupts one's normal functioning or when the disabling impact of the experience is prolonged beyond a reasonable period' (1996: 68).

In Striggio's original libretto, as in Virgil's, Ovid's, and Poliziano's versions of the myth, the Bacchic women now appear, though Striggio does not actually show them tearing Orfeo to pieces as the other authors relate—in other words, they do not enact in front of the audience the physical fragmentation symbolic of the psychic fragmentation resulting from Orfeo's failed individuation. Striggio's libretto does refer to Orfeo's fate to come, but leaves it to the audience's imagination and concludes with a dance around Orfeo by the taunting women. This, of course, is not the conclusion we know from Monteverdi's published scores of the opera. There is no proof that Monteverdi ever composed music for this original ending, though an unusual transposition rubric in the score of Act IV suggests that a change in plans had taken place sometime after the composition of the first half of that act, a change that may well have been required by the new text for Act V, and perhaps its music.[32] Prompted by one or more reasons

we can only speculate about, Monteverdi either became dissatisfied with the first conclusion or was asked to change it by his patron.[33]

The new ending of Act V has been criticized for its *Deus ex machina* resolution of
Orfeo's dilemma, whereby Apollo descends on a cloud from Heaven and carries Orfeo
off with him to see Euridice configured eternally in the stars.[34] I have quite a different
view of this ending, however, which I think, whatever its shortcomings, rounds out the
opera much better than Striggio's original conclusion. In rescuing Orfeo, Apollo criti-
cizes his son for his lack of moderation between emotional extremes (a criticism which
represents a fundamental tenet of Platonic philosophy). He had rejoiced too much in
his good fortune and now he grieves too much over his bitter fate. He has not learned
that all earthly pleasures are only temporary.

Apollo's descent symmetrically balances the paean to the sun (Apollo himself) in
Act I (*Rosa del ciel*) where the sun god was witness to Orfeo's excessive outpouring of
love; now he is witness to Orfeo's excessive effusion of sorrow. In fact, the chorus had
already sung a warning against abandoning oneself to sadness at the end of Act I, and
after Orfeo loses Euridice for the second time comments *Degna d'eterna gloria fia sol
colui ch'avrà di se vittoria* ('only he who has mastered himself is worthy of eternal
glory'—an admonition that meshes well with Jung's theory of individuation); but the
thought was left hanging, so to speak, in Striggio's original libretto. Thus the moral to
the story can only be brought home by completing the significance of that thought
with Apollo's criticism of Orfeo's overbearing grief in Act V. The Act V revision also
produces symmetry between Orfeo's earthly experiences in his initial lamentations
over Euridice's resistance turned into happiness by her eventual acquiescence, and his
otherworldly experiences involving even greater lamentation and a different kind of
satisfaction in being transported by Apollo to Heaven to see her configured there.

There is likewise a psychological level on which the new ending of Act V can be
considered successful. In Jung's theory, when one is faced with an irresolvable dilemma, one can indeed fragment psychologically as Orfeo does in Striggio's version; but
one can also be presented with an unexpected solution produced spontaneously by the
unconscious, what Jung calls the 'third way', when caught on the horns of a binary
dilemma.[35] The descent of Apollo and his bearing of Orfeo off to Heaven can be
viewed as that third way, a solution generated by the unconscious, which is quite different from what Orfeo consciously sought. This unexpected solution enables him to
see his relationship to Euridice in an entirely new way, as a constellation in Heaven,
rather than as an *anima* projection. In *Tu sei morta*, cited above (see Example 20.3),
Orfeo had declared that he would carry Euridice with him out of Hades to see the stars
again. Now she herself has become the stars and he is the one transported upwards.
Jung's 'third way' is indeed a *deus ex machina*, where the *machina* is the unconscious,
the original source of all god images, mythologies, and creative solutions.

Obviously, Striggio, Monteverdi and the author of the revised last act knew nothing
of psychoanalytic theory. Jungian psychology, however, provides us with a means of
interpreting and understanding the psychological phenomena presented to us by
these figures. What I find so remarkable about Monteverdi, taking what his librettist(s)
gave him, is the psychological insight with which he responded to Orfeo's circumstances; how clearly he understood psychological principles that Jung later enunciated

in his own psychoanalytic terms, and how imaginatively and convincingly Monteverdi presented Orfeo's psychology in his music. Orfeo was a man beset by a typically human problem, the impingement of the unconscious on conscious life and activity. His tragedy, like that of many people, was his failure to recognize that impingement and to come to grips with the subsequent catastrophes of his life by making use of the unconscious to understand, change, and renew himself in the face of these disasters—his failure, in Jung's terminology, to 'individuate', leading inevitably to psychic disintegration.

If there is a moral lesson in Monteverdi's opera, as Galilei thought drama in music should have, it is not only about the need for moderation in balancing the emotional extremes of life and not expecting the permanence of earthly happiness; but also about the need for psychological growth, for individuation, in the face of life's inescapable challenges and tragedies. Perhaps we ourselves instinctively (i.e. unconsciously) recognize this in the story and in Monteverdi's music, and that is why the opera continues to attract, fascinate, and move us over 400 years after its creation.

Acknowledgements

This chapter is expanded from papers read at the University of Toronto, the University of Kentucky, the conference of the International Association for Jungian Studies at the University of Greenwich, and the International Conference on Music and Consciousness at the University of Sheffield. I would like to thank Elizabeth Aurbach, Richard Aurbach, David Clarke, Eric Clarke, Beverly Field, Rose Holt, and Brian Vandenberg for their invaluable comments on and criticism of earlier versions of this essay.

References

Anderson, W.S. (1985). The Orpheus of Virgil and Ovid: *flebile nescio quid*, in J. Warden (ed.), *Orpheus: The Metamorphoses of a Myth*, 25–50 (Toronto: University of Toronto Press).

Carter, T. (1999). Singing *Orfeo*: on the performers of Monteverdi's first opera. *Recercare*, 11, 75–118.

Carter, T. (2002). *Monteverdi's Musical Theatre* (New Haven, CT: Yale University Press).

Donington, R. (1968). Monteverdi's first opera, in D. Arnold and N. Fortune (eds.), *The Monteverdi Companion*, 257–76 (London: Faber and Faber).

Edinger, E.F. (1999). *The Psyche in Antiquity, Book One: Early Greek Philosophy* (ed.), D.A. Wesley (Toronto: Inner City Books).

Fenlon, I. (1986). The Mantuan *Orfeo*, in J. Whenham (ed.), *Orfeo*, 1–19 (Cambridge: Cambridge University Press).

Hanning, B.R. (2003). The ending of *L'Orfeo*: Father, son, and Rinuccini, in *Journal of Seventeenth-Century Music, 9/1: In Armonia Favellare*. Available at: http://sscm-jscm.press.illinois.edu/v9/no1/hanning.html.

Hill, J.W., (ed.) (2003). In *Armonia Favellare*: Report of the International Conference on Early Opera and Monody to Commemorate the 400th Anniversary of the Italian Music Dramas of 1600, Held at the University of Illinois, Urbana-Champaign, October 5–8, 2000. Available at: http://sscm-jscm.press.illinois.edu/v9no1.html.

Hollis, J. (1996). *Swamplands of the Soul: New Life in Dismal Places* (Toronto: University of Toronto Press).

Jung, C.G. (1953). *Two Essays on Analytical Psychology*, trans. R.F.C. Hull, *Bollingen Series* XX, vol. 7 (Princeton, NJ: Princeton University Press).

Jung, C.G. (1971). *Psychological Types*, trans. H.G. Baynes, rev. R.F.C. Hull, *Bollingen Series* XX, vol. 6 (Princeton, NJ: Princeton University Press).

Jung, E. (1957). *Animus and Anima*, trans. C.F. Baynes and H. Nagel (Dallas, TX: Spring Publications).

Kerman, J. (1956). 'Orpheus: the neoclassic vision', in Kerman, *Opera as Drama*, 25–49 (New York, NY: Vintage Books); reprinted in J. Whenham (ed.) (1986), *Orfeo*, 126–37 (Cambridge: Cambridge University Press).

Kurtzman, J. (2003). Deconstructing gender in Monteverdi's *L'Orfeo. Journal of Seventeenth-Century Music*, 9. Available at http://sscm-jscm.press.illinois.edu/v9/no1/kurtzman.html.

Lax, E. (ed.) (1994). *Claudio Monteverdi: Lettere* (Florence: Leo S. Olschki Editore).

McClary, S. (1989). Constructions of gender in Monteverdi's dramatic music. *Cambridge Opera Journal*, 1, 203–23.

Mioli, P. (1993). *Claudio Monteverdi: L'Orfeo, Favola in Musica* in *Archivium Musicum, Musica Drammatica, I* (Florence: Studio per Edizioni Scelte).

Palisca, C.V. (1989). *The Florentine Camerata: Documentary Studies and Translations* (New Haven, CT: Yale University Press).

Pryer, A. (2007). Approaching Monteverdi: his cultures and ours, in J. Whenham and R. Wistreich (eds.), *The Cambridge Companion to Monteverdi*, 1–19 (Cambridge: Cambridge University Press).

Robbins, E. (1985). Famous Orpheus, in J. Warden (ed.), *Orpheus: The Metamorphoses of a Myth*, 3–23 (Toronto: University of Toronto Press).

Scavizzi, G. (1985). The myth of Orpheus in Italian renaissance art, 1400–1600, in J. Warden (ed.), *Orpheus: The Metamorphoses of a Myth*, 111–62 (Toronto: University of Toronto Press).

Segaller, S. (director and producer) (c. 1989). *The Wisdom of the Dream: Carl Gustav Jung*, vol. 1 (Wilamette, IL: Public Media Video).

Steinheuer, J. (2007). Orfeo (1607), in J. Whenham and R. Wistreich (eds.), *The Cambridge Companion to Monteverdi*, 119–40 (Cambridge: Cambridge University Press).

Stevens, D. (1972). *Claudio Monteverdi: L'Orfeo, Favola in Musica, Venice 1615* (London: Gregg International Publishers).

Stevens, D. (trans. and ed.) (1995). *The Letters of Claudio Monteverdi*, rev. edn (Oxford: Clarendon Press).

Strunk, O. (1950). *Source Readings in Music History* (New York, NY: W.W. Norton & Co.).

Tomlinson, G. (1993). *Music in Renaissance Magic: Toward a Historiography of Others* (Chicago, IL: The University of Chicago Press).

Warden, J. (1985). Orpheus and Ficino, in J. Warden (ed.), *Orpheus: The Metamorphoses of a Myth*, 85–110 (Toronto: University of Toronto Press).

Notes

1. As Galilei put it (Strunk 1950: 313, 315, 319):

> let men, who have been endowed by nature with all these noble and excellent parts, endeavor to use them not merely to delight, but as imitators of the good ancients, to improve at the same time … [P]assion and moral character must be simple and natural, or at least appear so, and their sole aim must be to arouse their counterpart in others … [I]f the musician has not the power to direct the minds of his listeners to their benefit, his science and knowledge are to be reputed null and

vain, since the art of music was instituted and numbered among the liberal arts for no other purpose.

For the principal documents relating to the background of opera see Palisca (1989).

2. The Renaissance belief in the magical powers of music is examined extensively in Tomlinson (1993).

3. Galilei's programme is described in his *Dialogo della musica antica et della moderna* (1581). For an English translation of the relevant passages see Strunk (1950), especially pp. 306–7, 312, 317.

4. *Euridice* was first performed in the Pitti Palace on 6 October 1600 as part of the wedding ceremonies of Henry IV and Maria de' Medici. It comprised mostly music by Peri, but with some insertions by Caccini. Both composers published their competing versions in the next few months.

5. A facsimile edition of the 1607 libretto and 1609 score was published with an introduction in Mioli (1993). A facsimile of the 1615 edition was published with an introduction in Stevens (1972).

6. The power of music to penetrate directly to the soul is an important theme in the *Republic* and other writings of Plato, as well as for such diverse Renaissance figures as Ficino and John Calvin.

7. In this and subsequent quotations from this source, I have omitted Jung's original footnotes and cross-references.

8. Jung also explores the significance of the *anima* and the *animus* in many of his other writings, including a chapter in his *Two Essays on Analytical Psychology* (C.G. Jung 1953), first published in 1917, but revised and reissued several times up to 1943. The most focused and comprehensive discussion of this subject was written by his wife: see Emma Jung (1957).

9. Quoted from a London interview in English, featured in Segaller (1989).

10. Dream analysis was a principal focus of Jung's therapeutic practice and many of his writings study mythology and such 'mythological' activities as alchemy.

11. 'Cryptomnesia' is a term Jung coined for the phenomenon of unconsciously appropriating for oneself someone else's thought, writing, or image and later reproducing it as one's own, not recognizing that it had an external source.

12. The myth has a variety of versions. Those of the Roman poets Virgil and Ovid are the best known, but there are several fragments with other, sometimes variant details as well. For an account of the Virgilian and Ovidian versions, see Anderson (1985). On the origins and variant early versions, see Robbins (1985).

13. This oft-quoted letter was sent from Venice, where Monteverdi was employed at the time as *maestro di cappella* at St Mark's. The original Italian may be found in Lax (1994: 19).

14. On Orfeo's Act I song to Euridice and her response see McClary (1989); for my response to McClary see Kurtzman (2003).

15. All translations from Striggio's libretto are mine. I have opted for a literal rendering in order that readers unfamiliar with Italian can, as far as possible, relate each word in the associated music example to its English counterpart.

16. The significance of the tritone as a symbol of the loss of Euridice is penetratingly explored in Donington (1968: 263–4, 272).

17. For a fuller analysis of the tonalities of this passage and their dramatic significance see Steinheuer (2007: 128–9).

18. The version of the text given here is that found in the scores of the opera published in 1609 and 1615 (Mioli 1993; Stevens 1972). The version originally published in Striggio's 1607 libretto differs in a few details.

19. *Cantus mollis* refers to a staff systemwith a single-flat signature, indicating the soft hexachord.

20. See Steinheuer (2007: 136–9). *Terza rima* is the poetic form of Dante's *La Divina Commedia*. Dante, like Striggio, follows Virgil in describing a descent into the Underworld.

21. Pryer (2007: 12–14) calls attention to a close relationship between Monteverdi's unadorned line and Giulio Caccini's aria *Qual trascorrendo* from *Il Rapimento di Cefalo* of 1600, published in his *Le Nuove Musiche* of 1601—a piece originally sung by Francesco Rasi. Steinheuer (2007: 137) observes that Monteverdi's ornamentation is not merely embellishment of the simple line, but deviates from it 'for purposes of harmonious enrichment of the declamation'.

22. Anderson makes a parallel judgement on Ovid's text at this point in the story:

> the song he assigns Orpheus is anything but unique: it makes no emotional appeal whatsoever, but works with cheap, flashy, and specious rhetoric to persuade Hades to go against his own nature. As a consequence, Orpheus strikes us as a third-rate poet-orator who, assigned the task of creating an inimitable song and trying to regain Eurydice, can only mouth commonplaces or try to devise clever but lifeless points ('colores') and so win applause. . . . Ovid presents it [love] as a chill abstract noun, a calculated point in persuasive discourse that has nothing in the previous narrative or in Orpheus' character to support it. (1985: 40)

23. This line is the *commiato* of the *capitolo*.

24. Steinheuer (2007: 138–9) summarizes the aria as follows: 'In "Possente spirto" . . . Monteverdi paints a singer certain of his abilities at the outset, who is first disturbed and finally overwhelmed by his emotions but then controls them again in the final stanza.'

25. Steinheuer (2007: 139–40) describes this passage as 'rapid, restless declamation soaked with dissonance to give Orfeo's despair free rein, culminating in a refrain section at the end'. Steinheuer continues: 'In this passage Orfeo achieves exactly that affective style, seemingly artless and spontaneous, despite its refined compositional technique'.

26. Kerman (1956: 33, 1986: 131–2) interprets the song egoistically: 'In Act IV, when Eurydice is released, the drama quickens as it reveals Orpheus' rather terrible insufficiency. His reaction is neither gratitude nor real affection, but a hymn of praise to himself and to his lyre'. Steinheuer (2007: 133–4) also notes the parallelism between this strophic song and those of Act II, but in addition outlines its unequal line lengths and strophic variations over a walking bass. Steinheuer considers these strophic songs representatives of a 'low' style in contrast to passages in the 'middle' and 'high' styles.

27. The reading of this line is taken from Striggio's libretto. Both editions of the score substitute *Io* for *con*, which makes no sense.

28. Kerman (1956: 33, 1986: 132) also observes that 'Orpheus learns nothing'. Anderson (1985: 32) likewise comments on Orpheus's failure to come to grips with his passions and to make room for a new future.

29. This idea also echoes Ficino's concept of the power and priority of love, as described in Warden (1985: 101–2).

30. Steinheuer (2007: 129–31) analyses the tonal structure of the entire passage, indicating the dramatic references of the constantly changing tonalities that Orfeo and Euridice pass through.

31. The libretto differs from the text of the published scores in some details: *Dove te'n vai mia vita? ecco i' ti seguo./Ma chi me'l vieta ohime: sogno, o vaneggio?/Qual poter, qual furor da questi orrori,/Da questi amati orrori/Mal mio grado mi tragge, e mi conduce/A l'odiosa luce?*

32. The rubric, in a solo tenor part on p. 76 of the 1609 and 1615 scores, reads 'Un tono più alto', which unequivocally means transposition a tone higher. Such a rubric was a means of avoiding rewriting or reprinting the music at the sounding pitch that had already been notated a step lower. See Carter (1999: 103–5, 2002: 98, 121) for one possible explanation of why this rubric was required.

33. There has been much speculation as to who might have revised the text of the last act as published in 1609 and 1615—whether Striggio, Prince Francesco Gonzaga, or someone else. Recently, however, Hanning (2003), through a close and sophisticated textual analysis, has concluded—quite convincingly in my view—that the new Act V ending was written by Ottavio Rinuccini. Rinuccini was not only the librettist of the Florentine *Euridice* several years earlier, but also the author of the librettos for Monteverdi's second opera, *Arianna*, and for his dramatic ballet, *Il ballo delle ingrate*, both performed as part of the 1608 Mantuan wedding festivities.

34. See, for example, the comments in Kerman (1956: 32, 37, 1986: 132, 135).

35. Jung first introduces this concept in his chapter on Friedrich Schiller's *Letters on the Aesthetic Education of Man* (C.G. Jung 1971: 88–9). The Jungian scholar Edward Edinger explains the 'third way' in this manner: 'If problems on the concrete level of personal human existence are irreconcilable within the usual terms of understanding, then with the help of material from the unconscious such as dreams or fantasies—thus raising the problem to a symbolic level—the dilemma can often be resolved' (1999: 27).

VI

WHAT MAKES CLAUDIO DIVINE? CRITERIA FOR ANALYSIS OF MONTEVERDI'S LARGE-SCALE CONCERTATO STYLE

Claudio Monteverdi enjoyed in his lifetime what few creative artists achieve-a level of fame commensurate with his artistic achievements. Where the first contemporary reference to Claudio as "il Divino" comes from, I do not know, but it is a sobriquet that his name has carried ever since it was first applied. Monteverdi himself bears witness to the esteem in which he was held in Venice in his letter to Alessandro Striggio of March 13, 1620: "nè vi è Gentilhomo che non mi stimi et honori, et quando vado a far qualche musica o sia da camera o chiesa giuro a V.S. Ill.ma che tutta la città corre"[1].

That Monteverdi's contemporaries regarded him as extraordinary in the field of composition is apparent. Today he retains an equally elevated stature. He is the only composer of the 17th century whose surviving works we know virtually in their entirety. He is performed and recorded everywhere, some works over and over again. His operas are staged, despite their many difficulties, and his large sacred works are presented in elaborate productions in churches from St. Mark's to Westminster Abbey.

His stature is also confirmed, at least for me, by the still very limited quantity of contemporaneous music that has to this time been published and recorded. Although I consider myself a very sympathetic listener to 17th-century music, the music of Caccini, Peri, Cavalieri, Gagliano, Viadana, Grandi, Rovetta and Cavalli, as excellent as some compositions are, does not strike me as "divine." Why does the music of Monteverdi ascend to the celestial kingdom? Why is only he worthy of being called "divine"?

This is not a simple question, for it opens the Pandora's box of issues of value and relative value, not only in our own terms, but in terms of 17th-century aesthetics and taste. Is there any way we can determine what made and still makes Claudio "divine" aside from the immediate judgment of our ears? Or to address the question from a different angle, given the judgment of our ears, how can we justify that judgment in terms of what actually happens in Monteverdi's music?

---

[1] DOMENICO DE'PAOLI, *Claudio Monteverdi: lettere, dediche e prefazioni*, Roma, Edizioni de Santis, 1973, p. 150.

One of the obvious approaches to this question is through whatever analytical methods we can apply to any individual work of Monteverdi's. And from the examination of individual pieces, we may be able to establish general criteria that help define the nature of his art as well as allow us to grasp some of the essential characteristics and values of that art. In order to understand why Monteverdi is so palpably superior to his contemporaries, individual works of his must be compared with similar works by other composers, and the generalities of his compositional method must be compared with the generalities of method of other composers. All of these are difficult tasks, but especially the last, because we have so little of his contemporaries' music available in modern editions. At this stage, we can only begin the process, hoping to lay enough groundwork to have some idea where we stand; so that the basics of Monteverdi's compositional process can be generally understood.

Gary Tomlinson has attempted something of this kind with his recent study of the relationship between music and text in Monteverdi's music[2]. Whether or not one agrees with Tomlinson's conclusions regarding specific pieces, his effort is useful, for it seeks to explain how significant features of the musical artifact reached their particular form. Tomlinson is interested principally in the Mantuan madrigals and the early operas, for he holds to a view, with which I heartily disagree, that Monteverdi abandoned the strengths of his rhetorically oriented compositional aesthetic after the opera *Arianna* and pursued a more superficial style outside the realm of Renaissance Humanism. What we would call the early Baroque works of Monteverdi Tomlinson describes as "musical simplification" whose result "was expressive improverishment"[3]. He characterizes madrigals of Book VIII as "sonorous, grandiloquent, but after all hollow works"[4]. For Tomlinson, the shift in Monteverdi's musical direction beginning at about the time of his move to Venice represented a decline in his creative and expressive powers.

I hold to quite a different view: that is, that the development of the *concertato* style in the latter half of the first decade and the early part of the second decade of the *Seicento* represents an adjustment to a new aesthetic, with its own purposes and values, fully equal in importance to the Renaissance Humanism whose abandonment Tomlinson laments *all'ostinato*. While this is not the place to delve into the details of this aesthetic, it is obvious that rhetoric, contrasts, activity and color are among its salient features. It is astonishing how quickly and with what a sure hand Monteverdi changed directions and mastered, indeed, helped define, the new techniques. Monteverdi was surely a composer for all seasons. And I find his

---

[2] GARY TOMLINSON, *Monteverdi and the End of the Renaissance*, Berkeley, University of Califonia Press, 1987.
[3] *Ibid.*, p. 164.
[4] *Ibid.*, p. 210.

Venetian season as expressive, as imaginative and as rewarding as his Mantuan season.

What is often overlooked about this shift in style is that it not only changed the basic sonorous characteristics of Monteverdi's music (and I grant their adumbration in his early madrigals as well as the persistence of Renaissance techniques in his Vespers of 1610 and the madrigals of Books VI and VII); it required of him a fundamentally different approach to musical structure. No longer did the musical idiom consist of short, sometimes almost aphoristic statements, where a single musical idea or a couple of ideas could carry a piece through from beginning to end. The contrasts of the *concertato* style resulted in more extended compositions, requiring careful thought about large-scale organizational issues far beyond the scope of the five-voice madrigal. This is, of course, already the case with *L'Orfeo* and presumably *Arianna*, as well as the 1610 Vespers.

These latter works exhibit a variety of techniques for expanding the musical space over large spans of time. In the *concertato* compositions of Monteverdi, the management of time becomes a crucial issue; and one of the prime features, one of the "divine" characteristics of Monteverdi's art is the organization of time - its structuring, its coherence and its sense of passage through the process of change. While I have not yet examined compositions of his contemporaries from this standpoint, my intuition in hearing their music suggests that one of the most significant factors differentiating "il Divino" from "i più mondani" is Monteverdi's management of time through the structuring of the musical time span; in other words the sense of both coherence and change that articulates the passage of time.

At this stage of the game and in this kind of forum, I can only sketch out a starting point by sampling some of the details of a single *concertato* work as a model from which to derive specific characteristics. The results will have to be compared with numerous other works of Monteverdi in order to test their validity and in order to establish a set of general observations about his compositional method. Such general observations can then serve as a basis for comparison with music by other composers. Only at that stage might we gain some real insight into what makes Claudio "Divine".

Granted that my presentation today is only a point of departure, I must nevertheless emphasize that as soon as we begin dissecting the "divine", we begin to tarnish its divinity. Analysis can only proceed by one item at a time, and it is, of course, the total combination of items, the network of relations and effects a composer has created which form the Gestalt we call "the piece". Piecemeal study of a composition yields piecemeal results. But these results can still improve our understanding in important ways, and if we have enough piecemeal results, our own intellectual and creative intuition can perhaps give us insights that go beyond the individual bits of information themselves. Analysis, therefore, does not provide answers for our larger questions; analysis, rather, is a process of discovery that eventually leads to deepened understanding.

The piece I have chosen for this opening sortie is the first *Dixit Dominus* from the *Selva morale et spirituale* of 1641. The piece was essentially chosen at random. If one wishes to begin the massive task of understanding Monteverdi's large-scale *concertato* style, one can begin anywhere, and where else makes more sense than the first in the lengthy series of *concertato* psalms in this massive collection? At this point I would like to play a recording of the entire piece to fix in your ears the subject of our discussion. I don't agree with all of the performance practice choices on this recording, but it was the best I had available[5].

(Recording of entire *Dixit* was played)

It is my belief that one gathers more information faster by beginning with large issues and then moving toward smaller ones rather than vice versa. And so I would like to start with a discussion of the piece as a whole, or rather, with the main components that make up the whole.

We can begin where Monteverdi began, with a given text with a specific liturgical function. The text of *Dixit Dominus* is distributed throughout the piece as follows:

> *Dixit Dominus Domino meo: Sede a dextris*
> *meis,*   92 bars)
> *Donec ponam inimicos tuos, scabellum*
> *pedum tuorum.*
> *Virgam virtutis tuae emittet Dominus ex Sion:*
> *dominare in medio inimicorum tuorum.*   (57 bars)
> *Tecum principium in die virtutis tuae in*
> *splendoribus sanctorum: ex utero ante luciferum*
> *genui te.*   (34 bars)
> *Iuravit Dominus, et non paenitebit eum: Tu*
> *es sacerdos in aeternum secundum ordinem*
> *Melchisedech.*

---

[5] CLAUDIO MONTEVERDI, *Selva Morale e Spirituale* (Selections). Kammerchor Stuttgart and Barockensemble Stuttgart, conducted by Frieder Bernius, 1982/84 (Pantheon Music International, Inc., D 07108, 1983).

Dominus a dextris tuis, confregit in die irae
suae reges.
Iudicabit in nationibus, implebit ruinas: (44 bars)
conquassabit capita in terra multorum.

De torrente in via bibet: propterea exaltabit   (17 bars)
caput.
Gloria Patri, et Filio, et Spiritui Sancto.
Sicut erat in principio, et nunc et semper et in   (59 bars = 9 + 50)
saecula saeculorum. Amen.

For purposes of this discussion, I am using the barring and bar numbers in the Malipiero edition, which for this piece, are accurate[6]. To the right of each line of text is a number indicating the quantity of bars devoted to each line or pair of lines. The first thing to note is that they are drastically unequal. By the time of the *Selva morale*, Monteverdi no longer felt bound to present psalm texts straightforwardly, running from one line to the next in approximately equal time spans. The text becomes a much more flexible constituent of the compositional process, malleable, stretchable, even subject to rearrangement for purposes of musical structure.

Nevertheless, the principal subdivisions of the overall structure do correspond with particular lines of text. These subdivisions are as follows:
Dixit Dominus-Donec ponam inimicos (bars 1-92)
Virgam virtutis (bars 93-149)
Tecum principium-Iuravit Dominus (bars 150-183)
Dominus a dextris (bars 184-227)
De torrente (bars 228-244)
Gloria Patri-Sicut erat (bars 245-303)
The means of subdividing the composition into these segments are various. Important cadences are obvious marking points, although insufficient in and of themselves, since some of the sections have equally strong internal cadences resulting from a shift of texture or meter. Other factors contributing to the deliniation of subdivisions are the texture or combination of successive textures, consistency of thematic material, consistency of harmonic patterns, consistency of rhythmic patterns, and the completion of lines of text themselves.

The question for the analyst is, "Are these sections simply successive passages, their length and relation to one another a chance result of how long it takes Monteverdi to traverse a given line of text with the musical figures he has chosen,

---

[6] GIAN FRANCESCO MALIPIERO (ed.), *Tutte le opere di Claudio Monteverdi*, Vol. XV/2, Wien, Universal Edition, 1967, pp. 195-245.

VI

or do the sections themselves form a larger, coherent pattern?" To put the question in Platonic terms with which Monteverdi would have been familiar, "Is there an overall structure, reflecting a permanent, ideal harmony, behind the sensual manifestation that we hear as a transitory earthly experience?" And if so, "Is that 'ideal harmony' a factor in the perception of Monteverdi as partaking of the divine?"

The conception of the Platonic harmonic ideal was, of course, proliferated widely in the Renaissance, and not just through Marsilio Ficino. It permeated thinking about architecture, about painting, about literature, about celestial mechanics, and about music. Rudolph Wittkower has related Palladio's and Zarlino's conceptions of proportions both to one another and to the Platonic ideal.[7] Platonic balance and moderation is behind Pietro Bembo's analysis of Petrarch in the *Prose della volgar lingua*. Both High Renaissance painting and architecture depend on the symmetries and balances generated by the static Platonic ideal. And the difficulties encountered by both Johannes Kepler and Galileo Galilei were in part due to their seeming refutation of the accepted celestial Platonic harmony.

We know, of course, that Monteverdi was familiar with at least the ordinary assumptions of his time about Plato, whatever his sources may have been. Plato is dragged forth as a justification for both the *seconda prattica* and the *genere concitato*[8]. But it is also true that Monteverdi, even though interested in as metaphysical a topic as alchemy, was a practical rather than a theoretical musician[9]. His projected treatise on the *seconda prattica* was never written; even his copy of the 1573 edition of Zarlino's *Istitutioni Harmoniche*, which has his autograph across the title page, contains no annotations anywhere in the book[10]. His use of Plato as a justification for the *seconda prattica* and the *genere concitato* is a bow to Humanistic tradition, a citation of classical authority to strengthen his case. Plato did not give Monteverdi the idea for either the *seconda prattica* or the *genere concitato* - these concepts arose out of Monteverdi's musical sensibility, invention and practical needs. Plato only served as

[7] RUDOLPH WITTKOWER, *Architectural Principles in the Age of Humanism*, New York, W.W. Norton & Company, Inc., 1971 [first published 1949]. See especially Part IV, "The Problem of Harmonic Proportion in Architecture."

[8] The *seconda prattica* is described in the preface to the *Scherzi musicali a tre voci* of 1607. The *genere concitato* is described in the preface to the Eighth Book of Madrigals, *Madrigali guerrieri, et amorosi* of 1638. Both prefaces may be found in DE' PAOLI, *op. cit.*, pp. 394-404 and 416-418.

[9] Monteverdi's interest in alchemy is documented in five letters of 1625-1626: August 23, September 19, February 15, February 24 and March 26. See DE' PAOLI, *op. cit.*, pp. 222 ff., 226, 230, 231, 235.

[10] The title page is reproduced in GUSTAVE REESE, *Music in the Renaissance*, New York, W.W. Norton & Co., 1954, Plate IV facing p. 366. The copy, formerly in the library of Dragan Plamenač, is now owned by Yale University.

justification after the fact.

There are also numerous instances in Monteverdi's works where the text might have led him to some kind of abstract or mathematical symbolic interpretation. However, Monteverdi normally avoided abstract musical symbols. His interest lay not in the abstract or the symbolic, but rather in concrete, sonorous results. As a consequence, we should be wary of seeking hidden, abstract structural patterns in Monteverdi, at least as evidence of an *a priori* attempt to impose a Platonic harmony on his compositions.

However, there is another side to this issue as well-a more practical one, much more in tune with Monteverdi's own proclivities. This more practical side of the ideal harmony is the tradition of rhythmic and structural proportions manifested in compositions from the early 14th-century onward. Composers of so-called "isorhythmic motets" (what I would prefer to call "periodic motets") were quite concerned with the sense of balance and proportion in sound of sections of equal or different lengths, and in rhythmic patterns structured in hierarchies of duple and triple subdivisions.

Composers in the fifteenth and sixteenth centuries were clearly interested in the durational relationship between successive sections of larger compositions. Brian Trowell was the first to demonstrate proportional structural schemes and numerological symbols in the music of Dunstable[11]. Dufay obviously took care with durational proportions in his *cantus firmus* masses, and several motets have been found to display Golden Section structuring, the *sectio aurea* or *divina proportione*, as well as the Fibonacci number series and numerical symbolism[12]. A recent article by Alan Atlas has illustrated the presence of both balanced symmetries and the Golden Section in a wedding ballade of 1423[13]. My own analyses of motets by Josquin and Obrecht have also revealed Golden Section structuring and recent studies of specific pieces by Busnois and Josquin have emphasized careful proportional planning[14].

---

[11] BRIAN TROWELL, *Proportion in the Music of Dunstable*, "Proceedings of the Royal Musical Association", CV (1978/79), pp. 100-141. The endnotes on pp. 140-141 cite numerous other studies of proportion and numerology in both music and other fields.

[12] See MARGARET VARDELL SANDRESKY, *The Golden Section in Three Byzantine Motets of Dufay*,"Journal of Music Theory", XXV, 1981, 2, pp. 291-306.

[13] ALLAN W. ATLAS, *Gematria, Marriage Numbers, and Golden Sections in Dufay's 'Resvellies vous'*, "Acta Musicologica", LIX, 1987, 2, pp. 111-126.

[14] The editions of Obrecht's *Missa Sub tuum praesidium* and *Missa Maria Zart* by M. van Crevel in JACOB OBRECHT, *Opera Omnia*, Amsterdam: Vereniging voor nederlandse musiekgeschiedenis, 1959 and 1964, contain detailed, if controversial, studies of proportions and number in these works. For Busnois and Josquin, see RICHARD TARUSKIN, *Antoine Busnoys and the L'Homme armé Tradition*, "Journal of the American Musicological Society", XXXIX, 2 (1986), pp. 255-293; and CHRISTOPHER REYNOLDS, *Musical Evidence of Compositional Planning in the Renaissance: Josquin's*

This should not surprise us, for interest in numbers and proportions, especially symmetries and the Golden Section, sometimes called the Golden Mean, ran high during the Renaissance. This interest, of course, traces its roots to Pythagoras and Plato. The Golden Section was one of those laws of nature embodying the underlying ideal harmony of the Universe.[15] However, symmetrical proportions, duple and triple proportions and the Golden Section all have their immediate practical significance as well. A building constructed with balanced, symmetrical sections has a different visual impact from a building where the *sesquialtera* or the Golden Section predominate. The complex proportions of a Gothic cathedral have a completely different impact from the simple, duple proportions of Brunelleschi. The same is true in music. Evenly balanced sections, proportional sections, and sections related by the Golden Mean all have a different sonorous effect. And Monteverdi's direct cultural heritage consisted of music in which all of these methods of structuring larger pieces were used.

Now, an important difference I alluded to earlier between a brief madrigal and a large-scale *concertato* work is the significant structural demands the latter makes on the composer. The large-scale work absolutely requires the composer to think about formal organization, to consider the length of the piece and the temporal and other relationships between its sections. I think we can assume that those composers who do not give thought to such issues, who simply compose out a piece by beginning at one point and writing until the text has been completed, are aesthetically inferior. Indeed, I would argue that one of the chief differences between mediocre or poor composers and great composers is the inability of the former to conceive of large-scale structural patterns that make sense to listeners in their experience of the passage of time through the composition.

Therefore, Monteverdi did not need the impetus of an abstract Platonic ideal to be concerned about durational proportions and other relationships between sections of his large-scale works. He was concerned about such matters from the purely practical standpoint of how one writes good music. The fact that contemporaneous listeners associated him and his work with the divine simply illustrates the link that Renaissance and Baroque intellectuals and artists drew between their concept of celestial harmony and its manifestation in the world through individual, concrete examples. By the same token, the immediate aesthetic beauty of a composition by Monteverdi was evidence for the 17th-century listener of its participation in the divine harmony of the Universe.

In examining several large-scale Monteverdi compositions from a structural

---

(*Plus nulz regretz*), "*Journal of the American Musicological Society*", XL, (1987), 1, pp. 53-81. Reynolds also makes brief reference to symmetrical structuring in Monteverdi's *Cruda Amarili* (pp. 72-73).

[15] See MATILA GHYKA, *The Geometry of Art and Life*, reprint ed., New York, Dover Publications, 1977, for an overview of natural and man-made forms displaying the Golden Section.

point of view, I have found that durational balances and proportions, including the Golden Section, do indeed play a prominent role in his structural thinking. Equally characteristic of Monteverdi is that these means of durational structuring are not used systematically-there is no single pattern or group of patterns that permeate all, or even many pieces, at least as far as I have been able to determine to this point. Each piece has its own pattern, depending on the length of the text and on the musical figures Monteverdi has chosen for that particular setting. Different settings of the same text may have very different structural patterns. This fact illustrates once again Monteverdi's eminent practical sense and his reliance on *inventio* rather than abstract mathematics as his driving force. It also reveals another fundamental characteristic of his compositional process, evident throughout his career: Monteverdi's *inventio* results in continual variety. *Varietà* was highly prized in the 16th and early 17th centuries, both as an aesthetic concept and as one of the principal means of achieving artistic grace and elegance. The quest for *varietà* has been linked to Aristotle's concept of the marvelous-novelty and variety are opposed to the commonplace and are consequently among the sources of the marvelous[16].

There is another way in which the notion of variety reflected Aristotelian philosophy and 16th-century Aristotelianism. The Aristotelian view was that the world consisted of multiple varieties of experience within any category of experience, whether biological, political or poetic. And rather than seeking an underlying, permanent ideal form for these multiplicities like Plato, Aristotle saw the role of the philosopher as describing the varieties of experience and deriving from them common truths permeating all examples of a particular kind. Aristotle was a classifier and categorizer, who worked from the detail of individual instances toward underlying, empirically verifiable generalities, whereas Plato had assumed eternal, unobservable truths of which individual instances were only shadowy, transitory and partial representatives.

Monteverdi, then, also falls into the Aristotelian traditions of empiricism and *varietà*. One of the chief characteristics of his *inventio* is his ability to create variety while maintaining underlying common threads that unite the multiplicity of individual differences. On the one hand, *varietà* is palpable, it strikes and delights the senses directly and immediately. On the other hand, the underlying similarities behind the *varietà* provide that larger, less obvious coherence that allows us to relate different manifestations of variety to more general, central ideas. And these central ideas represent an underlying harmony, something of a Platonic ideal if you will, valid for the individual piece if not for Monteverdi's *oeuvre* as a whole.

Let us look now at the structural divisions of our *Dixit Dominus* to see what

---

[16] BAXTER HATHAWAY, *Marvels and Commonplaces: Renaissance Literary Criticism*, New York, Random House, 1968, p. 160.

they yield in terms of underlying durational relationships. It becomes quickly apparent that bars 1-92, encompassing the first two lines of the text, form a coherent unit. This section is tied together through both text and thematic repetition, enlivened by *varietà*. Continuing on through the piece, the two sections defined by *Virgam virtutis* and the paired lines *Tecum principium-Iuravit Dominus* combine to form a larger unit comprising bars 93-183. The bases for joining these two sections are both textural and motivic. All three verses are set principally to duet textures (*Tecum principium* has double duets), even though full chorus eventually emerges in *Virgam virtutis*, a point I'll get to later. These two sections also differ from the rest of the psalm in thematic and harmonic patterns, but share among themselves certain thematic and harmonic procedures, which will also be discussed below.

The two larger sections that I have now described, bars 1-92 and 93-183, are of almost precisely equal length in terms of the *tactus* (92 bars vs. 91 bars). Here is a large portion of the composition where even balance has been the structural principal behind the organization of the music.

If we proceed through the rest of the text, we find that *Dominus a dextris* and *Iudicabit* form one continuous section, and *De torrente* forms a second. The *Dominus a dextris-Iudicabit* combination runs from bars 184-227, and *De torrente* from 228-244. Now, the beginning of *Dominus a dextris tuis* forms an important dividing point in the piece, because it presents, in varied form, music that is already familiar to us from early in the psalm where the text reads *Dixit Dominus* and *sede a dextris meis*. The passages in question are compared in **Examples 1a** and **1b**. Note that the passage from *Dominus a dextris*, that is from 184-191, places in direct juxtaposition musical ideas that are separated by some space in the first part of the piece.

Moreover, the music is by no means identical for either the choral passage or the solo passage; nevertheless, *Dominus a dextris tuis* is close enough to *Dixit Dominus* and *sede a dextris meis* to sound familiar and to make this passage sound as a structural dividing point in the composition. At the same time it is different enough not to suggest a *ritornello* figure and different enough to convey Monteverdi's sense of *varietà*. One might say that the relationship between the two passages, while discernible to the ear, is indirect enough to suggest the shadowy world of Platonic relationships-relationships which can only be vaguely sensed rather than directly perceived.

These comments underscore the role of *Dominus a dextris* in the large-scale structure of the composition. The following *De torrente* is quite different, however, returning to the duet texture encountered in the second half of the first part of the psalm, that is, in *Virgam virtutis* through *Iuravit Dominus*. Comparing *Dominus a dextris tuis* with *Dixit Dominus... Sede a dextris meis* and *De torrente* with *Virgam virtutis- Tecum principium-Iuravit Dominus*, we might draw a modest structural parallel between the two segments 184-227 and 228-244 and the two halves of the first part of the piece (1-92 and 93-183).

Concluding the psalm, from bar 245 to the end (bar 303), we have the *Doxology*, clearly demarcated by a choral tutti and rapid shift away from the prevailing G major.

Now that the major structural subdivisions of the piece have been defined, an examination of their temporal relationship proves very interesting. These subdivisions are outlined in **Example 2.** I've already noted that bars 1-92 and 93-183 form an almost perfectly balanced pair. I've also noted a major subdivision at 183-184 and a major division between the end of the psalm text and the beginning of the *Doxology* at 244-245. If we calculate the Golden Section of the entire 303-measure piece, it would fall at bar 187. Am I forcing matters if I suggest that Monteverdi's major subdivision at 183-184 reveals a Golden Section structuring on his part? I don't think so. In the first place, my way of calculating the figures may be skewed by a small degree. Are the semibreves with fermatas concluding each section to be considered as single *tactus* ? Is the final *longa* of the piece to be counted as a single *tactus?* I'm not sure, but I don't think that this ambiguity is of great enough significance to affect my basic conclusions.

Moreover, the work I have done so far on Golden Sections in Monteverdi suggests that in this domain as well, he is consistent with his basic, practical orientation and uninterested in abstract mathematics. A composer concerned with the perfection of his proportions would have placed the major subdivision precisely at bar 187, assuming that he treated the cadential notes as single *tactus*. But Monteverdi is rarely interested in that degree of mathematical precision. In fact, for our ability to hear and recall the passage of time, bar 184 is well within the limitations of temporal memory to make the subdivision sound like a Golden Section structuring. Indeed, in this 10-minute piece, I believe we would perceive the same large-scale structuring whether the subdivision occurred in bar 180, bar 184, bar 187, or bar 192. Our temporal hearing is simply not that precise. One psychophysical study suggests that we cannot perceive durational differences of less than 10% in time spans of under 2 seconds[17]. Other studies suggest 8% and 16% as the limits of accuracy of durational perception for time spans between 4 and 30 seconds[18]. Longer durations are presumably subject to even greater perceptual variability, depending as much on the nature of the content of a time

---

[17] Robert Cogan and Pozzi Escot deduce the 10% subliminal level of durational perception from C.D. CREELMAN, *Human Discrimination of Auditory Duration,* "*Journal of the Acoustical Society of America,* XXXIV (1962), pp. 582-93. See COGAN and ESCOT, *Sonic Design: The Nature of Sound and Music,* Cambridge, Publishing Contact International, 1976, pp. 240-243. Experiments about the accuracy and variability of time perception are discussed in LEONARD DOOB, *Patterning of Time,* New Haven, Yale University Press, 1971, pp. 101-106, 118-121, 127-129.

[18] Studies by François Macar and A.B. Kristofferson are reported in JONATHAN D. KRAMER, *The Time of Music,* New York, Schirmer Books, 1988, p. 332.

span as on our abilities to guage time in the abstract[19]. Over the time span of Monteverdi's 10-minute psalm, the differential between the mathematical Golden Section at bar 187 and Monteverdi's subdivision at bars 183-184 is perceptually inconsequential. Monteverdi has created and articulated a major subdivision of the piece near enough to the Golden Section for us to hear it like we would hear a precise Golden Section proportion. By the same token, the subdivision is close enough to demonstrate that Monteverdi, in composing this piece, thought of at least some aspects of the structure in Golden Section terms. This is confirmed by other Golden Section ratios on a smaller scale in this very piece as well as in other compositions.

Let us turn now to the review and further examination of smaller structural segments of the psalm. The opening portion of the piece (1-183), that is, the larger segment of the Golden Section, we have already seen subdivided into almost precisely evenly balanced sections of 92 and 91 bars. Once again, mathematical precision isn't as important as the aural effect.

If we look at the second part of the piece, that is, the smaller segment of the Golden Section, it consists of 120 bars (184-303). The principal subdivisions are 184-244 (61 bars) and the *Doxology*, 245-303 (59 bars). The smaller segment of the Golden Section is therefore also divided into two nearly equal halves, certainly close enough for our temporal perception and memory to sense the balance.

A study of even shorter segments of the composition reveals similar structural principles carried out on a smaller scale. In the opening section (bars 1-92), text subdivision is not Monteverdi's basis for structural divisions, for the two verses are integrated throughout the entire passage. Musical style, rather, articulates the formal organization. In **Example 2** it can be seen that this large section has three principal subdivisions. The first is at bars 32-33, where the opening passage comes to a cadence with the full chorus, followed by a solo voice, announcing a new texture. The solo then continues unabated until its own cadence in bar 61. From 61-92 there is a choral section which repeats the text and some of the music (most of it varied) from the first and second sections already completed. These three sections thus divide the first 92 bars into segments of almost equal length, comprising 32 bars, 29 bars and 31 bars.

In addition, these three sections have a dynamic of their own, dependent on texture and repetition of musical material. The first section itself divides neatly in half, beginning with a 16-bar introduction presenting the opening text as a kind of exordium and simultaneously establishing the tonic of the psalm and the principal thematic shape. This thematic shape, which will be discussed in more detail

---

[19] The complex and uncertain nature of this issue is explored in KRAMER, *op. cit.*, pp. 322-374. Kramer avoids definitive conclusions, but suggests that repeated hearing and a correspondingly more complete memory of a composition bring our perception of temporal durations into closer approximation of the actual elapsed time. See *Ibid.*, p. 368.

below, recurs in various guises throughout the psalm. The second half (17-32), presents the same material for full choir: the exordium is fully harmonized, and the thematic shape is now diminished by a 2:1 ratio and treated through imitation. Here we have the concept of *varietà* operating on thematic, harmonic, rhythmic and structural levels.

The second and third sections take the dynamic established by the first and double its dimensions. The second section (33-61) comprises the solo, now almost twice as long as the opening 16-bar solo. Moreover, the thematic material of this longer solo is related to and an extension of bars 6-16. The third section, in relation to the second section, fulfills the same function as bars 17-32 in relation to 1-16. That is, a solo texture is now transformed into a polyphonic texture for full choir, utilizing the music from both the first and second sections, including a 2:1 rhythmic diminution of a motive from the second section (bars 40-51) treated in imitation (bars 73-77), just as in bars 22-32. In this way Monteverdi has created not only three almost evenly balanced sections, but the symmetry is overlaid with a forward-moving dynamic of solo-to-full choir textures, first on a small scale and then on a larger scale, the whole thoroughly integrated through thematic materials, repetitions, variations and parallel instances of rhythmic diminution.

If we turn our attention now to the passage from bars 93-183, we find a different structural process at work. In this section, the first line of text, *Virgam virtutis*, is sung twice. The first setting is in the form of a tenor duet (bars 93-112). The text repetition begins with full choir, returns to a duet texture, this time in the sopranos, accompanied by the psalm tone in one of the tenors, and then closes with full choir (bars 113-149). The two statements of *Virgam virtutis* occupy 57 bars of the total section of 91 measures (93-183). Now the Golden Section of 91 is 56.238, so that Monteverdi has divided the passage 93-183 right at the Golden Section point, separating *Virgam virtutis* from *Tecum principium*. This division can be seen in **Example 2**.

As I have just observed, *Virgam virtutis* is presented twice, but these two segments are unequal in length. The first runs from bars 93-112 (20 bars), and the second from 113-149 (37 bars), totalling the 57 bars just mentioned. The Golden Section of 57 is 35.226, with the smaller segment being 21.774. In the two statements of *Virgam virtutis*, Monteverdi has subdivided the 57-bar passage itself by approximately a Golden Section ratio, but this time the smaller segment comes first, while the larger segment is second. See **Example 2**.

If we proceed now to bars 150-183, that is, the smaller segment of the Golden Section between 93 and 183, we find the two lines of text *Tecum principium* and *Iuravit Dominus*. These two lines are nearly run together, but there is a brief cadence in bar 166, with *Iuravit* beginning immediately afterward (See **Example 3**). This cadence and the new line of text, which is taken up by the tenors, who had been silent throughout *Tecum principium*, divides the 34-bar passage into almost equal groups of 16-1/2 bars and 17-1/2 bars (See **Example 2**). That Monteverdi indeed thought of these two lines as parallel structural passages is demonstrated by the fact that *Iuravit Dominus* repeats in only slightly varied form the music of *Tecum principium*, but transposed a fourth lower. The reason the two segments are not perfectly balanced is also clear: a cadential extension for *Iuravit Dominus* is required to bring it to a close in the desired key rather than the key that a perfect parallel with *Tecum principium* would have produced (a deviation in bars 179-180, in comparison with 163-164, causes *Iuravit Dominus* to cadence in the same key and with nearly the same cadence as *Tecum principium*).

Next let us turn to the passage after bar 183, that is, the smaller Golden Section segment of the entire psalm. As we have already seen, the 120-bar passage is divided almost exactly in the middle at bar 244 by the end of the psalm text and the beginning of the *Doxology*. However, the first half of the final section is further subdivided at 227, where the two lines *Dominus a dextris-Iudicabit*, which Monteverdi has run together and set for full choir, come to a cadence and are followed by *De torrente* as a soprano duet. Thus we have a 61-bar passage (184-244) subdivided after 44 measures, leaving 17 bars remaining. This subdivision is substantially larger than the Golden Section of 61 (37.698), Leaving only a brief space for the line *De torrente*. And long before I had begun examining the structural organization of this piece, I can recall hearing this passage as disproportionately short in relation to others in the composition.

However, even though *Dominus a dextris* and *Iudicabit in nationibus* are continuous, the two lines of text are distributed over nearly equal portions of the passage 184-244. *Dominus a dextris* occupies 20 1/2 bars, while *Iudicabit* takes 23 1/2 bars.

The *Doxology* is also somewhat irregularly structured, consisting of a 9-bar passage at the opening of the *Gloria Patri*, followed by a 23-bar duet presenting the first part of the *Sicut erat*, and finally a 27-bar setting of the *Et in saeculum*, which itself comprises twelve bars of *Et in saeculum* and 15 bars of *Amen*. But once again, the text itself is distributed in a specific way. Monteverdi actually presents the word *Amen* for the first time before he has concluded with the *et in saecula* (See **Example 4**). At this point the full choir yields to two bass voices in imitation intoning *Amen*. This happens at bars 280-281, which is precisely the Golden Section point of the *Doxology* (See **Example 2**).

An overview of the smaller Golden Section segment of the psalm (184-303), shows that Monteverdi divides things almost evenly on the largest scale (61 bars + 59 bars), and even employs one reasonably balanced pairing (184-205 and 205-227) as well as a Golden Section subdivision (245-280 and 281-303) on the middle level, but seems less interested in rational structures at the smallest level. Monteverdi may not have felt the need in the shortest time spans to concern himself with durational proportions the way he does in the larger sections. Indeed, in one of these passages, bars 184-227, Monteverdi creates an unusual quantity of

VI

smaller segments, consisting of 4 bars, 11 bars, 10 bars, 5 bars and 14 bars. The three longer segments of these each divide themselves into a 4-bar duet followed by a *tutti*, with the duet identical each time it recurs. Thus the duet acts as a kind of *ritornello* for this section, organizing it by a means altogether different from durational proportions.

The *Doxology*, occupying the final 59 bars of the piece, also divides into the several irregular smaller sections already mentioned (9 bars, 23 bars, three segments of 4 bars each, and 15 bars). But once again, thematic repetition provides a cohesive factor (bars 254-258, 281-284 and 289-293). The final 120 bars of the piece, from 184 to the end, perhaps contain more rapid changes of texture in order to facilitate the drive toward the final cadence. In other words, there is a different dynamic, a less patterned one, from the first section of the piece, in order to generate an increasing thrust toward the final cadence by foreshortening many of the smaller structural subdivisions, leading to more rapid changes of texture, especially in the *Et in saeculum*.

If we retreat now and survey where we've been, we find Monteverdi to have been concerned with large-scale structural organization based on both balanced symmetries and subdivisions at the Golden Mean. The broadest organizational patterns are replicated in smaller units in both of the main segments of the composition, but never in precisely the same way. *Varietà* in structural patterns is effected by subdividing each of the two large Golden Section segments into two almost equally balanced sections, and then varying considerably the further subdivisions of these evenly balanced sections. In some cases the smaller subdivisions are symmetrical, in others they are related by the Golden Mean; and the Golden Mean may be presented in two ways: with either the larger or the smaller segment first. The structural organization of the composition seems more carefully planned in the first, larger segment (1-183).

What Monteverdi seems to be striving for is an underlying sensibility that the composition is rationally organized, but with enough complication and variety in the structuring that the patterns are not immediately obvious. This variety and complication provide a foil to the perceptually obvious contrasts of texture, meter and rhythmic activity that characterize the surface of the composition. To put it another way, the immediacy of the surface contrasts is countered by a more sophisticated and less obvious underlying structure.

The structural elements I have been discussing up to this point are defined principally by contrasts-contrasts articulated by voicings and the textures of voicings, by rhythmic figures, by harmonic patterns, by solo-tutti oppositions, by shifts of meter, by verses of text. Contrasts, of course, have the tendency to separate and fragment the various parts of a composition. Symmetrically balanced and proportional sectioning is one way to rationalize these fragments, this *varietà*, and bond them together in a coherent whole. I have also pointed out some structural links and parallels between various sections of the work that contribute to its coherence. Monteverdi also uses many other methods, however, that are more direct and immediately apparent to the listener. These other methods will be addressed in Part II.

Part II

I now would like to turn to other elements of underlying unity in *Dixit Dominus* as well as facets of Monteverdi's compositional style that reveal more variety than unity. Beginning with elements of coherence, the most important of these in *Dixit Dominus* is thematic direction based on the underlying tonality of G major.

G major is introduced at the very outset in the simplest manner possible-reiteration of the tonic pitch supported by reiteration of the tonic triad (bars 1-5). G is also established as tonic through a thematic process in the solo passage immediately following (see **Example 5a**). **Examples 5b, 5c** and **5d** show this melody in successively reduced form (the black notes represent less fundamental pitches in each reduction). The final reduction, **5d**, reflects the overall melodic direction I believe we hear, consisting of a principal motion of a 5th descent from d^2 to g^1, with the important upper neighbor of e^2. Quite typical of Monteverdi is that the descent does not appear in simple form until near the end of the original melodic line. At the beginning, the melodic motion is complicated by sequences of broken thirds, a characteristic Monteverdian thematic motion from early in his career until the very end. These broken thirds also characterize the underlying organ continuo part, as can be seen in **Example 6**. Simple descending scales underly many thematic and harmonic patterns throughout Monteverdi's *oeuvre*.

The reiterated G (1-5) and subsequent melodic pattern (6-16) permeate the entire first section through bar 92 in various ways. Bars 17-32 comprise a varied repetition for full choir of what has just been heard in the first 16 bars. This time the reiterated G is fully harmonized (17-21), and the following descending figure for *Sede a dextris meis* becomes the subject of an imitative texture, with its speed doubled by a 2:1 ratio (22-32).

The next section, bars 33-61, as you may recall from the discussion of the psalm's structure, is for soprano solo throughout. The soprano's solo line, as shown in **Example 7**, is obviously closely related in its first several measures to the thematic motion of bars 6-16, but this time is extended below the tonic to the leading tone (33-39). At bar 40 the first significant thematic ascent begins, moving in broken-fourth sequences back up to the high e^2 (bar 44). This ascent, repeated sequentially a step lower, but leading only to c^2 (bars 45-49), ultimately descends again, but this time even lower than $f\#^1$ (bars 49-52). By arpeggiation it drops all the way to d^1, then leaps quickly back up the octave to d^2 in bar 54. This d^2 ultimately leads, through some twists and turns, including an extended ornamental flourish on e^1 (58-60), to a final cadence on d^1. A reduction of the motion of the entire section is shown in **Example 8**. The main point I wish to emphasize is that not only has the melodic idea of bars 6-16 permeated this passage, but it has also been expanded from a fifth descent d^2-g^1 (with upper neighbor e^2) to a full octave descent d^2-d^1 (again with the upper neighbor e^2).

The third segment (62-92) of the opening section then repeats the choral *Dixit Dominus* exordium (62-65) followed by a choral version of the solo soprano passage I have just been discussing (66-92). Once again Monteverdi treats one of the thematic figures in imitative polyphony with a 2:1 rhythmic diminution (73-92).

I would like now to skip to the final large section of the psalm, the passage from bars 184-303, which comprises the smaller segment of the overall Golden Section. Near the very beginning of this passage, a thematic descent from e^2-a^1 (188-192), then to g^1 (192-195) and finally to e^1 (196-198) is patently obvious (see **Example 9**). Note that this portion of the piece exploits the A tonality, in minor form, suggested at the opening of the psalm by the e^2-$c\#^2$ neighbor tones (bars 7 and 9-10). The thematic reductions in **Example 10** illustrate the thematic direction of this passage as well as the remainder of the piece. Their relationship to the fifth and octave descents of the opening two sections is manifest. Indeed, the psalm closes with a descending fifth d^2-g^1 ornamented by the leading tone.

As I pointed out earlier, the opening section from bars 1-92 has a sense of dynamic growth in the way texture and thematic materials are used. Likewise, the smaller segment of the overall Golden Section, from 184 to the end, is dynamic in its more rapid changes in texture. But what about the passage from bars 93-183? This section has changes of texture, but seems more static in its thematic material and in its consistent use of duets. **Example 13** shows the motive of bars 96-99, just after the initial repeated pitch on *Virgam virtutis*, reminiscent of the psalm tone. The derivation from the e^2-$c^2\#$ neighbour notes of bars 7 and 9-10 is apparent. But in bars 104-110 the thematic pattern changes to triadic outlines that both rise and fall, often simultaneously as two voices are joined in contrary motion (see **Example 12**). The reduction in **Example 13** shows the thematic patterns of bars 93-149, together with their harmonic functions. The descending fifth d^2-g^1 re-emerges at critical points, even the descent e^2-$f\#^1$ recurs in bars 130-135, but the predominant motion consists of triadic outlines articulating rapid harmonic movement, most often around the descending circle of fifths.

In bars 150-183, that is, *Tecum principium* and *Iuravit Dominus*, descending scalar patterns return, but complicated by contrary motion as just encountered with the triads. Moreover, this section has fairly frequent tonal shifts as well, as can be seen from the reduction in **Example 14**.

It is now apparent that Monteverdi introduces the greatest harmonic interest in precisely those sections that are texturally and melodically more static (93- 183). It is in this portion of the composition that series of secondary dominants moving around the descending circle of fifths are introduced (**Example 13**), and later, other, less regular modulations in the sequence C major, D minor, F major, C major, D minor, D major (= V/G), G major, A minor, A major (= V/D) and finally D major (= V/G) (**Example 14**). As a consequence, there is a sense of increased energy throughout this section, despite the static character of repetitive thematic patterns and the persistence of duet textures. This large section thus provides a significant contrast within the context of the entire psalm. Monteverdi has decreased the dynamism of one set of parameters, but has compensated by increasing the energy and motion of another set of parameters.

From the standpoint of thematic unity, this section also contributes to the underlying structural organization outlined in Part I of this paper. Here again we have the same unifying principal, that of the descending fifth and octave, but in constantly varied form. In hearing the piece, the listener becomes immediately aware of the variety of Monteverdi's melodic *inventio*, but as the composition progresses, there soon develops a growing awareness of a shadowy coherence to the variety of thematic motions, a coherence which only the timeless process of analysis can reveal in clearer outlines.

Turning now to the question of tonality in the psalm, the most obvious factor in tonal coherence has already been mentioned-the prevailing key of G major. Tonal movement throughout the course of the piece tends to correspond with the large structural subdivisions. The first section, bars 1-92, is mostly in G major, with a few important cadences on D major and occasional excursions to A major or minor, as suggested by the neighbor-notes e^2-$c\#^2$ near the beginning. But the harmonically active second section, 93-183, begins in a new key, C major, further articulating the subdivision between this section and the previous one. *Virgam virtutis* finally ends on G major, but *Tecum principium*, at the Golden Mean of this section, begins again in C. After passing through the tonalities already outlined in **Example 14**, the section concludes on D major, which serves as dominant of the next section, the small segment of the largest Golden Section. As the motivic diagram of bars 183-227 in **Example 10** illustrates, this section is heavily laced with A minor, but also has internal cadences and a final, plagal cadence in C, before finally returning to G for *De torrente* (bar 228). G major is sustained as the principal tonality until the *Doxology* (bar 245). Although the *Doxology* begins on G, it, too, heavily emphasizes A, both major and minor, before finally closing in G.

There is a large-scale pattern to the harmonic motion in this piece, the broader outlines of which can be seen in **Example 2**. The tonic of G major is firmly established in bars 1-92; the symmetrically balanced section, bars 93- 183, moves farther afield, beginning on C but involving rapid modulation to related tonalities primarily around the circle of descending fifths, before it finally returns to D major as dominant of G. But despite the harmonic activity, the prevailing tonality of this section is C major. The smaller Golden Section segment from bars 184 onward begins in G major, but is principally in A minor, albeit with some important cadences in C, all the way to bar 227, where the two verses *Dominus a dextris tuis* and *Iudicabit* conclude with a plagal cadence in C. At this point, the final verse of the psalm, *De torrente*, returns solidly to G major, re-establishing the tonic after the long excursus beginning in bar 93. The *Doxology* then surveys with its cadences all of the tonalities emphasized in the piece, but most prominently A major and minor. Only mid-way through the *Doxology*, at the conclusion of *et nunc et semper* (bar 276), is G major re-established, only to be displaced again by A minor and major, before eventually settling back to G at the final cadence. It is as if the return to G, first effected at *De torrente*, is ultimately strengthened for the final cadence by keeping much of the *Doxology* out of G, mostly around A, before the last few bars of the psalm.

Rhythmic patterns also contribute to the shape of the various sections of the composition and from time-to-time serve as cohesive links throughout the work. The manner in which rhythms function structurally depends on their speed rather than on specific patterns. There are four fundamental rhythmic types in the psalm. The first is presented at the opening, in triple meter (see **Example 15a**). The second consists of slow movement in semibreves (see **Examples 15b**). A third type has prevailing motion in semiminims, scattered with some minims (see **Examples 15c**).

Finally, there is rhythmic activity mixing semiminims and cromas, sometimes emphasizing mostly cromas (see **Example 15d**). A special version of the semiminim-croma combination is a dotted rhythm (see **Examples 15e**). On the local level, particular rhythmic patterns are often the result of text declamation. But on the larger scale, the prevailing rhythms of various sections articulate dynamic patterns of increasing rhythmic motion.

The opening of the psalm illustrates such a pattern quite clearly. The initial triple meter is succeeded by motion predominantly in semiminims in bars 6-16 (see **Example 5a**). A return to the triple meter in bars 17ff. is then succeeded by the 2:1 diminution (22-32), so that the prevailing motion is now in semiminims and cromas. A similar pattern emerges in bars 61-92, where the beginning is again in triple meter, then moves to a combination of minims, semiminims and semibreves before settling into dotted rhythms of semiminims and cromas (another 2:1 diminution) for most of the passage.

Virgam virtutis is another section which begins slowly, but then becomes ore rapid. In this case the exordium is followed by declamatory cromas. And in keeping with the rapid harmonic activity of the entire passage from bars 93-183, cromas define the prevailing rhythmic motion.

I will confine myself to just one other passage, the beginning of the *Doxology*, to illustrate the pattern of increasing rhythmic motion (see **Example 16**). The *Gloria Patri* begins in minims and semiminims, introduces a few dotted semiminims and cromas, and then slows to semibreves for the cadence. After this slow opening, the duet begins, first with minims and semiminims (254-258), then with semiminims and cromas (258-260), and finally adding even semicromas (261-262). Having explored nearly all of the rhythmic levels used elsewhere in the piece, Monteverdi then turns to his last-triple meter-which also begins in semibreves and then moves to minims (263-272). Only at the very end of the psalm, in the *Amen*, does the pattern of increasing speed reverse itself to create a slowing of the rhythmic activity for the final cadence.

These cycles of slower-to-faster rhythmic activity occur throughout the psalm, but since the number of levels of rhythmic values is limited, these cycles operate within the smaller segments of the piece rather than the larger sections (see **"Rhythmic cycles"** in **Example 17**). The longest such cycles are about 30 bars in duration. Nevertheless, the pattern of such motions, generally building toward rhythmic climaxes, then retreating to slower motion at the commencement of another cycle, becomes a reliable expectation for the listener and helps define the character of time-passage for this piece.

Other aspects of rhythm help give the psalm coherence in other ways. Rhythms associated with particular thematic shapes are often repeated when the thematic shape is repeated. Dotted rhythms contribute to the energy of the rising sequence of broken fourths at *inimicos tuos* and to the semantic meaning of the word at *conquassabit* (see **Examples 15e**). Descending scalar fifths are often cast in sustained notes. But the strongest rhythmic links throughout the piece are declamatory cromas, such as at *emittet Dominus* in **Example 11** and *in splendoribus* in **Example 15d**. Numerous passages in the psalm rely on such declamatory cromas; less often, on declamatory semiminims. The declamatory cromas derive from Monteverdi's *concitato* style, described in the preface to the Eighth Book of Madrigals. It is no accident that these rhythms, conceived for the "warlike" style in the Eighth Book, are introduced in this psalm near the very beginning in the verses *Donec ponam inimicos tuos scabelum pedum tuorum* and *Virgam virtutis tuae emittet Dominus ex Sion: dominare in medio inimicorum tuorum*. The repeated use of these declamatory rhythms contributes to our sense of consistency among the contrasting sections of the piece.

Levels of rhythmic activity are also frequently associated with particular types of textures. For example, strictly chordal textures are most often cast in long notes. Imitative polyphonic textures normally rely on semiminims and cromas. Duets are likewise usually in semiminims and cromas. Solos, on the other hand, are predominantly in minims and semiminims.

These differing textures are also used very cleverly by Monteverdi throughout the psalm. There is a pattern, employed numerous times throughout the composition, whereby a solo or duet is succeeded by a homphonic tutti and then a polyphonic tutti. However, this cyclic pattern corresponds only partially with the structural segments of the composition (see **"Textural cycles"** in **Example 17**). Some structural segments are introduced by a solo or duet, while others commence with a homophonic tutti. Both main segments of the last part of the piece (184-244 and 245-303) are introduced by homophonic tuttis. Indeed, in this final section, the homophonic and polyphonic tuttis exceed the thin-textured soloistic passages in duration and importance. The thicker textures thereby contribute further to the sense of increased activity, marked by more rapid changes of texture, already discussed above. The final section thereby also gathers its energy through desnity ot texture for the denouement.

The alternation of soloistic and tutti sections makes an important contribution to the sense of variety throughout the piece. Moreover, the choice of voices in the main soloistic sections also varies, beginning with the soprano as soloist and moving to a tenor duet, a double duet of altos and basses, another tenor duet, a soprano duet and finally a tenor duet (see **Example 17**). The very fact that the textural cycles in the psalm do not coincide fully with the structural segments is evidence of the complexity and sophistication of Monteverdi's compositional process. Here we have one parameter organized rather differently from another, but without the two being mutually contradictory. The same can be said for the rhythmic cycles, which overlap the textural and structural patterns with yet a third layer. **Example 17** illustrates, albeit in a somewhat crude fashion, this threefold overlapping of the structural segments (central horizontal line), textural cycles (bracketed areas above the horizontal line) and rhythmic cycles (brackets below the horizontal line).

In examining facets of Monteverdi's compositional technique that function within shorter time spans, phrase structures are especially fascinating, for Monteverdi continually sets off regular and predictable phrase structures against irregular and unpredictable phrases. For example, at the very outset of the piece he establishes a nearly palindromic phrase based on the palindromic syllable structure of the text (see **Example 15a**). The very next passage, however, is quite irregular, consisting of a   2-bar phrase, followed by a phrase of 2-1/2 bars (combining to form a 4 1/2 bar unit), succeeded in turn by phrases of 3-bars and 3-1/2 bars (see **Example 15a**). Contrasting with this unpredictability is the passage based on the same thematic material but in imitation and 2:1 rhythmic diminution (22-32). Here the imitative phrase consists of orderly two-bar units, and the imitative entries are consistently at one-bar intervals. The regularity of this passage is one of its most salient characteristics, and its predictability contributes powerfully to the build-up of texture, sonority and energy in this section until just before the cadence at bars 31-32. Regular phrase structures tend to occur especially in imitative passages, and their association with imitation enhances the forward drive of such passages through the inevitability of each successive entrance. It is, of course, the same effect on a smaller scale that Bach often achieves in fugues with regularly spaced entries of the subject.

Regular phrase structures may appear not only in imitative tuttis, but also in duet passages, and sometimes elsewhere as well. The tenor duet at *Virgam virtutis* (bars 93-112) is an example of a duet with regular phrase structure (see **Example**

18). On the other hand, irregular phrases are also very common, especially in soloistic passages, homophonic passages and non-imitative polyphony. In these passages the phrase structure is often determined, or at least strongly influenced, by the number of syllables and speech rhythm in a given line of text. Since the verses of the psalm are irregular in Length and do not display any poetic meter, irregular phrase structures emerge quite naturally.

The variety of Monteverdi's phrase structures and patterns of imitative entry is remarkable. Moreover, this facet of the compositional process is only partially related to textures and rhythms and only occasionally to larger structures. Phrase structure is primarily a short-term issue, determined by the exigencies of the moment. The variety and constant change in phrase structures confront us with passages that are wholly predictable, contrasted with others that are equally unpredictable. Nor can we be sure of any pattern or cycle of phrase structures. Phrase structures function almost entirely on the sonorous surface of the composition where variety is the most important aesthetic goal. They do not form hierarchical large-scale structures as in music from the very late 17th-century onward. Monteverdi's phrase structures, rather, reflect the rhetorical orientation of his compositional technique, either shifting constantly as the text itself progresses, or helping define a particular musical gesture characterizing a passage, such as in the imitative segments described above.

I have by now examined most of the main elements of Monteverdi's compositional practice in *Dixit Dominus*. The road has been long, perhaps even a bit tedious. Nevertheless, I cannot claim to have exhausted the items of interest in this psalm; indeed, there is much more to be said about the details of the composition and perhaps about larger issues as well. Nor would I claim that this analysis has discovered what is "divine" in Monteverdi. But perhaps the discussion has shed some light on the complexity and sophistication of Monteverdi's compositional process. We have seen him engage in a complex, but coherent large-scale structure based on the Golden Mean and evenly balanced sections. We have seen him indulge in fairly tight thematic coherence, but somewhat looser rhythmic coherence. Tonalities establish and center around the main tonic, but local cadences are unsystematic in their organization. Textures tend to follow a pattern of alternation, but one not fully corresponding to the structural subdivisions. Phrase Lengths range from the highly predictable to the irregular and unpredictable, and bear only a passing relationship to other features we have studied.

The process of analysis has required breaking the piece into structural fragments and separate parameters. But the secret of any composer's success lies in the way all of these disparate elements are forged into a satisfying whole. That is something the analyst cannot do, and it is precisely the way that everything fits together, the almost infinitely complex web of relationships, the sophisticated interactions among several parameters acting simultaneously, that give the work its richness and rewards us for the time spent listening to and studying it.

Were we to compare this work with a *Dixit Dominus* setting by a lesser composer, I venture to say that we would find in the lesser composer less complex structural organization, less coherent thematic ideas, and less variety of phrase structures, rhythms and harmony, all as a consequence of a less fertile imagination and poorer judgment as to how to assemble all of the features of a composition into a whole work. The network of relationships in any great work of art are theoretically inexhuastible, a circumstance which may help us distinguish great works and great artists from mediocrities, where the networks are limited and much less rich in the variety of their interactions. Contrary to Tomlinson's assertion that Monteverdi's later works are "hollow" and the result of "musical simplification," his first *Dixit Dominus* from the *Selva morale et spirituale* reveals an inexhaustible inventiveness and extraordinary sophistication in the compositional process, but based on other aesthetic aims than the humanistically oriented madrigals and early operas Tomlinson rightly values so highly. The large-scale *concertato* works represent a different kind of art for a different society from the Gonzaga court at Mantua, but they are no less sophisticated, no less expressive and no less valuable than Monteverdi's earlier works.

In shaping his *Dixit Dominus*, Monteverdi has applied principals inherited from both the Platonic and Aristotelian traditions as they were voiced in the 16th century. *Dixit Dominus* is basically Aristotelian in its sonorous surface, in the *varietà* of the many elements it presents to the listener's ear. Yet underlying this variety is a complex sense of organization and unity, based principally on thematic shape and structural proportions, but also involving harmony, rhythm and texture. This organization and unity only partially reaches our perception and consciousness, but without that underlying sense of coherence and logic, I assert that the composition would sound fragmentary, strange, unfulfilling, and ultimately uninteresting. The background unity and logic reflect the Platonic mentality, the world of vague images that give us a glimpse of the eternal ideas. While we cannot through analysis fully demonstrate what makes Claudio "divine", perhaps by grasping the magnitude of his achievement in combining Aristotelian empirical variety with the Platonic ideal of structures based on the eternal verities of the Golden Section and symmetrical balance, we can at least glimpse the shadow of his genius.

VI

282

Example 1a

Example 1b
17 (cf. also 62)

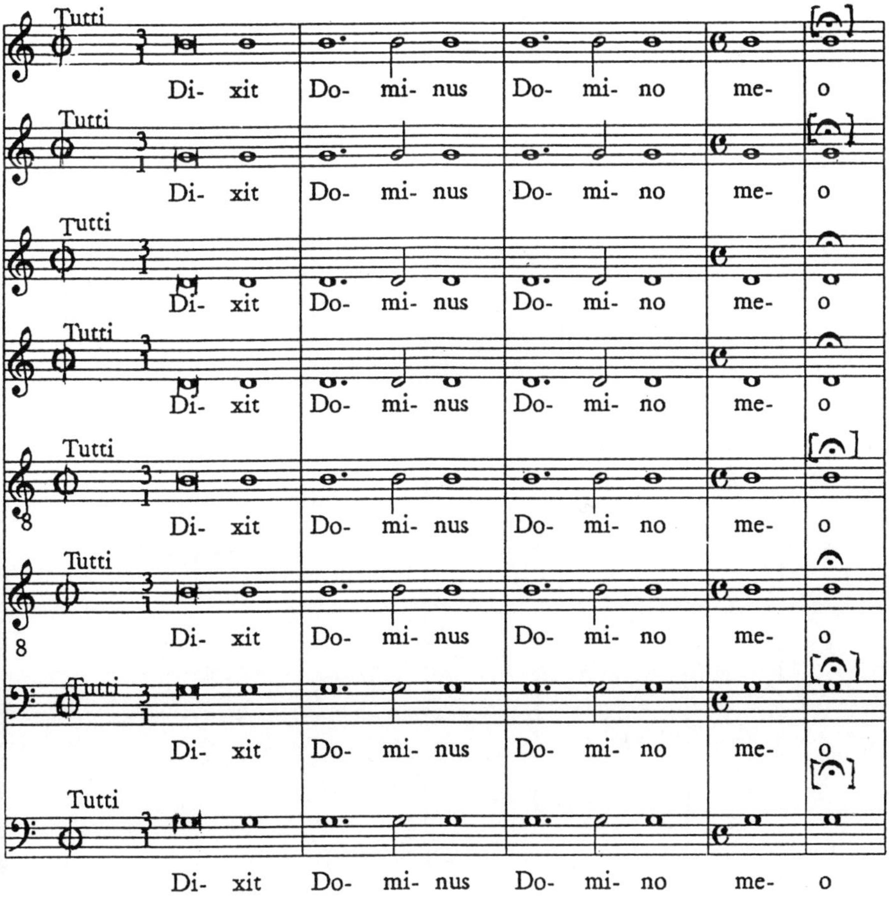

Example 1b
(continued)

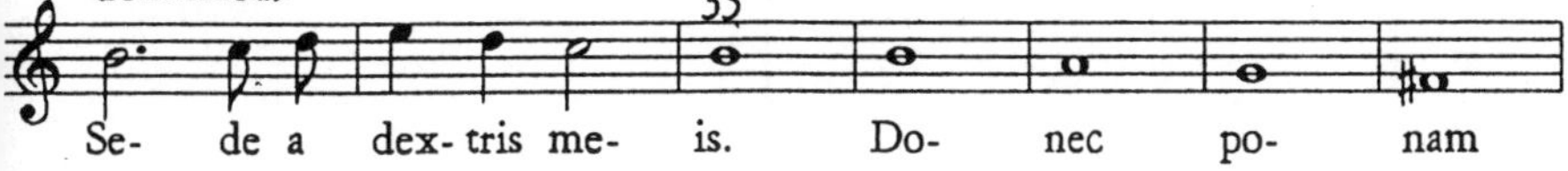

Example 2

G. S. (187)

92 bars · 91 bars · 61 bars · 59 bars

G. S. (148)

G. S. (280)

reverse G.S. (114) · 37 bars

32 bars · 29 bars · 31 bars · 20 bars

16 bars 16 bars

16 | 17 | 32 | 33 | 61 | 62 | 92 | 93 | 112 | 113 | 149 | 150 | 166 | 167 | 183 | 184 | 204 | 205 | 227 | 228 | 244 | 245 | 280 | 281 | 303

16/2 bars · 17/2 bars · 20/2 bars · 23/2 bars · 17 bars · 23 bars · 36 bars

Dixit Dominus - Donec ponam	G major
Virgam virtutis	C major
Virgam virtutis	C major / A major cadence / Rapid modulation by descending 5ths
	Rapid modulation by descending 5ths
Tecum principium	Rapid modulation / C major / G major cad. = V/C
Iuravit Dominus	G major
Dominus a dextris	A minor / G major / D major = V/G
Iudicabit	
De torrente	G major / C major cadence
Doxology	G major
Amen - et in saecula	(A minor) / Varied / G major / (A major) / A major = V/D / G major

Example 3

164
-ci- fe- rum ge- nus- i- te.
-ci- fe- rum ge- nus- i- te.
a2
Ju-
-ci- fe- rum ge- nu- i- te.
-ci- fe- rum ge- nu- i- te.

286

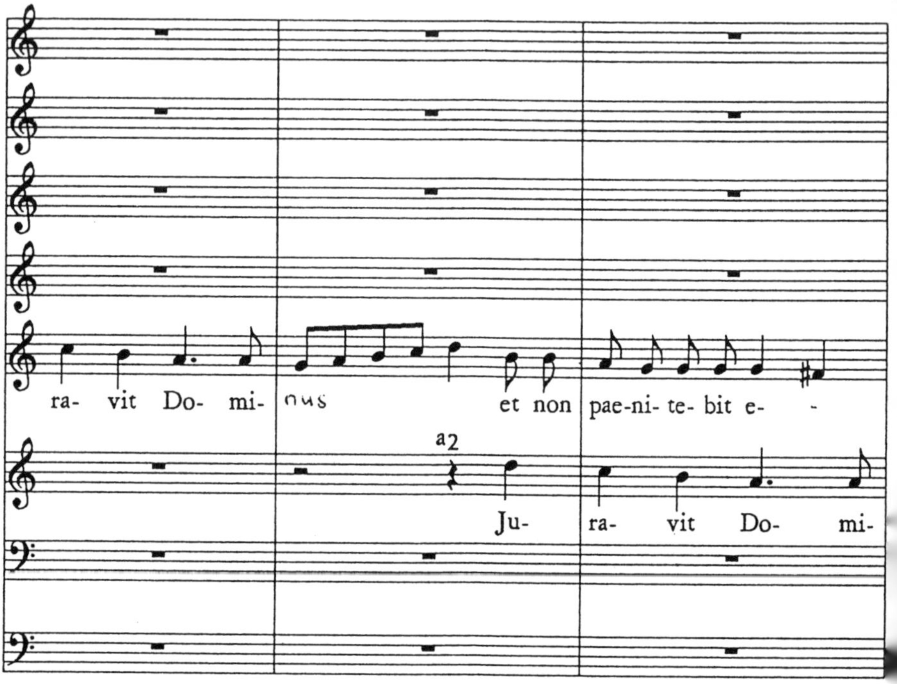
ra- vit Do- mi- nus et non pae-ni- te- bit e- -
a2
Ju- ra- vit Do- mi-

Example 4

Example 5a

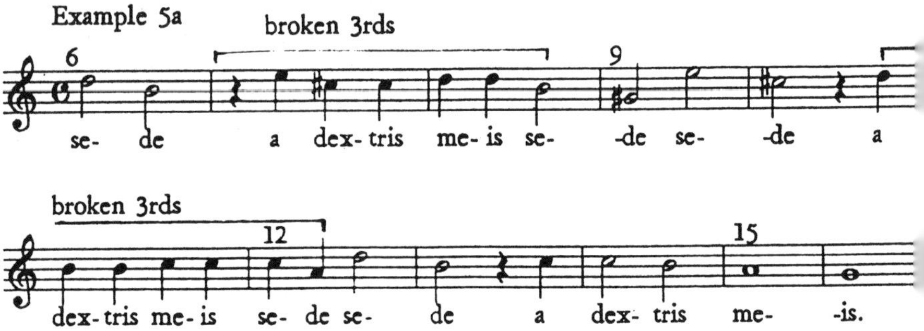

Example 5b

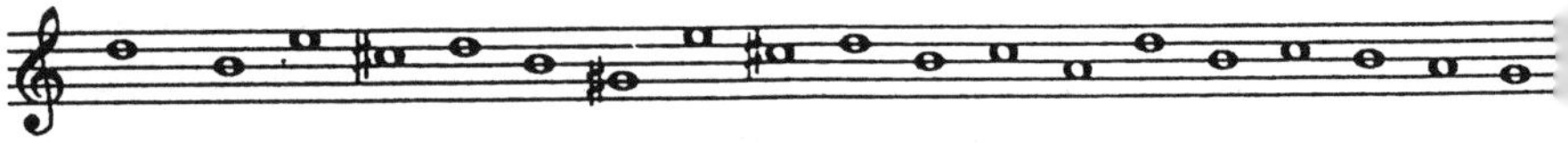

Example 5c

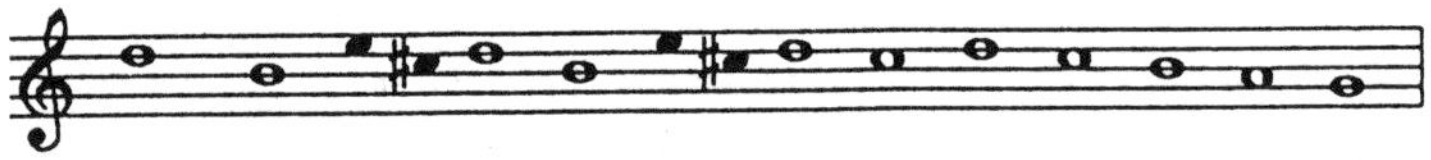

Example 5d

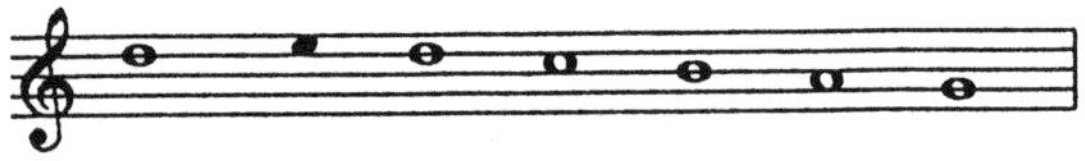

Example 6

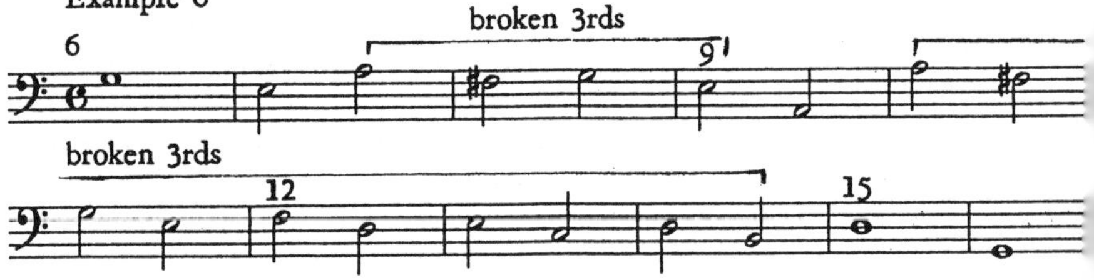

Example 7
33 Solo   36

se-   de a   dex- tris me-   is.   Do-   nec

39   42

po-   nam   i-   - ni- mi-   - cos i-   - ni- mi-

45

- cos tu- os i-   ni- mi-   cos i-   ni- mi-   - cos tu-

51   54

-os sca-bel-lum pe- dum tu- o-   rum sca-bel-lum pe- dum tu- o-

57   60

rum sca-bel-lum pe- -   - dum tu- p-   rum

Example 8
33-39   40-45

45-52   53-61

Example 9

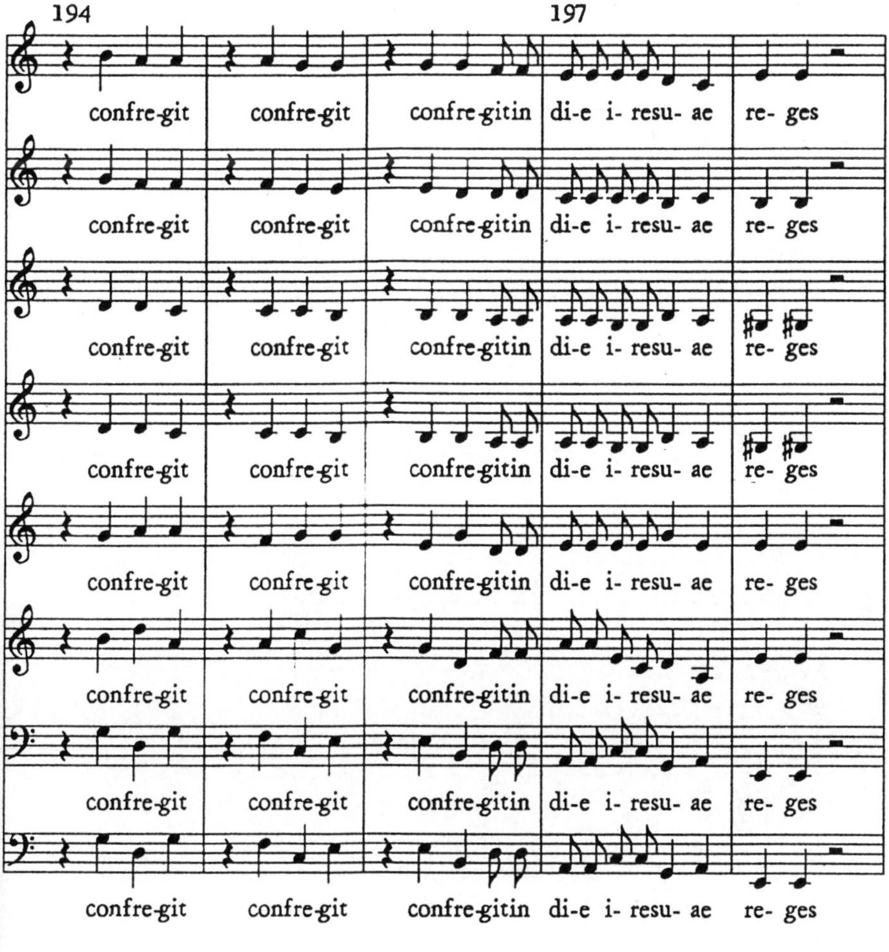

Example 10

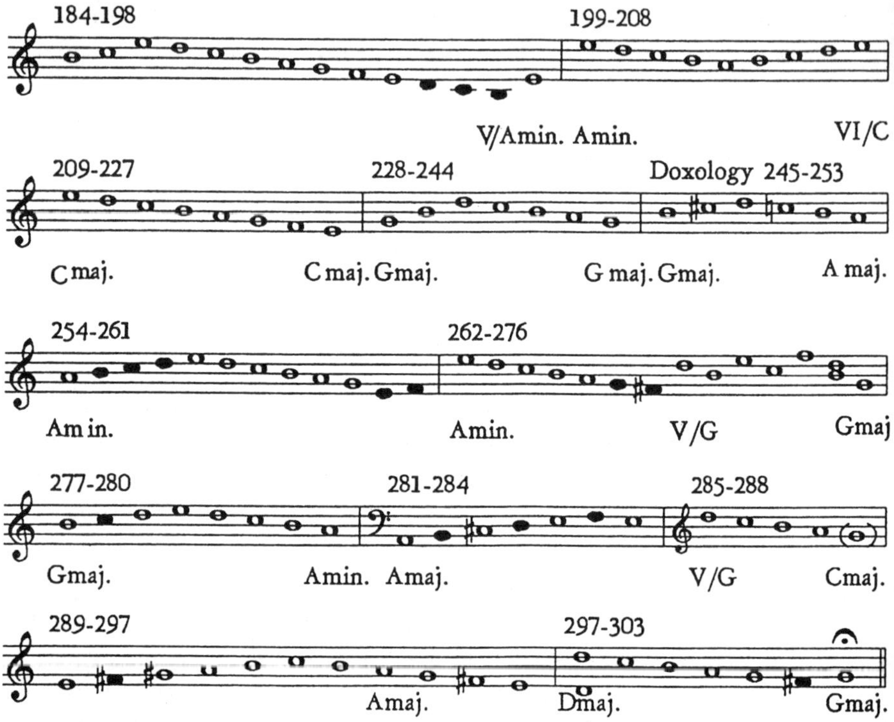

Example 11

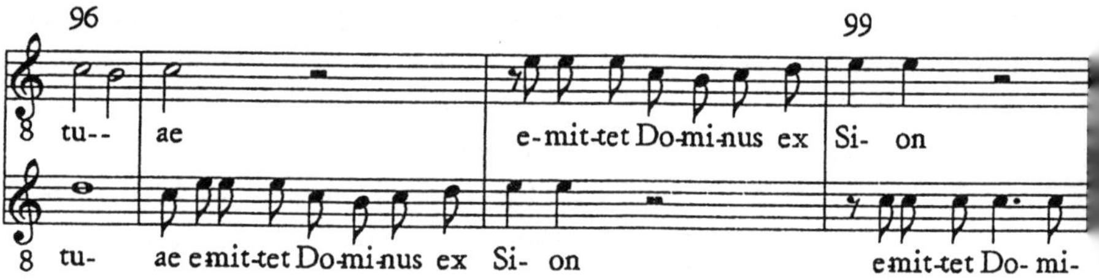

Example 12

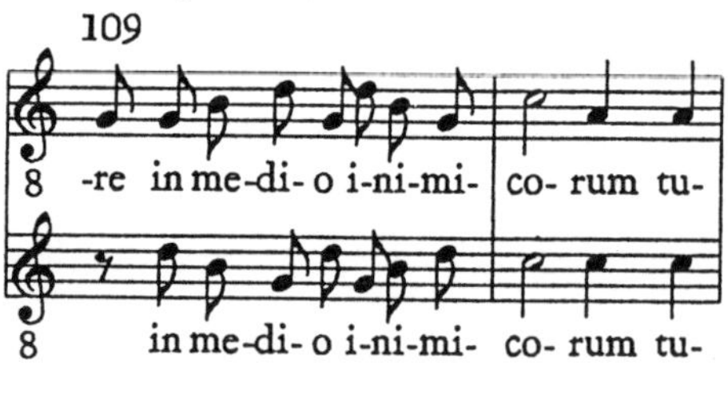

Example 13

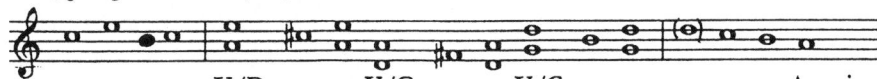

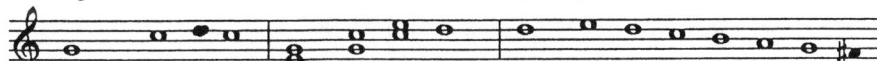

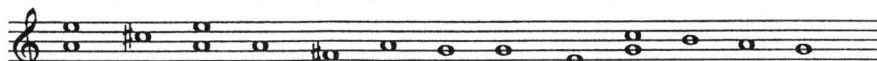

Example 14

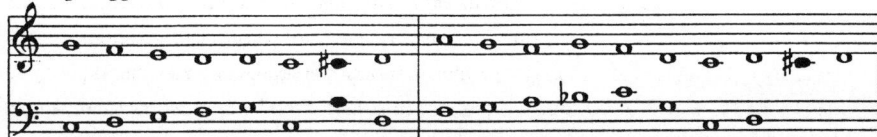

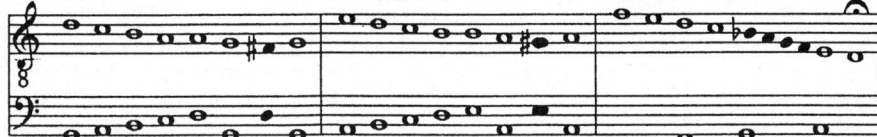

294

Example 15a

Di- xit Do- mi- nus Do- mi- no me o

Example 15b.1

-is Do- nec po- nam

Example 15b2
[a 2]

dex- tris tu-

a 2

a dex- - tris tu- - -

Example 15c.1
8   11   14

me-is se- de se- de a dex-tris me-is se- de se- de a dex-tris

Example 15c.2
51   54   57

-os sca bellum pedum tu- o- rum sca bellum pedum tu- o- rum sca bellum

Example 15b.3

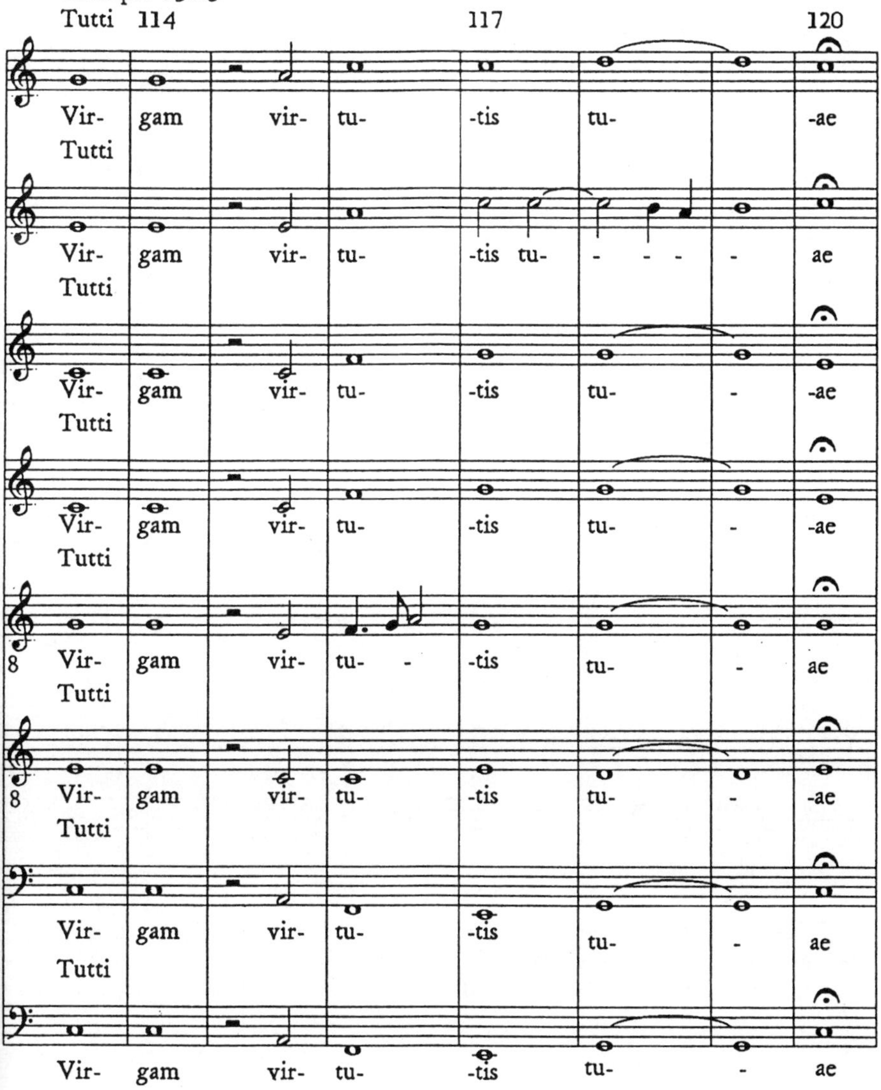

Example 15d

150
[A4]
Te- cum prin-
A4
Te- cum prin- ci- pi- um in di- e vir-
A4
Te- cum prin- ci- pi- um
A4
Te- cum prin-
153
ci- pi- um in di- e vir- tu-tis tu- ae
tu-tis tu- ae in splen- do ri- bus san- cto- rum
in di- e vir- tu-tis tu- ae
ci- pi- um
in splen- do ri- bus san- cto- rum ex u- te- ro ex
[ex u- te- ro] ex u- te- ro an-
ex
in splen-do-ri- bus sa- cto- rum ex u- te- ro

Example 15e.1
73

Example 15e.2

Example 16

Example 16
(continued)

Example 17

Textural cycles

Cycle	Texture	Description
8th cycle	tutti	Homophonic & Polyphonic tutti
	duet	Bass duet
7th cycle	tutti	Homophonic tutti
	duet	Tenor duet
6th cycle	tutti	Homophonic tutti
	duet	Soprano duet
5th cycle	tutti	Homophonic & Polyphonic tutti with Soprano duet as "Ritornello"
	duets	Tenor duet
		Alto & Bass double duet
4th cycle	tutti	Homophonic & Polyphonic tutti
	duet	Soprano & Alto duet
3rd cycle	tutti	Homophonic tutti
	duet	Tenor duet
2nd cycle	tutti	Homophonic & Polyphonic tutti (2 x bars 17-32)
	solo	Soprano solo (2 x bars 1-16)
1st cycle	tutti	Homophonic & Polyphonic tutti
	solo	Soprano solo

Rhythmic cycles

Bar numbers: 16 | 17 | 32 | 33 | 61 | 62 | 92 | 93 | 112 | 113 | 149 | 150 | 166 | 167 | 183 | 184 | 204 | 205 | 227 | 228 | 244 | 245 | 280 | 281 | 303

1st cycle, 2nd cycle, 3rd cycle, 4th cycle, 5th cycle, 6th cycle, 7th cycle

Example 18

93
A 2
96
Vir- gam vir- tu- tis tu- - ae
A 2
Vir- gam vir- tu- tis tu- ae e- mit-tet Do-mi-nus ex
99
e- mit-tet Do-mi-nus ex Si- on e- mit-tet
Si- on e- mit-tet Do- mit- nus ex
102
Do-mi-nus ex Si- on do- mi- na-
Si- on do- - mi-na- -re in me-di- o i-ni-mi-
105
108
-re in me-di- o i-ni-mi- co- rum do- - mi-na-
co- rum in me-di- o i-ni-mi- co- rum
111
-re in me-di- o i- ni- mi- co- rum tu- o- - -rum
in me-di- o i- ni- mi- co- rum tu- o- rum

VII

The Mantuan sacred music

When Monteverdi was hired by Duke Vincenzo Gonzaga to join the court musicians at Mantua, he described himself as a player of the *vivuola*. Yet it is obvious that he was also expected to compose, for he had already published several collections of music for three and four voices, two of which were of sacred music. Indeed, Monteverdi's very first publication, at the age of fifteen (1582), was a set of twenty-three three-voice motets, many based on antiphon texts for various of the Offices, which he entitled *Sacrae cantiunculae tribus vocibus*. In the very next year the young Claudio displayed his growing compositional skill by expanding his texture to four voices for a set of eleven *Madrigali spirituali*, only the bass voice of which survives today. It was only after these initial forays in religious music that the young composer turned his hand to three-voice secular *Canzonette* (1584) and his first two books of five-voice madrigals (1587 and 1590). So by the time he entered Gonzaga service, Monteverdi had already established himself as a significant composer of both sacred and secular music in northern Italy.

Only one more book of madrigals appeared during Monteverdi's first decade in Mantua (in 1592), but during that time he had already composed those madrigals on texts of Giambattista Guarini's *Il pastor fido* that would make him both famous and notorious because of the polemics with the conservative theorist Giovanni Maria Artusi that lasted from 1600 to 1608. Several of these madrigals were contrafacted and published with Latin spiritual texts by a Milanese rhetorician, Aquilino Coppini, in 1607. Before 1610, Monteverdi published no more sacred music, a gap of twenty-seven years from his *Madrigali spirituali*, yet that does not mean he was completely silent in the religious sphere during this period. Unfortunately, so much of Monteverdi's music, especially his sacred music, was never published, and far more was lost than ever appeared in print. We only have hints of what he must have produced from various remarks and citations in letters and other documents. The first such reference is from late 1595 when Monteverdi and four or five other singers accompanied Duke Vincenzo on a military expedition against the Turks in Hungary.[1] Monteverdi may well have provided the Mass sung in S. Andrea prior to the departure of the troops. According to the report of the expedition's chronicler, four or five masses were said in the duke's quarters every day, and on solemn feasts Vespers were sung by the singers accompanied by an organ. Most of the masses were likely sung in chant, but polyphony, presumably composed by Monteverdi, who was listed as *maestro di cappella* of the expedition, was probably performed at solemn Vespers.

In summer 1599 Monteverdi again accompanied Duke Vincenzo on a journey, this time to Spa in Flanders. Although we have no accounts of music on this excursion, it is again probable that Monteverdi provided not only secular music, but also the music for sacred services during this trip.[2] Monteverdi's own first mention of sacred music comes from two years later in his first surviving letter. Written while the duke was again in Hungary on a military expedition (though this time Monteverdi was left behind with his wife, who was shortly expecting their first child), the letter seeks appointment as *maestro di cappella* of both the chamber and the church ('e della camera e della chiesa'), a position most recently occupied by Benedetto Pallavicino, who had just died. In this letter Monteverdi expresses his desire for 'greater opportunity' to demonstrate his capacities to the duke's 'most refined musical taste as of some worth in motets and masses too' (letter of 28 November 1601). He seems here to be speaking of his eagerness to write motets and masses rather than referring to music he had already written.

What did Monteverdi mean by 'the chamber and the church'? The ducal church of S. Barbara already had its own *maestro di cappella*, Giacomo Gastoldi, who served in that role from 1588–1609. In Chapter 4 of this book, Roger Bowers cites the church of S. Croce at the edge of the ducal palace and Vincenzo Gonzaga's chapel in the Corte Vecchia as locations where Monteverdi and his predecessors as *maestro di cappella* were active as composers of sacred music. In addition, there was a chapel in the Castello S. Giorgio, another edifice in the palace complex. Yet these facilities were small and unlikely venues for the five- and six-voice masses and eight-, twelve- and sixteen-voice motets published by Pallavicino, and if Monteverdi had provided sacred music for any of these locations, it would have had to be for few-voiced ensembles. Moreover, if he had done so, why would he have expressed his desire to demonstrate his capacities to the duke in motets and masses, since the duke would already have been well acquainted with his sacred music? In my view, it is more likely that the service music in these private venues normally comprised plainchant and *falsobordone*, with possibly music of a more elaborate nature on rare occasions composed by the succession of *maestri di cappella* at the court. Had any of them produced substantial quantities of elaborate polyphony for these chapels, it is likely that some documentary trace would by now have come to light.

By 1603, Monteverdi had indeed been appointed *maestro di cappella* for Vincenzo Gonzaga (Bowers argues plausibly for December 1601), but the most likely venues for any sacred music Monteverdi wrote in this capacity were the cathedral church of Mantua, San Pietro, which lies directly across the piazza from the ducal palace and had no permanent *maestro di cappella* of its own, and the church of S. Andrea, constructed by the famous architect Leon Battista Alberti, just around the corner. The duke's *cappella* performed with some frequency in S. Pietro, and the Gonzagas celebrated numerous major events in S. Andrea, such as the Feast of the Ascension, which included the annual 'Sensa' festival celebrating Gonzaga rule in Mantua. On this feast in 1608 Duke Vincenzo established in S. Andrea a new order of knighthood in honour of Christ the Redeemer.[3] Special events at other churches in the city were also organised by the Gonzagas, and it is highly likely that the duke's *cappella* provided the music. The installation in the Jesuit Church of the Holy Trinity of an altarpiece by Peter Paul Rubens figuring Vincenzo Gonzaga and his family adoring the Holy Trinity could have featured a performance of the trinitarian motet 'Duo seraphim', or an early version of it, eventually published with the 1610 Vespers (Bowers suggests the consecration of Luigi Gonzaga in the same church at the end of the same year, which is also a possibility). Mantuan reaffirmation of the cult of the Virgin Mary in 1611 included the consecration of the Immacolata in the Capuchin Church and the renewal of the confraternity of the Immacolata in the Church of San Francesco.[4] Such events at other churches in Mantua suggest that by 'della chiesa' in his 1601 letter, Monteverdi may well have been using the term generically rather than specifically, i.e., he was asking to be responsible for all church music sponsored by the duke outside S. Barbara, rather than to be the *maestro di cappella* of any particular church.

That Monteverdi provided sacred music for liturgical celebrations is clear from a passage in the famous *Dichiaratione* of 1607, published in the *Scherzi musicali* of that year, in which Giulio Cesare Monteverdi, speaking for his brother, answered the charges of Artusi with his famous doctrine of the *prima pratica* and *seconda pratica*. Giulio Cesare justified responding in place of Claudio because his brother did not have the time, 'not only because of his responsibility for both church and chamber music, but also because of other extraordinary services'.[5]

Monteverdi's interest in sacred music was reasserted a year later when, exhausted and sick from preparations for the Gonzaga wedding festivities of May and June 1608, he retired to his father's house in Cremona. From there his father, a physician, wrote to the duke on 9 November requesting his son's dismissal from service, fearing that Claudio would perish from the bad Mantuan air should he return. But in the event that he could not obtain dismissal, his father pleaded, 'If Your Most Serene Highness commands only that he serves in the church, that he will do.'[6] In this instance the word 'church' probably referred specifically to S. Barbara, for Giovanni Gastoldi, its *maestro di cappella*, was very ill at the time and not expected to live long. Subsequent letters from Monteverdi's father and the composer himself, however, were in vain, for when Gastoldi died in January 1609, an interim *maestro* was appointed to S. Barbara and Monteverdi was ordered to return to court, though the duke did confirm a previously promised annual pension of a hundred *scudi* for the composer in recognition of his service and merit.

During 1608 and 1609, Coppini issued two more books of Latin sacred *contrafacta* of Monteverdi's madrigals in Milan. Italian spiritual *contrafacta* of three of his *Scherzi musicali* from 1607 and two otherwise unknown pieces appear in a Brescian manuscript entitled *Canzonette e madrigaletti spirituali* dated 1610.[7]

Monteverdi's hectic, difficult and penurious life at Mantua certainly prompted him to think about seeking another position, as hinted in another passage of his father's letter of 9 November 1608:

> I . . . beseech you that . . . you permit him the requested discharge, assuring Your Most Serene Highness that all his well-being he will always recognise as coming from your generosity, for if from the favour of your generous dismissal it happens that he serves a prince, I know that in this respect he will be viewed favourably.[8]

However, Monteverdi could not be hired by another court without the duke's permission or without being honourably dismissed from his service. Moreover, since court life had proved unpredictable and unbearable to him in so many ways, the only alternative was to seek a position as *maestro di cappella* of a major church, where the duties followed the liturgical calendar and were not subject to unanticipated pressures and sudden whims. However, Monteverdi had published no sacred music for twenty-seven years and no music for any liturgy at all. This lacuna in his public profile appears to have been the impetus for embarking on the publication of what would come to be known as the Mass and Vespers of 1610.[9] This print is a very large collection of fifteen compositions, and Monteverdi must have assembled it from music he had already written as well as a number of new works. By the summer of 1610 the collection was well under way and the vice *maestro di cappella*, Bassano Cassola, reported in a letter to Cardinal Ferdinando Gonzaga:

Monteverdi is having printed an *a cappella* Mass for six voices of great
studiousness and labour, having obliged himself to handle for every note and in
every way, always reinforcing the eight [*recte* ten] points of imitation that are in
the motet 'In illo tempore' by Gombert, and together [with it] he is also having
printed psalms for Vespers of the Madonna, with various and diverse manners
of invention and of harmony – and all are on the *cantus firmus* – with the idea
of coming to Rome this autumn to dedicate them to His Holiness.[10]

The Mass Cassola describes was apparently Monteverdi's musical answer
to Artusi's public attacks on his compositional technique (the last of which
had been published only two years previously). In this Mass, as will be
discussed further below, Monteverdi wove a dense, imitative polyphonic
texture not only based on a motet dating from at least seventy-three
years earlier, but in several respects also reflecting the style of polyphony
from that period. Cassola's letter emphasises the strenuous effort it took
Monteverdi to produce this work, suggesting that perhaps Monteverdi
was not as practised and skilled in the *prima pratica* as his brother had
declared. Cassola also mentions the variegated psalms (Magnificats were
often listed under the rubric *salmi*) and their foundation in the *cantus firmus*
of the psalm tone, a procedure in composing psalms that was largely out of
date by 1610. What Cassola does not mention are the introductory Response,
four virtuosic few-voiced motets, the 'Sonata sopra "Sancta Maria"', and the
hymn 'Ave maris stella', which are also included in the collection.

The print is entitled *Sanctissimae Virgini missa senis vocibus, ac vesperae pluribus decantandae, cum nonnullis sacris concentibus, ad sacella
sive principum cubicula accommodata. Opera a Claudio Monteverde nuper
effecta ac Beatiss. Paulo V. Pont. Max. consecrata.*[11] It thereby has a double
dedication in honouring the Virgin, but with Monteverdi's personal
dedication addressed to Pope Paul V. The Vespers psalms and hymn
Monteverdi chose are those of the eight major feasts of the Virgin in
Monteverdi's day, prompting that entire section of the print to carry the
heading *Vespro della Beata Vergine*. Even though the publication was
evidently designed to assist Monteverdi in obtaining another position,
it had close ties to the Gonzagas, who honoured Mary as the patroness
and protectress of the city of Mantua, and who claimed a special relationship with Pope Paul V as well. Indeed, a general papal indulgence was
declared for the city in the church of S. Andrea in 1607 and the city
celebrated a reaffirmation of the cult of Mary in 1611.

The introductory Response of the Vespers service is even based on the
toccata fanfare that opened Monteverdi's *Orfeo*, a work commissioned
by Prince Francesco Gonzaga, whose fanfare has been understood by
several scholars as a kind of Gonzaga family entrance piece. Moreover,

the chant used in the hymn 'Ave maris stella' reflects a variant found in the rite of the ducal church of S. Barbara at Mantua.[12] In fact, there is no incompatibility between Monteverdi's having written some, possibly even most, of the compositions in the Mass and Vespers of 1610 for specific occasions in Mantua, and their subsequent function in print as an advertisement of his skill and invention for a possible appointment elsewhere.

The dedication of the print is dated 1 September 1610, and later that autumn Monteverdi did indeed go to Rome to present the collection to the Pope as Cassola had said he would. He also had hopes of obtaining a position in the Roman seminary for his son Francesco. Monteverdi seems to have travelled to Rome somewhat surreptitiously, for a letter from the Mantuan official, Rainero Bissolati, of 7 October speaks of bumping into the composer accidentally on the street and learning that he was staying at an inn.[13] As a representative of the Duke of Mantua, Monteverdi would normally have lodged in the palace of Vincenzo's brother, Cardinal Ferdinando, and the official insisted Monteverdi move to the palace for the remainder of his visit. Perhaps the composer was secretive at this stage of his journey because he was feeling out the possibility of employment at one or another major Roman church or with a cardinal or Roman noble-man. In any event, Monteverdi returned to Mantua by Christmas, and despite high praise from Cardinals Montalto and Borghese, two of the most important cardinals in the Roman curia, he came home empty-handed – without a post for his son in the seminary, and without a new job for himself. Remnants of his visit to Rome are a copy of the Missa 'In illo tempore' in a Sistine Chapel manuscript and an alto part-book of the 1610 print leather-bound and embossed with the coat of arms of Pope Paul V in the Biblioteca Doria Pamphilij.[14]

A few months after his return to Mantua, Monteverdi sent to Prince Francesco Gonzaga a setting of the Vespers psalm 'Dixit Dominus' for eight voices 'which Your Highness ordered me to send, together with which I am also sending you a little motet for two voices to be sung at the Elevation, and another for five voices for the Blessed Virgin' (letter of 26 March 1611). Attempts to identify these compositions with Monteverdi's published church music are probably in vain, since, as indicated above, he composed far more, especially in the field of sacred music, than he ever published. No sign of either the Elevation motet or the motet for the Virgin survives. Even though Monteverdi and his publisher eventually issued four settings of 'Dixit Dominus' for eight voices, he must have composed many more over the course of his long career, and it is far more likely that the 'Dixit' sent to Prince Francesco perished with so many other Monteverdi manuscripts in the sack of Mantua by Imperial troops in 1630.

On 11 May 1611, the vigil of the Feast of Christ the Redeemer (Ascension Day) was celebrated in S. Andrea with Vespers by Monteverdi.[15] One is tempted to think this was the first performance of the recently minted Vespro della Beata Vergine, but the feast of the Redeemer would normally have required the psalm cycle for most male feasts and a hymn proper to that feast instead of the cycle for the Virgin. The eight-voice 'Dixit Dominus' Monteverdi sent to Prince Francesco in late March could have been performed as the first psalm on this occasion, and he could well have written additional music between his return from Rome and the middle of May. Nevertheless, four of the compositions in the 1610 print – the Response, the psalms 'Dixit Dominus' and 'Laudate pueri', and the Magnificat – are also suitable for Ascension Day, so it is indeed possible that at least some of Monteverdi's Vespers music published in 1610 was heard on this occasion, together with other new music that fulfilled the liturgical requirements of that particular service.

There exists a report from Christmas 1611 of another performance of Vespers music by Monteverdi in the cathedral of Modena. A local chronicler declared that the *maestro di cappella* there 'had certain psalms sung, by Monteverdo [sic], *maestro di cappella* of the Duke of Mantua, which were to everyone's disgust'.[16] Speculation that these were the psalms from the 1610 Vespers are again somewhat misguided, since the psalm cycle for Christmas Vespers is not the same as for the Virgin, except for the overlap of 'Dixit Dominus' and 'Laudate pueri' (the latter for First Vespers only).

At some time in the period between summer 1610 and 1612, Monteverdi composed a sacred solo madrigal on a text by Angelo Grillo, which was sung by the famous court singer Adriana Basile, 'a sublime singer and an angelic voice ... who, marrying the voice with the instrument, and with gesture giving soul and speech to the strings, brings forth the sweet tyranny of our souls, while leaving them in our bodies on earth, takes them with the hearing to heaven'.[17]

In July 1612, both Claudio and Giulio Cesare Monteverdi were dismissed from their posts at the Mantuan court by the new duke, Francesco Gonzaga, who had succeeded his recently deceased father. We hear no more of sacred music by Monteverdi from his Mantuan years with the exception of his audition for the position of *maestro di cappella* at S. Marco in Venice, where the 1610 print is mentioned in the document announcing his election.

The music of the Mass and Vespers of 1610

Monteverdi's first sacred collection is grandiose in style and scope. Its fifteen compositions are as follows:

148

Missa 'In illo tempore' for six voices
'Domine ad adiuvandum': Response to versicle 'Deus in adiutorium' for six voices
and twelve instruments
'Dixit Dominus': psalm for six voices with optional six-part instrumental ritornellos
'Nigra sum': motet for solo tenor
'Laudate pueri': psalm for eight solo voices
'Pulchra es': motet for two solo sopranos
'Laetatus sum': psalm for six voices
'Duo seraphim': motet for three solo tenors
'Nisi Dominus': psalm for ten voices in *cori spezzati*
'Audi coelum': motet for solo tenor and tenor echo, concluded by six-voice chorus
'Lauda Jerusalem': psalm for seven voices
'Sonata sopra "Sancta Maria"': instrumental sonata with prayer 'Sancta Maria ora
pro nobis' intoned as an eleven-fold litany in the soprano voice
'Ave maris stella': hymn for eight voices with five-part instrumental ritornellos
Magnificat: canticle for seven voices and six instruments
Magnificat: canticle for six voices

Monteverdi's print opens with the contrapuntal *tour de force* described in Bassano Cassola's letter, the Missa 'In illo tempore' for six voices. This work is almost archaic in its rigid adherence to a highly imitative six-voice texture, though with organ continuo added. The organ part, however, almost exclusively follows the lowest sounding note of the vocal parts, and any organist of the time would have played much of the rest of the vocal texture as well. In fact, a manuscript organ *partitura* of this piece survives in the Cathedral of Brescia in which all the vocal parts are reproduced.[18]

Monteverdi advertises his contrapuntal technique, in a manner unique among contemporary sacred music publications, by listing at the beginning of the piece the ten motifs drawn from Nicolas Gombert's motet of the same name (Ex. 8.1). It is apparent from this ploy and from Cassola's letter that Monteverdi conceived the Mass as displaying his contrapuntal expertise, demonstrating to Artusi that he was not only the foremost practitioner of the *seconda pratica*, but also a master of the *prima pratica*.

Gombert's motet was first published in 1538. It is noteworthy that Monteverdi reached this far back into the sixteenth century for his first large-scale effort in the imitative polyphonic style rather than drawing on a more recent work. His choice of the Gombert motet was probably influenced by two factors: its motives have a strong harmonic profile, and it is in the C-Ionian mode with no trace of the traditional eight Church modes. Monteverdi's almost reactionary contrapuntal style yields a composition that is nearly unremitting in its six-voice texture based on time-honoured contrapuntal complexities: pervasive imitation at varying time intervals, canon, inversion, retrogression, augmentation, diminution, paraphrase, sequences, countersubjects and invertible counterpoint. The first of

Ex. 8.1

the borrowed motifs is the most important, appearing in both the opening Kyrie and the closing Agnus Dei II (expanded to seven voices), as well as functioning as the head motif and closing motif in several other sections. At times Monteverdi uses more than one of Gombert's motifs simultaneously, while all ten make prominent appearances at various points throughout the Mass–all of them, for example, in the Gloria.

Monteverdi's unrelenting six-voice polyphony contrasts with more recent contrapuntists, such as Lassus, Palestrina, and Victoria, who were much more flexible in their handling of textures, motifs, and imitation. Only two sections of the Mass, the 'Et incarnatus est' in the Credo and the Benedictus, are principally homophonic. Both begin on an E major triad, expressively contrasting in their texture and tonality with the prevailing, almost monotonous Ionian mode of the rest of the Mass in order to highlight the mystery and uniqueness of their common textual reference to the incarnated Son of God. Despite the emphasis on Gombert's motifs and conservative style, many sections of the Mass conclude with descending

Ex. 8.2a Kyrie II

Ex. 8.2b Kyrie II

sequences based on scales or broken thirds, generating a more modern, forceful, harmonic impetus toward final cadences. These sequences also occur with some frequency within individual sections, providing relief to the ubiquity of Gombert's motifs (see Exx. 8.2a, 8.2b). Such sequences constitute the entirety of the Sanctus, with the exception of the homophonic Benedictus. Following the Mass, the fourteen pieces listed above fulfil in succession almost all the musical needs for a Vespers service on any feast of the Virgin in the Roman Rite. The psalms and Magnificat (with two alternative choices of the latter) are also those required for the Common of virgin saints. The four motets and the 'Sonata sopra "Sancta Maria"' have generally been recognised as substitutes for the plainchant psalm antiphons from the Proper in the Roman Rite, though a few scholars have disputed

Ex. 8.3 Second Psalm Tone

Ex. 8.4 Sancta Maria ora pro nobis

Sancta Maria ora pro nobis

San - cta Ma - ri - a o - ra pro no - bis

this on the grounds of liturgical impropriety (see below). Monteverdi provided no motet or instrumental piece to substitute for the Proper Magnificat antiphon. Thus, Monteverdi's Vespers are designed for a single category of feast, though as indicated above, the Response, the Magnificat, and the first two psalms can also serve for most other feasts, and there is no reason to exclude the possibility that a choirmaster might have chosen only certain elements from this and any other publication for a particular Vespers service.

As Monteverdi's own rubrics indicate, all the psalms and the Magnificat are based on Gregorian chant psalm (and Magnificat) tones (see the second psalm tone, Ex. 8.3). In addition, the Response is built upon its Gregorian recitation tone, the 'Sonata sopra "Sancta Maria"' employs a simple litany chant addressed to the Virgin (see Ex. 8.4), and the hymn employs its traditional melody as the upper voice (see Ex. 8.5, close to the version in the rite of S. Barbara). These chants are utilised in a number of different ways in these compositions. In the two Magnificats and the 'Sonata', and sometimes in the psalms as well, it appears as a long-note cantus firmus in one or another voice. In the Response and the psalms the chant is thoroughly integrated into the texture, often moving at the same speed as the other voices. Only in the hymn, where the chant is far more melodious than the psalm tones, does it occupy a prominent melodic role as the upper part of four- and eight-part textures, and as the solo line in the three monodic verses.

In all these pieces the chant is ubiquitous rather than simply making an occasional appearance, as in most other uses of a Gregorian cantus firmus in the early seventeenth century. Since the psalm tones are melodically limited and repetitious, Monteverdi builds around them the most varied textures, ranging from virtuoso solo and duet textures, to six-, seven- and eight-part polyphony and homophony. These varied textures generate what came to be known as the *concertato* style: the division of a

Ex. 8.5 Ave maris stella: Monteverdi's apparent unknown source

A - ve_____ ma - ris stel-la, De - i ma-ter al - ma, At-que sem-per Vir - go, Fe-lix coe-li por-ta.

composition into several different contrasting segments through changes of texture, metre and rhythm, performing forces, tempo and style. This differentiation between modern, *concertato* techniques and the conservative, traditional cantus firmus is one of the chief characteristics and highlights of Monteverdi's chant-based compositions in the 1610 Vespers. He opposes modern, opulent variety against the conservative rigidity of the cantus firmus, creating a palpable tension that is a major factor in the aesthetic effect of these settings.

Among the elements in this opulence is the employment of instruments, whether optional or obbligato, in several of the cantus firmus pieces. As already mentioned, the Response is contrafacted from the instrumental toccata that opened the opera *Orfeo*. The harmonic stasis of this toccata is ideally suited to function as a counterpoint to the chant, which consists almost entirely of the static reiteration of a single tone. Monteverdi introduces greater variety into the Response by interpolating an instrumental ritornello in triple metre, which, in its third statement, is accompanied by the voices. Nevertheless, Monteverdi denotes the instruments as optional.

Obbligato instruments are a main feature of the seven-voice Magnificat, which restructures the six-voice Magnificat by assigning many of its vocal roles to instruments. Here the instruments, like the voices, sometimes engage in virtuoso ornamentation, but also play ritornellos, provide counterpoint to the vocal cantus firmus, or, as in the first and last verses, double the voices. The instruments also play ritornellos in 'Dixit Dominus', where they are optional, and in the hymn, where they are not indicated as optional, but might well be considered so. The inclusion of a version of the Magnificat without instruments and the possibility of omitting instruments in other pieces allows for a performance of the main elements of the service by a choirmaster who did not have such instruments at his disposal.

The single composition primarily instrumental in its conception is the 'Sonata sopra "Sancta Maria"' for eight string and wind instruments with organ in addition to the solo soprano voice. This piece is also *concertato* in style, changing metre frequently, and shifting textures from eight-voice polyphony to virtuoso duets of violins or cornetts and quick antiphonal responses between strings and wind instruments. Modern dotted rhythms abound, engaging even the bass instruments. The short vocal cantus firmus appears in the soprano voice only intermittently – eleven times – above the instrumental ensemble.

Apart from the instrumental parts notated by Monteverdi, contemporary performance practice allowed for generous instrumental doubling of vocal parts, especially in thicker textures. Many early music performers today make ample and appropriate use of instruments for doubling in the psalms, the six-voice section of the motet 'Audi coelum' and the four- and eight-voice verses of the hymn. While Monteverdi's own instrumental ensemble provides sufficient instrumental colour, it is not inappropriate to employ other contemporary instruments, such as recorders or flutes, as well.

The remaining four pieces comprise motets for solo voices and continuo, which could just as well be a theorbo, or theorbo with organ, as organ alone (the harpsichord is generally not a suitable continuo instrument for sacred music). These pieces have no connection to a cantus firmus and represent the most modern style of solo singing, requiring a wide vocal range, excellent intonation and well-developed oratorical skills on the part of performers. 'Nigra sum', for solo tenor, is one of Monteverdi's greatest achievements in its consistent melodic and harmonic construction around the principal concept expressed in the text, 'surge' (arise).[19] 'Pulchra es', for two sopranos, illustrates the modern, virtuosic duet style in which one voice takes the lead and the other follows in imitation, often running in parallel thirds with the first. 'Duo seraphim', for three tenors, exhibits extraordinary virtuosity, comparable to Orfeo's aria, 'Possente spirto' in Monteverdi's opera. The motet divides into two segments, the first for two voices, representing the two seraphim, and the second for three voices in response to the Trinitarian text 'et hi tres unum sunt' (and these three are one). All three tenors sing the most extreme virtuoso embellishments, a tour de force of vocal exhibition, which is also characterised by a strong sense of melodic and harmonic direction. The final motet, 'Audi coelum', a prayer to the Virgin for solo tenor with an echo voice responding to the final syllables of several of its words, eventually expands its texture to an imitative six-voice choir when the text reads, 'omnes hanc ergo sequamur' (let all of us, therefore, follow her). The solo first part is largely in recitative style with virtuoso melismas interpolated on several occasions. The echoes sometimes form puns on the words they imitate, since the final letters or syllables echoed constitute words in their own right (e.g., 'gaudio'/'audio', 'benedicam'/'dicam', 'orientalis'/'talis'). A service without instruments other than organ could even include these motets if singers of sufficient capacity were available.

As with most collections of music in the seventeenth century, there are many unknowns regarding the origins and functions of the print itself as well as suitable ways of performing its music. Early commentary debated whether the collection was intended for a single service or constituted a random assemblage of pieces.[20] Graham Dixon has proposed that the music was originally designed for a Vespers of S. Barbara and only later redirected toward the Virgin Mary.[21] The fiercest controversies have raged over the role of the four motets and the 'Sonata sopra "Sancta Maria"', interspersed in the original print between the psalms. In earlier writings on the Vespers, scholars tended to consider them separate from the Vespers liturgical service, since they do not match (though two of their texts overlap) any of the liturgical antiphons for a Marian Vespers. Nevertheless, four of the five texts are Marian in their orientation, and ever since a seminal article by Stephen Bonta in 1967, the growing weight of evidence has pointed to a widespread contemporary practice of substituting texts and even instrumental music for the liturgical antiphons in Vespers services, and most scholars have come to believe that the print was intended to provide music for a single liturgical service, though choirmasters could easily have extracted individual items from the collection.[22]

In recent years, controversy has also arisen regarding the proportional relationships in performance of sections in duple metre versus those in triple metre. Roger Bowers has argued in favour of a strictly mathematical proportional relationship, while I have proposed a more flexible approach based not strictly on numerical proportions, but rather on the unit of beat, the *tactus*.[23] Four of the pieces in Monteverdi's 1610 print employ high clefs, so-called 'chiavette', in the notation of the voices (G_2, C_2, C_3, and C_4 or F_3 clefs; the 'standard' clefs are C_1, C_3, C_4, F_4). Many scholars, myself included, have presented substantive evidence arguing that the high clefs entailed transposition downward, typically by a fourth, in performance. Bowers has recently disputed this point as well, though other scholars have found his arguments deficient.[24] Although there will always be some questions remaining open regarding Monteverdi's Mass and Vespers of 1610, many of the issues confronting earlier scholars are gradually becoming better understood and resolved through the accumulation of evidence from a wide variety of contemporary sources.

NOTES

1. The expedition is described in V. Errante, '"Forse che sì, forse che no": la terza spedizione del duca Vincenzo Gonzaga in Ungheria alla guerra contro il Turco (1601) studiata su documenti inediti', *Archivio storico lombardo*, 42 (1915), 29–34.
2. Documents relating details of this trip are found in S. Parisi, 'The Brussels–Mantua connection: Vincenzo Gonzaga's state voyages to the Low Countries in 1599 and 1608', forthcoming in *Alamire Yearbook*, vol. 6/7.
3. I. Fenlon, 'The Monteverdi Vespers: suggested answers to some fundamental questions', *Early Music*, 5 (1977), 383. Fenlon is mistaken in applying a Marian liturgy to a feast of Christ. The papal indulgence proclaimed in S. Andrea in 1607 at the request of the duke would have been in the context of a solemn, probably musically ostentatious, service.
4. I am grateful to Licia Mari for information on the 1611 events as well as evidence of the duke's chapel of musicians performing in both S. Pietro and S. Andrea.
5. O. Strunk, *Source Readings in Music History*, vol. IV, rev. M. Murata, *The Baroque Era*, New York and London, 1998, p. 29.
6. Fabbri, *Monteverdi*, Cambridge, 1994, p. 102.
7. J. Kurtzman, 'An early seventeenth-century manuscript of *Canzonette e madrigaletti spirituali*', *Studi musicali*, 8 (1979), 149–71.
8. Fabbri, *Monteverdi*, p. 102.
9. The principal studies of this publication are J. Kurtzman, 'The Monteverdi Vespers of 1610 and their relationship with Italian sacred music of the early seventeenth century', Ph.D. dissertation, University of Illinois at Champaign-Urbana, 1972; Kurtzman, 'Some historical perspectives on the Monteverdi Vespers', *Analecta musicologica*, 15 (1974), 29–86; Kurtzman, *Monteverdi: Essays on the Monteverdi Mass and Vespers of 1610*, Houston, 1978; Kurtzman, *The Monteverdi Vespers of 1610: Music, Context, Performance*, Oxford, 1999; and J. Whenham, *Monteverdi: Vespers (1610)*, Cambridge, 1997.
10. Fabbri, *Monteverdi*, p. 109.
11. The title of the Bassus generalis part-book differs somewhat, beginning *Sanctissimae Virgini missa senis vocibus, ad ecclesiarum choros ac vesperae pluribus decantandae*.
12. See P. Besutti, '"Ave Maris Stella": La tradizione mantovana nuovamente posta in musica da Monteverdi', in P. Besutti, T. M. Gialdroni and R. Baroncini (eds.), *Claudio Monteverdi: studi e prospettive, atti del convegno (Mantova, 21–24 ottobre 1993)*, Florence, 1993, pp. 57–77.
13. S. Parisi, 'New documents concerning Monteverdi's relations with the Gonzagas', in Besutti, Gialdroni and Baroncini (eds.), *Claudio Monteverdi*, p. 495.
14. The Mass is in the manuscript Cappella Sistina 107.
15. This information is contained in a letter recently discovered by Licia Mari in Mantova,

Archivio di Stato, Archivio Gonzaga, busta 2721, fasc. III, cc. 55–56.
16. Quoted in Fabbri, *Monteverdi*, p. 120.
17. Quoted from an undated letter by Grillo to Monteverdi in Fabbri, *Monteverdi*, p. 118.
18. The manuscript, possibly from the late seventeenth or early eighteenth century, is found together with one of the cathedral's copies of Monteverdi's print. It was penned by one Lorenzo Tonelli, about whom we currently have no other information. The six vocal parts of the Mass are transposed down a fourth in this *partitura*, in keeping with the standard practice of performing compositions notated in high clefs a fourth or a fifth lower than notated.
19. For a detailed analysis of 'Nigra sum', see Kurtzman, *The Monteverdi Vespers of 1610*, pp. 308–24.
20. See the account and bibliography of the vitriolic debate between Hans Redlich and Leo Schrade in Kurtzman, *The Monteverdi Vespers of 1610*, pp. 16–19.
21. G. Dixon, 'Monteverdi's Vespers of 1610: "della Beata Vergine"?', *Early Music*, 15 (1987), 386–9.
22. S. Bonta, 'Liturgical problems in Monteverdi's Marian Vespers', *Journal of the American Musicological Society*, 20 (1967), 87–106. On the practice of antiphon substitutions, see also J. Armstrong, 'The Antiphonae, seu sacrae cantiones (1613) of Giovanni Francesco Anerio: a liturgical study' *Analecta musicologica*, 14 (1974), 89–150; A. M. Cummings, 'Toward an interpretation of the sixteenth-century motet', *Journal of the American Musicological Society*, 34 (1981), 43–59; and J. Kurtzman, '*Per fare il Vespro meno tedioso*: Don Pietro Maria Marsolo and the "antiphon problem"', in B. H. Haggh (ed.), *Essays on Music and Culture in Honor of Herbert Kellman*, Paris, 2001, pp. 411–22. See also the discussion of the substitution issue in Kurtzman, *The Monteverdi Vespers of 1610*, pp. 56–78.
23. R. Bowers, 'Some reflection upon notation and proportions in Monteverdi's Mass and Vespers of 1610', *Music and Letters*, 73 (1992), 347–98; Kurtzman, *The Monteverdi Vespers of 1610*, pp. 433–66.
24. See the recent discussion in R. Bowers, 'An "aberration" reviewed: the reconciliation of inconsistent clef-systems in Monteverdi's Mass and Vespers of 1610', *Early Music*, 31 (2003), 527–38; A. Parrott, 'Monteverdi: onwards and downwards', *Early Music*, 32 (2004), 303–18; and A. Johnstone, "High" clefs in composition and performance', *Early Music*, 34 (2006), 29–54; see also Chapter 14, 'Monteverdi in Performance', below. As indicated in note 20 above, the manuscript organ partitura of the *Missa in illo tempore* in Brescia transposes all voices of the mass, which were originally notated in the high clefs, downward by a fourth.

VII

Bibliography

Armstrong, James. "The Antiphonae, seu sacrae cantiones (1613) of Giovanni Francesco Anerio: a liturgical study," *Analecta Musicologica* 14 (1974), 89–150.

Besutti, Paola. "'Ave Maris Stella:' La tradizione mantovane nuovamente posta in musica da Monteverdi," in Paola Besutti, Teresa M. Gialdroni and Rodolfo Baroncini (eds), *Claudio Monteverdi: studi e prospettive, atti del convegno (Mantova, 21-24 ottobre 1993)* (Florence: Leo S. Olschki, 1993), 55–77.

Bonta, Steven. "Liturgical problems in Monteverdi's Marian Vespers," *Journal of the American Musicological Society* 20 (1967), 87–106.

Bowers, Roger. "Some reflection upon notation and proportions in Monteverdi's Mass and Vespers of 1610," *Music & Letters* 73 (1992), 347–98.

_____. "An 'aberration' reviewed: the reconciliation of inconsistent clef-systems in Monteverdi's Mass and Vespers of 1610," *Early Music* 31 (2003), 527–38.

Cummings, Anthony M. "Toward an interpretation of the sixteenth-century motet," *Journal of the American Musicological Society* 34 (1981), 43–59.

Dixon, Graham. "Monteverdi's Vespers of 1610: 'della Beata Vergine'?" *Early Music* 15 (1987), 386–9.

Errante, Vincenzo. "'Forse che sì, forse che no:' la terza spedizione del duca Vincenzo Gonzaga in Ungheria alla guerra contro il Turco (1601) studiata su document inediti," *Archivio storico lombardo* 42 (1915), 29–34.

Fabbri, Paolo. *Monteverdi*, translated by Tim Carter (Cambridge: Cambridge University Press, 1994).

Fenlon, Iain. "The Monteverdi Vespers: suggested answers to some fundamental questions," *Early Music* 5 (1977), 380–87.

Johnstone, Andrew. "'High' clefs in composition and performance," *Early Music* 34 (2006), 29–54.

Kurtzman, Jeffrey. "An early seventeenth-century manuscript of Canzonette e madrigaletti sprirituali," *Studi musicali* 8 (1979), 149–71.

_____. "Per fare il vespro meno tedioso: Don Pietro Maria Marsolo and the 'antiphon problem'," in Barbara H. Haggh (ed.), Essays on Music and Culture in Honor of Herbert Kellman (Paris, Minerve, 2001), 411–22.

_____. *The Monteverdi Vespers of 1610: Music, Context, Performance* (Oxford: Oxford University Press, 1999).

_____. "The Monteverdi Vespers of 1610 and their relationship with Italian sacred music of the early seventeenth century" (Ph.D. dissertation, University of Illinois at Urbana-Champaign, 1972).

_____. "Some historical perspectives on the Monteverdi Vespers," *Analecta Musicologica* 15 (1975), 29–86.

_____. *Essays on the Monteverdi Mass and Vespers of 1610* (Houston: Rice University Studies, 1978).

Parisi, Susan. "The Brussels-Mantua connection: Vincenzo Gonzaga's state voyages to the Low Countries in 1599 and 1608," *Alamire Yearbook* 7 (2008), 275–98.

_____. "New documents concerning Monteverdi's relations with the Gonzagas," in Paola Besutti, Teresa M. Gialdroni and Rodolfo Baroncini, eds, *Claudio Monteverdi: studi e prospettive, atti del convegno (Mantova, 21–24 ottobre 1993)* (Florence, Leo S. Olschki, 1993), 77–511.

Parrott, Andrew. ""Monteverdi: onwards and downwards," *Early Music* 32 (2004), 303–18.

Stevens, Denis. *The Letters of Claudio Monteverdi*, revised ed. (Oxford: Clarendon Press, 1995).

Strunk, Oliver. *Source Readings in Music History* 4, revised by Margaret Murata, *The Baroque Era* (New York and London, 1998).

Whenham, John. *Monteverdi: Vespers (1610)* (Cambridge: Cambridge University Press, 1997).

VIII

'Laetatus sum' (1610)[1]

Seven of the fourteen compositions comprising Monteverdi's *Vespro della Beata Vergine* are based on psalm or Magnificat tones, so it is appropriate that this analysis be devoted to one of those pieces. However, with the exception of the two settings of the Magnificat, which are parallel in many respects, the role of the psalm tone in the construction of each psalm differs significantly, and the psalms differ radically from the Magnificats. Therefore, the analysis of no single composition can serve as a model for the others, and each must be addressed separately, with quite different observations to be drawn from each. Of these seven compositions, the six-voice Psalm 121 (*Book of Common Prayer* 122), 'Laetatus sum', is the most complexly organised and the one whose compositional techniques most adumbrate methods of organising *concertato* psalms in subsequent decades. Rather than the chant serving as an organising force, as in the other psalms and the two Magnificats, the structure of the text is the principal organising element. The cantus firmus is mixed together with repetitive bass patterns, imitative polyphony, chordal homophony, virtuoso solo melismas, duets, trios and *falsibordoni*. The chant appears only intermittently, either as a solo vocal line or as a single voice in a four- or six-part texture. When it does appear, the chant is usually accorded some prominence either by its position in the texture or by long note values.

Psalm texts normally consist of two-verse couplets, with each verse divided into two hemistiches. Even if a psalm text does not strictly follow this pattern (such as a grouping of three verses, or a single verse with three separate segments), the structure of the psalm tones – which are rigidly divided into two hemistiches (see Ex. 8.3 in the preceding chapter) – force this two-part organisation upon the text.

The text of 'Laetatus sum', as found in the Latin Vulgate, is as follows (the first word in each couplet is in bold type):[2]

156

1. **Laetatus** sum in his quae dicta sunt mihi:	I rejoiced in what was said to me:
In domum Domini ibimus.	We will go to the house of the Lord.
2. Stantes erant pedes nostri	Our feet were standing
In atriis tuis, Jerusalem.	In your halls, Jerusalem.
3. **Jerusalem**, quae aedificatur ut civitas,	Jerusalem, which is built as a city,
Cuius participatio eius in idipsum.	Is one with itself.
4. Illuc enim ascenderunt tribus, tribus	For there the tribes ascended, the tribes of the Lord,
Domini, Testimonium Israel,	The witness of Israel,
Ad confitendum nomini Domini.	For acknowledging the name of the Lord.
5. **Quia** illic sederunt sedes in judicio,	For there the thrones sit in judgment,
Sedes super domum David.	The thrones over the house of David.
6. Rogate quae ad pacem sunt Jerusalem,	Pray for the peace of Jerusalem,
Et abundantia diligentibus te.	And prosperity for those who love you.
7. **Fiat** pax in virtute tua,	Let there be peace in your strength,
Et abundantia in turribus tuis.	And abundance in your ramparts.
8. Propter fratres meos et proximos meos,	For the sake of my brothers and my neighbours,
Loquebar pacem de te.	I was saying, 'Peace be with you.'
9. Propter domum Domini Dei nostri,	For the sake of the house of the Lord our God,
Quaesivi bona tibi.	I sought good things for you.
10. **Gloria** Patri et Filio et Spiritui Sancto,	Glory to the Father and the Son and the Holy Spirit,
11. Sicut erat in principio et nunc et semper,	As it was in the beginning and now and forever,
Et in saecula saeculorum. Amen.	For all ages. Amen.

The psalm proper consists of four couplets and one additional verse, while the last two verses comprise the lesser doxology, which is appended to the end of all psalms when serving in the liturgy. Monteverdi, as he typically does, sets the beginning of the doxology off from the rest of the psalm to emphasise its role as a distinct textual unit. His approach to the structure of the text is highly original: he sets each couplet's first verse, as well as the isolated final verse of the psalm proper (i.e., every odd-numbered verse), to an identical walking bass in steady crotchets

157 *'Laetatus sum'* (1610)

Ex. III.1

Ex. III.2

Ex. III.3

(Ex. III.1). This is the first known appearance of a repetitious bass in an Italian psalm setting; later, in the 1630s and 1640s, ostinato basses became common in Italian psalmody. The walking bass as well as the remainder of the psalm is in the second mode, transposed a fourth upward to G by means of a one-flat signature (*cantus mollis*), as was normal for this mode. The note E is also quite often flattened by means of an accidental, making the mode analogous in many respects to the modern G minor. The second mode serves to harmonise the second psalm tone chant (see Ex. 8.3 in the preceding chapter), likewise transposed up a fourth.

What prompted Monteverdi to devise such a rhythmically steady, repeated bass is likely the concept of stasis and durability conveyed in the text through the perennial prosperity and peace of Jerusalem. The walking bass, with its octave leaps and reversals of direction, also has a lively character suitable to the ethos of rejoicing with which the psalm begins and continues. Another bass pattern, slower in its movement and with some variation in its repetition, supports verses 2 and 6 (Ex. III.2). This pattern is not entirely new, but rather a variant of the walking bass which begins in the major (*cantus durus*) rather than the minor (*cantus mollis*) (see Ex. III.3, in which the two basses are compared). Moreover, as John Whenham has pointed out, its second phrase bears a notable resemblance to the typical *Romanesca* bass.[3] Yet another two bass patterns are employed for verses 4, 8, and the doxology (Exx. III.4a and III.4b).

Ex. III.4a

Ex. III.4b

Ex. III.5

The first of these, a sustained G minor triad interrupted briefly by its dominant, underlies lengthy virtuoso melismas at the beginning of verses 4 and 8 (see Ex. III.5, verse 4). At the beginning of the doxology the sustained triad turns to G major, yielding at first not to its dominant, but rather to another sustained chord on C, finally turning back to D as dominant after the second G major triad. The fourth bass, which each time follows immediately after the third, is varied through truncation and diminution in verse 8, and the varied version returns once more for the final verse of the doxology. Following Gioseffe Zarlino's classification and description of the twelve modes, the regular cadences of the second mode, transposed to G, are on D, B-flat and G.[4] According to Monteverdi's contemporary, the theorist and composer Adriano Banchieri, the most common cadence notes for the second psalm tone transposed up a fourth are also D, B-flat and G.[5] In fact, Monteverdi's most prominent cadences are on the major triads of G and D (both half- and full-cadences on D), with only three cadences on B-flat in the entire psalm, embedded in the fourth bass pattern.

As indicated above, the psalm tone appears irregularly in 'Laetatus sum'. The psalm text begins with the tenor voice alone singing the second tone in comparatively slow note values, though with its leading note sharpened in order to create a strong cadence on G. The psalm tone is not heard again until verse 4, after the lengthy melismas on 'Illuc', where the cantus part sings the first hemistich to the recitation tone, harmonised in measured *falsobordone* by the other voices. For the second hemistich ('ad confitendum nomini Dei nostri'), the recitation tone shifts to the altus voice at its original *cantus durus* pitch level of F, then is repeated in the cantus back in *cantus mollis* on B-flat, both times in long note values, distinguishing the psalm tone from the rest of the texture. The psalm tone is next heard after the lower voices have presented the first hemistich of verse 6 ('Rogate quae ad pacem sunt Jerusalem'). At that point the cantus alone sings the entire first hemistich of the tone, including its *initium*, joined by the lower voices as the tone continues for the second hemistich. The other soprano voice, the sextus, takes up the tone in verse 7 ('Fiat pax in virtute tua') for another full statement, accompanied throughout by the three lowest voices. The chant is more hidden in the texture of verse 8 ('Propter fratres'), appearing after the opening melismas in the sextus voice as a recitation tone for the first hemistich, then in the altus a fourth lower (*cantus durus*) for the second hemistich ('Loquebar pacem de te'), only to be repeated in the sextus, once again in *cantus mollis*. Parallel to verse 4, the second hemistich is sung in longer note values by both the altus and sextus. The chant then disappears until the final verse of the doxology ('Sicut erat in principio'), where the first hemistich of the recitation tone is again heard in the cantus part, commencing with an unmeasured *falsobordone*.

Whether in this psalm, where the repetitive bass patterns enforce not only a certain continuity, but also a degree of uniformity, or in the other psalms and the two Magnificats, where the psalm or Magnificat tone is a principal unifying factor in its repetitions, Monteverdi's imagination and skill are revealed in the variety of textures and modes of expression he opposes to these elements of conformity. Indeed, the aesthetic effect of these compositions based on the psalm and Magnificat chants is due in substantial measure to the tension Monteverdi achieves between repetitious consistency on the one hand and substantial variety on the other. This compositional principle can readily be seen by comparing the beginnings of verses 1, 3 and 9 of 'Laetatus sum', all built over the walking bass pattern, which supports gradually increasing textures in each of its reiterations (see Exx. III.6a, III.6b, III.6c). The second bass pattern also supports a variety of textures and styles, ranging from a solo intonation of the psalm tone to paired duets to imitative textures. The fourth bass pattern normally underlies a full six-voice sonority. This type of structural process, whereby the bass remains the same or largely the same, while the upper parts are varied, is known as strophic variation. Monteverdi is sparing in his madrigalesque interpretations of words of the text in his 1610 psalm settings, and 'Laetatus sum' offers limited scope for the analyst seeking word-tone relationships. The suitability of the

160

Ex. III.6a

Ex. III.6b

Ex. III.6c

lively walking bass to the general emotional orientation of the text has already been mentioned. John Whenham has called attention to the first verse's first-person singular, set for a single voice part, while the first-person plural of the second verse results in a six-voice texture.[6] The words 'civitas' (city, in reference to Jerusalem) in verse 3, and 'pax' (peace) and 'abundantia' (prosperity or abundance) in verse 7 also receive modest melismatic emphasis. Otherwise one can only point to such vague relationships as the solid, steady imitative descending scales in the first hemistich of verse 2 figuring 'Stantes erant pedes nostri' (our feet were standing) or the energetic reiterations of 'ad confitendum' (for acknowledging) in the second hemistich of the fourth verse. Whenham has also taken the *Romanesca* bass as a possible reference to Rome as the centre of the Christian world, analogous to the text's 'Jerusalem' as the centre of the Hebrew world of King David's time.[7] Even though Monteverdi is often praised for his attention to the rhetorical setting of his texts and to careful word declamation, that is not always true, for there are many instances in his works where purely musical factors clearly take precedence over the text.[8] Such is the case at the beginning of verses 4 and 8, where the first word of the fourth verse is the adverb 'Illuc' (there), while the first word of the eighth verse is the preposition 'Propter' (because of or for the sake of). Although both words fulfil important grammatical functions in their respective verses, neither is the type of word that justifies either by itself nor by its significance in the verse such extraordinary melismatic treatment, and Monteverdi's only reason for setting them in this manner is his obvious desire to interrupt the regularity of the musical verse patterns he has already established in order to begin these two verses with virtuosic display. At the beginning of the doxology, however, when the sustained bass that supported these virtuoso melismas returns in its major version, the melisma abandons its virtuosic character in favour of a six-voice, imitative texture. Here the melisma is fully appropriate to the first word of the verse, 'Gloria', which Monteverdi sets melismatically several times in the course of the 1610 Vespers. The shift to a six-voice imitative texture, supported now by G major and C major harmonies, underscores the separateness of the doxology as a textual unit.

In 'Laetatus sum', it was not so much words, but rather the musical structure that was foremost in Monteverdi's mind. Although that structure is organised around the verse structure of the psalm text, individual words and phrases count for little in his compositional workshop in this piece.

VIII

1. For other analytical comments on this psalm, see John Whenham, *Monteverdi: Vespers (1610)*, Cambridge, 1997, pp. 67–72; and Jeffrey Kurtzman, *The Monteverdi Vespers of 1610: Music, Context, Performance*, Oxford, 1999, pp. 223–30.
2. I am grateful to Judith Evans-Grubb for assistance with details of the English translation.
3. Whenham, *Monteverdi: Vespers (1610)*, p. 71. The beginning of the walking bass itself follows the typical *Romanesca* outline.
4. See G. Zarlino, trans. V. Cohen, *On the modes: part four of 'Le istitutioni harmoniche'*, 1558, New Haven and London, 1983, pp. 58–61.
5. A. Banchieri, *Conclusioni nel suono dell'organo*, Bologna, 1609; reprinted New York, 1975, p. 39; and Banchieri, *Cartella musicale nel canto figurato fermo, & contrapunto*, Venice, 1614; reprinted Bologna, 1968, p. 71.
6. Whenham, *Monteverdi: Vespers (1610)*, p. 71.
7. Ibid., pp. 71–2.
8. On this subject, see T. Carter, 'Two Monteverdi problems, and why they matter', *Journal of Musicology*, 19 (2002), 417–33.

Bibliography

Banchieri, Adriano. *Cartella musicale nel canto figurato fermo, & contrapunto* (Venice: Giacomo Vincenti, 1614; facs. ed. Bologna: Arnoldo Forni, 1968).

_____. *Conclusioni nel suono dell'organo* (Bologna: Heredi Di Gio Rossi, 1609; facs. ed. New York: Broude Brothers, 1975).

Carter, Tim. "Two Monteverdi problems, and why they matter," *Journal of Musicology* 19 (2002), 417–33.

Cohen, Vered, trans. *On the modes: part four of "Le istitutioni harmoniche,"* 1558 (New Haven and London: Yale University Press, 1983).

Kurtzman, Jeffrey. *The Monteverdi Vespers of 1610: Music, Context, Performance* (Oxford: Oxford University Press, 1999).

Stevens, Denis. *The Letters of Claudio Monteverdi*, revised ed. (Oxford: Clarendon Press, 1995).

Whenham, John. *Monteverdi: Vespers (1610)* (Cambridge: Cambridge University Press, 1997).

Zarlino, Gioseffe. See Cohen, Vered.

IX

Licia Mari and Jeffrey Kurtzman

A Monteverdi Vespers in 1611

In a letter dated 14 May 1611, one Lorenzo Campagna, a servant of Mantua's Duke Vincenzo Gonzaga, wrote to the Marchese Fabio Gonzaga regarding a Vespers service with music newly composed by Claudio Monteverdi:

Lorenzo Campagna to the Marchese Fabio Gonzaga

My most Illustrious Lord and most revered Patron

Tomorrow the [Feast of the] Sensa ends, and its vigil, when His Serene Highness went to Sant'Andrea, with all the Cavaliers of the Order, in a gorgeous cavalcade, where, as usual, solemn Vespers were sung with most beautiful music, newly composed by Signor Claudio Monteverdi. Present were the most serene *infante* and Monsignor, the most illustrious Cardinal, and Signor Don Cesare, Prince of Guastalla, in an enclosure [*ghabinetto*] made especially for him in order not to require any formality. Near it was another larger one with some 50 Jesuit fathers, who were here for a meeting of the Chapter. His Highness wanted them to see the ceremony.[1] In addition, he himself had shown them his treasures with his own hands.[2] Then came the Signor Prince of Bozzolo, who did not come to Sant'Andrea the day of the Sensa, but yesterday kissed the hand of His Highness, and His Highness showed him his jewels and the treasures he possesses [which] he usually displays to princes. Before the Mass the day of the Sensa, Signor Marchese Gian Thomaso Canossa was made a Cavalier of the Order of the Redeemer, in place of the Marchese his brother; and His Most Serene Highness promised in the coming year to make Signor Conte Rivara [a member of the Order]. And yesterday morning the Office was celebrated for the soul of the aforesaid Marchese, with the greatest solemnity. This is all that has newly occurred, but in order not to annoy you further, I recommend myself to the good graces of Your Illustrious Lord, and pray God our Lord all the greatest prosperity for you.[3]

Like so many documents mentioning musical performances in this period, the letter is frustratingly short on details (it is transcribed in Appendix 1 and reproduced in facsimile as illus.1). But just the opening lines raise several questions: (1) what was the Sensa and what was its significance? (2) what is the Order of Cavaliers and why were they taking part (see Appen-

dix 2)? (3) what was the music by Monteverdi that was performed? and (4) why did this Vespers service with Monteverdi's music take place in Sant'Andrea?

The Feast of the Sensa in Mantua has some parallels with the much better known feast of the Sensa in Venice, an extended annual spring festival with overtones of fertility rites that climaxed on Ascension Sunday with the elaborate ceremonial marriage of Venice to the sea.[4] As such, it represented a conjoining of one of the most important Christological feasts of the year with the celebration of the city's source of civic wealth and political power. The marriage included a procession of the Doge and Signoria from St Mark's to the ceremonial civic barge, the *bucintoro*, docked at the piazzetta, embarkation of the procession onto the barge, sailing out to the mouth of the lagoon while motets were sung, and consummating the traditional marriage of Venice to the sea by dropping a consecrated ring into the waters, thereby establishing the city's dominion over the sea. The *bucintoro* then returned to the dock and everyone disembarked for further festivities.[5]

In Mantua, the Feast of the Sensa had also for a long time been a spring festival with fertility implications coupled with the Feast of the Ascension. The festivities, from at least the late 16th century, included fair and elaborate processions, including one in a small barge, the *burchiello*, from which fish were thrown out to the populace. As in Venice, the Sensa in Mantua joined religious and civic functions, celebrating the legitimacy, authority and wealth of the Gonzaga dukes and the prosperity they brought to Mantua. Unique to the Mantuan Sensa and a central focus of the festivities was the exposition of the city's most treasured relic, the drop of blood of the wounded Christ, mixed with a small amount of the earth of Golgotha, which was kept under lock and key in a special crypt in the Church of Sant'Andrea.

1 Letter dated 14 May 1611 from Lorenzo Campagna, servant of the Duke of Mantua, to the Marchese Fabio Gonzaga regarding a Vespers service with music by Monteverdi (Mantua, Archivio Gonzaga 2721, fasc.II. ff.55–56)

The relic also included a small piece of the sponge soaked in vinegar that a Roman soldier had offered to Christ on the cross after He had called for water.

The festivities encompassed processions and prayers on Monday, Tuesday and Wednesday (called Rogation days), a first exposition of the blood of Christ at First Vespers on the vigil of Ascension Day; the procession in the *burchiello*, a pontifical Mass and a second exposition of the blood of Christ on Ascension Day itself (Thursday), followed by a third exposition of the blood that evening at Second Vespers; and funeral rites for deceased members of the Knights

1 continued

of the Order of the Redeemer on Friday.[6] As with the Venetian Sensa, visitors came from afar to witness the event, especially the exposition of the blood.[7] In 1611, Ascension Day was on 12 May with the vigil the evening of 11 May. While the Venetian Sensa continued to the end of the Republic in 1797, the Mantuan version declined after the imperial sack of Mantua in 1630 and the end of Gonzaga domination.[8]

Campagna's letter mentions a procession of cavaliers on horseback. The reference is to the Knights of the Order of the Redeemer, founded by Vincenzo Gonzaga on Sunday 25 May 1608 in the Church of Sant'Andrea. The first knight of the order had been his son Francesco and the service had formed part of the ceremonies surrounding the wedding of Francesco with Margherita of Savoy for which

Monteverdi's opera *Arianna* was written and premièred three days later.[9] In 1608, Ascension Day had been on 15 May, but the Ascension Day services and the Sensa had been postponed to the day after Pentecost in order to coincide with Francesco and Margherita's wedding festivities.[10] Further reunions of the Knights of the Order of the Redeemer were irregular, the first occurring on 29 June 1609 and the second as part of the Sensa celebrations on 14 May 1611.[11]

In addition to the palace church of Santa Barbara the Gonzaga dukes celebrated many important events in both Sant'Andrea and the cathedral of San Pietro, larger and more public venues than Santa Barbara. The dukes exerted considerable influence over ceremonies in both Sant'Andrea and San Pietro; Sant'Andrea was a collegiate church and the *primicerio* was often a Gonzaga (Lodovico Gonzaga, son of Prospero of the Rodolfo branch of the family, was elected *primicerio* in 1610).[12] A register of 1588–90 indicates that payment for the master of ceremonies, the bell ringer and the instrumentalists in Sant'Andrea came from the court.[13] As noted above, Duke Vincenzo had postponed the Ascension Day festivities in Sant'Andrea until the day after Pentecost in 1608, and in 1610 the duke had again postponed the Ascension Day ceremonies to Pentecost itself because he had been away for a 'purge'.[14] Claudio Monteverdi, as *mastro e de la camera e de la chiesa*, would have been responsible for the music for this and other major services involving the Gonzaga court in whatever church the function took place.[15] Indeed, it is probable that Monteverdi had been annually responsible for the music for the Feast of the Sensa for several years before 1611.

Ippolito Donesmondi has left us two overlapping accounts of the principal festivities of the Ascension Day ceremonies.[16] The other accounts of these festivities, by Giovanni Battista Cremonesi and Federigo Amadei, are more detailed, but do not conflict in any significant way with those of Donesmondi.[17] The ceremonies began before Vespers with a procession of the bishop and the cathedral chapter from the cathedral to Sant'Andrea. From the ducal palace there arrived a cavalcade of the Knights of the Order of the Redeemer preceding the duke. At First Vespers, attended by a large quantity of the populace, a Carmelite monk recited an oration in praise of the holy blood, half in Latin for the benefit of foreigners,

and half in Italian.[18] The bishop then intoned solemn Vespers while the musicians sang; at the Magnificat, the duke and the Knights of the Order of the Redeemer were incensed by the *Prima Dignità* of the cathedral, the master of ceremonies of the bishop, the master of ceremonies of the ducal church of Santa Barbara, and the head chaplain. Upon completion of Vespers, the holy blood and the sponge, each in its own vessel, were transported from the high altar to a specially built platform covered with the finest brocade to the sound of trumpets and various instruments while the large bell of the piazza tower rang in a unique manner reserved for this occasion. The duke and princes of Mantua personally carried the baldachin above the relics, which were returned to the high altar after a benediction by the bishop. When the service was over, the relics were placed in a location where they were continuously guarded.[19]

The next day saw a lay procession from the cathedral to Sant'Andrea of all the professions (*offitij*) and artisan-trades (*arti*) of the city. According to an ancient tradition, a small boat (*burchiello*) was carried from the Porta di San Giorgio to Sant'Andrea, from which three men dressed as fishermen and representing the apostles Peter, John and Andrew, threw fish out to the populace as symbols of divine grace. After the procession, the bishop performed a pontifical Mass during which the holy blood was exposed again to the populace with the assistance of the princes and principal citizens, accompanied by instruments, singing and the ringing of the same tower bell as the previous evening. All the professions and artisan-trades again processed to present their offerings to the sacred relic, and gifts were also presented to the duke. Cremonesi places the oration in Latin and Italian by a Carmelite monk in the morning's celebrations rather than at First Vespers as described above.[20]

After Second Vespers was said in the afternoon (without a sermon), the holy blood was once again exposed as at First Vespers, this time in an ebony chest from the church of Santa Barbara encrusted with crystals and ornamented with silver. At the end of the service, to the accompaniment not only of the tower bell, but the others of the city, the relics were ceremoniously returned to the crypt where they were stored throughout the year.[21]

Other letters than the one quoted above, mostly to Fabio Gonzaga, who was ill and could not attend,[22] describe additional aspects of the Sensa of 1611. Prince Francesco arrived with his wife Margherita by 9 May, and, according to Campagna, 'a most beautiful Ascension was being prepared'.[23] On 11 May, the Prince of Bozzolo was expected to arrive and several individuals were to be made 'Knights of the Order of the Most Holy Blood of our Lord Jesus Christ' (evidently another appellation for the Knights of the Order of the Redeemer, who were inducted on 11 May).[24] On 13 May, Scipione, the son of the Prince of Bozzolo, arrived in Mantua to kiss the hand of the duke (Campagna's letter names the Prince of Bozzolo himself who kissed the duke's hand).[25] A letter at the end of the Sensa described it as

a very beautiful fair, both of goods and of people in large quantity and much more beautiful for those ladies for whom the duke paid, each costing some five or six hundred *scudi*. The Signor Marchese Giovanni Tommaso Canossa was inducted into the Order on Ascension Day, and the Signor Conte Rivara was promised induction the next time he attended chapel in Sant'Andrea. It is said that His Highness will leave Tuesday for Lago di Garda.[26]

Campagna's letter of 14 May mentions only First Vespers as featuring music by Monteverdi. What music was this, and was it entirely new? Monteverdi had published his *Missa Senis vocibus* and *Vespro della Beata Vergine* in September 1610 (the dedication is dated 1 September). However, the Vespers liturgy for Feasts of the Virgin and for Ascension Day are different. Table I shows the principal texts (apart from antiphons and the hymn) for First and Second Vespers for Feasts of both the BVM and Ascension Day. Only two of the psalms and the Magnificat overlap the two cursus, so that it is conceivable that the music performed on 11 May 1611 included *Dixit Dominus*, *Laudate pueri* and one of the Magnificats from the *Vespro della Beata Vergine*, though Campagna's phrase *nuova inventione* suggests even more recent settings by Monteverdi. A letter of 26 March 1611 from Monteverdi to Prince Francesco Gonzaga conveys with it a *Dixit* for eight voices that had been requested by him, along with two motets. However, these pieces were for Francesco's own chapel at Casale Monferrato, and it is not obvious that this *Dixit* would have also served for the Sensa in Mantua.[27] If Monteverdi composed a new *Dixit* for the Sensa rather than using the one from the 1610 print, then he may well have composed a new

Laudate pueri and Magnificat as well. The remaining three psalms would have had to have been different from those of the 1610 print and were certainly newly composed rather than resurrected from some earlier celebration. Vincenzo Gonzaga's demand for new music was insatiable, and it does not seem to have been the practice in Mantua to rehash large amounts of older music for major celebrations.[28]

When might Monteverdi have written this music of 'new invention'? We know he was away in Rome from at least early October 1610 to sometime before Christmas, since he wrote on 28 December from Mantua to Cardinal Ferdinando Gonzaga entreating assistance in having his son Francesco accepted into the Roman seminary.[29] That leaves a period of some four months, during which he wrote the *Dixit* he sent to the duke on 26 March, and whatever other music it was necessary to compose for the Ascension Day Vespers on 11 May.

Unfortunately, Campagna says nothing at all about the style of the music or what singers and instrumentalists may have taken part. It is hard to imagine, though, that for such an important feast, putting on public display the city's most sacred relic, the Order of the Redeemer, and Gonzaga ducal authority, that the music was not of a splendid character, employing voices and instruments in the *concertato* style similar to the first three psalms or the Magnificat *a7* of the *Vespro della Beata Vergine*. Whether there were again motets or perhaps instrumental music substituting for plainchant antiphons is anyone's guess, though by this time it had become quite common to insert motets and

Table 1 The principal texts (apart from antiphons and the hymn) for First and Second Vespers for Feasts of the BVM and Ascension Day

Psalm cursus for Feast of the Ascension	Psalm cursus for Marian Vespers
First and Second Vespers	First and Second Vespers
Dixit Dominus	Dixit Dominus
Confitebor tibi	Laudate pueri
Beatus vir	Laetatus sum
Laudate pueri	Nisi Dominus
Laudate Dominum	Lauda Jerusalem
Magnificat	Magnificat

instrumental music into Vespers services as substitutes for antiphons.[30] Perhaps the opening Respond, like that of the 1610 Vespers, also employed the fanfare adapted from the toccata of *Orfeo* as the Respond published in 1610, considered by some scholars as a kind of 'entrance' piece for the Gonzagas. All this is speculative, but within the scope of Monteverdi's duties at Mantua and consistent with the character of the composer's already published Vespers.

Campagna's letter, like several other documents,[31] highlights the fact that what sacred music we have by Monteverdi, almost all of it published, may well be a truncated torso of a much larger body of music forever lost. If Monteverdi had been responsible for the music for previous Sensa festivities, as he most likely had been, then there is a substantial amount of lost, festive Vespers music for this service alone, not to speak of other important celebrations over the previous decade, of which the *Missa senis vocibus* and *Vespro della Beata Vergine* represent only a single, if magnificent, echo.

Appendix I

Letter of Lorenzo Campagna, 14 May 1611
Mantua, Archivio Gonzaga 2721, fasc. III. ff.55–56

Lorenzo Campagna al Marchese Fabio Gonzaga

Illustrissimo signor mio et Padrone Colendissimo

Domani finisce la Senssa, et la uigilia di essa, che *Sua Altezza Serenissima* ando in santo Andrea, con tutti li Cauaglieri, del'ordine, con bellissima caualcata, doue si canto al solito Il Vespro solene, con bellissima musica, et Nuoua inventione, del signor Monte Verdi, doue ui era la serenissima Infante, et Monsignor Illustrissimo Cardinale, et Il signor Don Cesare Principe di Guastalla, in vn Ghabinetto fattogli à Posta, per non metterssi in necessita, de cirimonie, à Presso a quello, ve ne era vn altro più Grande, doue gli era, da 50 Padri Glesuiti, che per l'occasione del Capitolo fatto qui, Sua Altezza à voluto, che uedi quella cirimonia, oltre, che lui proprio, gli ha mostrato di propria mano quanto tiene, di Poi vene Il signor Principe di Buozzolo, Il qual Il Giorno della Senssa non vene, in santo Andrea; ma hieri bacciò le mani à Sua Altezza, et se gli mostro le Gioie, et tutto, quello, che tiene detta Altezza, solitti à Mostrarsi a Principi. Il signor Marchese Gian Thomaso Canossa fu fatto il Giorno della Senssa, avanti la Messa, Cauagliero dell'ordine del Redentore, in loco del Marchese suo fratello, et questo Anno che uiene, Sua Altezza Serenissima à Promesso far Il signor Conte Rivara. Et Hieri mattina si cellebro l'ufficio,

per l'anima del soddetto Marchese, con Grandissima solenita; che è quanto di nouo occore, et per non fastidirla piu, mi racomando nella buona Gratia di Vostra Signoria Illustrissima col Pregargli da Dio nostro signore ogni maggior Prosperita.

Di Mantova li 14 Maggio 1611

Di Vostra Signoria Illustrissima

Vmilissimo et devotissimo servitore

Lorenzo Campagna

Appendix 2
Identification of individuals named in Campagna's letter

CAMPAGNA, LORENZO. Together with his brother Giulio, Master of the Ducal Wardrobe. Performed various duties, such as custodian of the duke's possessions and organizer of events.[32]

GONZAGA, FABIO (1546–after 1616). Natural son of Alessandro Gonzaga, who was himself the natural son of Federico, former Duke of Mantua. Cousin and servant to Duke Vincenzo I. Governor of Monferrato and Mantua, General of the armies of Duke Vincenzo. Recipient of dedications of several sonnets by Torquato Tasso.[33]

GONZAGA, VINCENZO (1562–1612). Duke of Mantua. Identified in letter as *Sua Altezza Serenissima*.

MARGHERITA DI SAVOIA (1589–1655). Wife of Prince Francesco Gonzaga. Identified in letter as *serenissima infante*.

GONZAGA, FERDINANDO (1587–1626). Second son of Duke Vincenzo Gonzaga. Created cardinal in 1607. Identified in letter as *Monsignor Illustrissimo Cardinale*.

GONZAGA, CESARE (1592–1632). Prince of Guastalla. Member of another branch of the Gonzaga family who ruled in Guastalla.

GONZAGA, SCIPIONE (1594–1670). Prince of Bozzolo. Son of Ferrante Gonzaga. Ferrante was the brother of Giulio Cesare Gonzaga (1552–1609), previous prince of Bozzolo. Giulio Cesare was made a Knight of the Order of the Redeemer in 1608. When Giulio Cesare died, Scipione, his nephew, became prince of Bozzolo. Still a youth in 1611 under regency of his mother Isabella.

CANOSSA, GIAN TOMMASO. Marquis of Calliano in Monferrato (Asti). Made a Knight of the Order of the Redeemer in 1611. Served as valet to Duke Vincenzo I, captain of a company of lancers, and the head waiter to Ferdinando Gonzaga.

CANOSSA, GALEAZZO. (By then deceased) Marquis of Calliano in Monferrato (Asti). Made a Knight of the Order of the Redeemer in 1608. Identified in a letter as *il Marchese suo fratello*, for whom funeral services were held on Friday, 13 May 1611.

RIVARA, CONTE. Presumably Giacomo Antonio Valperga di Rivara, a member of one of the important noble families of the Piedmont. From 1612 Governor of the citadel of Casale Monferrato. The letter says he was promised by Vincenzo to be made a knight the next

year, but Vincenzo died in 1612 and Rivara was not named a Knight of the Order of the Redeemer until 1614.

NOTES

1 Just three weeks earlier, on 23 April 1611, the Jesuit Church of Santa Trinità had been consecrated by the Bishop of Mantua, and the Jesuit fathers had come to the city for a provincial chapter meeting (un Capitolo). Cited by Francesco Tonelli, Ricerche storiche di Mantova, iv (Mantua, 1800), p.36, and F. Amadei, Cronaca Universale della città di Mantova, ed. G. Amadei, E. Marani and G. Praticò, III (Mantua, 1956), p.267. See A. Bilotto-Flavio Rurale, Istoria del Collegio di Mantova della Compagnia di Giesù scritta dal padre Giuseppe Gorzoni, pt.1 (Mantua, 1997), p.118.

2 Probably comprising the duke's collection of antiquities and relics.

3 See Appendix 1 for the original text. The document is summarized in the online Herla Project, www. capitalespettacolo.it, C1275. We are grateful to Michael Sherberg and Tim Carter for their suggestions regarding the translation.

4 Ascension Day itself, which followed Easter Sunday by 40 days, was therefore always on a Thursday.

5 A thorough and rich interpretation of the history, ritual and symbolism of the Sensa is found in E. Muir, Civic ritual in Renaissance Venice (Princeton, 1981), pp.98, 101, 105, 107 and 119–34.

See also L. Urban, Processioni e feste dogali (Venice, 1998), pp.89–96; and M. Casini, I gesti del principe: La festa politica a Firenze e Venezia in età rinascimentale (Venice, 1996), pp.168–711, 310–12.

6 The most important study of the Mantuan Sensa is R. Capuzzo, 'La festa dell'Ascensione mantovana nelle descrizioni seicentesche', Civiltà mantovana, xxxiv/108 (1999), pp.7–35. Capuzzo draws on documents by the contemporaneous Mantuan chroniclers Ippolito Donesmondi and Federico Follino and the 18th-century writers Federigo Amadei and Giovanni Battista Cremonesi, who both relied on a lost 17th-century manuscript. Unlike the Venetian Sensa, we have few details regarding the liturgy of the celebration.

7 See note 18.

8 R. Capuzzo, 'Il "Preziosissimo Sangue" nella religiosità mantovana in epoca moderna (secc. XII–XX)', Sulle orme del Preziosissimo Sangue: Catalogo della mostra (Mantua, 1998), pp.37–47, and Capuzzo, 'La festa dell'Ascensione', pp.7–35.

9 Federico Follino, Compendio delle sontuose feste fatte l'anno MDCVIII nella città di Mantova per le reali nozze del Serenissimo Prencipe D. Francesco Gonzaga, con la Serenissima

Infante Margherita di Savoia (Mantua, 1608), pp.19–26. A brief description of the ceremony is found in I. Fenlon, 'The Monteverdi Vespers: suggested answers to some fundamental questions', Early Music, v (1977), pp.380–7. Fenlon suggests this event as a possible origin of the 1610 Vespers, but the psalms for a Marian Vespers constitute a somewhat different cursus from a Christological Vespers. Overlapping elements between the two services are the Respond, the psalms Dixit Dominus and Laudate pueri and the Magnificat.

10 Capuzzo, 'La festa dell'Ascensione mantovana', p.27, n.12. Margherita arrived in Mantua on 24 May.

11 Mantua, Archivio Storico Diocesano, Archivio di Sant'Andrea, b.112, fasc.2, 'Carte concernenti l'Ordine del Redentore', f.15.

12 See Ippolito Donesmondi, Dell'istoria ecclesiastica di Mantova ... parte seconda (Mantua, 1616), p.452.

13 Mantua, Archivio Gonzaga 410B, reg.43, c.[25v], 5 February 1589.

14 Indicated in a letter of Bassano Casola of 21 May 1610 (Mantua, Archivio Gonzaga 2718, fasc.XVII, ff.524–525).

15 See J. Kurtzman, 'The Mantuan sacred music', in The Cambridge

IX

companion to Monteverdi, ed. J.
Whenham and R. Wistreich (Cambridge,
2007), pp.142–3. Roger Bowers has
argued that Monteverdi composed and
performed a substantial amount of
sacred music for the small church of
Santa Croce on the edge of the ducal
palace. See Bowers, 'Monteverdi at
Mantua 1590–1612', in The Cambridge
companion to Monteverdi, pp.53–6.
However, the documents Bowers cites to
support his contention actually
contradict it. These documents will be
discussed more fully in J. Kurtzman,
'Monteverdi's missing sacred music',
forthcoming in the Festschrift for Piotr
Pozniak. More plausible is Bowers's
suggestion that Monteverdi was named
maestro of the ducal cappella by
December 1601 (p.61). There is, however,
no firm evidence of Monteverdi's
appointment at this time, even though
Bowers states it simply as fact.

16 Capuzzo, 'La festa dell'Ascensione',
pp.12–14, where he has laid out the two
descriptions in parallel columns in
order to clarify their similarities and
differences.

17 Cremonesi's account is excerpted in
Capuzzo, 'La festa dell'Ascensione',
pp.15–18; the accounts of Cremonesi,
Amadei and Federico Follino are
compared with those of Donesmondi
on pp.18–21.

18 Among the most likely foreign
visitors were those from the
Benedictine Monastery of Weingarten
near Lake Constance, which also
possessed a small portion of the same
relic of the holy blood.

19 Compiled from the accounts of
Donesmondi, Cremonesi, Amadei and
Follino in Capuzzo, 'La festa
dell'Ascensione', pp.13, 16–17, 19.

20 Donesmondi places the procession
before the Mass, while Cremonesi
describes the procession as occurring
after the Mass, beginning with the
offering. It is conceivable that there
were processions both before and after
the Mass—the first to the church, the
second to present the offerings and
exiting from the church. The latter is
the interpretation taken in the body of
our text. See Capuzzo, 'La festa
dell'Ascensione', pp.13–14, 17–18, 20.

21 Capuzzo, 'La festa dell'Ascensione',
pp.14, 18, 21.

22 Letter from Fabio Gonzaga to
Alessandro Striggio of 10 May 1611
(Mantua, Archivio Gonzaga
2722, fasc.I, doc.16).

23 'Si prepara una belissima Senssa'.
Letter from Campagna to Fabio
Gonzaga of 9 May 1611 (Mantua,
Archivio Gonzaga 2721, fasc.III, c.54)
(Herla, www.capitalespettacolo.it, C1275).

24 'Ogi si aspetta il prencipe di Bozollo
[Bozzolo] che viene alla Sensa et si
farano alcuni Cauaglieri del ordine del
santisimo sangue di Nostro Signore
Giesu Cristo.' Letter from Giovan
Battista Thesis to Fabio Gonzaga, 11
May 1611 (Mantua, Archivio Gonzaga
2722, fasc.VI, doc.33).

25 Letter of 13 May 1611 from Isabella
Gonzaga to Fabio Gonzaga (Mantua,
Archivio Gonzaga 2722, fasc.I, doc.17).

26 'Qui ui e stata assai bella fiera cosi di
robba come di gente in bona quanttita
e molto piu bella per quelle Damme à
quali e stata pagata Dal signor Ducca
essendone toccata à bona parte il ualore
di cinque e sei cento scudi per una. Fù ·
dato l'ordine il giorno dell'assensione al
signor Marchese Giovanni Tomaso
Canossa, e prommesso al signor Conte
Riuara per dargliedo alla prossima
occasione che si tenghi Capella in Santo
Andrea. Per quanto si dice Sua Altezza
partirà Martedi per il lago di Garda.'
Letter of 15 May 1611 from Vincenzo
Nuvoloni to an unknown recipient
(Mantua, Archivio Gonzaga 2722, fasc.
XII, doc.132).

27 E. Lax, ed., Claudio Monteverdi:
Lettere (Florence, 1994), pp.35–6. English
translation in D. Stevens, The letters of
Claudio Monteverdi (Oxford, rev.1995),
pp.77–81. In this letter Monteverdi also
promises Francesco two madrigals after
Holy Week has passed, for whose
liturgy he was also likely occupied in
composing and directing the music.

28 These demands led, after the
wedding festivities of May and June
1608, for which Monteverdi had
composed Arianna and the Ballo delle
Ingrate, to Monteverdi's withdrawal
from Mantua to his father's home in
Cremona in early July 1608 and his
request for dismissal from the ducal
service or at least appointment as
simply maestro della chiesa. See the
letters of 9 November and 26
November from Monteverdi's father

Baldassare to the duke and duchess
and Monteverdi's own letter of 2
December to the duke's councillor,
Annibale Chieppio, all published in
P. Fabbri, Monteverdi, Eng. trans.
T. Carter (Cambridge, 1994), pp.100–3.
Monteverdi's original letter is
published in Lax, Lettere, pp.20–4, and
Stevens, The letters, pp.50–4. Vincenzo's
response was to order Monteverdi back
to Mantua for new work.

29 Lax, Lettere, pp.31–3; Stevens, The
letters, pp.71–2. That Monteverdi was
already in Rome by 7 October is
demonstrated by a letter from a
Mantuan official, Rainero Bissolati,
who bumped into Monteverdi on the
street in Rome. See S. Parisi, 'New
documents concerning Monteverdi's
relations with the Gonzagas', in Claudio
Monteverdi: Studi e prospettive, Atti del
Convegno (Mantua, 21–24 ottobre 1993),
ed. P. Besutti, T. M. Gialdroni and R.
Baroncini (Florence, 1998), pp.477–511.

30 See J. Kurtzman, 'Per fare il vespro
meno tedioso': Don Pietro Maria
Marsolo and the "Antiphon problem"',
in Essays on music and culture in honor
of Herbert Kellman, ed. B. Haggh
(Paris, 2001), pp.411–21.

31 See, for example, the citation of a
letter concerning the performance of
Monteverdi psalms in Modena at
Christmas 1611 in Fabbri, Monteverdi,
p.120; documents pertaining to
Monteverdi's audition at St Mark's,
which may refer to one or more
unknown Masses, cited in Kurtzman,
The Monteverdi Vespers, pp.53–4;
Monteverdi's letter of 29 December
1616, in which he says he was occupied
the entire month of December in
composing and copying the annual
Mass for Christmas Eve, Lax, Lettere,
p.51, Stevens, The letters, p.113;
Monteverdi's letter of 21 April 1618, in
which he says he is responsible for a
concerted Mass and motets for Holy
Week, Lax, Lettere, p.64, Stevens, The
letters, pp.136–7; Monteverdi's letter of
17 April 1621 discussing his responsibility
for the Requiem Mass of 25 May 1621
for Cosimo II, Grand Duke of Tuscany,
Lax, Lettere, p.118, Stevens, The letters,
pp.237–40; Monteverdi's letter of 27
November 1621 offering a Solemn Mass
to the Duchess of Mantua, Lax, Lettere,
pp.121–2, Stevens, The letters, p.246;
Monteverdi's letter of 1 May 1627,

554

offering Vespers or a Mass to the Duke
of Mantua, Lax, *Lettere*, p.151, Stevens,
The letters, pp.316–17; Monteverdi's
letter of 30 October 1627, in which he
says that his annual duties at St Mark's
are greatest at Christmas Eve, Lax,
Lettere, p.113, Stevens, *The letters*, p.381;
and Monteverdi's letter of 2 February
1634, indicating that he was responsible
for composing a new Mass for
Christmas Eve every year, Lax, *Lettere*,
pp.203–4, Stevens, *The letters*, p.424.

32 R. Morselli, *Le collezioni Gonzaga.
L'elenco dei beni del 1626–1627* (Milan,
2000), pp.114–15.

33 M. L. Chappel, 'Appunti sulla vita
di Fabio Gonzaga', *Civiltà mantovana*,
iv/21 (1970), pp.184–94.

X

Monteverdi's Mass of Thanksgiving: Da Capo

I

Venice is well known for its collection of stories and legends purporting to recount the history of the *Serenissima*. These tales, repeated in various forms by a variety of Venetian authors over the centuries[1] and enshrined in the iconography of Venetian painting,[2] are often subsumed under the broad category of the "Myth of Venice." Like many myths, there are kernels of truth in most or all of the stories, elaborated and conflated over the centuries to a legendary and heroic history of the Republic. For Venetians of earlier times, these stories were part of their very identity as citizens of the city, prompting both attitudes and action in numerous situations throughout the centuries.

---

[1] The most important of these accounts, summarizing numerous previous authors, are found in Francesco Sansovino, *Venetia città nobilissima, et singolare* (Venice, 1581). Sansovino's book was enlarged with additional material by Giovanni Stringa in the early seventeenth century and published as *Venetia città nobilissima, et singolare, descritta già in XIIII. Libri da M. Francesco Sansovino et hora con molta diligenza corretta, emendata, e più d'un terzo di cose nuove ampliata dal M.R.D. Giovanni Stringa, canonico della Chiesa Ducale di S. Marco. Nella quale si contengono tutte le cose, così antiche, come moderne, che nell'ottava facciata di questo foglio si leggono . . . In Venetia, presso Altobello Salicato. MDCIIII.* A second enlargement was published almost sixty years later by Giustiniano Martinioni as *Venetia, città nobilissima et singolare, descritta in XIIII. Libri . . . nella quale si contengono tutte le guerre passate, con l'attioni illustri di molti senatori, le vite de i principi, & gli scrittori Veneti del tempo loro, le chiese, fabriche, edifici, & palazzi publichi, & privati, le leggi, gli ordini, & gli usi antichi, & moderni, con altre cose appresso notabili, & degne di memoria; con aggiunta di tutte le cose notabili della stessa città, fatte, & occorse dall'Anno 1580, fino al presente 1663 da D. Giustiniano Martinioni . . . In Venetia, appresso Steffano Curti, MDCLXIII* (reprint ed., Venice: Filippi Editore, 1968). For a discussion of the historical myths of Venice, see Edward Muir, *Civic Ritual in Renaissance Venice* (Princeton: Princeton University Press, 1981), 103–19. The basic Italian article on the emblems of Venetian legendary history is Agostino Pertusi, "Quedam regalia insignia: ricerche sulle insegne del potere ducale a Venezia durante il medioevo," *Studi veneziani* 7 (1965): 3–123.

[2] The historical paintings in the doge's palace and the collection of large paintings of historical "events" in Venetian history by Gentile Bellini in the Academia delle Belli Arte constitute the most prominent sets of depictions of such events. Many other historical paintings of recent events, which also quickly took on a legendary cast, are found in the Museo Correr. Of the many books on painting in Venice, see especially Bernard Berenson,

The initial version of this essay appeared in *FIORI MUSICALI: Liber amicorum Alexander Silbiger*, edited by Claire Fontijn with Susan Parisi, Detroit Monographs in Musicology/ Studies in Music, No. 55, Harmonie Park Press, 2010.

It is rare that any of these legends involves music or musical instruments, apart from the tale of the presentation of six large silver processional trumpets to Doge Sebastiano Ziani by Pope Alexander III in 1177 in recognition of the doge's assistance in negotiating a treaty between Frederick Barbarossa and the pope.[3] However, much more recently, in the modern era, a story has arisen regarding the Mass of Thanksgiving performed under the direction of *maestro di cappella* Claudio Monteverdi in St. Mark's on November 21, 1631 to celebrate the official end of the plague that had devastated Venice in the years 1630–31.[4] That such a mass was indeed performed as part of the more extensive ceremonies of the day that included the dedication of the site of the future church of Santa Maria della Salute, pledged by the government in seeking relief from the plague from the Virgin, is fully documented and indisputable.[5]

Italian Pictures of the Renaissance; a List of the Principal Artists and their Works with an Index of Places: Venetian School, 2 vols. (New York: Phaidon Publishers, 1957); Carlo Donzelli and Giuseppe Maria Pilo, *I pittori del seicento veneto* (Florence: R. Sandron, 1967); Augusto Gentili, Giandomenico Romanelli, and Philip Rylander, *Paintings in Venice* (Boston: Bulfinch Press, 2002); Peter Humfrey, *Painting in Renaissance Venice* (New Haven: Yale University Press, 1995); Rodolfo Pallucchini, *La pittura veneziana del cinquecento*, 2 vols. (Novara: Istituto geografico De Agostini, 1944); idem, *La pittura veneziana del seicento*, 2 vols. (Milan: Electa, 1981, 1993); Terisio Pignatti, ed., *Il Museo Correr di Venezia: dipinti del XVII e XVIII secolo* (Venice: N. Pozza, 1960); idem, ed., *Le scuole di Venezia* (Milan: Electa, 1981); Giovanna Nepi Sciré, *Treasures of Venetian Painting: The Gallerie dell'Accademia* (New York: Vendome Press, 1991); and Staale Sinding-Larsen, *Christ in the Council Hall: Studies in the Religious Iconography of the Venetian Republic*, vol. 5 of *Acta ad Archaelogiam et Artium Historiam Pertinentia* of the Institutum Romanum Norvegiae (Rome: "L'Erma" di Bretschneider, 1974): 156–66.

[3] A painting depicting this scene is reproduced in Pallucchini, *La pittura veneziana del seicento*, 2:489, plate 126. See Ellen Rosand, "Music in the Myth of Venice," *Renaissance Quarterly* 30 (1977): 511–37 for a survey of music in Venetian ritual life in the Cinquecento and Seicento.

[4] The plague was brought to Venice by the Mantuan ambassador Alessandro Striggio, former court secretary to Duke Vincenzo I of Mantua and librettist of Monteverdi's *L'Orfeo*, who was en route to Vienna to appeal to Emperor Ferdinand II for peace in the War of Mantuan Succession. The first account of the plague appeared on November 29, 1631 in a long, published letter, entitled *La Liberatione di Venetia*, from Marco Ginammi to Marc'Antonio Padavino, the Venetian Resident in Naples. A transcription of the entire letter may be seen in Jeffrey Kurtzman and Linda Maria Koldau, "*Trombe, Trombe d'argento, Trombe squarciate, Tromboni*, and *Pifferi* in Venetian Processions and Ceremonies of the Sixteenth and Seventeenth Centuries," *Journal of Seventeenth-Century Music* 8, http://www.sscm-jscm.org/jscm/v8/no1/Kurtzman/Doc.1.html. A much lengthier and more detailed account of the plague was published just three years later in Michael Angelus Rota, *De peste Veneta anno 1630 Michaelis Angeli Rotae ciuis Veneti artium, et medicinae doctoris quaestiones disputatae, siue Apologeticum ad syllogisticam disputationem* (Venice: Ghirardum de Imbertis, 1634), which I have not yet had the opportunity to see. For more recent accounts of the plague, see below.

[5] The documentation is cited *in extenso* in James H. Moore, "*Venezia favorita da Maria*: Music for the Madonna Nicopeia and Santa Maria della Salute," *Journal of the American Musicological Society* 37 (1984): 299–355. Moore cites and quotes from Ginammi's pamphlet rather than a remarkably similarly worded letter by Antonio de' Vescovi (see further in n. 9) previously published by the historians cited in nn. 9–13, who do not mention Ginammi. Moore seems to have been unaware of de' Vescovi's letter as the source for the accounts

The story of the Mass of Thanksgiving identifies the mass performed on that occasion with the Kyrie, Sanctus, and Agnus Dei of the *Messa a quattro voci* as well as the Gloria *a 7* and three segments of a concertato Credo published in Monteverdi's *Selva morale e spirituale* in 1641.[6] It has generally been assumed that the three Credo segments are the only remaining fragments of a complete Credo, and that the rubrics in the *Selva morale* permitting their substitution for the corresponding verses of the

of the thanksgiving ceremonies by modern Venetian writers, though he does mention the letter in his *Vespers at St. Mark's: Music of Alessandro Grandi, Giovanni Rovetta and Francesco Cavalli*, 2 vols. (Ann Arbor, MI: UMI Research Press, 1981), 1:348, n. 198. I am grateful to John Whenham for calling this citation to my attention. On the basis of Ginammi's pamphlet as well as other documentary sources, Moore emended the word *uscir* to *unir* in the sentence about Monteverdi's mass and corrected the date of the thanksgiving ceremonies to November 21. The wording of Ginammi's pamphlet is reproduced almost verbatim in a letter published in Giovanni Francesco Loredano's *Lettere del Signor Gio: Francesco Loredano . . . divise in cinquantadue capi e raccolte da Henrico Giblet, cavalier, 17a impressione* (Geneva: Appresso Gio. Herm. Widerhold, 1669), 369–77, the earliest surviving edition of which was published in 1653. Loredano's undated letter is headed by the rubric "Per Altri" and addressed to the same Venetian resident in Naples as Ginammi's pamphlet. This rather vague rubric may indicate that the letter was by someone other than Loredano himself. In any event, the relationship between de' Vescovi, Ginammi, and Loredano is both confusing and intriguing and invites further investigation. Contributing further to the confusion is the fact that Henrico Giblet, cavalier, the "collector" of Loredano's letters is, in fact, a pseudonym for Loredano himself. I am grateful to John Whenham for bringing Loredano's letter to my attention and supplying me with its text, and to David Bryant, Mauro Calcagno, Massimo Ossi, Giulio Ongaro, and Michael Scherberg for their suggestions regarding the meaning of the rubric "Per Altri." Other contemporary references to the Mass of Thanksgiving from the Archivio di Stato di Firenze, Archivio Mediceo del Principato, have also been discovered by Whenham. The Florentine Resident in Venice, Ippolito Buondelmonti, wrote to Andrea Cioli, First Secretary of State to the Grand Duke of Tuscany, on November 17, 1631, "Hieri si cominciorno a fare allegrezze *per* la Città *per* la libera*zione* dal Cons.o, e la giouentù, che è rimasta uiua, spende gran denari in far caccie de Tori, guerre de pugni, fuochi, e festini e balletti. Venerdi dicesi, che si canterà di nuouo la Messa solennissima pro gratiar actione . . ." (Reg. 5, f. 261v). Buondelmonti's remark, "canterà di nuouo la Messa," is intriguing, suggesting that Monteverdi's mass had already been performed at least once before November 21, though no record of such a performance has yet been found. Buondelmonti's letter to the Grand Duke of November 22 describes the procession and ceremonies of November 21, including the sentence, "A S. Marco si cantò la messa della Madonna con una musica insignissíma, e piena di artifiziosa allegria" (Reg. 5, ff. 263v–264v). I am most grateful to Prof. Whenham for his generosity in sharing these documents with me and granting permission to use them in this article.

[6] SELVA / MORALE / ET / SPIRITVALE / DI CLAVDIO / MONTEVERDE / Maestro Di Capella della Serenissima / Republica Di Venetia / DEDICAT A / ALLA SACRA CESAREA MAESTA / DELLA IMPERATRICE / ELEONORA / GONZAGA / Con Licenza de Superiori, & Priuilegio. / IN VENETIA M DC XXXXI / Appresso Bartolomeo Magni. The copy at the Civico Museo Bibliografico Musicale in Bologna has two different title pages, one dated 1640, the other, as given above, in 1641. The dedication of the print is dated May 1, 1641. The 1640 title page is reproduced in facsimile in Gianfrancesco Malipiero, ed., *Claudio Monteverdi: Tutte le Opere* (Vienna: Universal Edition, 1927–32 & 1966–68), XV, part 1, ii. Both title pages are reproduced in facsimile in Denis Stevens, ed., *Claudio Monteverdi: Selva morale e spirituale*, vol. XV of "Claudio Monteverdi: Opera Omnia" (Cremona: Fondazione Claudio Monteverdi, 1998), 81. For a discussion of these two title pages, see Jeffrey Kurtzman, "Monteverdi's 'Mass of Thanksgiving' Revisited," *Early Music* 22 (February 1994): 65–66.

Credo of the *Messa a quattro voci* was an expedient by the publisher, Bartolomeo Magni, to make these three surviving segments appear useful.[7] This story has been accepted as common knowledge in the musicological community and has even generated a commercial recording of the "Mass of Thanksgiving."[8] However, in just the past few years, new scholarship has begun to cast doubt on this "common knowledge." Is the story true, or are we in the presence of a modern "myth of Venice," elaborated by musicologists from grains of fact into a story that transcends any reasonable veracity?

The question is best addressed by going back to the beginning of historical references to the actual mass performed on November 21, 1631 and tracing the lineage of scholarly investigation and commentary that has led to the present commonly shared assumptions. The first writer after the seventeenth century to mention the mass was the Venetian historian Giambattista Gallicciolli in his *Delle memorie venete antiche profane ed ecclesiastiche* of 1795, quoting from a long letter by one Antonio de' Vescovi.[9] After describing the official announcement of the end of the plague in St. Mark's square and the procession into the church itself, this letter includes the following oft-quoted sentence:

> Quivi si cantò una solennissima messa, facendo il Signor Claudio
> Monteverdi maestro di cappella, gloria del nostro secolo, alla Gloria
> e al Credo uscir il canto con le trombe squarciate con isquisita e
> maraviglia armonia.[10]

---

[7] This idea was first proposed by Denis Stevens in 1967 and repeated and embellished by him on numerous other occasions. See the discussion below.

[8] EMI CDS 749876 2. See the discussion of this recording below.

[9] Giambattista Gallicciolli, *Delle memorie venete antiche profane ed ecclesiastiche*, 10 vols. (Venice: Domenico Fracasso, 1795), 2:224–31. Gallicciolli's account is based on a certain Ms. Svajer, which I have not seen. Gallicciolli also included a substantial portion of a letter of November 29, 1631 "scritta a certo suo amico da Antonio de' Vescovi Clerico e Cittadino ciò che, omesse le cose di ceremonia, io qui produrrò colle stesse sue parole" (p. 226). This letter runs quite parallel to the published pamphlet of Ginammi cited in n. 4 above, but I have not been able to make a full comparison between the letter and Ginammi's pamphlet, since Gallicciolli omitted some portions of the original without including any ellipses to indicate where material was excised. According to James H. Moore (see n. 5 above), de' Vescovi's letter was printed in Giovanni Nicolò Doglioni's *Le cose notabili et meravigliose della città di Venezia* (Venice, 1675), which I have also not yet been able to examine. Antonio de' Vescovi [Antonius de Episcopis] provided two anagrams at the end of Ginammi's pamphlet, published the same day as the former's letter. Clearly there was very close collaboration between the two, producing parallel accounts with parallel, but not always identical, wording. Ginammi's pamphlet appears to be a slightly expanded version of the letter, which may have served as the pamphlet's first draft. Gallicciolli's of this letter is the origin of the mistaken date of November 28, 1631 for the thanksgiving ceremonies, as well as the mistaken *uscir* [recte *unir*] in the phrase "alla Gloria e al Credo uscir il canto con le trombe squarciate." Both errors were reproduced by later historians until they were finally corrected by Moore in 1984.

[10] Gallicciolli, 228.

In 1830, another Venetian, Giovanni Casoni, published a much enlarged account of the plague and its ceremonies in a monograph devoted to the history of the erection of the church of Santa Maria della Salute.[11] In this small book, Casoni also quoted Antonio de' Vescovi's letter, copied from Gallicciolli, with only a couple of words altered. Some twenty years later the Venetian historian Giuseppe Cappelletti included a description of the horrible scourge in his monumental history of Venice.[12] Cappelletti drew much of his material on the epidemic from Casoni's book, including a great deal of both paraphrase and direct quotation. Among the direct quotations is Antonio de' Vescovi's letter, copied from Casoni with only a single word added.

At the same time that Cappelletti was writing, Francesco Caffi was assembling and publishing his history of music at St. Mark's.[13] In this study Caffi quoted the same passage from Antonio de' Vescovi's letter as Cappelletti, but drew no connection between the mass performed at the celebration of the end of the plague and any music in the *Selva morale e spirituale*.[14] The same is true of the first monographic study of Monteverdi by Emil Vogel in 1887, whose own source of information on the thanksgiving ceremonies was Cappelletti.[15] Vogel, however, laid one important stone in the foundation of the story of the Mass of Thanksgiving in his German translation of the brief passage quoted above from de' Vescovi: "beim Gloria und beim Credo liess er den Gesang durch Posaunen begleiten, damit einen vortrefflichen und wunderbaren Zusammenklang hervorbringend."[16] In the early history of the trombone the German word *Posaunen* could mean either trumpets or trombones, just as in Italian of the period, *trombe* could refer to either instrument.[17] However, by Vogel's time there was a distinct difference

---

[11] Giovanni Casoni, *La peste di Venezia nel MDCXXX: Origine della erezione del tempio S. Maria della Salute* (Venice: Tipografia di Alvisopoli, 1830).

[12] Giuseppe Cappelletti, *Storia della repubblica di Venezia dal suo principio sino al giorno d'oggi; opera originale del prete veneziano Giuseppe Cappelletti*, 13 vols. (Venice: G. Antonelli, 1850–55), x. The description of the plague is found in the first two *Capi* of Book 39, 189–206.

[13] Francesco Caffi, *Storia della musica sacra nella già cappella ducale di San Marco in Venezia dal 1318 al 1797*, 2 vols. (Venice: G. Antonelli, 1854; reprint, Bologna: Forni Editore, 1972).

[14] Ibid., 230.

[15] Emil Vogel, "Claudio Monteverdi. Leben, Wirken im Lichte der zeitgenössischen Kritik und Verzeichniss seiner im Druck erschienenen Werke," *Vierteljahrsschrift für Musikwissenschaft* 3 (1887): 315–450.

[16] Ibid., 393.

[17] The primary Italian dictionary of the period is the *Vocabolario degli Accademici della Crusca* (Venice: Giovanni Alberti, 1592), reissued in numerous editions in the seventeenth and eighteeth centuries. The standard dictionary of the Venetian dialect is Giuseppe Boerio, *Dizionario del dialetto veneziano* (Venezia: A. Santini, 1829), reprinted numerous times in the nineteenth and twentieth centuries. A Venetian-German dictionary

between *Trompeten* and *Posaunen*, and by choosing *Posaunen*, Vogel set the stage for a subsequent series of English renderings of *trombe squarciate* as "trombones" (often translated directly from Vogel's German rather than from the Italian original).

In 1914, Antonio Tirabassi published a modern edition of the *Messa a quattro voci*, with an introduction by Charles Van den Borren.[18] In noting that much of Monteverdi's musical production remained in manuscript and was subsequently lost, Van den Borren mentions the 1631 thanksgiving mass, and following Vogel, declares that, "D'après la description qui nous a été laissée de cette solennité, des trombones accompagnaient le chant pendant le *Gloria* et la *Credo*," translating Vogel's *Posaunen* into French without recourse to the original Italian text.[19] Tirabassi's edition also appends at the end the three substitute *concertato* Credo segments from the *Selva morale*, which Van den Borren likewise describes in some detail, finding their stylistic discontinuity with the *Messa a quattro voci* puzzling. Nowhere, however, does Van den Borren connect either the *Messa* or the Credo segments with the Mass of Thanksgiving cited earlier in his preface.

After Vogel, no further extended studies of Monteverdi appeared until Louis Schneider's book on the composer in 1921.[20] In this volume, Schneider erroneously described Monteverdi's mass as a Requiem and quoted the same passage from Cappelletti as Vogel, translating the phrase *trombe squarciate* in French as "trombones," following in the footsteps of Van den Borren.[21] A little later in his book Schneider describes the mass and Credo fragments from the *Selva morale et spirituale*, but makes no mention of the Gloria *a 7*, nor does he associate the *Selva* mass with the ceremonies of November 1631.

Three years later, Henri Prunières published his first monograph on Monteverdi, in which he described in some detail the *Messa a quattro voci* from the *Selva morale* based on the edition and commentary by Tirabassi and Van den Borren.[22] In an expanded

---

of the fifteenth century was published by A. Rossebastiano Bart, ed., *Vocabolari Veneto-Tedeschi del secolo XV*, 3 vols. (Edizioni L'Artistica Savigliano, 1983).

[18] Antonio Tirabassi and Charles Van den Borren, eds., *Selva morale et spirituale. Venetia 1641, Claudio Monteverde: "Messa a quattro da cappella"* (Brussels, Leipzig, Berlin, London, New York, Paris: Breitkopf & Härtel, [1914]).

[19] Ibid., iv.

[20] Louis Schneider, *Un précurseur de la musique italienne aux XVIe et XVIIe siècles. Claudio Monteverdi (1567–1643) l'homme et son temps, le musicien* (Paris: Perrin et cie., 1921).

[21] Ibid., 200–01.

[22] Henri Prunières, *Claudio Monteverdi* (Paris: Librairie Félix Alcan, 1924, 1931). The passages regarding the *Messa a quattro voci* are on pp. 92–95. Two years later Prunières published a much expanded work on Monteverdi, *La Vie et l'oeuvre de Claudio Monteverdi* (Paris: Les Éditions Musicales de la Librairie de France, 1926), which appeared in the same year in an English translation by Marie D. Mackie as *Monteverdi: His Life and Work* (London and Toronto: J.M. Dent & Sons Ltd., 1926). This was the first study of the composer to be published in English.

biography of 1926, Prunières noted the "style archaïque" of the *Messa a quattro voci*, contrasting it with the concertato style of mass composition, which he introduced by citing the historical references to the mass of 1631 "pour célébrer la fin de la peste au cours de laquelle des *'trombe squarciate'* accompagnaient le chant du *Gloria* et du *Credo*, produisant 'une exquise et marveilleuse harmonie.'"[23] Although the source of Prunières's quote was Vogel, he did not follow Vogel's, Van den Borren's or Schneider's example by translating *trombe squarciate*, preferring instead to retain the original Italian terminology. Immediately afterward in the text, Prunières describes the concertato Credo fragments from the *Selva morale*, but only by way of examples of the concertato style, not in terms of any direct connection with the Mass of Thanksgiving.[24] Nowhere in the volume does Prunières mention the Gloria *a 7*.

The first Italian monograph on Monteverdi was published by Domenico de' Paoli in 1945. De' Paoli also quotes the passage referring to the Mass of Thanksgiving from Cappelletti, but only in the historical context of the plague.[25] His brief description of the *Messa a quattro voci*, including the substitute Credo fragments, appears later in the volume within the discussion of the *Selva morale*, and he draws no inferences with regard to this mass and the Mass of Thanksgiving.[26] Like Prunières, de' Paoli doesn't even mention the Gloria *a 7*.

Hans Redlich was the author of the first German language monograph on Monteverdi in the twentieth century, published in Switzerland.[27] Redlich briefly notes Monteverdi's role in the Mass of Thanksgiving of 1631 (without quoting the passage from either Cappelletti or Vogel), and declares that the music has been lost.[28] His commentary on the *Messa a quattro voci* and the Credo fragments is reserved for another section of the book, and like those before him, Redlich says nothing to relate the

---

[23] Prunières, *La Vie et l'oeuvre*, 126. Mackie, *Monteverdi*, 117. Prunières's source for the Mass of Thanksgiving quotation was Vogel.

[24] Nevertheless, Prunières hinted indirectly at a connection, if only in declaring that when writing "a mass or a motet for the great public religious ceremonies which were frequent in Venice, he wrote in the *concertato* style, but when he had to write a mass for some strictly liturgical service he contrived to write in the style of the old masters. . . ." See Mackie, *Monteverdi*, 117–18. Prunières's distinction between "great public religious ceremonies" and a "strictly liturgical service" is specious, since "strictly" is a meaningless adjective when applied to the liturgy and all "great public religious ceremonies" were also liturgical.

[25] Domenico de' Paoli, *Claudio Monteverdi* (Milan: Editore Ulrico Hoepli, 1945), 288.

[26] Ibid., 311–12.

[27] Hans Ferdinand Redlich, *Claudio Monteverdi: Leben und Werk* (Olten: Verlag Otto Walter, 1949). An English translation appeared three years later by Kathleen Dale, *Claudio Monteverdi: Life and Works* (London, New York, Toronto: Oxford University Press, 1952).

[28] Ibid., 62. English edition, 35–36.

Messa a quattro voci to the Mass of Thanksgiving. He does, though, mention the Gloria *a 7* as the highest example of Monteverdi's writing in the concertato style, immediately after he describes the concertato Credo fragments (the Gloria *a 7* is positioned between the *Messa a quattro voci* and the Credo fragments in the *Selva morale*).[29]

To summarize the first hundred years of writing on the Mass of Thanksgiving, the sentence extracted from Antonio de' Vescovi's letter was quoted repeatedly, but no writer through 1949 had made any connection whatsoever between this description and music from the *Selva morale e spirituale*. However, in 1887 Vogel had already set the stage for misinterpretation of the letter by translating *trombe squarciate* as *Posaunen*. Van den Borren and Louis Schneider, both possibly in emulation of Vogel, had translated the Italian phrase as "trombones" in their own references to this passage.

II

The first attempt to assign any surviving music of Monteverdi's to the Mass of Thanksgiving was made in 1950 by Leo Schrade, who was interested in trying to relate Monteverdi's published sacred music to documentary evidence. Schrade begins with the citation of three letters of Monteverdi from 1618, 1621, and 1627 that mention specific mass compositions and then goes on to demonstrate how neither the *Messa a quattro voci* from the *Selva morale* nor the *Messa a quattro* from Monteverdi's posthumous 1650 collection, published in Venice by Alessandro Vincenti, could be any of those mentioned in the letters.[30] On the other hand, while the concertato Gloria *a 7* could fit the description of any of the masses mentioned in the three Monteverdi letters, Schrade preferred to relate it to Antonio de' Vescovi's sentence regarding the Mass of Thanksgiving. Apart from the grandiose, celebratory style of the work, it is clear that Schrade's association of the Gloria *a 7* with the Mass of Thanksgiving depended on the optional trombones mentioned in Monteverdi's performance rubric for the Gloria in the *Selva morale*, coupled with Vogel's translation of *trombe squarciate* as *Posaunen*. Schrade's argument is best conveyed by quoting his entire paragraph:

> In a totally different style is the *Gloria a 7 voci concertata con due violini et quattro viole da brazzo overo 4 Tromboni*, in which, according to instructions, the trombones can be left out if circumstances do

---

[29] Ibid., 142–43. English edition, 125–26.

[30] Leo Schrade, *Monteverdi: Creator of Modern Music* (New York: W.W. Norton & Co., 1950), 318–19.

not allow their use.[31] The dating of this work involves difficulties
of a different kind. In the first place, this Gloria can be part of any
of the Masses Monteverdi speaks about in 1618, 1621, and 1627.
But there is another occasion for which an extraordinary solemnity
of the Mass is recorded. In 1630 Venice was afflicted by the plague,
whose horrors lasted till late in 1631. Since the epidemic wrought
great havoc among the Venetians, it is understandable that the Doge,
Francesco Erizzo, ordered a general thanksgiving in St. Mark's when
it was over, and on 28 November 1631 [recte 21 November], this
service took place. It has been described by Antonius de Episcopis
[Antonio de' Vescovi], who also wrote some laudatory poems in
dedication to Monteverdi: "There was sung the most solemn Mass,
composed by Claudio Monteverdi, the Maestro di Cappella, the glory
of our century; in Gloria and Credo the voices were joined by trombones which produced an exquisite and marvellous harmony."[32]
This description exactly fits the Gloria which Monteverdi selected
for his *Selva Morale*, and since it has the beauty and maturity of stylistic
technique that distinguish the late compositions of Monteverdi,
we may believe that it belongs to the mass he composed for the
thanksgiving of 1631.[33]

Schrade did not consult Cappelletti or Caffi for de' Vescovi's Italian text, but
rather relied entirely on Vogel, leading him to assume that the instruments mentioned
in the Venetian's letter were actually trombones. Thus there appeared to be a plausible
documentary link between the rubrics for the Gloria *a 7* in the *Selva morale* and the
contemporaneous description of the Mass of Thanksgiving—all hinging on Vogel's
translation of *trombe squarciate* as *Posaunen*.

Only one page later Schrade describes the *Messa a quattro voci* and its unusual
rubrics for the substitution of the Credo fragments that follow the Gloria *a 7* in the
print, but made no attempt to connect either the mass or the Credo fragments to the
Mass of Thanksgiving. Schrade's sole focus was on the Gloria *a 7*, even though the
rubric in the index for the third of the Credo fragments, the *Et iterum*, is very similar
to that for the *Gloria*.[34]

---

[31] Schrade's footnote: "*Selva Morale*, ibid., xv, 117."

[32] Schrade's footnote: "Vogel, *VfMW*, III, 393, n. 3."

[33] Schrade, 319–20. Bracketed text here and in subsequent quotations mine.

[34] Ibid., 321. The rubric for the *Et iterum* reads *Concertato con quatro Tronboni o viole da brazzo quali si
ponno anco lasciare*. The full rubric from the index for the *Gloria* is *concertata con due violini & quattro viole da brazzo
ouero 4. Tromboni quali anco si ponno lasciare se occoresse l'acidente.*

Denis Arnold was the first to relate the *Messa a quattro voci* and the Credo fragments to the Mass of Thanksgiving. In 1962, Arnold published an edition of the *Messa a quattro voci* in the series of Eulenburg miniature scores.[35] In his preface, Arnold overstated and distorted Schrade's comments, shifting them from the Gloria *a 7* to the Credo fragments and the *Messa a quattro voci*:

> The present mass, published in 1641 in the collection of his
> church music called *Selva Morale*, belongs to his *stile antico*. In its
> original form, it had two [recte: three] strange interpolations, a *Cruci-*
> *fixus* and *Et Resurrexit* in which the voices are joined by trombones,
> and the vocal style becomes *concertante* in the most up-to-date manner.
> This has led L. Schrade to identify this mass as that performed on
> 28 November [recte: 21 November] 1631 in S. Marco in thanksgiving
> for the relief from the terrible plague which in the previous months
> had reduced the Venetian population to about one-third.[36]

Here, for the first time, the claim appears that the *Messa a quattro voci*, with its substitute Credo fragments, represents the 1631 Mass of Thanksgiving. The story takes an odd twist, however, in Arnold's Monteverdi monograph of the next year, where the Gloria *a 7* is mentioned in connection with the Mass of Thanksgiving but not the *Messa a quattro voci* nor the Credo fragments.[37] Unwittingly, Arnold undermined Schrade's rationale for drawing a relationship between the Gloria *a 7* and the Mass of Thanksgiving by his English translation of Antonio de' Vescovi's description as quoted by Vogel: "there was sung a solemn Mass, composed by Sig. Claudio Monteverdi, *maestro di cappella*, the glory of our century, in which during the Gloria and Credo the singing was joined by loud trumpets (*trombe squarciate*) with exquisite and marvelous harmony."[38] Arnold avoided Vogel's *Posaunen* and Schrade's "trombones," understanding by *trombe squarciate* some type of trumpets. While Arnold does not describe the type other than by the adjective "loud," he would eventually be proved accurate in this assumption. However, later in the book, in his discussion of the music of the *Selva morale e spirituale*, the *Messa a quattro voci* and the Credo fragments receive no mention whatsoever. Only the Gloria *a 7* is associated with the plague ceremonial music: "Perhaps the most splendid

---

[35] Denis Arnold, ed., *Messa a 4' voci da cappella by Claudio Monteverdi (1641)* (London, Zurich and New York: Ernst Eulenburg, Ltd., 1962). This edition was no. 990 in Eulenburg's series of miniature scores.

[36] Arnold, *Messa a 4 voci*, preface.

[37] Denis Arnold, *Monteverdi* (London: J.M. Dent and Sons Ltd., 1963), 44, 150.

[38] Ibid., 44.

of all his church music is to be found in the *Gloria* with trombones and strings which he composed in 1631 for the Mass in thanksgiving for the relief from the plague."[39]

The inconsistency is obvious, for in Arnold's 1962 Eulenburg edition, the Mass of Thanksgiving is only related to the *Messa a quattro voci* and the Credo fragments, while in his book, only the *Gloria a 7* is mentioned in connection with the Mass of Thanksgiving. Moreover, Arnold's translation of the description of the Mass of Thanksgiving cites the *trombe squarciate* (loud trumpets) in the Gloria and Credo of that mass, while his commentary on the Gloria *a 7* appropriately includes the trombones mentioned in its rubrics. Thus the link that Schrade had argued between the Gloria *a 7*, with its trombones, and the Gloria of the Mass of Thanksgiving, with its "loud trumpets," was actually disjoined by Arnold, while Schrade's conclusion remained intact.

When Arnold's book was reissued in 1990 in a posthumous, revised third edition by Tim Carter, the only change made was in substituting James H. Moore's more recent translation of the passage from Ginammi's pamphlet for Arnold's translation of de' Vescovi's letter [the wording of the two are actually identical in this passage], thereby leaving the phrase *trombe squarciate* in Italian, but without Arnold's earlier English rendering.[40] However, in the meantime, Arnold had published in 1982 a book devoted exclusively to Monteverdi's sacred music.[41] In this slim volume Arnold reconciled the contradiction in his earlier writings, first by declaring unequivocally that the Gloria *a 7* was performed at the Mass of Thanksgiving: "We have no way of dating these works, but one piece can be assigned to a particular occasion.... The work is a *Gloria à 7 voci* printed in the *Selva morale*."[42] Secondly, apparently having recognized that he had previously undermined the connection between de' Vescovi's description and the rubrics for the Gloria *a 7* in the *Selva morale* by interpreting *trombe squarciate* as "loud trumpets," he revised his translation of the passage to read "trombones." Arnold also realized the need to reconcile the differences between the preface of his 1962 edition of the *Messa a quattro voci* and his 1963 book on Monteverdi. He therefore also brought the mass and the Credo fragments into the discussion, but this time not insisting on the position he had taken in 1962 regarding their employment in the 1631 Mass of Thanksgiving:

---

[39] Ibid., 150. The 1975 revised edition of Arnold's book makes no change in the passages relating to the *Messa a quattro voci*, the Credo fragments, the *Gloria a 7* or the Mass of Thanksgiving. See pp. 44 and 151–52.

[40] Denis Arnold, *Monteverdi*, 3rd ed., rev. Tim Carter (London: J.M. Dent & Sons Ltd., 1990), 41. Carter quotes from Moore, "*Venezia favorita*," 313.

[41] Denis Arnold, *Monteverdi Church Music* (London: British Broadcasting Corporation, 1982).

[42] Ibid., 56.

X

106

In the *Selva morale* there are two [recte: three] alternative sections to the Credo in the modern style which may, it is said, take the place of those in the *stile antico* in the Mass for four voices. . . . There has been some discussion as to whether that means that the Mass for this day of thanksgiving consisted of the Kyrie, Sanctus and Agnus Dei of the Mass for four voices, together with the Credo given with three interpolations and the large-scale Gloria which is next to them in the volume; or whether really only the Gloria survives in full and the interpolations to the Credo are part of a grander conception, a true *Missa concertata*, of which most of the music has disappeared. Either is a possible view.[43]

In 1964, Roger Tellart became the first Frenchman since Prunières to publish a book on Monteverdi.[44] This work, a relatively thin volume in the series *Musiciens de tous les Temps*, did not take into account recent scholarship, however. Tellart mentions the Mass of Thanksgiving and quotes the by then well-known passage from de' Vescovi's letter in a French version, but does not translate the phrase *trombe squarciate*.[45] In a different section of the book Tellart mentions the *Messa a quattro voci* only in passing, but does follow Schrade in assigning the Gloria *a 7* to the Mass of Thanksgiving: "Il fut, selon toutes vraisemblances, chanté pour la première fois à l'occasion du service d'actions de grâces qui salua la fin de la grande épidémie de 1631."[46] Like Prunières, Tellart issued a much expanded version of his biography in 1997, in which the author acknowledged his debt to Paolo Fabbri's *Monteverdi*, published in 1985.[47] Once again Tellart quotes the famous letter in French, not translating the phrase *trombe squarciate*, but adding in brackets: "[certainement des trombones, comme le suggère Fabbri]."[48] Similarly, Tellart renews his attribution of the Gloria *a 7* to the thanksgiving ceremonies, but does not do the same in his discussion of the *Messa a quattro voci* and the concertato Credo fragments.[49]

---

[43] Ibid.

[44] Roger Tellart, *Claudio Monteverdi: L'homme et son œuvre* (Paris: Éditions Seghers, 1964).

[45] Ibid., 85: "une messe solennelle composé par le seigneur Claudio Monteverdi, Maestro di Cappella, la gloire de notre siècle, au cours de laquelle les chants du *Gloria* et du *Credo* étaient accompagnés de *trombe squarciate* qui créaient de merveilleuses harmonies."

[46] Ibid., 148–49.

[47] Roger Tellart, *Claudio Monteverdi* (Paris: Librairie Arthème Fayard, 1997), 645. Tellart's reference is to Paolo Fabbri, *Monteverdi* (Turin: Edizioni di Torino, 1985). Fabbri's book was published in an English translation by Tim Carter (Cambridge: Cambridge University Press, 1994).

[48] Tellart, 1997, 411.

[49] Ibid. "De ces musiques d'apparat exécutés le 28 (ou 21) novembre 1631, rien, là non plus, ne nous est parvenu, à ceci près que le Gloria de la messe d'action de grâce semble bien être l'irrésistible *Gloria a 7 voci*

The 1967 monograph on Monteverdi authored by Guglielmo Barblan, Claudio Gallico, and Guido Pannain in celebration of the four-hundredth anniversary of the composer's birth reiterates what had by then become the most common assumption about the Mass of Thanksgiving and its connection with Monteverdi's surviving music.[50] In the biographical section of the book, written by Barblan, the Mass of Thanksgiving is mentioned and a brief extract from de' Vescovi's letter quoted (not requiring a translation of *trombe squarciate* into another language, of course), but Barblan leaves the matter with the simple historical facts and does not speculate on any extant music of Monteverdi's as pertaining to the ceremony.[51] That role is left to Guido Pannain, who, in the section on Monteverdi's secular and sacred polyphony, assigns the Gloria *a 7* to the Mass of Thanksgiving: "pagina veemente, di gioiosa accensione ritmica, scritta nel 1631 in occasione di una cerimonia religiosa di ringraziamento per la fine della peste."[52] The *Messa a quattro voci* and the Credo fragments, however, remain separately described and unconnected to the Gloria *a 7* and the Mass of Thanksgiving.[53]

The same year saw a mobile conference in Venice, Mantua, and Cremona in which Denis Stevens spoke at length about the *Selva morale* and the Mass of Thanksgiving. Stevens took pains to note the similarity in orchestration between the *Et iterum* Credo fragment and the Gloria *a 7* to draw for the first time a direct association between the three Credo fragments on the one hand, and the *Gloria*, which immediately precedes them in the *Selva morale*, on the other. This association led him to further speculation regarding the origin of the anomalous substitution rubrics for the Credo fragments:

> The history of the *Gloria*, whose orchestration is so similar to that of the Credo section, goes back a decade before the publication of the *Selva*, for it is generally associated with the Thanksgiving Mass ordained by the Doge on November 28 [recte: November 21], 1631. . . . The predominance of duets, first for sopranos, then tenors, then violins, reminds us of the duets in the fragment "Et resurrexit"; and since the "Et iterum" calls for trombones, we surely have in this *Credo* section all that remains of the *Credo* referred to

---

concertata qui figurera dans le *Selva morale e spirituale* de 1640: une liturgie jubilatoire, fleurie d'exubérantes arabesques en double croches au tutti et, telle quelle, admirablement adapté à la dimension festive de la célébration" (p. 411).

[50] Guglielmo Barblan, Claudio Gallico, and Guido Pannain, *Claudio Monteverdi: nel quarto centenario della nascita* (Turin: Edizioni RAI Radiotelevisione Italiana, 1967).

[51] Ibid., 122.

[52] Ibid., 348–49.

[53] Ibid., 346–48.

by Antonio de' Vescovi. It is strange that historians have been quick to associate his *Gloria* with the one in the *Selva*, but slow to realize that the *Credo* he mentions might also be preserved—at least partially—in the same publication. But the printer's or Monteverdi's idea of substitution led them astray, although it seems fairly clear that the music was found to be incomplete at the very moment when it was due to be handed over to Magni.[54]

Stevens facilitated joining the Gloria *a 7* and the Credo fragments with the Mass of Thanksgiving by a sleight of hand regarding the discrepancy between de' Vescovi's *trombe squarciate* and the trombones cited in the rubrics of the *Et iterum* and Gloria *a 7* in the *Selva morale*. First quoting the letter's sentence in Italian, Stevens goes on to note:

> Emil Vogel, who was the first to reprint this passage from Cappelletti's *Storia della Repubblica di Venezia*, translated "trombe squarciate" as "Posaunen" (tromboni), on the assumption that this clerical commentator did not know the correct term "tromboni" and so invented "trombe squarciate"—trumpets that were torn asunder by the hard-working right arms of their players. . . . If Antonio de' Vescovi did invent the term "trombe squarciate" he was not far wrong, for a later Italian term for the slide trumpet was "tromba spezzata." Denis Arnold, in his translation of de' Vescovi's words, uses the term "loud trumpets," presumably on the analogy of "squarciagola," which means "at the top of one's voice," or "loud and shrill."[55]

Vogel, however, had not impugned de' Vescovi's knowledge of terminology, and Vogel's "assumption" was purely the invention of Stevens. Stevens then noted that cornetti were the usual soprano brass instruments in the instrumental ensemble at St. Mark's according to the testimony of both the contemporaneous Venetian historian Francesco Sansovino and the payment accounts of St. Mark's. Thus Stevens concludes that "To sum up, we have Sansovino, Vogel, and the account-books in favour of trombones, together with the evidence in the partbooks of the *Selva*. But there are no actual trombone parts, since it was the custom to let them double the tenor and bass chorus lines."[56]

---

[54] Denis Stevens, "Claudio Monteverdi: *Selva morale e spirituale*," *Congresso internazionale sul tema Monteverdi e il suo tempo: relazioni e comunicazioni*, ed. Raffaello Monterosso (Verona: Stamperia Valdonego, 1969), 424–26.

[55] Ibid., 425.

[56] Ibid.

Stevens, in fact, had ignored several uses of the phrase *trombe squarciate* by Sansovino and simply passed off the discrepancy between *trombe squarciate* and trombones as an "invention," also ignoring the fact that the Mass of Thanksgiving was a special occasion that might well have called for special instrumentation. In the round-table discussion that followed Stevens's oral presentation, Nino Pirrotta suggested that *trombe squarciate* were larger than trumpets but smaller than trombones, while Denis Arnold changed his earlier position to warn against "a too exact translation." Arnold now said he would avoid the issue and translate *trombe squarciate* as "loud brass instruments."[57] Thus the phrase *trombe squarciate* and its meaning continued to bedevil scholars, but rather than questioning the identification with trombones that had led to the hypothesis that the Gloria *a 7* was the Gloria from the Mass of Thanksgiving, these and other scholars preferred to dance around the original terminology, each opting for one or another manner of explaining away the discrepancy between *trombe squarciate* and *tromboni*, the latter a term also used with great frequency by Sansovino and in the St. Mark's account books and certainly available to Antonio de' Vescovi.

At the same time Stevens was presenting his hypotheses on the Mass of Thanksgiving and the *Selva morale*'s Gloria *a 7* and Credo fragments at the Monteverdi Congress, John Steele was preparing an edition of the Gloria *a 7* for the Penn State Music Series, published in 1968. In that edition, Steele assumed that the hypotheses put forward by Schrade and Arnold were widely accepted.[58] His preface begins, "It is commonly agreed by scholars that the *Gloria concertata* is a surviving portion of a complete Mass composed by Monteverdi for performance at a great thanksgiving in St. Mark's on 28 November [recte: 21 November] 1631." Steele goes on to quote from Arnold's 1963 book de' Vescovi's description of the mass in which Arnold had interpreted *trombe squarciate* as "loud trumpets." Steele then continues:

> "Trumpets" is probably a misreading for "trombones," since the natural trumpets of the time did not take part in concerted church music. With this correction, the identity of the *Gloria concertata* with that of the Thanksgiving Mass is reasonably certain. Other portions of the "lost" Mass may perhaps be traced in the same printed source (*Selva morale*, 1641) as the *Gloria concertata*; here there is a *Messa a 4 voci da cappella*[59] with alternative *concertato* settings of *Crucifixus* and

---

[57] Ibid., 433–34.

[58] John Steele, ed., *Gloria Concertata by Claudio Monteverdi* (University Park, Pennsylvania and London: The Pennsylvania State University Press, 1968), preface.

[59] Steele's footnote: "See the recent edition by D. Arnold, Eulenburg, London (1962)."

> *Et resurrexit.* These settings may well have been salvaged from the
> Thanksgiving Mass either by Monteverdi or his publisher, Magni.[60]

Thus Steele, drawing on both Arnold's edition and his book, was the first to join together in print the *Gloria a 7*, the Credo fragments, and the *Messa a quattro voci* as all stemming from the November 1631 ceremonies, though that conjunction was already implicit in Arnold's writings. However, Steele rejected Arnold's translation of *trombe squarciate* as "loud trumpets," assuming that de' Vescovi's original description was in error, and returned to the trombones that had been the link between the Mass of Thanksgiving and the Gloria *a 7* in Schrade's book.

Despite the confidence with which Denis Stevens had argued in 1967 that *trombe squarciate* were trombones, he became somewhat unsure of the matter later, as revealed in 1978 when he published a small book on Monteverdi's sacred, secular, and occasional music.[61] In that volume, after citing the 1631 thanksgiving ceremonies, Stevens says that "a report by one who was present confirms that the *Gloria* and *Credo* by Monteverdi sounded fourth [*sic*] with 'trombe squarciate'—probably slide-trumpets or narrow-bore trombones.[62] These two movements were eventually, though imperfectly, published in the *Selva morale* of 1641."[63] Why he would have suggested specifically "narrow-bore" trombones is not at all obvious, but Stevens's ambivalence about the instruments did not extend to the role of the Gloria *a 7* and the Credo fragments in the Mass of Thanksgiving, which he states as a simple matter of fact.

Once again, in his 1980 translation of Monteverdi's letters, Stevens claimed un-equivocally that the complete Gloria *a 7* and the fragmentary Credo of the *Selva morale* were those performed for the Thanksgiving Mass. This time, to bolster his 1967 contention that *trombe squarciate* were trombones, he cited a rubric by Giambattista Guarini from an intermezzo for the author's *Il pastor fido* to be performed in Mantua utilizing "trombone di quelli che chiamano 'squarciati'."[64] By this time Stevens entertained no

---

[60] Steele, *Gloria Concertata*, preface.

[61] Denis Stevens, *Monteverdi: Sacred, Secular, and Occasional Music* (Rutherford, NJ: Fairleigh Dickinson University Press, 1978).

[62] Stevens's footnote: "Vogel, 'Claudio Monteverdi,' 393. See also the discussion of 'trombe squarciate' in *Claudio Monteverdi e il suo tempo* (Verona, 1969), 433. A reliable performing edition of the *Gloria*, by John Steele, is published in the Penn State Music Series, No. 18 (University Park, 1968)."

[63] Stevens, *Monteverdi: Sacred, Secular, and Occasional Music*, 69–70.

[64] Denis Stevens, trans., *The Letters of Claudio Monteverdi*, rev. ed. (Oxford: Clarendon Press, 1995), 413–14. The passage from Guarini is found in Marziano Guglielminetti, ed., *Opere di Battista Guarini*, 2nd ed. (Turin: UTET, 1971), 722. This rubric by Guarini is at odds with almost all other uses of the term *squarciate* in connection with instruments, which is almost invariably found as a participial adjective to *trombe*, very often

doubts that *trombe squarciate* were trombones; nevertheless, on the basis of later evidence, he once again hedged on the translation in his 1995 second edition of the letters. Stevens repeats exactly the same wording as in the first edition, but adds a footnote, saying "The account of Antonio de' Vescovi (Vogel, 393) has given rise to varying interpretations of the term, but it is certain that brass instruments were used. This theory is elaborated in Morre, [*sic*] 'Venezia', 234ff., and in Kurtzmann, [*sic*], 63ff."[65]

In 1998, Stevens published his critical edition of the *Selva morale e spirituale* in the *opera omnia* of Monteverdi published by the Fondazione Claudio Monteverdi in Cremona.[66] In the introduction to this volume Stevens provides a detailed description of the performance of the Mass of Thanksgiving and its aftermath:

> When the Thanksgiving Mass was performed on 21 November 1631, a state of enormous excitement prevailed. Something had to go wrong, and what happened was that since the musical forces required two basic positions in the basilica and two extra *palchi*, four sets of music had to be prepared for two small groups and the double choir which as usual occupied the *pergolo* and other sections of the edifice. After the service, the fireworks, the cannon, and the inevitable liquid refreshments, a man deputed to return the music to Monteverdi was robbed, probably by one of the composer's enemies. It was never recovered.
>
> The composer was of course upset, since nobody had made a safety copy. As he had no intention of reconstructing the missing parts of the *Credo*, one of Magni's assistants probably suggested using a Mass already submitted, and "troping" it with the surviving *concertato* items.[67]

According to Stevens's footnote, the source of this description is G. Ridolfi, *Le meraviglie di Venezia*, Venezia, Curti, 1642. However, no such book can be found in the Biblioteca Marciana in Venice, in any of the Italian online catalogues, or in any other

---

paired with *tamburi* as an ensemble. By contrast, I have never seen a reference to trombones paired with *tamburi*. See Kurtzman and Koldau, "*Trombe, Trombe d'argento, Trombe squarciate, Tromboni,* and *Pifferi*," discussed below.

[65] Stevens, *The Letters*, 2nd ed., 414, n. 5. In this note, Stevens also reiterates the information about Guarini's rubric referring to "trombone di quelli che chiamano 'squarciati'." The citation of Moore in this note is to his "*Venezia favorita da Maria*." The citation of Kurtzman is to my "Monteverdi's 'Mass of Thanksgiving' Revisited," to be discussed below.

[66] Stevens, ed., *Claudio Monteverdi: Selva morale e spirituale*.

[67] Ibid., 15. The same story is repeated with only slight variants of wording in Stevens's subsequent book, *Monteverdi in Venice* (Madison and Teaneck, NJ: Fairleigh Dickinson University Press, 2001), 51.

X

112

of the world's major libraries. The closest match is Carlo Ridolfi's *Le meraviglie dell'arte, ovvero le vite degli illustri pittori veneti e dello stato* (Venice: Giovanni Battista Sgava, 1648). In this book Ridolfi, from personal experience, graphically describes Venice during the plague years and mentions the procession to the site of Santa Maria della Salute in late 1631, but says nothing about the Monteverdi mass and nothing about a score being stolen.[68] At this time, Stevens's description of the performance of the mass and the theft of its score appears to be a figment of his imagination with no evidentiary foundation.[69]

On the basis of a slight similarity between the principal motive of the *Messa a quattro voci* and a madrigal printed in his *Primo Libro dei madrigali* of 1587, *La vaga pastorella*, Stevens makes the highly dubious claim that the *Messa a quattro voci* is a parody mass on the madrigal, written in that same year of 1587.[70] His final word on the Mass of Thanksgiving, derived in part from James H. Moore (see the discussion of Moore's 1984 article below), is that:

> The concertante *Gloria* and *Credo*, together with a magnificent bass aria *Ab aeterno ordinata sum* were first performed at the ceremonies on 21 November 1631 as part of a general thanksgiving for the cessation of the plague. Extra singers and instrumentalists were hired for the occasion, which Marco Ginammi, a Venetian man of letters, described in a pamphlet addressed to the city's official Resident in Naples [there follows the famous quotation regarding the mass, in the version published by Moore]. The loud *trombe squarciate* were sometimes called *tromboni*, as at Mantua in 1592 when the young Monteverdi had just joined the establishment as a string player. He might have noticed, in the Third Intermezzo for Guarini's *Il pastor fido*, that the actor representing Austro, the south wind, had "in mano trombone di quelli che chiamano *squarciati.*"[71]

---

[68] A second, corrected edition of Ridolfi's book was published in Padua by the Tipografia e Fanderia Cartallier, 1835–37. Ridolfi's description of the thanksgiving ceremony is on p. 568 of this edition. Ridolfi's activity as a painter and writer is the subject of a monograph by Domenico Vitaliani, *Carlo Ridolfi, pittore e scrittore* (Lonigo: Tip. Papolo e Panozzo, 1911). There is a Giulio Antonio Ridolfi in this period who wrote plays and poetry, but published nothing in Venice and nothing even remotely similar to the title Stevens gives.

[69] Throughout his career, Stevens was given to describing in detailed, concrete terms events in Monteverdi's life that were only hinted at in the sources, often creating elaborate scenarios with varying degrees of probability which Stevens simply presented as fact. This practice is especially frequent in his commentaries on the Monteverdi letters in his volume of translations. However, I have never seen another instance by Stevens of a fabrication of a scenario *ex nihilo* as seems to be the case in the paragraph describing the circumstances of the Mass of Thanksgiving.

[70] Stevens, ed., *Claudio Monteverdi: Selva morale e spirituale*, 15.

[71] Ibid., 20–21. This passage, too, is repeated in Stevens's *Monteverdi in Venice*, 58–59.

At approximately the same time as Stevens was making his claims about the *Selva morale*, Claudio Gallico's Monteverdi book of 1979 presented no new thoughts on the issue of the Mass of Thanksgiving, suggesting only the probability of the Gloria *a 7* having been performed for that event.[72] Gallico discusses the *Messa a quattro voci* and the Credo fragments separately from the Gloria *a 7* and does not draw them into the Mass of Thanksgiving.[73] Also in 1979, de' Paoli published a much expanded version of his 1945 monograph on Monteverdi, but made no changes with respect to the *Messa a quattro voci* and the Mass of Thanksgiving other than rewording his previous, separate comments on the thanksgiving celebrations and the mass from the *Selva morale*.[74] De' Paoli does, however, add discussion of the Gloria *a 7* to his earlier monograph and, following closely Schrade's language, declares that "Il carattere del lavoro e la sua corrispondenza con testimonianze dei contemporanei fanno pensare che il *Gloria* appartenga a quella *Messa di Ringraziamento* per la liberazione dalla peste, composta nel 1631, ed eseguita il 28 novembre [recte: 21 novembre] dello stesso anno."[75]

Silke Leopold, however, in her 1982 monograph on Monteverdi, included both the Gloria *a 7* and the Credo fragments in her brief discussion of the mass music of the *Selva morale* and its presumed relationship to the Mass of Thanksgiving. Leopold made no definitive statement on this relationship, simply noting that "Diese Meßordinariums-Teile sind immer wieder mit der Dankesmesse für das Ende der Pest in Verbindung gebracht worden. . . ." Her subsequent reference to Antonio de' Vescovi's account of the mass is rendered in German as "daß beim *Gloria* und beim *Credo* laute Blechblas-instrumente den Gesang begleitet hätten."[76] The adjective *laute* is obviously derived from Denis Arnold, but the use of the term *Blechblasinstrumente*, in its generality, avoids the issue of whether these were some kind of trumpets or trombones.

---

[72] Claudio Gallico, *Monteverdi: Poesia musicale, teatro e musica sacra* (Turin: Giulio Einaudi Editore, 1979), 132: "Non v'è modo d'accertare le date delle singole opere comprese nei due libri [*Selva morale e spirituale* and *Messa a quattro voci e salmi* of 1650]. Con l'eccezione, forse, del *Gloria a sette voci concertato con due violini e quattro viole da braccio ovvero quattro tromboni*. Esso potè risuonare la prima volta nel 1631. Terminato l'orrore della peste, il doge Francesco Erizzo ordinò una funzione di ringraziamento in San Marco, il 26 [recte: 21] novembre 1631." Gallico then quotes from Vogel the description of the Gloria and Credo by Antonio de' Vescovi and continues: "Era verosimilmente il *Gloria* concertato, compreso poi nella *Selva*."

[73] Ibid., 133–34.

[74] Domenico de' Paoli, *Monteverdi* (Milan: Rusconi, 1979), 420, 458–59.

[75] Ibid., 463.

[76] Silke Leopold, *Claudio Monteverdi und seine Zeit* (Laaber: Laaber-Verlag, 1982), 215–16. Leopold also describes the plague and the Mass of Thanksgiving as a historical event in her chronology of Monteverdi's life on pp. 39–40. These passages remain unchanged in the second revised edition (Laaber: Laaber-Verlag, 1993), 38–39, 197.

X

114

Thus, by the early 1980s, scholars had commonly accepted, with varying degrees of certainty, that at least the Gloria *a 7* from the *Selva morale*, and in many authors, the Credo fragments as well, were written for and performed in the Mass of Thanksgiving on November 21, 1631. The Credo fragments were considered remnants of a complete Credo, and their interpolation into the *Messa a quattro voci* as substitute segments, was merely an expedient to justify their inclusion in the *Selva morale*. John Steele had argued that the other three movements of the *Messa a quattro voci* formed the remainder of the Mass of Thanksgiving.

III

In 1984 James H. Moore, for the first time, went far beyond the brief passage Venetian historians and Vogel had quoted from one another all the way back to Antonio de' Vescovi's letter first published by Gallicciolli in 1795.[77] In an impressive article, supported by frequent quotation from Venetian sources of 1630 and 1631, Moore argued that not only the *Messa a quattro voci*, the Gloria *a 7*, and the Credo fragments belonged to the Mass of Thanksgiving, but that the entire first half of the *Selva morale*, up to the sequence of psalm settings, represented music for various events during the course of the plague.[78] In a *tour de force* of archival research, Moore had discovered that the Mass of Thanksgiving was the culmination of a long series of events and ceremonials that extended back to September of 1629 with the first efforts of the city to ward off the plague, and continued in response to its horrific spread throughout 1630–31.[79] The day of the thanksgiving celebration was not November 28, as consistently reported in the sources going back to Gallicciolli, but rather November 21. The Mass of Thanksgiving itself, held in St. Mark's, preceded a procession to the site of the future Church of Santa Maria Salute for a ceremony there. The church was to be constructed in fulfillment of the vow made by the Senate and Doge for relief from the plague in October of 1630.[80] The hope had been that this vow would have the same salutary effect as the one made during the plague of 1575–77 (still within the memory of elderly Venetians) which had resulted in the construction of Palladio's Church of the Redeemer

---

[77] See n. 9.

[78] Moore, *Venezia favorita*. See especially the author's table of plague music on p. 353.

[79] Ibid., 317–26.

[80] The fulfillment of this vow by the erection of the church was one of the subjects of Casoni's *La peste di Venezia* of 1830. See the full title in n. 11.

(Il Redentore) on the Giudecca island. The end of this earlier plague is still celebrated annually in Venice on the third Sunday in July as the *Festa del Redentore*, and includes a procession over a pontoon bridge across the Giudecca canal to a ceremony in the church in emulation of the original sixteenth-century processions across a bridge formed from gondolas.[81]

Among Moore's discoveries was the pamphlet authored by Marco Ginammi, whose wording overlapped very closely the letter by Antonio de' Vescovi quoted by Venetian historians and repeated by Vogel and all recent scholars.[82] Another was a second account of the Mass of Thanksgiving, inscribed in the Collegio Ceremoniale (a series of large books describing in chronological order special ceremonies at St. Mark's), which records each of the ceremonies associated with the plague that were held in the ducal church.[83] The account of the mass on November 21, 1631 closely resembles that of de' Vescovi and Ginammi: "Si cantò solenissima Messa sonandosi alcuna volta le trombe al Gloria in excelsis et al credo; si fece una salva di codette al vangelo et alla consacratione, si cominciò la processione."[84] The Collegio's version, however, omits the adjective *squarciate* attached to *trombe*, as found in the two other sources.

From the Collegio account, one could indeed assume that the instruments playing in the Gloria and Credo were trombones, since the term *trombe* in that period covered both instruments.[85] However, de' Vescovi's and Ginammi's more detailed description, identifying the *trombe* specifically as *squarciate*, throws an entirely different light on the matter. Moore was the first to recognize unequivocally that these must be trumpets, not trombones, and assumed that they were natural trumpets in C.[86] As Moore pointed out, the phrase *trombe squarciate* is found frequently in Venetian sources, and the instruments are often associated with drums in processions and other public ceremonials.

---

[81] Moore, *Venezia favorita*, 318–19.

[82] Ibid., 314–17. See n. 4 and the discussion above. In Ginammi's pamphlet, Antonio de' Vescovi was merely the author of a couple of anagrams printed at its conclusion, where he signs himself in Latin as "Antonius de Episcopis Clericus & Ciuis Venetus." Moore, unaware of Antonio's letter as a separate entity, assumed that previous scholars had taken Ginammi's pamphlet as their source and had mistaken the name of the author. See n. 5.

[83] Ibid., 319–24. Moore notes that a number of these accounts were later copied into I-Vas, San Marco, Procuratia de Supra, Registro 99. For details, see Moore, *Venezia favorita*, 319, n. 70.

[84] Quoted in ibid, 324, n. 94. I have myself checked Moore's transcription for accuracy against the Collegio Ceremoniale.

[85] See the discussion of terminology in Kurtzman and Koldau, *Trombe*, section V.

[86] Moore, *Venezia favorita*, 345. Moore's argument in favor of trumpets and his speculation on their use in the Gloria *a 7* of the *Selva morale* are on pp. 343–48.

X

Unlike Arnold, Moore realized from the beginning that by identifying the instruments as trumpets, he was undercutting the very foundation of the association between the Mass of Thanksgiving and the concertato mass music published in the *Selva morale*, where *tromboni* are specifically identified in the rubrics.[87] Therefore, immediately upon completing his discussion arguing that the *trombe squarciate* must be trumpets rather than trombones, he argues:

> Since it seems clear that the *trombe squarciate, trombe,* and two *trombetti* [the latter term taken from pay records] refer to trumpets, not trombones, we are faced with a dilemma. Either some unknown Mass must have been performed, one with obbligato parts for two trumpets, or trumpets must have performed in the Gloria and Credo of the *Selva morale* even though no trumpet parts were published. . . . However, the publication of the Gloria, Credo, and *Ab aeterno ordinata sum* [a motet following the Credo fragments in the *Selva morale*] as a unit makes it nearly certain that all three pieces were part of the mass of thanksgiving. Thus, trumpets must somehow have played in the two movements that survive.[88]

Moore subsequently explains that trumpets could well have been used in those parts of the Credo that don't survive and also illustrates passages in the Gloria *a 7* where trumpets might have doubled the printed violin parts rather than having separate obbligato parts of their own.

The crux of Moore's association of the *Selva morale* mass movements with the Mass of Thanksgiving has now shifted from the instrumentation described by de' Vescovi, Ginammi and the Collegio Ceremoniale to his extended argument that the motet *Ab aeterno ordinata sum* was also performed at the Mass of Thanksgiving.[89] We need not follow this argument in detail here, other than to proceed to Moore's conclusion: "Since the association of this motet with the Mass of Thanksgiving seems so clear, and since it was printed alongside a *concertato* Gloria and Credo, it seems evident that the Gloria and Credo are, in fact, the very movements performed on this day, as scholars have surmised."[90]

---

[87] By this time *tromboni* clearly referred to a slide instrument larger than the typical trumpet in C. Moreover, *tromboni* are not coupled with drums in any Venetian source I have seen. See Kurtzman and Koldau, *Trombe*, section V, especially paragraph 44.6.

[88] Moore, *Venezia favorita*, 345 (brackets mine).

[89] For this argument, see ibid., 339–42.

[90] Ibid., 342.

But the association of the motet with the Mass of Thanksgiving is much more circumstantial than Moore asserts, and even if he were correct, the motet's position in the *Selva morale*, another crucial point in Moore's argument, may not have the weight he ascribes to it with regard to the role of the Gloria *a 7* and Credo fragments. Both bookends of his argument are required to accept his conclusion, and both are tentative and susceptible to other explanations. As will be shown below, the motet was more likely destined for another purpose, and its position in the *Selva morale* print, at the end of the section labeled A in the index, may have been a matter of convenience in the typesetter's layout of the part-books rather than association with the Gloria *a 7* and the Credo fragments.[91]

Moore's claim that the entire first half of the *Selva morale* as well as one psalm and the motets at the end of the *Selva* were performed at various plague ceremonies in the years 1629–31 is based on even more circumstantial, even wholly speculative evidence. For example, Moore asserts that the five spiritual madrigals that open the *Selva morale* print were performed at five successive services at the cathedral church of San Pietro di Castello on five successive days in 1629. But the only evidence Moore adduces linking the madrigals with these services is the quantity five, scarcely convincing testimony.[92]

As far as the *Messa a quattro voci* is concerned, Moore again tacitly resorts to the argument of contiguity in the *Selva morale* print: "It is probable that the Kyrie, Sanctus, and Agnus Dei used for the Mass of thanksgiving came from the *Messa a quattro voci* later printed in the *Selva morale*, although it is also possible that they were merely chanted."[93] Once again, Moore undercuts his argument, for if these sections of the mass ordinary were chanted on November 21, 1630, then the four-voice Kyrie, Sanctus, and Agnus Dei printed in the *Selva morale* (as well as the Gloria and Credo *a quattro voci* in this complete mass), did not form part of the Mass of Thanksgiving, and therefore the first half of the *Selva morale* does not represent, in its entirety, music from the plague ceremonies. Moore seems not to have considered the possibility that an entirely different Kyrie, as well as perhaps a Sanctus and Agnus Dei, all concertato, might have

---

[91] See my discussion of the organization of the part-books in, "Monteverdi's 'Mass of Thanksgiving' Revisited," 65–67.

[92] Moore, *Venezia favorita*, 328–29. Robert Holzer, in a recent paper entitled "Monteverdi's *Rerum vulgarium fragmenta*: The Italian-Texted Pieces of the *Selva morale et spirituale*," delivered at Princeton University in 2005, makes a very different case for the role of the *madrigali spirituali*, exploring at length their literary forbears and explaining their theme of *vanitas* as both the personal confession of an elderly man and a public statement of the wisdom and perspective of old age on the transitoriness of earthly endeavors and values. I am grateful to Professor Holzer for sharing a copy of his paper with me.

[93] Moore, 348.

formed the other movements of the original Mass of Thanksgiving.[94] If so, then the
Gloria and Credo of the November 21, 1631 mass might also have been different
compositions from those published in the *Selva morale*.

Moore's entire argument derives from the understandable desire, seen prominently
in the writings of Denis Stevens as well, to associate surviving published music with
specific events described in documents. Moore's tendency in this direction is so strong
that where he cannot find pieces in Monteverdi's extant repertoire to match those
cited in the accounts of the plague ceremonies, he looks to the publications of Giovanni
Rovetta, *vice maestro di cappella* at St. Mark's, for their representation. Yet it is apparent
that what survives of Monteverdi's Venetian sacred music must be only very small
remnants of what he actually produced (the same is likely true for Rovetta). As Stevens
himself pointed out, two of Monteverdi's letters refer to the requirement that the *maestro
di cappella* of St. Mark's compose a new mass for every Christmas eve.[95] We are not
told whether the style of the mass must be concertato, *coro spezzato*, or in a more conservative imitative polyphony, but whatever the style, Monteverdi apparently composed
thirty masses for this service alone during his tenure in Venice. The *Messa a quattro voci*
from the *Selva morale* and the *Messa a quattro* published posthumously in 1650 are the
only masses of Monteverdi to survive from his Venetian years, and they may have been
written for other occasions altogether. In addition to these many Christmas masses,
Monteverdi's Requiem mass (portions of which were composed by Francesco Usper
and Giovan Battista Grillo) for the Florentine Grand Duke Cosimo II of 1621 is lost.[96]
And what of masses for such important feasts as Easter, Corpus Christi, the Finding
of the Holy Cross, and the Assumption of the Virgin, when Venice renewed each year
its marriage to the sea, as well as the feast of the Redeemer celebrating the end of the
1575–77 plague, or the annual celebration of the anniversary of the Battle of Lepanto
in the church of San Giustina, or the many masses he must have written for important
occasional events, or for the *scuole grandi* of Venice?[97] Any of these feasts might well have
elicited as celebratory a piece as the Gloria *a 7* and/or the concertato Credo segments.

---

[94] As Moore notes on p. 348, the Sanctus and Agnus Dei were often abbreviated or omitted altogether
in Venetian mass ordinaries.

[95] Letters of October 30, 1627 and February 2, 1634. Monteverdi also comments in a letter of
December 29, 1616 that he was occupied the entire month of December with the mass for Christmas Eve.
See *Letters*, ed. Stevens, 2nd ed., pp. 113, 381, 424.

[96] For a contemporary account of this mass, see Fabbri, *Monteverdi*, 240 (Carter translation, 179).

[97] The principal feasts that occupied Monteverdi in new composition are enumerated in Fabbri,
Monteverdi, 185–90 (Carter translation, 132–38). A letter of April 21, 1618 and other documents make it clear
that some of these masses were in *concertato* style. The question of Monteverdi's lost sacred music is examined
in Kurtzman, "Monteverdi's Missing Sacred Music" forthcoming in the Festschrift for Piotr Pozniak.

Given the loss of such large quantities of masses by Monteverdi (as well as other sacred music), the greatest likelihood, from a purely statistical point of view, is that *none* of the music performed on November 21, 1631 survives at all.

Prompted by Moore's article, Andrew Parrott and the Taverner Consort, Choir and Players issued in 1989 a recording entitled *Monteverdi: Mass of Thanksgiving, Venice 1631*.[98] The program notes, penned by Hugh Keyte, repeat many of the conclusions from Moore's 1984 article, but suggest that the missing sections of the concertato Credo that together with Monteverdi's three Credo fragments would have completed this movement of the mass, were composed by St. Mark's *vice maestro di cappella* Giovanni Rovetta. Keyte declares that the Credo from Rovetta's *Messa e Salmi* of 1639 "is closely modeled on Monteverdi's *Selva morale* Gloria, which it matches in scoring and key."[99] Keyte finds that the three segments of Rovetta's Credo corresponding to those Monteverdi published in the *Selva morale* are "in a noticeably different style from the rest of the piece," and therefore Keyte speculates that "the Credo was planned as a collaboration, with Monteverdi reserving the textual plums for himself, and that Rovetta added this section at a later date. Monteverdi may have been anxious to unload part of his composing burden onto his assistant. . . ."[100] Keyte also assumes that the Kyrie, Sanctus, and Agnus Dei on November 21, 1631 were from the *Messa a quattro voci* of the *Selva*. The mass on the recording inserts a trumpet toccata and sonata after the Gregorian Introit and concludes with a trumpet sonata, all by the Medici court trumpeter, Girolamo Fantini.[101] The Proper portions of the mass are filled out with motets and instrumental music by Monteverdi and other composers associated with St. Mark's. Segments such as the Prayer, Epistle, and Evangelist are in Gregorian chant.

This is not only a purely speculative reconstruction, but also quite suspect, since the Rovetta mass was commissioned by the French ambassador in September 1638 for a service in the Palladian church of San Giorgio, on the island of that name, to celebrate the birth of the French dauphin, the future King Louis XIV.[102] It does not

---

[98] See n. 8.

[99] EMI CDS 749876 2, program booklet, 9.

[100] Ibid.

[101] In 1638 Fantini had published a treatise on the trumpet, containing a number of fanfares and other compositions: *Modo per Imparare e sonare di Tromba tanto di Guerra Quanto Musicalmente: in Organo, con Tromba Sordina, col Cimbalo e con ogn'altro istrumento* (Frankfurt: Daniel Wastch, 1638; facs. ed., Edward H. Tarr, Nashville: The Brass Press, 1978).

[102] A detailed account of the birth of the dauphin, the commission, and the celebration in the church of San Giorgio was published by Fausto Ciro, *Venetia festiva per gli pomposi spettacoli fatti rappresentare dall'Illustriss. & Eccellentiss. Sig. d'Hussè Ambasciatore di S. M. Christianissima, per la nascita del Real Delfino di Francia* (Venice: Andrea Baba, 1638). The dauphin was born on September 5, and news of his birth reached Venice on

seem likely that such a prestigious commission would have been filled by resurrecting an older work composed for another occasion, though the psalms published together with the mass in 1639 must represent an assemblage accumulated over an extended period of time. Nor is Rovetta's Credo on an aesthetic par with Monteverdi's Credo fragments or the Gloria *a 7*.

A decade after Moore's article appeared, I published an article of my own critiquing Moore's arguments and conclusions.[103] In this study I found Moore's logic and contentions to be weak in many respects, but still accepted the "presumption (probable, perhaps, but certainly not proven) that the Mass in F, the Gloria *a 7* and the three substitute Credo segments were indeed performed at the 'Mass of Thanksgiving' on 21 November 1631."[104] My re-examination of the evidence was summarized as follows:

> The preceding discussion makes it clear that the linking of the Mass in F, the Gloria *a 7* and the concertato Credo segments through the substitution rubrics for the latter is a separate issue from the association of these compositions with the "Mass of Thanksgiving" of 21 November 1631. Moore's disentangling of the *trombe squarciate* from trombones has eliminated the rationale for this association put forward by earlier scholars (i.e. the rubrics calling for optional trombones), and the connection between these compositions and the "Mass of Thanksgiving" on the Feast of the Presentation now depends on the likelihood that the *trombe* mentioned by the payment documents and by the contemporaneous witnesses could have been used in the Gloria and Credo segments.[105]

Earlier in my article I had examined the possibilities for using trumpets in the Gloria *a 7* and the Credo *a quattro voci* with the three concertato fragments substituting for the equivalent four-voice segments as indicated by the rubrics in the *Selva morale*.[106]

September 16. See Ciro, 12–13. The performance of Rovetta's mass, a Te Deum, and the psalm *Omnes gentes plaudite manibus* is described by Ciro on pp. 28–34. The mass was published together with a collection of Vesper psalms by Rovetta the next year, with a dedication of March 1, as *Messa e Salmi concertati a cinque, sei, sette, otto voci, e due violini . . . opera quarta . . .* (Venice: Vincenti, 1639). Rovetta's entire print has been published in a modern edition by Linda Maria Koldau, *Giovanni Rovetta: Messa, e salmi concertati, op. 4 (1639)*, 2 vols. (Middleton, WI: A-R Editions, Inc., 2001). The mass alone has also been published in Anne Schnoebelen, ed., *Seventeenth-Century Italian Sacred Music: Masses*, 10 vols. (New York and London: Garland Publishing, Inc., 1995–99), 5:3–100.

[103] Kurtzman, "Monteverdi's 'Mass of Thanksgiving' Revisited," 63–84.

[104] Ibid., 70.

[105] Ibid., 78.

[106] Ibid., 72–75.

Noting that there was no evidence that the remainder of a concertato Credo had ever been composed, my speculations focused on the existing concertato fragments as well as the possibility of introductory music for trumpets before the Credo and a fanfare before the *Et resurrexit*.[107] I did not at that time find troublesome the well-known stylistic and tonal dichotomy between the Credo segments and the rest of the *Messa a quattro voci*, including its own four-voice Credo.[108] However, now that Anne Schnoebelen has published a sizable sample of Italian mass music from the seventeenth century and has completed her inventory of mass publications from that period, the contrast between the motivically unified, consistent imitative polyphony of Monteverdi's four-voice mass and the concertato Credo fragments appears much more likely to be the publishing expedient assumed by John Steele and Denis Stevens than a valid aesthetic enterprise in the musical language of seventeenth-century Venice and Italy.[109]

But why would Monteverdi have sanctioned such an expedient? In fact, he might not have; the decision to include these fragments in the print and justify their existence by rubrics in the Credo of the *Messa a quattro* allowing for their substitution in that piece may well have been the work of the publisher, Bartolomeo Magni, as hypothesized by both Steele and Stevens.[110] Monteverdi's dedication to the *Selva morale* is apologetic for the imperfections of the collection, which are indeed prolific, and which Monteverdi

---

[107] "I should note that the Credo in concertato style has frequently been described as fragmentary, with only three segments of a complete Mass movement surviving in the *Selva morale*. However, there is nothing in the surviving descriptions that justifies an unquestioned assumption that the Credo performed on November 21, 1631 was in the modern concertato style throughout. It is equally possible that the Credo never contained more than the three concertato segments printed in the *Selva morale*, a point which will be discussed further below." Ibid., 70. The discussion of the possible use of trumpets in the Credo is on pp. 72–73. In light of Linda Koldau's and my subsequent research on *trombe squarciate* (see n. 4), I no longer entertain the notion of trumpets doubling or substituting for the violin parts in the *Et resurrexit*.

[108] Ibid., 70, 74, 78.

[109] Schnoebelen, ed., *Seventeenth-Century Italian Sacred Music: Masses*, 10 vols. Although there are a multitude of masses in the seventeenth century with contrasting textures and styles within individual movements, these are mostly either compositions in the *concertato* style throughout or multi-choir masses with segments for smaller numbers of voices and possibly instruments. I know of no other masses for three, four, or five voices in a consistently conservative, imitative polyphonic style with a few sections utilizing radically contrasting, more modern techniques. However, it is common in both sixteenth- and seventeenth-century polyphonic Credos for the *Crucifixus* and sometimes one or more subsequent sections to be set for a reduced number of voices, as in Monteverdi's own *Missa in illo tempore*.

[110] Steele and Stevens first made this suggestion in the same year (1968). See Steele, *Gloria Concertata*, preface, i. Stevens, in his imaginative way, suggests a couple of scenarios leading to the inclusion of the Credo fragments, as shown in the discussion above. See Stevens, *Claudio Monteverdi: 'Selva morale e spirituale'*, 425; idem, *Monteverdi: Sacred, Secular, and Occasional Music*, 70; idem, ed., *Selva morale e spirituali*, I, 15; idem, *Monteverdi in Venice*, 51.

clearly did not have an opportunity to correct.[111] Indeed, he may not even have had complete control over the print's final contents. The year 1641 was just two years before the composer's death, and we know he was indisposed and unable to complete the last act of *L'incoronazione di Poppea* himself approximately a year later.[112] Moreover, it was not Monteverdi to whom the French ambassador in Venice had turned in 1638 for a festive mass in honor of the birth of the dauphin, but the *vice maestro di cappella* of St. Mark's, Giovanni Rovetta. This fact alone suggests that Monteverdi was at that time not healthy enough to fulfill the commission, for it would have been strange for the ambassador not to have first solicited the far more famous *maestro di cappella* before approaching Rovetta, and equally strange for Monteverdi, if he had been able, to have declined such an important commission.

The conclusion of my article questioned the validity of Moore's thesis that the entire first half of the *Selva morale* and other additional pieces in the print constituted music for the various plague ceremonies of 1630–31:

> In sum, Monteverdi's *Selva morale* contains a group of Mass composi-
> tions that have been linked through contemporaneous descriptions
> with the "Mass of Thanksgiving" celebrating the official end of the
> Venetian plague of 1630–31, although not without some difficulties
> of interpretation. The evidentiary thread supporting this link is
> tenuous, and the evidence Moore adduces connecting other compo
> sitions from the *Selva morale* to the plague ceremonies is weaker still.
> Yet Moore's thesis is a very attractive one, appealing to our natural
> tendency to want coherent, all-embracing explanations for what appear
> to be complicated, puzzling circumstances. By weaving documentary,
> liturgical, and iconographic evidence into a coherent tapestry of
> explanation, Moore may have hit on the correct origin and function
> of at least some of this music; but his explanations arise more out
> of his imagination than from the evidence itself. His is a brilliant
> historical reconstruction; but we cannot be sure of the truth of
> most of his assertions or of the origins of the music of the *Selva
> morale* without considerable additional documentary evidence.[113]

---

[111] The dedication includes the sentence, "Per lo che supplico la Maestà Vostra con ogni humiltà possibile a degnarsi di riceverla, anchorchè ella non sia forse in quel grado di perfettione, ch'io desidererei, che'ella fosse. . . ."

[112] See Alan Curtis, "*La Poppea impasticciata* or, Who Wrote the Music to *L'incoronazione* (1643)?" *Journal of the American Musicological Society* 42 (1989): 23–54.

[113] Kurtzman, "Monteverdi's 'Mass of Thanksgiving' Revisited," 79–80.

Not long after the appearance of this article, it was subjected to attack by Peter Downey in an article replete with misquotation, self-contradiction, unsubstantiated "facts," and logical fallacies. In his conclusion, Downey reasserted the proposition that *trombe squarciate* were trombones, but then proceeded to discuss the role of trumpets in the Gloria and Credo, declaring that "the contribution of the trumpeters in the 'Mass of Thanksgiving' may be established to a high degree of certainty." In sum, Downey's methodology and mode of argumentation do not permit his theses to be taken seriously, and these need not detain us further here. [114]

However, Downey's attack did prompt me, with the assistance of Linda Koldau, to investigate further the question of *trombe squarciate*—what they were and how they were used in Venice. The results of this inquiry were published in 2002.[115] This study traced the use of trumpets in Italian cities from the late middle ages through their frequent employment in Venice in ceremonies of many kinds in the sixteenth and seventeenth centuries. We found the phrase *trombe squarciate* to have been used with considerable frequency in Venice during the Cinquecento and Seicento, and to be often associated with drums, whether in military or civilian surroundings. Trombones, on the other hand, are never associated with drums except when both *pifferi* (normally cornetti and trombones in this context) and trumpets with drums were employed on the battlefield. Despite a couple of problematic uses of the term *squarciato* with trombones outside of Venice, *trombe squarciati* in Venice clearly were not only trumpets, but small four-foot straight trumpets with wide bells used for fanfares and celebrations where their ability to resound afar was an important criterion.[116] Moore's conclusion that the *trombe squarciate* were trumpets was indeed correct.

Meanwhile, Koldau was completing her University of Bonn dissertation on Monteverdi's Venetian Sacred Music, subsequently published by Bärenreiter-Verlag.[117] For the first time Koldau posited a plausible alternative to the thesis that the *Selva morale*

---

[114] Peter Downey, "Monteverdi's 'Mass of Thanksgiving'—Aspects of Tension in Historical Musicology," *Irish Musical Studies* 4: The Maynooth International Musicological Conference 1995, Selected Proceedings: Part One, ed. Patrick F. Devine and Harry White (Dublin: Four Courts Press, 1996), 152–88. For quotation, see pp. 178–81. I presented a paper entitled "A Response to Peter Downey" at the Biennial Baroque Conference at Trinity College, Dublin, Ireland in July 2000 in which only a few of the misquotations, self-contradictions, and distortions in Downey's article were demonstrated.

[115] Kurtzman and Koldau, "*Trombe, Trombe d'argento, Trombe squarciate, Tromboni,* and *Pifferi.*"

[116] Ibid., Sections IV and V in particular.

[117] Linda Maria Koldau, *Die venezianische Kirchenmusik von Claudio Monteverdi* (Kassel: Bärenreiter-Verlag, 2001). See also her "Giovanni Antonio Rigattis 'Messa e salmi, parte concertati' (1640) und die Entwicklung des Concertato-Stils," *Schütz-Jahrbuch* 24 (2002): 85–88, where the same points (discussed below) are stressed as in her dissertation.

was prepared, at least in part, as a reflection of the plague ceremonies of 1630–31. Koldau takes as her point of departure the dedication of the *Selva* to Eleonora Gonzaga, daughter of Monteverdi's first employer at Mantua, Duke Vincenzo Gonzaga, widow of the Habsburg Emperor Ferdinand II and mother of Emperor Ferdinand III.[118] Koldau, following others, also cites ongoing contacts with the Habsburgs throughout Monteverdi's career in Venice.[119] Moreover, compositions from the *Selva morale* that Moore had associated with Venice prove to be just as appropriate for Eleonora's personal devotion to the Madonna and for the highly developed Marian worship at the Habsburg court. Eleonora had instituted her passiontide *Mysterienandachten* (Fifteen Mysteries) in 1637 in the Augustinian Church, which three years earlier had been elevated to the official court chapel. Her mysteries had a central focus on the rosary; moreover, the court chapel also regularly celebrated the Saturday service of the Madonna and the controversial doctrine of the immaculate conception.[120] In addition, Eleonora had also founded her own smaller personal court chapel in 1637, after the death of her husband earlier that year, in order to have more elaborate music than the masses her priests, presumably Jesuit fathers, had been able to provide.[121]

---

[118] Ibid., 110. As Koldau emphasizes, Monteverdi's Eighth Book of Madrigals, the *Madrigali guerrieri, et amorosi*, was dedicated in 1638 to Ferdinand III. The volume was originally intended for Ferdinand II, who died in 1637. Steven Saunders has argued that some of these compositions had been sent to Ferdinand II as early as 1633. See Saunders, "New Light on the Genesis of Monteverdi's Eighth Book of Madrigals," *Music & Letters* 77 (1996): 183–93. Several of the madrigals make direct reference to Ferdinand III, and Margaret Mabbett has shown that some stylistic aspects of these madrigals can be found in Viennese madrigals of the same period, but are rare in Italy. See Mabbett, "The Italian Madrigal, 1620–1655," 2 vols. (Ph.D. diss., King's College, University of London, 1989), 1:237–38; and idem, "Madrigalists at the Viennese Court and Monteverdi's *Madrigali guerrieri, et amorosi*," *Monteverdi und die Folgen: Bericht über das Internationale Symposium Detmold 1993*, ed. Silke Leopold and Joachim Steinheuer (Kassel, Basel, London, New York, Prague: Bärenreiter, 1998), 291–310; and in the same volume, Herbert Seifert, *"Monteverdi und die Habsburger,"* 77–92.

[119] Koldau, *Die venezianische Kirchenmusik*, 110–13, where she summarizes the research on this issue. In addition to the Seifert article cited in n. 118, see Fabbri, *Monteverdi*, 242–44 (Carter translation, 180–83); Jonathan Glixon, "Was Monteverdi a Traitor?" *Music & Letters* 72 (1991): 404–06; and Saunders, "New Light on the Genesis," 183–93.

[120] See the summary of research on this topic in Gabriela Krombach, "Die Musik zu den Mysterien-Andachten in der Wiener Augustiner-Kirche," *Johann Joseph Fux und seine Zeit: Kultur, Kunst und Musik im Spätbarock*, ed. Arnfried Edler and Friedrich W. Riedel (Laaber: Laaber-Verlag, 1996), 205–06. Koldau also sees the five *madrigali spirituali* that open the *Selva morale*, with their theme of vanity, as fitting the spiritual climate of Vienna in these years. Koldau notes that the *madrigali spirituali* at the beginning and the *Pianto della Madonna* at the end, the only Italian-texted pieces in the *Selva*, frame the mass and Vesper music that form the bulk of the *Selva*. As in Monteverdi's first piece in the *Madrigali guerrieri, et amorosi* of 1638, it was common to place in the first position of a collection a work or works that were particularly appropriate to the dedicate.

[121] Herbert Seifert, "Die Musiker der beiden Kaiserinnen Eleonora Gonzaga," *Festschrift Othmar Wessely zum 60. Geburtstag* (Tutzing: Schneider, 1982), 528.

Koldau begins her study of the *Selva morale* by observing that only a limited quantity of the Vesper music in the print could have served for major feast days at St. Mark's, which required a different, *coro spezzato* style from the majority of the concertato psalms in the collection.[122] Koldau sees the simpler style of the *Messa a quattro voci* as suitable for the Jesuit fathers who sang mass in Eleonora's private chapel, and the psalms, hymns, and motets of the *Selva morale* as fitting the needs of the feasts of lesser rank celebrated there.[123] Even if not definitively proven, Koldau's thesis that the *Selva morale* may have been conceived to serve the religious and liturgical needs of its dedicatee, as well as its being useful for a broad range of circumstances in Venice and northern Italy apart from St. Mark's, is based on firmer grounds than Moore's speculations about the first half of the print representing music for the plague ceremonies. Indeed, the collection may represent music not only for Eleonora's modest personal chapel, but for the larger court chapel as well.

If Moore's disassociation of the *trombe squarciate* of the Mass of Thanksgiving from trombones had broken the link previously used to claim that the Gloria *a 7* and Credo fragments from the *Selva morale* matched the contemporary descriptions of the Mass of Thanksgiving, the evidence for a Viennese orientation of the collection brought forth by Koldau throws an entirely different light on the *Selva* and the question of the Thanksgiving Mass. The connection between the print and the plague ceremonies that I had described as tenuous and circumstantial in my 1994 article was severed altogether by Koldau.

Further support for Koldau's thesis came shortly afterward from Andrew Weaver in his dissertation on motets at the Habsburg court during the reign of Ferdinand III.[124] Weaver suggested that the *Stabat Mater* for soprano solo, labeled *Pianto della Madonna*, published in 1638 by Giovanni Felice Sances, the Viennese court composer, as well as the *Pianto della Madonna* (also for solo soprano) in Monteverdi's *Selva morale*, were both "intended to be performed during the celebration of the Fifteen Mysteries in the court chapel . . . each of which is the final piece in a publication dedicated to Eleonora I Gonzaga."[125] Weaver also relates Sances's solo bass motet *Dominus possedit me* and

---

[122] Koldau, *Die venezianische Kirchenmusik*, 105–10. This observation is based on James H. Moore's study of the uses of the *coro spezzato* style for major feast days at St. Mark's when the famous *Pala d'oro* was opened. See Moore, The *Vespero delli cinque Laudate* and the Role of *Salmi Spezzati* at St. Mark's," *Journal of the American Musicological Society* 34 (1981): 249–78.

[123] Koldau, *Die venezianische Kirchenmusik*, 115.

[124] Andrew Hudsco Weaver, "Piety, Politics, and Patronage: Motets at the Habsburg Court in Vienna during the Reign of Ferdinand III (1637–1657)" (Ph.D. diss., Yale University, 2002).

[125] Ibid., 152–55. Sances's *Pianto* is in his *Motetti a voce sola* (Venice: Bartolomeo Magni, 1638), 133–45. A facsimile edition is available in Anne Schnoebelen, ed., *Solo Motets from the Seventeenth Century: Facsimiles of Prints from the Italian Baroque*, 10 vols. (London and New York: Garland, 1987–88), 8:133–45.

Monteverdi's *Ab aeterno ordinata sum* from the *Selva morale*, likewise for solo bass, to the Habsburgs' devotion to the Virgin (see below).[126] Thus Weaver concurs with and strengthens Koldau's suggestion that the music of the *Selva morale* was closely associated with Eleonora Gonzaga and the Viennese court rather than with the plague ceremonies of 1630–31.

In a paper, delivered at the annual meeting of the American Musicological Society in November 2002 and subsequently published, Weaver explored further the relationship between the *Selva morale*'s *Ab aeterno ordinata sum* and *Pianto della Madonna* and the liturgical emphases of Eleonora and the Viennese court.[127] For Weaver, the position of these two motets, each closing one of the two main sections of the *Selva*, is itself significant, as are pieces serving as structural pillars in other publications of Monteverdi.[128] Like Koldau, Weaver reviews the long history of Monteverdi's relationship with the Habsburg court.[129] The author notes probable points of contact between Sances and Monteverdi and suggests "conscious emulation and perhaps even a direct rivalry between the two composers," echoing a suggestion already made by Silke Leopold.[130] Weaver documents the intense piety of the Habsburg court, focused on the Virgin and the Cross, the two elements represented in both Sances's and Monteverdi's *Pianto della Madonna* settings, which may have been particularly suitable for the celebration of the "dolorous mystery" of the crucifixion in Eleonora's *Mysterienandachten*.[131] Weaver observes even closer connections between the two composers and Habsburg court worship in the two motets already discussed in his dissertation, Monteverdi's *Ab aeterno ordinata sum* and Sances's *Dominus possedit me*, the latter including the same text from Proverbs as set by Monteverdi (see table 6.1).[132] These rarely set verses were taken in the seventeenth century as prefiguring

---

[126] Weaver, "Piety, Politics, and Patronage," 384–89. Sances's motet appears in Schnoebelen, *Solo motets*, 104–13. Moore had also shown the relationship between Monteverdi's text, Divine Wisdom, and the Virgin, but in the context of Venetian adoration of Mary.

[127] Andrew H. Weaver, "New Light in the Forest: A Context for the Solo Motets in Monteverdi's *Selva morale et spirituale*," paper delivered at the annual meeting of the American Musicological Society, Columbus, Ohio, November 1, 2002. I am grateful to Professor Weaver for sharing the more extended version with me before its publication as "Divine Wisdom and Dolorous Mysteries: Habsburg Marian Devotion in Two Motets from Monteverdi's *Selva morale et spirituale*," *Journal of Musicology* 24/2 (Spring 2007): 237–71.

[128] Ibid., 239–42.

[129] Ibid., 242–45.

[130] Ibid., 249, n. 41, 15. For Leopold's comments, see Silke Leopold, "Al modo d'Orfeo: Dichtung und Musik im italienischen Sologesang des frühen 17. Jahrhunderts," *Analecta Musicologica* 29 (Laaber: Laaber-Verlag, 1995), 273.

[131] Weaver, "Divine Wisdom," 250–63.

[132] The text is from Proverbs, VIII:22–32 in Sances's longer version.

Table 6.1   Texts of Monteverdi's *Ab aeterno ordinata sum* and Sances's *Dominus possedit me*

Monteverdi, *Ab aeterno ordinata sum*

Ab aeterno ordinata sum & ex antiquis antequam terra fieret.

Nondum erant abyssi & ego iam concepta eram; necdum fontes aquarum eruperant; necdum montes gravi
   mole constiterant: ante omnes colles ego parturiebar.

Adhuc terram non fecerant, & flumina & cardines orbis terrae.

Quando preparabat caelos, aderam; quando certa legge & giro vallabat abyssos.

Quando ethera firmabat sursum, & librabat fontes aquarum; quando circundabat mari terminum suum, &
   lege ponebat acquis ne transient fines suo; quando apendebat fundamenta terrae.

Cum eo eram cuncta compones.

& delectabar per singulos dies, ludens coram eo omni tempore, ludens in orbe terrarum & delitiae meae esse
   cum filiis hominum.

Sances, *Dominus possedit me*

Dominus possedit me in initio viarum suarum ante quam quicquam faceret; a principio ab aeterno ordinata
   sum & ex antiquis antequam terra fieret.

Nondum erant abissi & ego iam concepta eram.

Necdum fontes aquarum eruperant; necdum monte, gravi mole constiterant; ante omnes colles ego parturiebar.

Adhuc terram non fecerat & flumnia & cardines orbis terrae.

Quando praeparabat Coelos aderam; quando certa lege & giiro vallabat abiissos; quando ethera firmabat
   sursum & librabat fontes aquarum; quando circundabat mari terminum suum & legem ponebat aquis
   ne transirent fines suos; quando appendebat fundamenta terrae.

Cum eo eram cuncta componens & delectabar per singulos dies ludens coram eo omni tempore; ludens in
   orbe terram & delitiae meae esse cum filiis hominum.

Nunc ergo filii audite me: Beati qui custodiunt vias meas.

the Immaculate Conception of the Virgin, a doctrine fervently promoted by Ferdinand
against the objections of Rome.[133] Weaver finds it striking that Monteverdi, who rarely
wrote for bass, not only employed the same voicing and virtuosic style as Sances's
motet, a style "avidly cultivated for bass singers at the Habsburg court," but also utilized
similar structural features as Sances.[134]

---

[133] Weaver, 250–55. The only other known setting was by another Habsburg court composer, Antonio
Bertali. The importance at the Habsburg Court of the Immaculate Conception and musical settings of texts
relating to this doctrine are explored further in Weaver, "Music in the Service of Counter-Reformation Politics:
the Immaculate Conception at the Habsburg Court of Ferdinand III (1637–1657)," *Music & Letters* 87/3
(2006): 361–78.

[134] Weaver, "Divine Wisdom," 256–58. Among the similarities between the two pieces, apart from the
general virtuosity demanded of the bass, are the openings in slow, repeated-note dotted rhythm, low-pitched
cadences at *fieret* and *abissi*, similar virtuoso melismas for *ego iam concepta* (Monteverdi's melisma is on *ego*,
Sances's longer ornament is on *concepta*), identical (except for pitch level) descending-scale melismas at *aquarum*
eruperant (Monteverdi places the melisma on *aquarum*, while Sances sets it to *eruperant*), a similar scalar rise at
monte (though only Monteverdi drops the pitch dramatically on the next word *gravi*), a long melisma at *colles ego*

The direct evidence of the *Selva morale*'s dedication to Eleonora Gonzaga, combined with the more circumstantial evidence adduced by Koldau and Weaver of the appropriateness of the *Selva* to the liturgical needs of the Habsburgs, including Eleonora's own private chapel, contrasts sharply with the absence of any evidence that the Gloria *a 7*, the Credo fragments, and the *Messa a quattro voci* constituted part of the Venetian plague ceremonies. The rationale for the arguments that one or more of these compositions represented the Mass of Thanksgiving of November 21, 1631, was severely attenuated by Moore's identification of the *trombe squarciate* as trumpets, not trombones, and Linda Koldau's and my confirmation of that identification in more detailed terms removed any remaining grounds for asserting such a connection. On the basis of the work of Koldau and Weaver, we now have far more reason to believe that the *Selva morale* was conceived and organized specifically for Eleonora and the Habsburg court, as its own dedication would naturally suggest, rather than reflecting any music from the plague ceremonies, for which there is no evidence whatsoever.

It is logically impossible to prove a negative except under certain special conditions, so the possibility cannot be excluded that the Gloria *a 7* and the Credo fragments, or even the *Messa a quattro voci*, originated with the Venetian plague ceremonies and were subsequently accommodated by Monteverdi to the needs of the Habsburg court and entered into the *Selva morale*. However, the quantity of lost mass music by Monteverdi is so large that even this possibility would represent an unlikely coincidence and statistical anomaly for which there is no support of any kind. In sum, the evidence is much more persuasive that we should relegate the claims that the *Selva morale*'s Gloria *a 7*, Credo fragments and *Messa a quattro voci* represent music from the Mass of Thanksgiving of 1631 to the category of one of those charming "myths of Venice," an appealing story, no doubt, but a modern invention, in all probability having nothing to do with historical reality.

---

parturiebar (Monteverdi places the melisma on the last word, Sances on the first), similar melismas on *flumina*, a similar gesture and cadence at *orbis terrae*, very similar declamatory presentations of *quando praeparabat Coelos*, a long melisma on *giro* proceeding to a low-pitched cadence at *abissos*, shift to triple meter at *Cum eo eram*, and a scale-oriented melisma concluding both motets. Despite a number of differences between the two motets, these similarities are sufficient to support Weaver's suggestion of emulation between the two pieces.

XI

Monteverdi's missing sacred music:
evidence and conjectures

Throughout modern Monteverdi research, scholars have attempted to assign individual sacred compositions in Monteverdi's surviving *oeuvre* to particular events or ceremonies that are documented, but for which the music is either unidentified, or identified with insufficient precision. The underlying assumption behind such efforts is that Monteverdi's published sacred music and the few pieces surviving in manuscript represent most of the sacred music Monteverdi wrote, and that therefore any sacred music mentioned in documents should be traceable to the surviving repertoire. I have already demonstrated elsewhere with regard to the so-called "Mass of Thanksgiving" that such efforts are misguided, and the tacit assumption that we possess most of the sacred music Monteverdi wrote is clearly invalid.[1] It is now worth exploring the question of just what sacred music by Monteverdi we can determine is missing, and furthermore, what sacred music he is likely to have written of which we have no distinct record. The significance of this investigation is the broader and more accurate perspective it should shed on the surviving sacred music and the relationship between that music and Monteverdi's total sacred output.

In the case of Monteverdi's dramatic music, we probably know something about every work he composed, whether extant or not, with the possible exception of some minor ballets, since dramatic works necessarily generated significant correspondence and other documentation. With regard to madrigals and other secular vocal forms, there are also a number of references in letters and other documents to texts given or sent to Monteverdi and his response to them, though it is likely that he composed many more secular pieces than those that survive and

---

[1] See Jeffrey KURTZMAN, "Monteverdi's Mass of Thanksgiving: Da Capo," forthcoming in *Fiori Musicali: Liber Amicorum Alexander Silbiger*, Warren, MI.

those for which we have documentation. The sources of information with regard to his sacred output, however, are somewhat more complex than those for his dramatic and secular vocal works, since in discharging his responsibilities for sacred music, he had to fulfill the obligations of the annual liturgical calendar in addition to composing for special events and responding to commissions from individuals, organizations and institutions to which he was not otherwise accountable.

As with the dramatic music, the obvious place to begin the search is Monteverdi's correspondence as well as other letters and documents referring to his lost sacred music. These sources provide information ranging from references to particular compositions, to compositions in specific genres, to general responsibilities of the composer at certain times of the liturgical year, to much vaguer indications of ceremonies for which he may well have had responsibility because of his position. The quality of this evidence runs the gamut from documentary proof, to probabilities of varying degrees, to grounds for reasonable conjecture. In the end, many of my conclusions must of necessity remain speculative, though I hope they will at least be plausible and give us pause to think about Monteverdi's professional responsibilities, the music that is forever lost, and the place in our understanding of Monteverdi of the treasures that do survive.

To begin with the most concrete forms of evidence, the first items we know are missing are the upper three parts of his *Madrigali spirituali a quattro voci* published in 1583, only the bass part-book of which survives in a single copy at the Museo Internazionale e Biblioteca della Musica di Bologna (formerly Civico Museo Bibliografico Musicale).[2] But we also have several letters and documents mentioning specific sacred works that no longer survive.

The earliest of these is a letter to Prince Francesco Gonzaga of March 26, 1611, in which Monteverdi says he is sending the prince, who was establishing his own *cappella* at Casale Monferrato, a *Dixit* for eight voices and two motets, one for two voices for the Elevation and the other in five voices for the Blessed Virgin.[3] There is no reason to identify this *Dixit Dominus* with either of the eight-voice *Dixit*s published thirty years later in the *Selva morale e spirituale* of 1641 and to identify the two motets, whose texts are unknown, with *O bone Jesu* in the Johannes Donfrid anthology of 1622 (RISM 1622²) and *Venite sitientes* in the Lorenzo Calvi anthology of 1624 (RISM 1624²), as Denis Stevens has done. It is absurd

---

[2] RISM M3444.

[3] Eva Lax, ed.: *Claudio Monteverdi: Lettere* (Florence: Leo S. Olschki Editore, 1994), pp. 35–36. English translation in Denis Stevens, *The Letters of Claudio Monteverdi*, revised ed. (Oxford: Clarendon Press, 1995), pp. 77–81. Domenico de' Paoli, *Claudio Monteverdi: Lettere, Dediche e Prefazioni* (Rome: Edizioni de Santis, 1973), p. 56, reads the number of voices as 5. In this letter Monteverdi also promises Francesco two madrigals after Holy Week has passed.

to think that these are the only motets Monteverdi wrote for two voices and five voices or that served these liturgical functions. All three compositions are far more likely lost.[4]

The same year of 1611 produced two reports of vesper services with music by Monteverdi. The first is in a recently discovered letter of May 14, written by one Lorenzo Campagna, a servant of Duke Vincenzo Gonzaga, to the Marchese Fabio Gonzaga. In this letter the writer mentions First Vespers on the vigil of the feast of the Ascension, celebrated in the church of Sant'Andrea with music "newly composed by Signor Claudio Monteverdi."[5] Since only two psalms for Ascension Day overlap those of the *Vespro della Beata Vergine* published with a dedication of September 1, 1610, at least three of the psalms, and quite possibly all five and the Magnificat, had been newly composed and are now lost. Moreover, as with the *Vespro*, Monteverdi might well have composed a response, a hymn and even some motets as antiphon-substitutes for this service.

At the end of the year, Monteverdi provided the music for a Christmas Vespers at the cathedral of Modena, which, according to the account "were to everyone's disgust."[6] What caused this disgust is unknown—it may have been the novel style of concertato psalms, or even the quality of the performance; in any event, the psalm cursus for First Vespers on Christmas is the same as the Feast of the Ascension, but Second Vespers conclude with two different psalms. Again, the *Vespro* of 1610 has only two overlapping psalms with First Vespers at Christmas and just one with Second Vespers, so most of these compositions were either the same as those performed on Ascension Day earlier that year or composed at another time, perhaps even especially for the Modenese service. Once again, the music is lost. In addition, we know from an undated letter by the poet Angelo Grillo that sometime in the period 1610–1612, Monteverdi composed a sacred solo madrigal to one of Grillo's texts, no longer extant, but sung at court by Adriana Basile.[7]

When Monteverdi auditioned for the position of *maestro di cappella* at the ducal church of St. Mark's in Venice in August of 1613, he made demonstration

---

[4] STEVENS, p. 79.

[5] Mantua, Archivio di Stato b. 2721, fasc. III, doc. 8, cc. 55–56. The letter is also referenced online at http://www.capitalespettacolo.it/ita/ric_gen.asp by entering "Campagna" in the box *Persone Notevoli* and selecting *Segnatura* C–1275 from the resulting list. See Licia MARI and Jeffrey KURTZMAN, "A Monteverdi Vespers in 1611," *Early Music*, 36 (November 2008), 547–55.

[6] G. RONCAGLIA, "Di Bellerofonte Castaldi (con un document inedito)," *Deputazione di storia patria per le antiche provincie modenesi: atti e memorie*, VIII/10 (1938), p. 121. Cited in Paolo Fabbri, *Monteverdi*, trans. Tim Carter (Cambridge: Cambridge University Press, 1994), p. 120.

[7] See the letter from Grillo quoted in Fabbri, p. 118. The letter describing this performance, effusive in its praise, is undated.

of his compositions in St. Mark's with Mass and Vespers on the Feast of the Assumption of the B. V. M. (August 15). The payment records for extra instrumentalists on these occasions suggest the possibility of a concerted mass rather than the *Missa in illo tempore* published together with the *Vespro della Beata Vergine* in 1610.[8] In addition, the *Ceremoniale* of St. Mark's called for double-choir psalms on the Feast of the Assumption, so that unless an exception was made, only *Nisi Dominus* from the 1610 print could have been performed on that day.[9] The other psalms and Magnificat would have had to have been other compositions now lost. That these were different psalms and a different Magnificat from the 1610 print may be suggested by the document recording Monteverdi's election to the post. He is described as "recommended as the foremost candidate; of the quality and worth of whom the Procurators are greatly confirmed in this opinion, both from his published works and those which in these days the Procurators have sought to hear, to their complete satisfaction in the church of St. Mark with its musicians."[10] If "by his published works" is meant specifically sacred music, the wording would suggest that the Procurators heard different music from that which had been published, i.e., different from the Mass and Vespers of 1610.[11] On the other hand, the reference could be to Monteverdi's entire published repertoire up to that point.

Three years later, already well ensconced in his position at St. Mark's, Monteverdi wrote on December 29, 1616 to Alessandro Striggio in Mantua, excusing the delay in offering his opinion about the maritime fable *Le Nozze di Tetide* which

---

[8] The payment records are not entirely clear and consistent, either as to the numbers of instrumentalists paid or the liturgical function. However, they are clear and consistent in referring to Monteverdi's audition (*prova*). See the two documents quoted in Denis ARNOLD, *Monteverdi*, 2nd edition (London: J. M. Dent & Sons, 1975), p. 202 and the discussion in Jeffrey KURTZMAN, *The Monteverdi Vespers of 1610: Music, Context, Performance* (Oxford: Oxford University Press, 1999), pp. 53–54.

[9] See Giulio CATTIN, *Liturgia e Musica a San Marco*, 3 vols. (Venice: Edizioni Fondazione Levi, 1990), I, 88–90 for a discussion of the *Ceremoniale* of Bartolomeo Bonifacio, written before 1564 and still in use in the early 17th century. Bonifacio's description of each feast is given in Cattin, vol. III at the end of each feast listed in the Temporale and the Sanctorale. The description for the Feast of the Assumption reads, in part: "In primis Vesperis psalmi omnes Laudate [the *cinque Laudate* psalms], in secundis Vesperis psalmi de Domina, qui cantantur in utrisque Vesperis a cantoribus in duobus choris." See Cattin, III, p. 143. On the *cinque Laudate* psalms, see James H. MOORE, "The *Vespero delli Cinque Laudate* and the Role of *Salmi Spezzati* at St. Mark's," *Journal of the American Musicological Society*, 34 (Summer 1981), pp. 249–78.

[10] KURTZMAN, ibid., p. 53. Tim Carter's slightly different translation appears in FABBRI, *Monteverdi*, p. 124.

[11] In KURTZMAN, *The Monteverdi Vespers*, pp. 53–54, I had expressed the belief that the *Vespro della Beata Vergine* of 1610 had been performed on the Feast of the Assumption in St. Mark's, but the *Ceremoniale* of St. Mark's suggests otherwise, unless a special exception was made.

Striggio had submitted to him, explaining that he had been working all month composing and copying out the Mass for Christmas Eve.[12] Three other letters by Monteverdi testify that a new Christmas Eve mass was expected of the *maestro di cappella* of St. Mark's every year. On October 30, 1627, in a letter to the Marquis Enzo Bentivoglio of Ferrara, Monteverdi indicates that his duties require him to be at St. Mark's on Christmas Eve, the feast of his greatest duties in the entire year.[13] A letter of November 8 of the same year, written to a Procurator of St. Mark's from Parma, where he was busy preparing an *intermedio* for the wedding of Duke Odoardo Farnese with Margherita de' Medici, assures the Procurator that he would return to Venice in time for the Christmas Eve mass.[14] Another letter of February 2, 1634 to Giovanni Battista Doni in Rome confirms that he was required to compose a new mass annually for this feast.[15]

Stevens asserts that the mass for Christmas Eve 1616 must have been in the large-scale concertato style, but we have no information about the style expected of the Christmas Eve mass at St. Mark's.[16] We do not know whether it could have been in the imitative polyphonic style of the two four-voice masses published in the *Selva morale* of 1641 or the *Messa e Salmi* of 1650, respectively. But since Monteverdi served as *maestro di cappella* at St. Mark's for thirty years, he was responsible for thirty Christmas Eve masses, at least twenty-eight, and possibly all thirty of which, are lost. One mass in manuscript by Monteverdi, but no longer extant, was listed in a 1720 *Inventario de' libri musicali inservienti all'uso della cappella di S. Marco*.[17]

II

In addition to references to the mass for Christmas Eve, Monteverdi's letters mention a number of other occasions for which he wrote music for St. Mark's or ecclesiastical officials of St. Mark's. In most cases, only one such ceremony is cited, but because the liturgical calendar repeats itself annually, it is likely that for each of these feasts or occasions Monteverdi was expected to provide the same kind of music every year. This type of evidence provides, on the one hand, proof that Mon-

[12] LAX p. 51, STEVENS, p. 120.
[13] LAX, p. 113, STEVENS, p. 381.
[14] LAX, p. 114; STEVENS, p. 383. FABBRI, pp. 206–19 describes the preparations for the intermedio in considerable detail with numerous letters, many of which reiterate the necessity of Monteverdi's returning to Venice in time for the Christmas celebrations at St. Mark's.
[15] LAX, pp. 203–204, STEVENS, p. 424.
[16] STEVENS, pp. 119–20.
[17] Francesco CAFFI, *Storia della Musica Sacra nella già Cappella Ducale di San Marco dal 1318 al 1797*, 2 vols. (Venice: G. Antonelli Editore, 1854; reprint ed. Bologna: Forni Editore, 1972), I, p. 224; II, p. 100.

teverdi wrote music for particular events, and on the other, circumstantial evidence that he likely wrote similar music for the same events in other years. In fact, he may not have had to compose new music every year for such annual ceremonies, but simply directed the performances, whether of already existing music of his own, or the music of other composers. Nevertheless, it is highly probable that he did indeed compose a significant quantity of new music for these services over the thirty-year span of his tenure at St. Mark's.

On April 21, 1618 Monteverdi wrote to Prince Vincenzo Gonzaga in Mantua that he was responsible for a concerted mass and motets for the entire day on the Feast of Finding the Holy Cross, when the Most Sacred Blood would be displayed on the high altar.[18] In the same letter he speaks about rehearsing "a certain cantata in praise of His Serenity, which is designed to be sung every year in the *Bucintoro* when, with all the Signoria, he attends the wedding of the sea on Ascension Day."[19] Moreover he also had to rehearse "a Mass and solemn Vespers, which is sung in St. Mark's on such an occasion..." It is noteworthy that Monteverdi only says "rehearse" and not "compose" in reference to the Ascension Day mass and vespers, suggesting that he already had music available for this occasion, whether his own or written by someone else. But even if the latter were the case in 1618, the topical subject of this letter, excusing his delay in sending the Prince the music for *Andromeda*, doesn't exclude the possibility that he composed new music for these services in other years.

Yet another annual celebration requiring Monteverdi's participation was the Feast of the Redeemer, mentioned in a letter of July 19, 1620 to Alessandro Striggio: "the task has been given me of serving this Most Serene Republic tomorrow... at the Church of Our Redeemer, a day celebrated by this Most Serene Republic in memory of a favour received from the hand of God, which was the liberation of the city from a terrible plague."[20] The Palladian Church of the Redeemer on the Giudecca island had been built in fulfillment of a vow made by the doge in September 1576 in soliciting an end to the plague of 1576–1577. In commemoration of the plague's cessation, the Feast of the Redeemer was henceforth celebrated every year on the third Sunday of July. A principal feature of this feast, to this day an important event in Venice, is a procession across a pontoon bridge built over gondolas to Palladio's church for the services mentioned in Monteverdi's letter.

A somewhat different type of repetitive situation is represented by the thrice-weekly meetings on Wednesday, Friday and Sunday in the oratorio of the Primice-

---

[18] LAX, p. 64, STEVENS, pp. 136–37. This feast occurs annually on May 3.
[19] The *bucintoro* was the Venetian state's large ceremonial barge.
[20] LAX, p. 109; STEVENS, p. 219.

rius of St. Mark's for which Monteverdi claimed to supply music on a regular basis in a letter to Alessandro Striggio on March 17, 1620. Monteverdi does not specify what music he provides, saying simply, "I make music in a certain oratory of his, to which half the nobility come."[21] Given the frequency of these meetings, and the presumption from Monteverdi's letter that this was a continuous obligation, perhaps over a number of years, it is likely that most of the music was from other hands, but equally likely that some of it was of Monteverdi's own composition, whether in the form of motets, spiritual madrigals or spiritual canzonets.

III

Monteverdi's letters and other documents also offer proof of sacred compositions written for occasional events, most of which were unconnected with St. Mark's itself. In 1620, Constantin Huygens, serving as a Flemish diplomat, heard Vespers on June 24, the Feast of St. John the Baptist, at the Church of San Giovanni Elemosinario: "the most perfect music I had ever heard in my life… directed by the most famous Claudio Monteverdi, *maestro di cappella* of St. Mark's, who was also the composer." Huygens' description of the instruments and voices suggests that the style of the music was concertato rather than imitative or *coro spezzato*.[22] Paolo Fabbri suggests that the motets *Fuge anima mea mundum*, published in the Lorenzo Calvi anthology of 1620–21,[23] may relate to this feast and performance. Another motet from the same anthology, *O beatae viae*, is an antiphon for the Feast of St. Roch.[24] The archives of the Scuola San Rocco show payments to Monteverdi in 1623 and 1627 for directing music there on the feast of St. Roch.[25]

Another occasional event was a Requiem Mass for Duke Cosimo II de' Medici, composed and performed on behalf of the Florentine community in Venice in the church of Saints Giovanni and Paolo on May 25, 1621. In a letter of April 17,

---

[21] Lax, p. 97; Stevens, p. 196.

[22] Quoted in Fabbri, p. 177 from Frits Noske, "An Unknown Work by Monteverdi: the Vespers of St. John the Baptist," *Music & Letters*, 46 (1985), pp. 118–22.

[23] RISM Sammeldrucke 1620², 1621⁴.

[24] Fabbri, pp. 176–77.

[25] Venice, Archivio di Stato, Scuola San Rocco, II, Filze 166, August 1623: "Poliza de spese fatte per la festa de San Rocho… per contadi al signor maestro Monte Verde per la festa… £620; " and II, Filze 168: "A di 16 agosto 1627 in Venetia, Nota delle spese fatte il giorno di Santo Rocco per la festa di detto giorno… contadi al signor Don Claudio Mastro di Capella… £146." I am grateful to Jonathan Glixon for supplying these account records. The payments are noted in Denis Arnold, *Monteverdi*, Third edition, ed. Tim Carter (London, J. M. Dent & Sons, 1990), p. 35, but with the erroneous date of 1628 for the second one. The much smaller payment to Monteverdi in 1627 suggests that his responsibilities were significantly less on that occasion.

XI

of that year Monteverdi reports on the pressure he is under in composing portions of the mass.[26] The remainder of the mass was written by the organists of St. Mark's, Giovan Battista Grillo and Francesco Usper.[27]

On March 9, 1625, the visiting Polish monarch, Sigismond III, heard a mass by Monteverdi in St. Mark's, which "he took great delight in... never ceasing to praise the intelligence of Monteverde, *maestro di cappella*, the exquisiteness of the instruments, and in particular that of the organs of St Mark's."[28] The description suggests a concerted mass, in which the instruments and organs could be clearly distinguished, rather than a polyphonic mass with instrumental doubling. Six days later, on March 15, Monteverdi wrote to Alessandro Striggio in Mantua to apologize for not thanking him sooner for assistance he had provided the composer because of "the multitude of tasks I have had, and still have to do, in serving this Polish monarch both in his chapel and at his court..."[29] Evidently, Sigismond commissioned a substantial amount of music from Monteverdi, but we have no indication of what these compositions were, presumably all lost, like the mass Sigismond heard in St. Mark's.

Alessandro Striggio was also the recipient of a letter of July 24, 1627 in which Monteverdi wrote that he had been "pressed by the entreaties of many friends" to provide the music for First Vespers on the Feast of Our Lady of Mount Carmel for the Carmelite church.[30] Later in the letter he makes excuses about his progress on the comic opera *La finta pazza Licori*, citing church music that he had had to write. In the context of this letter, it seems likely that he is referring to the music for Vespers at the Carmelite church, though it is possible that other sacred music was meant.

Another occasional event is mentioned in Monteverdi's letter of February 23, 1630, written perhaps to Don Ascanio Pio of Savoy at Ferrara, which the composer uses as an excuse for not yet completing a commission. Monteverdi declares, "I was a little taken up with certain ecclesiastical compositions for some of the

---

[26] LAX, p. 118, STEVENS, pp. 237–240.

[27] The chronicler of the event, Giulio Strozzi, attributes the introit, the *Dies irae, De profundis* and the five responds *Subvenite sancti Dei, Qui Lazarum, Domine quando veneris* and *Ne recorderis* to Monteverdi, with the rest of the music composed by Grillo and Usper. See Fabbri: *Monteverdi*, pp. 178–79, quoted from STROZZI, *Esequie fatte in Venetia dalla natione fiorentina al serenissimo d. Cosimo II quarto gran duca di Toscana il di 25 maggio 1621* (Venice: Giovan Battista Ciotti, 1621). According to Strozzi, the music "was newly either concerted or composed by Signor Claudio Monteverdi."

[28] FABBRI, p. 192.

[29] LAX, p. 138; STEVENS, p. 289. Sigismond offered Monteverdi a position at his court in Warsaw, but Monteverdi declined. See Fabbri: p. 193.

[30] LAX, p. 166; STEVENS, p. 345.

194

nuns of S. Lorenzo who insisted no little on my doing it."[31] The most well-known of all these occasional events was the Mass of Thanksgiving, composed by Monteverdi and performed in St. Mark's on November 21, 1631 to celebrate the end of the great plague of 1630–31.[32] A scholarly tradition has built up over the years claiming that the *Gloria a 7*, the three Credo fragments, and possibly even the Kyrie, Sanctus and Agnus Dei of the Mass in F from the *Selva morale* of 1641 represent remnants of that mass, a tradition without any evidentiary foundation, however.[33]

Not all of the references in Monteverdi's letters to individual sacred compositions were for specific liturgical events. In a letter of November 27, 1621 to the Duchess of Mantua, thanking her for the commission of some *intermezzi*, Monteverdi offers her a "solemn Mass set to music, if it might please you to accept it."[34] The term "solemn mass" very likely refers to a concerted mass, and the phrasing of Monteverdi's offer suggests that it was a mass already composed and available. Another letter of May 1, 1627 to Alessandro Striggio, in response to a proposal to set an unnamed play to music, offers sacred music to the Duke of Mantua: "Then, if church music were needed, either for Vespers or for Mass, I rather think I might have something of this kind that would be to His Highness's liking."[35] In this case, Monteverdi clearly had such compositions already at hand.

IV

Apart from letters and documents citing individual compositions or groups of sacred compositions that we know Monteverdi wrote, there are also a number of references in his letters to his obligations for specific celebrations or for sacred music at various seasons of the year or for various institutions where it is obvious that Monteverdi was responsible for preparing the performances, but it is not as clear

---

[31] LAX, p. 198; STEVENS, p. 409. Lax indicates the addressee as the Marquis Enzo Bentivoglio, while Stevens suggests Don Ascanio Pio as the possible recipient.

[32] See James H. MOORE, "*Venezia Favorita da Maria:* Music for the Madonna Nicpopeia and Santa Maria della Salute," *Journal of the American Musicological Society*, 37 (Summer 1984), pp. 299–355 for the documentation pertaining to the 1631 celebration. I disagree with Moore's conclusion regarding the association of music in the *Selva morale e spirituale* with this and other plague-related services. See Jeffrey KURTZMAN, "Monteverdi's 'Mass of Thanksgiving' Revisited," *Early Music*, 22 (February 1994), 63–84.

[33] See Jeffrey KURTZMAN, "Monteverdi's Mass of Thanksgiving: Da Capo," for a full discussion of this tradition and an evaluation of the evidence.

[34] LAX, pp. 121–122, STEVENS, p. 246.

[35] LAX, p. 151, STEVENS, pp. 316–17. Stevens declares that these works were later published in the *Selva morale* of 1641, but there are no grounds to connect this music with the *Selva*.

that he would necessarily have composed the music himself. Some of the evidence refers to specific celebrations which are mentioned only once, but were annual feasts, while other evidence refers more generically to Monteverdi's responsibilities for sacred music at certain seasons of the year or commissions by institutions outside St. Mark's for recurring events. This type of evidence is circumstantial—it suggests the probability that Monteverdi composed an undetermined quantity of music for such occasional events or annual services, but offers no proof that he actually did so. Whether these events required new compositions from Monteverdi, or he resurrected old compositions or performed the music of others is an open question. The answer probably lies in between—at times he wrote and performed new music, and on other occasions simply performed either the music of others, or already existing compositions of his own. In such cases, we can only infer the likelihood of there having been a great deal of music from his pen, all of which is either lost, or only marginally represented in the *Selva morale* of 1641 and the *Messa e Salmi* of 1650 or the motets published in a variety of anthologies.

The earliest of this less definitive evidence comprises documents in reference to the expedition of Duke Vincenzo Gonzaga to Hungary in support of Imperial armies fighting the Turks in 1595, just a few years after Monteverdi joined Vincenzo's service. Monteverdi may have composed the mass performed in the church of Sant'Andrea prior to the expedition's departure, and the duke's chronicler indicates that he was responsible for leading four or five singers in singing four or five masses (probably in plainchant) per day in the duke's quarters as well as Vespers on solemn feasts accompanied by the organ.[36] It is probable that at least some of these Vespers included polyphony composed by Monteverdi, even if the style was simple rather than elaborate.

Another of Vincenzo's expeditions which Monteverdi accompanied was to Spa, north of Liège, in the summer of 1599.[37] Although the documents, several of which are letters by the singer Francesco Rasi, describe vocal chamber music and there is no mention of compositions or performances by Monteverdi, it was certainly the case that Monteverdi would have been responsible for the music for mass and vespers on a basis similar to his responsibilities in Hungary. Once again,

---

[36] The expedition is described in Vincenzo ERRANTE, "'Forse che si, forse che no': la terza spedizione del duca Vincenzo Gonzaga in Ungheria alla guerra contro il Turco (1601) studiata su documenti inediti," *Archivio storico lombardo*, 42 (1915), pp. 29–34. This article deals with the 1595 expedition as well.

[37] The documents pertaining to the visit to Spa are described in Susan PARISI, "The Brussels-Mantua Connection: Vincenzo Gonzaga's State Voyages to the Low Countries in 1599 and 1608," *Yearbook of the Alamire Foundation*, 7 (2008), pp. 275–305. I am grateful to Dr. Parisi for sharing a copy of this article with me in advance of its publication.

the probability is high that polyphonic mass and vesper music composed by Monteverdi for use on this voyage is lost.

When Monteverdi moved to Venice, they were also a number of feasts for which his letters indicate he had responsibility either to direct, or perhaps even compose, the music.

In a letter of February 11, 1617 to Annibale Iberti at Mantua, responding to a proposal that he travel from Venice to Mantua, Monteverdi mentions that many functions take place during Holy Week "in the presence of the Doge, who comes to church in that week."[38] The necessity of Monteverdi's presence and service during Holy Week is implied in this statement, and confirmed a year later in a letter of April 21, 1618, addressed to Prince Vincenzo Gonzaga, which begins, "The daily round at St. Mark's throughout Holy Week and Easter has kept me so busy that I have been unable before now to send Your Lordship the music for the *Andromeda* libretto."[39] The next year, on March 7, 1619, writing to Alessandro Striggio, Monteverdi remarks once more on "the many duties I shall have at St Mark's during Holy Week, and also because of the feast days, which are by no means few..."[40] Just a few days later, in writing to Prince Vincenzo Gonzaga, he declares that "throughout Holy Week I am at St Mark's, and the three feast-days likewise."[41] That his duties at this time of year were pressing is reiterated yet again the next year in a letter to Striggio of March 17, 1620, in which Monteverdi speaks of needing to be back in Venice "in time for Holy Week and the performance of my duty."[42] That Monteverdi's Eastertide responsibilities included Low Sunday is suggested by his letter of March 21, 1620 to Striggio, in which he asks for an extension of time before being expected in Mantua until Low Sunday is past.[43]

While Monteverdi's workload during Holy Week served him as an excuse in these letters for not doing or postponing something asked of him, there can be little doubt about the pressure he was under at this holiest time of the year, a pressure which he must have felt annually for thirty years. It seems highly unlikely that he only performed the music of others at this important season. He must have written some of the music that was sung during Holy Week, even if not everything

---

[38] Lax, p. 62; Stevens, p. 131.

[39] Lax, p. 64; Stevens, p. 136. This is the same letter in which Monteverdi mentions his concerted mass and motets for the Feast of the Finding of the Holy Cross.

[40] Lax, p. 68; Stevens, p. 143.

[41] Lax, p. 70; Stevens, p. 145. It is not clear what Monteverdi means by the three "feast-days," since he has already apparently included Maundy Thursday, Good Friday, and Holy Saturday in the phrase "throughout Holy Week."

[42] Lax, p. 97; Stevens, p. 196. This is the same letter in which Monteverdi mentions the thrice-weekly musical events in the oratorio of the Primicerius.

[43] Lax, p. 99; Stevens, p. 199.

and not every year. But his letters do not mention any specific compositions, and no lamentations, responsories, passions or settings of the *Benedictus* or *Miserere* survive from his hand. As with the Christmas Eve masses, he may have composed a large corpus of music for Holy Week accumulated over his thirty years' service in Venice that has all vanished.

Other letters comment on individual liturgical events for which Monteverdi was responsible, but since these were annual celebrations, his responsibilities may in most cases be justifiably projected from the single event to its annual recurrence. The earliest mention of a liturgical event in Venice requiring his services is in a letter of October 21, 1620 in which he wrote to Alessandro Striggio asking for assistance in obtaining the Mantuan musician Don Francesco Dognazzi for the Feast of St. Carlo Borromeo on behalf of the Milanese colony in Venice, who had asked Monteverdi to be in charge of the music.[44] Whether this meant composing the music or only preparing the performance is unclear, nor do we know whether the Milanese colony commissioned Monteverdi more than once or annually for this feast.

In the letter of May 1, 1627 cited above, in which Monteverdi indicates that he has music for vespers or a mass that might please the duke of Mantua, he also speaks of how busy he had been "looking after the music" for the Vigil of St Mark on April 24. The Feast of St. Mark, the patron saint of Venice, was obviously of great significance and celebrated with special pomp in the basilica of St. Mark. This is another of those feasts that annually must have occupied Monteverdi not only with preparations for the performance of the mass and vespers, but likely with the composition of new music as well, though we have no direct evidence of such compositions.

Another annual feast for which Monteverdi likely was required to provide music, whether or not it was new music of his own composition, was the anniversary celebration of the great naval victory over the Turks at Lepanto in 1571, which had occurred on October 7, the feast day of Saint Giustina, and was therefore attributed to her intervention. Monteverdi obliquely mentions his responsibility for this feast in a letter of September 18, 1627 to Striggio: "... in October... I have to attend to certain feasts ordered by our Most Serene Doge."[45] A week later, on September 25, he again mentions his obligation in a letter to the Marquis Enzo

[44] LAX, pp. 113–14; STEVENS, p. 228.
[45] LAX, p. 177; STEVENS, p. 369.

Bentivoglio.[46] The celebration included a ducal procession to the church of St. Giustina for the service.[47]

Not all of the major feasts for which Monteverdi would have had responsibility for the music are individually mentioned in his letters, but only implied. In his letter of July 11, 1620 to Alessandro Striggio, he begins by saying, "Now that my hectic days at St. Mark's are over (nor will they recur until All Saints' Day)..."[48] Implied in this statement are that Monteverdi was busy with several feasts prior to the date of the letter. Indeed, June 29 is the Feast of Peter and Paul, and the month of July begins with the Feast of the Most Precious Blood of our Lord Jesus Christ, followed the next day by the Feast of the Visitation of the Blessed Virgin Mary. All Saint's Day occurs on November 1, and evidently Monteverdi had responsibilities at St. Mark's on this day as well.

A somewhat vaguer and more generalized indication of what must have been frequent activity in composing and performing sacred music for institutions outside St. Mark's appears in a famous letter to Alessandro Striggio of March 13, 1620, in which Monteverdi declines an offer to return to the ducal court at Mantua. In this letter he declares that he is invited "again and again by the wardens of the guilds" (confraternities) from which he earns as much as his salary at St. Mark's "because whoever can engage the director to look after their music—not to mention the payment of thirty ducats, and even forty, and up to fifty for two vespers and a mass—does not fail to take him on, and they also thank him afterwards with well-chosen words." Monteverdi claims his popularity was such that "when I am about to perform either chamber or church music... the entire city comes running."[49] While Monteverdi may be engaging in hyperbole in comparing the positive aspects of his circumstances in Venice with his bitter experience in Mantua, there can be little doubt that he was frequently hired by the *guardiani* of the confraternities to provide first and second vespers as well as a mass on feasts important to the confraternities, especially the feast of each confraternity's patron saint. The wording of the letter implies that the payments were made for new compositions of his own, though there is enough ambiguity in Monteverdi's phrasing to leave open the possibility that his responsibility was simply for providing the music, not necessarily composing it. Indeed, if he were hired as frequently

---

[46] Lax, p. 181; Stevens, p. 377.

[47] The Venetian celebrations of the victory are recounted in Iain Fenlon: "Lepanto: Le arti della celebrazione nella Venezia del Rinascimento," in *Crisi e Rinnovamenti nell'autunno del Rinascimento a Venezia*, ed. Vittore Branca and Carlo Ossola (Florence: Leo S. Olschki, 1991), pp. 373–406.

[48] Lax, p. 107; Stevens, p. 216.

[49] Lax, p. 49; Stevens, p. 191.

as the letter suggests, he would scarcely have had time to compose so much music, given his remark in his letter of December 29, 1616 cited above that he had spent the entire month of December composing and copying the single Christmas Eve mass. Nevertheless, it is hard to imagine that at least some of this music didn't consist of new compositions of his own. Because so many of the major feasts at St. Mark's required double-choir psalms according to the *Ceremoniale* of Bonifacio, it may be that many of the concertato psalms and the Magnificats in the *Selva morale* and the *Messa e Salmi* originated as compositions for the confraternities rather than for St. Mark's. This matter will be discussed further below.

The death of Alessandro Striggio, who carried the plague to Venice in June of 1630, eliminated Monteverdi's principal correspondent, and his letters are thereafter far fewer in number. The only reference to sacred music in his letters after 1630 is to his obligation for a Christmas Eve mass every year in the February 2, 1634 letter to Giovanni Battista Doni cited above.

V

In addition to the assumptions about Monteverdi's responsibility for specific feasts discussed to this point, there are a number of more general suppositions that can be made regarding his responsibility for sacred music in both Mantua and Venice. This type of evidence is even more circumstantial, and the conclusions drawn can only be considered speculative.

Roger Bowers has claimed that Monteverdi was regularly engaged in composing and performing sacred music in the church of Santa Croce in the Corte Vecchia of the Gonzaga palace in Mantua as the principal locus of the duke's celebration of liturgical services.[50] This claim is dubious: the church was smaller than Bowers indicates,[51] and the large ducal church of Santa Barbara had been constructed by Vincenzo's father Guglielmo purposely to accommodate large-scale music for which Santa Croce was too small. The documents Bowers cites don't justify and even contradict the interpretations he has made of them.[52] It is far more likely

---

[50] Roger BOWERS, "Monteverdi at Mantua, 1590–1612," in *The Cambridge Companion to Monteverdi*, ed. John Whenham and Richard Wistreich (Cambridge: Cambridge University Press, 2007), pp. 53–58.

[51] Roger BOWERS, "Monteverdi at Mantua, 1590–1612," in *The Cambridge Companion to Monteverdi*, pp. 53–57. The source Bowers himself cites, Stefano L'OCCASO, "Santa Croce in Corte," *Quaderni di San Lorenzo*, 3 (2005), pp. 7–35, estimates the size of the entry-space at approximately 25 meters square, and the size of the altar-space at less than 20 meters square. I am grateful to Sig. L'Occaso for personally checking and confirming the dimensions of the space for me.

[52] As an example of the misinterpretation of documents, Bowers cites as his reference for the statement, "A remark made by a contemporary annalist identifies the church of S. Croce

that any services held in Santa Croce consisted primarily of plainchant, perhaps *falsobordone*, and possibly music for just a few voices and organ. There is no reason to assume, as Bowers does, that a High Mass must have necessarily been in polyphony and required the services of the court *cappella*. Whether or not Monteverdi ever composed any sacred music for Santa Croce, none survives.

The very first letter we have from Monteverdi's hand, dated November 28, 1601, a decade or more after he first entered Gonzaga service, constitutes a request to Duke Vincenzo, away in Hungary on another expedition against the Turks, to be appointed director of music of both the chamber and the church (*mastro e de la Camera e de la Chiesa sopra la musica*).[53] The former *maestro*, Benedetto Pallavicino, had died just days before, and Monteverdi was in haste to put his name before the duke, stressing that he would be remiss in not applying for "the position now

in Corte, standing within the Corte Vecchia of the palace and dating from c. 1425, as the established locale for much of the cappella's observance." The annalist cited is Ippolito DONES-MONDI, *Dell'istoria ecclesiastica di* Mantova, 2 vols. (Mantua, 1612–16), II, p. 201. The passage in question is about the reasons for constructing the church of Santa Barbara, indicating that the church of Santa Croce was too small for the *musica cantate* that Guglielmo Gonzaga and his wife wished to hear, since they liked to attend the divine hours every day. This statement is a direct contradiction of Bowers' claim that Santa Croce was "a building of modest but adequate size" (p. 53), later referring to "grand liturgical occasions known to have been conducted within S. Croce church" (p. 55). The passage cited by Bowers from Donesmondi reads: "[il principe Guglielmo], sì per sua devozione, come anche per comodo della Serenissima Eleonora Arciduchessa d'Austria sua consorte, et per gusto ch'ambidue havevano d'assistere ogni giorno alle hore divine, per ragion di musica cantate (al che non bastava la piccola chiesa di Santa Croce) diede principio quest'anno medesimo [1562] alla sontuosa fabrica del nobilissimo tempio di Santa Barbara …". Bowers gives no source for his statement about "grand liturgical occasions known to have been conducted within S. Croce church," nor is any such source known to me or, to the best of my knowledge, to those who work in the Archivio Diocesano in Mantua. His only citation about music in Santa Croce is a pastoral visitation of 1575–76. The passage relevant to Santa Croce reads "In ecclesia praedicta non celebratur per rectorem nisi in solemnitatibus sanctissimae Crucis, vel cum vocatus propter aliquos principes, vel magnatos foraenses in dicta Curia hospitantes, et mandato serenissimi ducis celebrat praesentibus dictis principibus et magnatis in dicta eccelsia pro commoditate dictorum foriensium. In quibus solemnitatibus conveniunt bini fratres mendicantes ex qualibet regula pro missis celebrandis et pro officio in primis vesperis, et secundis horis, et missa cantandis, modo decem et duodecim ex una illarum religione, modo ex altera quibus per dictum serenissimum elargitur elemosina." There is nothing in this statement that justifies speaking of "grand liturgical occasions," nor of any participation by musicians of the court cappella, nor anything other than quotidian plainchant services performed by monks within the precincts of the court for the convenience of visiting princes and dignitaries. I am grateful to Licia Mari for checking and transmitting the Donesmondi and visitation passages to me.

[53] LAX, pp. 13–14; STEVENS, p. 30. While Monteverdi had accompanied the duke on his Hungarian expedition in 1595, he did not in 1601. Monteverdi's wife was pregnant at the time.

vacant in this quarter of the church" (*il loco ora vacante in questa parte de la Chiesa*) in which he could seek "greater opportunity for showing [myself] to your most refined musical taste as of some worth in motets and masses, too."

The meaning of the word "church" is not clear here, for the church of Santa Barbara, within the palace grounds, already had its own *maestro di cappella* in Giovanni Gastoldi, who served there from 1588 until his death in 1609. Evidently, from shortly after the accession of Vincenzo Gonzaga in 1587, there had been two *maestri* responsible for the duke's sacred music—Gastoldi in Santa Barbara, and Giaches de Wert for sacred music in all other venues, whether inside the court, in the cathedral of San Pietro, in the basilica of Sant'Andrea, or in any other location where the duke may have sponsored a liturgical service requiring the presence of the court musicians.[54] When de Wert died in 1596, Pallavicino had succeeded to his post, for which Monteverdi was now applying upon the latter's death.

We have no documentation showing when Monteverdi was appointed to this position; perhaps it was immediately, or upon the duke's return to Mantua on December 19. The first proof we have of his new position is his self-identification as *maestro della musica* of the duke on the title page of *Il Quarto Libro de Madrigali a Cinque Voci* of 1603, whose dedication is signed March 1. But whenever he assumed this position, Monteverdi was clearly in charge of the duke's sacred music apart from Santa Barbara. In the *Dichiaratione* by Giulio Cesare Monteverdi that serves as preface to Claudio's *Scherzi musicali* of 1607, the composer's brother (also a composer and performer at the Gonzaga court) declares that Claudio had not had time to respond to the attacks on his music by the theorist Giovanni Maria Artusi (beginning in 1600) "because of his responsibility for both church and chamber music" as well as "other extraordinary services."[55]

---

[54] Sant'Andrea did not have its own *maestro di cappella* nor any professional singers at this time, and there is no record of a *maestro di cappella* at the cathedral between 1594 and 1600 or after February 4, 1602. See Pierre TAGMANN, *Archivalische Studien zur Musikpflege am Dom von Mantua (1500–1627)* (Bern: Paul Haupt, 1967), pp. 24–25, 30. The cathedral singers consisted of six *mansionarii* who sang chant and also polyphony, since important composers had served as *maestri di cappella* during much of the 16th century, and there are payment records for the copying of motets and a book of lamentations for Holy Week. See Susan PARISI, "Ducal Patronage of Music in Mantua, 1587–1627: An Archival Study" (Ph. D. dissertation, University of Illinois at Urbana-Champaigne, 1989), pp. 13–15. Gonzaga court musicians in this period performed in both the cathedral and Sant'Andrea, obviously supplementing or even replacing the cathedral musicians for certain celebrations. I am grateful to Licia Mari for this information.

[55] The most convenient translation is available in Oliver STRUNK, *Source Readings in Music History*, revised ed. Leo Treitler (New York: W. W. Norton & Co., 1998), pp. 536–44. The original text may be found in De' PAOLI, *Lettere, Dediche e Prefazioni*, pp. 394–404.

Unfortunately, we have very little information about what this church music might have been and can only assume that he was responsible for all major liturgical events where the duke's musicians participated, whatever the venue. Given Vincenzo Gonzaga's insatiable desire for new music, it is likely that much of this music was newly composed—it would have been far easier to re-use already-composed music for diverse institutions in Venice than to recycle music in the far narrower confines of the Mantuan court and in the presence of the duke.

Mantuan documents refer to a number of major liturgical events in the city for some of which Monteverdi may well have had some compositional responsibility. For example, in 1605 three large paintings by Peter Paul Rubens, one depicting the Gonzaga family honoring the Holy Trinity (worship of the Holy Trinity was the reason for Santa Barbara's martyrdom), were installed in the Jesuit church of the Holy Trinity with a ceremonial dedication on Trinity Sunday, quite possibly with music by Monteverdi.[56] In the same year Luigi Gonzaga, canonized as a saint in 1726, was consecrated in the same church, again a family event that may have required music from Monteverdi. Early in 1607, Pope Paul V, at the request of the duke, declared a perpetual indulgence for the church of Sant'Andrea, which was plenary on the feasts of Sant'Andrea, the Ascension, of our Lord and Good Friday.[57] These are major feasts for which Monteverdi may have annually been expected to provide new music in Sant'Andrea. Ascensiontide also marked the annual celebration of the Sensa, for which Monteverdi wrote new vesper music in May of 1611, as described above. But this could hardly have been a new obligation for him in 1611; rather, it is likely that he composed music for Ascension Day and the Sensa in other years as well. Also associated with the Sensa in 1611 was the celebration of the Order of Knighthood of Christ the Redeemer, founded by Vincenzo in 1608 on Pentecost.[58] The sporadic meetings of the Order mark an-

---

[56] See PARISI, "Ducal Patronage," pp. 18 and 50, note 61. Reproductions of the paintings may be seen in Michael JAFFÉ, *Rubens in Italy* (Ithaca: Cornell University Press, 1977), p. 11 and plates 239, 246 and 247.

[57] See Ippolito DONESMONDI, *Dell'istoria ecclesiastica di Mantova... parte seconda* (Mantua: Aurelio and Lodovico Osanna fratelli, 1616), p. 409: "Favorì nell'entrare del presente anno M.DC.VII. il Pontefice Paolo, la Chiesa di Sant'Andrea in Mantova, per rispetto del pretiosissimo Sangue di Christo, d'indulgenze molto ragguardevoli durante in perpetuo, ad istanza del Serenissimo; e fra l'altre, ne'giorni di Sant'Andrea, dell'Ascensione, di Nostro Signore, e per la notte del venerdi santi, è plenaria; ..." This account does not imply the actual presence of the pope in Mantua, which I suggested in *The Monteverdi Vespers of 1610*, p. 46.

[58] The founding of this order is described in Iain FENLON, "The Monteverdi Vespers: Suggested Answers to some Fundamental Questions," *Early Music*, 5 (1977), pp. 380–87. In 1608, the celebration of Ascension Day and Pentecost were conflated. Even though Ascension day in that year had been on May 15, the Ascension Day services and the Sensa had been postponed to the day after Pentecost (May 25) in order to coincide with the wedding festivities of Prince

other occasion for which the *maestro di cappella* might well have composed special music.[59]

Another feast day that was lavishly celebrated throughout Italy and Europe, and therefore probably in Mantua as well, was the Feast of Corpus Christi. This is an obvious occasion for which the services of the *maestro di cappella*, whether as composer or merely director, may have been required. Since the Gonzagas had long considered the Blessed Virgin the protectress of Mantua and there were important chapels dedicated to her in both the cathedral and Sant'Andrea, feasts of the Virgin, such as the Annunciation (March 25) or the Assumption (August 15), as well as other Marian feasts must have, at least from time to time, if not annually, been celebrated there with special pomp. In 1611, the city of Mantua reaffirmed the cult of the Virgin, consecrating the Immacolata in the Capuchin Church and renewing the confraternity of the Immacolata in the Church of San Francesco.[60]

As at Venice, Holy Week was another season of special emphasis, and we can assume that in Mantua, as in Venice, Monteverdi would have been expected, probably annually, to provide music for the extensive services of this week. Christmas celebrations may likewise have required new music from him as well, as they did in Venice. It is only happenstance that we have specific documentation of Monteverdi's vesper music for the Sensa of 1611 and for Christmas at Modena the same year; indeed, he probably was vastly more active in providing new music for particular liturgical events or seasons than this sparse documentation suggests. Unless a few of the pieces composed for specific events survive in the 1610 *Vespro della Beata Vergine* (*Duo Seraphim*, celebrating the Trinity, might have served for one of the services in the Jesuit church of the Holy Trinity in 1605), all of what must have been a large body of sacred music for Mantua has disappeared.

As noted above, Monteverdi's letters from Venice mention Holy Week and several feasts, such as the Finding of the Holy Cross, Ascension Day, St. Mark, and several others cited above, for which he was occupied with the music. But there are other feasts in the liturgical calendar that were significant in Venice and for which he very likely had to provide music as well. Pentecost, of course, was a

---

Francesco and Margherita of Savoy. Margherita arrived in Mantua on May 24. See Roberto CAPUZZO, "La festa dell'Ascensione mantovana nelle descrizioni seicentesche. Con un inedito di Ippolito Donesmondi," *Civiltà Mantovana*, XXXIV/108 (1999), p. 27, note 12. I am grateful to Licia Mari for this reference. Both the feasts of Pentecost and the Ascension require a different psalm cursus at vespers from that of Marian vespers, so that the service of the founding of the Knights of the Order of the Redeemer doesn't respond to the question of the origin of the 1610 Vespers as Fenlon suggests.

[59] Mantua, Archivio Storico Diocesano, Archivio di Sant'Andrea, b. 112, fasc. 2, "Carte concernenti l'Ordine del Redentore," 15. I am grateful to Licia Mari for this reference.

[60] I am grateful to Licia Mari for this information.

major feast, and as mentioned in connection with Mantua, Corpus Christi was celebrated with special pomp throughout Europe, and Venice was no exception. Giacomo Franco published in 1610 an engraving of the Corpus Christi procession in St. Mark's square, illustrating the thousands of people who took part, marching under a canopy that stretched from the doge's palace through the piazzetta, around the campanile to the bottom of the square, and then back along the other side to the door of St. Mark's.[61]

Although Monteverdi's letter of July 11, 1620, cited above, says "Now that my hectic days at St. Mark's are over (nor will they recur until All Saints' Day)…"[62], he may nevertheless have been responsible for music on the Feast of the Assumption (August 15). His duties at that time might simply not have been so "hectic." Indeed, his own audition at St. Mark's in 1613 had taken place on the Feast of the Assumption. If life were to become hectic for him again around All Saint's Day (November 1), it may be because the Feast of our Lord Jesus Christ the King occurs on the last Sunday in October, once again piling up two feasts in close succession.

Marian worship was just as strong in Venice as it was elsewhere in Italy, and other major feasts of the Virgin may also have required Monteverdi to prepare the music, whether occasionally or annually, whether at St. Mark's or at another Venetian church or confraternity. The Marian feasts that may have called for his services were the Feast of the Annunciation on March 25, the Feast of the Nativity on September 8, the Feast of the Presentation on November 21, and the Feast of the Conception on December 8.

The confraternities and churches of Venice themselves celebrated a variety of feasts, depending on the confraternity or church and its patron saint. The feasts emphasized by each confraternity (the six *scuole grandi* and over 200 *scuole piccole*, a few of which had larger memberships than the *scuole grandi*) were also annual events, recurring, like the Christmas Eve mass, thirty times during Monteverdi's tenure at St. Mark's.[63] How many times he was requested to provide music for these feasts we cannot know—our only testimony is the letter of March 13, 1620 quoted above. In addition to the confraternities, every active church in Venice engaged in some kind of special celebration on the feast day of its patron saint.

---

[61] Franco, Giacomo, Habiti d'huomeni et donne venetiane con la processione della Ser. ma Signoria et altri particolari, cioè trionfi feste et ceremonie publiche della nobilissima città di Venetia. [1610], Plate XXV. This engraving may be viewed at http://sscm-jscm. press. uiuc. edu/v8/no1/kurtzman/fig4. html.

[62] LAX, p. 107; STEVENS, p. 216.

[63] The definitive study of the Venetian confraternities is Jonathan GLIXON, *Honoring God and the City* (Oxford: Oxford University Press, 2003).

While the liturgical calendar was full, there were nevertheless stretches of time mentioned in Monteverdi's letters that were more fallow at St. Mark's. The period after Epiphany was unencumbered by obligations. In a letter of January 28, 1617 to Annibale Iberti at Mantua, he notes that "there is nothing going on at St Mark's," and he is free to travel to Mantua,[64] a statement that indicates he had no obligations at St. Mark's for the Feast of the Purification of the Blessed Virgin on February 2. The Feast of the Annunciation on March 25 is the first fixed date in this period that may have required his presence. Another period of relative leisure was between the middle of July and All Saint's day, mentioned in the letter of July 11, 1620. The feasts of the Nativity of the Blessed Virgin and of the Assumption are the only major celebrations before the Feast of Our Lord Jesus Christ the Redeemer at the end of October.

Just as it is not necessarily the case that Monteverdi composed new music for many of the services he directed in Mantua and Venice, it is also not necessarily the case that he himself was in charge of the music for all the significant feasts celebrated at St. Mark's. There was, after all, a *vice maestro di cappella* who may have taken over on many occasions, and even composed the music.[65] Nevertheless, it is obvious that Monteverdi composed vastly more sacred music in both Mantua and Venice than survives in his three major sacred publications or in anthologies. In the dedication of the posthumous *Messa e Salmi*, dated December 11, 1649, Alessandro Vincenti, the compiler, editor and publisher of the volume, relates how he barely saved Monteverdi's manuscripts from destruction (*che non senza miracolo doppo la morte di lui mi toccñ pietosamente raccogliere*). Without this "miracle," many works would have been lost. Yet it is unlikely that the manuscripts he gathered were either all that survived of Monteverdi's Venetian sacred music, nor that he published everything he did collect. Vincenti's print is very carefully ordered according to a typical pattern for publishing a mass and vesper music in the 17th century (see Table I). It begins with a single mass, and then proceeds with the five psalms for the "male cursus," which, because of the typical substitution of *Laudate Dominum* for *In exitu Israel*, also constitutes the Sunday cursus. The first two psalms are in two settings each. Then come the three additional psalms required for Marian feasts and feasts of female saints, all three of them in two settings. The psalm cycles close with a single Magnificat, by Cavalli rather than Monteverdi. Perhaps Cavalli was the source of the manuscripts, and Vincenti wished to honor him in this way,

---

[64] LAX, p. 25; STEVENS, p. 125.

[65] The *vice-maestri di cappella* during Monteverdi's years at St. Mark's were Marc'Antonio Negri (1612–1619), Alessandro Grandi (1620–c. 1624) and Giovanni Rovetta (interim c. 1624–1627; appointed vice maestro 1627; appointed maestro di cappella as Monteverdi's successor in 1644).

or there was no Magnificat among the manuscripts and Vincenti asked Cavalli for one to fill out the liturgical cycles. The collection closes with Monteverdi's single known litany, already printed twice in anthologies by Vincenti himself,[66] since litanies were often sung at the conclusion of Vespers. Nowhere in this collection do we find the additional psalms needed for some prominent feasts, such as *De profundis, Memento Domine David, Credidi, In convertendo* and *Domine probasti me* required for First and/or Second Vespers at Christmas, Corpus Christi, St. Agnes, St. Agatha, All Saints, St. Michael the Archangel, the Common of Apostles and Evangelists, the Commons of Martyrs, and several other saints and apostles.[67]

Perhaps even more significantly, the only double-choir psalms included in the collection are two settings of *Dixit Dominus*, and only the second is in the *coro spezzato* tradition of St. Mark's. According to the *Ceremoniale* of Bartolomeo Bonifacio, double-choir psalms were required at St. Mark's on all major feasts, and as mentioned before, the *Selva morale* of 1641 contains only two *coro spezzato* settings, *Credidi* and *Memento Domine David*, both of which name their psalm tone (*quarto tono*) and carry the rubric *da capella*. The two double-choir settings of *Dixit Dominus*, the two of *Laudate Dominum* and the single double-choir Magnificat in the *Selva* are in the *concertato* style rather than *coro spezzato*. While the *concertato* style of writing for two choirs may represent a modernized version of the double-choir psalms required at St. Mark's, the traditional character of *Credidi* and *Memento Domine David* would seem to argue instead for the maintenance of the long-standing tradition.

The careful liturgical ordering of the *Messa e Salmi* and the absence of any *coro spezzato* psalms or motets suggest that Vincenti didn't just publish whatever came into his hands, but rather produced a traditionally conceived collection that would have wide market appeal. It is obvious that the manuscripts he recovered must have been a far more random collection of compositions, containing more pieces, perhaps many more, that didn't fit into the scheme or scope of the intended publication.

The evidence assembled here, whether it comprises documents citing specific compositions, circumstantial evidence emanating from documents that are frustratingly vague, or consideration of the probable responsibilities of Monteverdi's employment, points to a very large body of sacred music, though of undetermina-

---

[66] The litany first appeared in *Libro secondo de motetti in lode della gloriosissima Vergine Maria nostra signoria*, ed. by Monteverdi's former Mantuan colleague Giulio Cesare Bianchi (RISM Sammeldrucke 1620⁴), and again in Lorenzo Calvi's anthology *Rosarium litaniarum Beatae V. Mariae* (RISM Sammeldrucke 1626³). The fact that Vincenti reprinted an already published work testifies to the significance of the carefully planned liturgical order of the *Messa e Salmi*.

[67] For a convenient listing of the various psalm cursus for major feasts, see KURTZMAN, *The Monteverdi Vespers of 1610*, Appendix A, pp. 500–502.

ble size, that must have dwarfed what survives in Monteverdi's published music or the few manuscripts containing sacred compositions attributed to him.[68] If we are to place Monteverdi's surviving sacred music in the perspective of his total output, we must admit that it is only a small torso of what he wrote, and that efforts to identify specific surviving compositions with particular liturgical ceremonies must fail on a statistical basis alone. Though we may lament the vast repertoire forever vanished, we can surmise that what survives must represent some of the best of what he composed, since he, and posthumously the publisher Alessandro Vincenti, selected this music for publication, and we must console ourselves with the treasures we have.

Table I
Contents of *Messa e Salmi* of 1650

Messa A 4. Voci. Da Capella.

Dixit Dominus A 8.

Dixit Dominus A 8. Voci, Alla Breue.

Confitebor tibi A Voce Sola con Violini.

Confitebor tibi A 2. Voci, con doi Violini.

Beatus vir A 7. Voci, con doi Violini.

Laudate pueri A 5. Alla quarta Bassa. Da Capella.

Laudate Dominum A Basso Solo.

Laetatus sum A 5. Istrumenti, & 6. voci. A 2. Sopr. e 2. Viol.

Laetatus sum A 5.

Nisi Dominus A 3. Voci, & duoi Violini.

Nisi Dominus A 6.

Lauda Ierusalem A 3.

Lauda Ierusalem A 5.

Magnificat A 6. Voci, & due Violini. Del Sig. Francesco Cavalli Organista di S. Marco.

Letaniae Della B. V. A 6. Voci.

---

[68] These consist of the motet *Exulta filia Sion a voce sola*, the motet *Exultent caeli a 5 voci*, the psalm *Confitebor tibi a 4 voci* (from a printed anthology) and a *Gloria a 8*, all published in Wolfgang Osthoff, *C. Monteverdi: 12 Composizioni vocali profane e sacre (inedite) con e senza Basso Continuo* (Milan: Ricordi, 1958). In 1974, Don Siro CISILINO of the Cini Foundation published three anonymous masses, attributing them, without foundation, to Monteverdi: *Claudio Monteverdi: Tre Missae* (Vienna: Universal Edition, 1974). More recently, Adolf WATTY has published a setting of the psalm *Confitebor tibi* from the Düben manuscript collection in Uppsala, arguing that it is by Monteverdi. See WATTY, "Studien zu Claudio Monteverdis Vertonungen des 110. Psalms: 'Confitebor tibi Domine'," (M. A. thesis, Ruhr-Universität Bochum, 1986). However, Erik KJELLBERG and Kerala J. SNYDER, editors of the *Düben Collection Database Catalogue*, have identified Johann Rosenmüller as the composer of this setting. See http://www.musik.uu.se/duben/Duben,vmhs 29:22 and 79:10 (consulted May 5, 2008).

XII

Collected Works of Claudio Monteverdi:
The Malipiero and Cremona Editions

Tutte le opere di Claudio Monteverdi, ed. Gian Francesco Malipiero

Gian Francesco Malipiero (1882–1973), known principally to the history of music as a prominent Italian composer of the 20th century, is better known to most musicologists for his pioneering edition *Tutte le opere di Claudio Monteverdi* (Asolo, Bologna, Vienna, 1926–1942) in 16 volumes, reprinted by Universal Editions of Vienna beginning in 1952 and again by the *Fondazione G. Cini* of Venice in 1966 with a revised version of Vols 15 and 16 edited by Denis Arnold in 1967–1968.[1] In 1966, Malipiero himself added Vol. 17, a supplementary volume with pieces not included in the earlier volumes. In a brief preface Malipiero rejects "non-autograph" manuscripts as well as a setting of the psalm *Confitebor tibi* published in Naples in 1627.[2] This edition was the first Italian effort at an *Opera Omnia* of any composer, reflecting the personal interests of Malipiero, the attitudes of Italian composers and other artists of his generation who rejected the immediate opera-dominated past of their country and sought a revival of early Italian music, and Italian nationalism, fostered by the fascist regime of Mussolini, who had personally supported Malipiero's project. Through his edition, Malipiero single-handedly made available the music of the Italian master, supplemented by a book

---

[1]   For an index of the compositions in Malipiero's edition, see *An alphabetical index to Claudio Monteverdi: tutte le opere nuovamente date in luce da G. Francesco Malipiero, Asolo, 1926–1942*, edited by the Bibliography committee of the New York Chapter, MLA. (New York: Music Library Association. [1964?]). The historical background of Monteverdi editions and Malipiero's undertaking is described in Gugliemo Barblan, *Malipiero e Monteverdi*, in: *L'Approdo musicale* 3 (1960), pp. 122–33; Chiara Bianchi, *Monteverdi e Malipiero: Storia di un'Edizione*, in: *Rassegna veneta di studi musicali* 15/16 (1999/2000), pp. 209–19; and Iain Fenlon, *Malipiero, Monteverdi, Mussolini and Musicology*, in: *Sing, Ariel: Essays and Thoughts for Alexander Goehr's Seventieth Birthday*, ed. Alison Latham (Aldershot: Ashgate Publishing Ltd., 2003), pp. 241–55. For Gabriele D'Annunzio's role in promoting Monteverdi and Malipiero's edition, see also Andrew dell'Antonio, *Il divino Claudio: Monteverdi and lyric nostalgia in fascist Italy*, in: *Cambridge Opera Journal* 8/3 (November 1996), pp. 271–84.

[2]   Published in Giovanni Maria Sabino, *Psalmi de vespere, a quattro voci. Napoli, Ambrosio Magnetta. 1627.* RISM S38, Sammeldrucke1627⁴.

containing a biographical sketch, the prefaces, dedications and facsimiles of the title pages of Monteverdi's printed works, and transcriptions of his letters in the Archivio di Stato of Mantua (Milan: Treves, 1929). For many years, Malipiero's edition and his separate piano-vocal scores of Monteverdi's first opera, *L'Orfeo*,[3] and *Il Combattimento di Tancredi e Clorinda*[4] were the primary access students, scholars, performers and the general public had to the composer's music.

Malipiero was famously antagonistic to musicologists, and his edition disdained the tools of contemporary scholarship in editing the collected works of a composer, referring to such approaches as "pedantic" and destructive of the composer's musical expressiveness. Malipiero, rather, justified his editorial decisions on the basis of what he felt to be an intuitive, mystical connection with Monteverdi.[5] As a consequence, there were many deficiencies in his edition, and in 1970 the Fondazione Claudio Monteverdi in Cremona, Italy, undertook a new edition of the complete works of the composer utilizing modern paleographical and musicological criteria. That series is not yet quite complete (see below). The purpose of the present article is to examine the criteria and methods of these two editions as a reflection of two very different perspectives on the objectives of an *Opera Omnia* edition.

Malipiero's goal at the outset was not a critical edition, but rather an edition that would make Monteverdi's music available to performers of the 1920s and 1930s for whom Monteverdi's music and most other music of the period had been virtually inaccessible. Palestrina's works had been available for quite some time in the Breitkopf und Härtel edition by Franz Xaver Haberl (1862–1907), but other than that, Italian music of the early modern period was largely unavailable to musicians before 1926, apart from a limited number of compositions in individual editions and anthologies.[6] Moreover,

---

3   London, J.W. Chester, 1923.

4   London, J.W. Chester, 1931.

5   In his "Farewell" at the end of Vol. 16 in 1942, Malipiero refers to Monteverdi as his "co-worker" and declares, "We do not know whether to ascribe it to our empathy or to another indeterminable feeling, but in any case we fancy that we have restored to the world 'all the works' of Claudio Monteverdi, without disfiguring them and without encountering difficulties of interpretation or doubts concerning the original notation; for the spirit of Claudio Monteverdi has been our guide."

6   The principal anthologies and editions of Italian music before 1926 were Carl von Winterfeld's *Johannes Gabrieli und sein Zeitalter* (Berlin: Schlesinger'sche Buch- und Musikhandlung, 1834), Robert Eitner's edition of Monteverdi's *L'Orfeo* (Berlin, 1881), adaptations of *L'Orfeo* by Vincent D'Indy (Paris: Schola Cantorum,1904) and Giacomo Orefice (Milan: Associazione italiana di Amici della Musica, 1909), Alessandro Parisotti's *Arie antiche italiane*, Milan: G. Ricordi,

contemporary musicians had little knowledge and even less interest in performing the music of the past according to what nowadays is generally called "historically informed performance." When Malipiero began his edition, there was virtually no understanding of vocal performance practices of the sixteenth and seventeenth centuries, and interest in early instruments was limited to such pioneers as Arnold Dolmetsch (1858–1940) and Wanda Landowska (1879–1959), whose efforts were ignored and even scorned by the vast majority of practicing musicians. Thus, Malipiero's endeavor must be understood in its own historical context, and whatever the failings of the edition itself, Malipiero deserves the credit for his heroic labors and the revival of Monteverdi's music in the twentieth century.

Malipiero's edition divides Monteverdi's works according to genre. The first nine volumes constitute the first eight books of madrigals (the eighth volume is divided into two parts) and the posthumous ninth book, the *Madrigali e Canzonette a due, e tre voci* of 1651. Vol. 10 comprises the lighter secular works: *Canzonette* and *Scherzi musicali*, while Vols 11–13 contain the operas. Monteverdi's sacred works are found in Vols 14–16, each in multiple parts, and Vol. 17 is a supplement, containing a facsimile of the sole surviving part-book of his *Madrigali spirituali* of 1583[7] and both secular and sacred works published in anthologies during Monteverdi's lifetime which had only come to light after 1942 (see Appendix for more detailed information).

From the very first volume, Malipiero's objectives and editorial methods were clear. Some of these are articulated in Malipiero's brief preface, which declares:

> In this edition there are neither deletions nor disfigurements of style. The original is reproduced completely and faithfully. Claudio Monteverdi's marvelous harmonic sensibility is respected because I don't consider printing errors those "accidents" that represent the graphic expression of a musician who did not live in 1848.

> Nor are the tonalities modified, even though it is known that these were transposed, adapting them to the voices at hand. Even today, one can do otherwise in performance.

1885–1890, Luigi Torchi's *L'arte musicale in Italia* (Milan: G. Ricordi, 1897–1903), the series *I Classici della Musica Italiana* (Milan: Società anonima notari, 1919–1921) and Robert Haas' edition of *Il ritorno d'Ulisse in Patria*, in: Denkmäler der Tonkunst in Österreich, Bd. 57 (Vienna: Universal-Edition, 1922).

   [7]   This facsimile was also originally printed in Vol. XVI, the plates of which were lost during World War II.

No reduction for pianoforte, so dear to dilettants, is added, but for convenience of reading the same distribution of the four voices is adopted: soprano, alto, tenor and bass (with the "quinto," which is merely the division of one of the four voices) and only violin and bass clefs (the tenor, however, is read an octave lower).

Sometimes the tenor is too high, other times the alto is too low: these inconveniences are eliminated by transposing the keys or modifying the distribution of the voices, always conforming to the means at hand.[8]

In this preface, which appears only in Vol. 1, Malipiero disavows any intention of providing analyses or discussion of the music, wishing to let Monteverdi's music "speak for itself." Thus we find nothing of the often extensive prefaces that are normal in modern critical editions, commenting on the sources of the music, its history and context, its analysis, and performance criteria. Nor is there any commentary on the texts Monteverdi sets or even any attempt to identify the authors of the texts.

Malipiero displayed sound instincts in wanting to present the music as it is, without the modifications, truncations, expansions and other editorial interventions that were so common in editions of early music in that period. He keeps the original names of voices, despite their actual tessitura, and even indicates their original clefs before the modern clefs in which the edition presents them. There are no transpositions and no reductions in note values: Monteverdi's semibreves and minims become Malipiero's whole- and half-notes, and modern barring is employed, with the measure in duple meter comprising a semibreve (whole note). When Monteverdi notated triple meter, Malipiero, unlike the Cremona edition to be discussed below, also maintains the original mensurations and note values, offering his own suggestions for proportional tempo relationships between the sections in duple and triple

---

[8]   Malipiero, *Tutte le opere*, Vol. 1, pp. i–ii: "In questa edizione non si troverranno nè amputazioni, nè deturpazioni dello stile. L'originale si riproduce integralmente e fedelmente. La prodigiosa sensibilità armonica di Claudio Monteverdi viene rispettata perchè non si considerano errori di stampa quegli "accidenti" che rappresentano l'espressione grafica di un musicista che non ha vissuto nel 1848. Nemmeno si modificano le tonalità, quantunque si sappia che queste si trasportavano adattandole alle voci di cui si disponeva. Anche oggi, in caso di esecuzione, si può fare altrettanto. Non si aggiunge il riassunto per pianoforte tanto caro ai dilettanti, ma per facilitare la lettura si adotta sempre la stessa distribuzione delle quattro voci: soprano, contralto, tenore e basso (col "quinto" che è soltanto la divisione di una delle quattro voci) e le sole chiavi di violino (il tenore si legge però l'ottava sotto) e basso. Talvolta il tenore è troppo acuto tal altra il contralto è troppo grave: questi inconvenienti si eliminavano appunto trasportando le tonalità, o modificando la distribuzione delle voci, sempre conformandosi ai mezzi materiali che si avevano sotto mano." (author's translation).

time. Only in the supplementary Vol. 17 published much later than the others did he resort to reductions of note values and meters in triple time. Triple meter is usually, but not always, barred in accordance with the principal unit that is triply subdivided. An exception is the *Lamento della Ninfa* from the *Madrigali guerrieri ed amorosi* in which the measure comprises two triply divided breves instead of one. At times, such as in *Il terzo libro de madrigali*, Malipiero changes a ¢ mensuration to C, obscuring the tempo significance of ¢.

Also in keeping with his intention to present Monteverdi's own notation, Malipiero openly corrects only the most obvious errors in the original print through footnote annotations at the bottom of the relevant page, though some of his corrections are dubious and Malipiero inevitably introduced new mistakes into his transcriptions.[9] Moreover, numerous passages were altered tacitly. Modern practice is followed in the notation of accidentals (an accidental is valid for the remainder of a measure unless altered again) and Malipiero adds a modest amount of *musica ficta* and other editorial accidentals in parentheses above the staff. Despite preserving Monteverdi's original notation, Malipiero didn't hesitate to add performance suggestions of his own without distinguishing them as editorial rather than Monteverdi's. Today, because of our familiarity with Monteverdi's original prints, it is an easy matter to separate Malipiero's editorial performance instructions from Monteverdi's original notation, but these would not have been obvious to readers in 1926–1942.

These added performance suggestions include tempo markings at the head of each piece (*e.g.* Andante; Andante, molto ritmato; Allegro ritenuto, in 2; Piutosto lento), which are at least in parentheses, indicating their editorial role as mere recommendations. In addition, Malipiero has added dynamic markings, including crescendos and diminuendos; phrase markings where there are both short or longer melismas in the music; and on rare occasions, editorial accidentals and *musica ficta*.[10] These volumes, therefore, are clearly performing editions, designed to be picked up by any musician and performed without need of much additional interpretive information on the part of performers. This is not to imply that Malipiero's suggestions are necessarily musically inappropriate; indeed, as the work of an excellent musician, they often enhance and convey appropriately the affect of the text

---

[9] See note 20 for articles critiquing Malipiero's edition, many of which enumerate specific errors.

[10] Late in his life, Malipiero declared that if he were to make a new edition of the works of Monteverdi, he would not add any expression marks, considering them superfluous. See Barblan, *Malipiero e Monteverdi*, p. 131.

at any given moment, though in the music of this period, there is often room for significant disagreement in interpretation, especially with regard to tempo.

From the standpoint of a critical edition, however, these scores are sorely lacking. Each volume begins with a facsimile of the title page of the original print used for the transcription, substituting one motto or another for the name of the voice of that part-book at the top of each title page, with additional facsimiles as noted below. In the case of *Il primo libro de madrigali*, Malipiero used the Alessandro Raverii reprint of 1607, the second of three editions of *Il primo libro*, clearly chosen because of its availability in the Museo internazionale e Biblioteca della musica (formerly Civico Museo Bibliografico Musicale) at Bologna. The only copy of the first edition of 1593 is in Gdansk, Poland (Danzig, Prussia in 1926), which Malipiero could have been aware of because of its listing in Robert Eitner's *Biographisch-bibliographisches Quellen-Lexikon*,[11] but which would have been rather remote of access. On the other hand, a complete copy of the 1621 edition by Bartolomeo Magni in Venice was available in the nearby Biblioteca Estense in Modena. Because Malipiero relies on only a single source throughout all the volumes of the edition (except for *Concerto settimo libro de madrigali* and *L'Incoronazione di Poppea*), he did not have the benefit of seeing the composer's and editors' later corrections or of comparing different readings of questionable passages. Consequently, we find none of the comparative editorial apparatus that would characterize a modern critical edition.

The characteristics of Malipiero's edition of *Il primo libro* also mark his editions of the remaining madrigal books, with some additional considerations. Since Malipiero's source for *Il terzo libro de madrigali* was the first edition, he includes a facsimile of the dedication as well as the title page. In *Il quarto libro de madrigali*, the madrigal *Sfogava con le stelle* begins with the *falsobordone* style notated in the source as a single breve in each voice, accommodating a number of syllables of text. Malipiero maintains Monteverdi's breve notation for this and subsequent *falsobordone* passages and for the first time, offers performance advice in a footnote: "free declamation, almost spoken."[12] *Il quinto libro de madrigali*, which is represented by facsimiles from the second edition of 1606, includes Monteverdi's note to readers apologizing for not yet responding to the published attacks of Giovanni Maria Artusi and promising his own

---

[11] Full title: *Biographisch-bibliographisches Quellen-Lexikon der Musiker und Musikgelehrten christlicher Zeitrechnung bis Mitte des neunzehnten Jahrhunderts*, Leipzig: Breitkopf und Härtel, 1900–1904.

[12] A similar footnote appears *in Il quinto libro* in the madrigal *Che dar più vi poss'io*, which also contains a passage in *falsobordone*.

treatise on the Seconda Pratica, which never appeared. The source Malipiero used for his transcription of *Il quinto libro*, however, was Ricciardo Amadino's reprint of 1615, which contains a number of hand-written corrections that Malipiero incorporated into his own edition without annotation except for the one he considered subject to question. Near the end of the final madrigal, the Tenore Primo Choro part is so corrupt as to be uncorrectable. Malipiero simply leaves the passage blank and prints the original passage at the bottom of the page as a footnote. *Il quinto libro* concludes with six madrigals with basso continuo, the first time a basso continuo appears in the composer's *oeuvre*. Monteverdi's basso continuo figures in this and all his works are sparse; Malipiero reproduces Monteverdi's figuring, but adds none of his own, although missing accidentals in the continuo line are notated beneath it in parentheses. Malipiero adds dynamic markings to this continuo part and provides a realization in simple harmonies with the upper parts on a staff of their own in a smaller font to distinguish them from the larger font of Monteverdi's own bass line, a practice that he will continue throughout the remaining volumes, with a few exceptions. One of these exceptions is found in *Il quinto libro*, where the final madrigal contains an instrumental *sinfonia* which Malipiero transcribes as a five-part score instead of the nine parts in two choirs with additional continuo originally printed by Monteverdi.[13] Malipiero again exercised sound instincts in the simplicity of his continuo realizations, recognizing the primacy of the voice and avoiding the thicker four-part realizations in 18th-century contrapuntal style that still mar some editions of 17th-century music.

Monteverdi's *Il sesto libro de madrigali* contains on the final page of the Basso part-book an anonymous sonnet in honor of the composer, which Malipiero prints in modern type. The next madrigal book, entitled *Concerto settimo libro de madrigali*, for which Malipiero used the 1641 edition according to his facsimile of the title page, nevertheless also contains a facsimile of the original 1619 dedication, as well as another sonnet in praise of the composer, again transcribed in modern type. Having more than one edition at his disposal in Bologna, this is the first time Malipiero made any attempt to compare differences between or among separate editions of the same opus, confined, however to a footnote annotation to the solo madrigal *Partenza amorosa* in which he indicates a different rubric for the piece in the 1623 edition. Also novel in Malipiero's edition of the *Concerto* is a realization of the basso continuo even when the upper parts of the harmonies are fully filled

---

[13] The Cremona edition, by contrast, reproduces all nine parts as well as the basso continuo with a full realization.

out by notated instruments, a practice that continues in the *Madrigali guerrieri et amorosi* and throughout all the subsequent volumes of the series.

The *Madrigali guerrieri et amorosi* of 1638, Monteverdi's *Libro ottavo*, contains an important theoretical preface, reproduced in facsimile by Malipiero in addition to the title page and dedication. In this volume there are stage and ballet works with stage directions or extensive verbal explanations, such as *Il combattimento di Tancredi e Clorinda* and *Il ballo delle ingrate*. Malipiero transcribes all of this verbal material, and in *Il ballo*, interprets in a footnote Monteverdi's directions that may be ambiguous or unclear. The differences between the versions of *Il combattimento* in the basso continuo part-book and the other part-books are substantial.[14] Where there are such differences Malipiero chooses without comment the basso continuo part as his source, although this is discernible from his footnotes annotating variants in the tenor and instrumental parts. In the *Madrigali guerrieri et amorosi*, Malipiero's practice of adding phrase markings makes it impossible to distinguish his editorial interventions from Monteverdi's own phrase markings, which are common in some of the madrigals, such as *Mentre vaga angioletta*.

Monteverdi's ninth book of madrigals, issued posthumously by the publisher Alessandro Vincenti in 1651, is actually entitled *Madrigali e Canzonette a due, e tre voci*. In addition to facsimiles of both the title page and Vincenti's dedication, the original index is transcribed in modern type, including Vincenti's brief message to readers explaining the reason for republishing some compositions that had already appeared in the *Libro ottavo*. At the end of this last volume of madrigals, Malipiero publishes facsimiles of the dedications of the first and second books of madrigals, which were lacking in the volumes of the edition containing those works.

Vols 11–13 of Malipiero's edition contain the operas and operatic excerpts. Vol. 11 consists of *L'Orfeo*, the *Lamento d'Arianna* from its 1623 publication, and a fragment *composta per la Maddalena* attributed to Monteverdi in an anthology of 1617. *Il Ritorno d'Ulisse* and *L'Incoronazione di Poppea* comprise Vols 12 and 13 repectively. *L'Orfeo* is based on the first edition of 1609 (the copies of which contain a number of variants) and ignores the corrected second edition of 1615.[15] *L'Orfeo* contains a variety of mensuration signs whose tempo relationships and note equivalencies are sometimes difficult

---

14   See Tim Carter, *Monteverdi's Musical Theatre*, New Haven and London: Yale University Press, 2002, pp. 176–7.

15   The stop-press corrections in the several extant copies of the 1609 edition have been studied and documented in Tim Carter, "Some Notes on the First Edition of Monteverdi's Orfeo (1609)," *Music & Letters*, 91, 2010, 498–512, first read as a paper at the conference *Orfeo*

to grasp. In such circumstances it is essential that an edition reproduce the original mensurations and note values, which Malipiero scrupulously does. Unlike the volumes of madrigals, Malipiero wisely avoids trying to suggest note equivalencies between passages in duple and triple meter except in a single instance in the first act. As in the *sinfonia* to the last madrigal in *Il quinto libro de madrigali*, Malipiero does not provide a continuo realization for the instrumental *sinfonia*s and ritornellos in *L'Orfeo*. On the other hand, he does publish a realization of the continuo line throughout *Il Ritorno d'Ulisse*, *L'Incoronazione di Poppea* and all subsequent volumes.

Vols 12 and 13, whose operas exist in manuscript versions only, open with *faux* facsimiles of printed title pages in the style of the 17th century, but dated MCMXXX and MCMXXXI respectively. Vol. 13 contains a facsimile of the first page of the Venetian manuscript of the opera, and a brief preface in each volume describes the manuscripts and provides a list of characters. Vol. 13 is the only volume in the entire series that actually compares two different sources, the Venetian and Neapolitan manuscripts of *Poppea*. Malipiero erroneously believed the first and third acts of the Venetian manuscript to be in Monteverdi's own hand, therefore giving the Venetian version priority, but he included at the end of the volume those portions of the 1651 Neapolitan manuscript that "complete" the Venetian one, i.e., passages or numbers lacking in the Venetian manuscript; full ritornellos, notated only by means of a basso continuo in the Venetian manuscript; and different versions of instrumental or vocal numbers. In each case he annotates the divergence between the two sources, although the annotations are not always clear. He also includes in his score those passages that are crossed out in the Venetian manuscript. Where words of characters or indications of scenes are missing from the manuscript, Malipiero supplies them from the 1646 Venetian libretto, and some missing vocal passages are reconstructed where the missing parts are obvious or are found in the Naples manuscript. In all of these editorial interventions, Malipiero is careful to indicate what his contributions are or where the missing Venetian passages may be found in the Naples manuscript, extending even to the point of including facsimiles of the same passage from both manuscripts to clarify a particularly problematic passage. On the other hand, he ignores the transposition rubrics, assuming that such transpositions were to accommodate particular performers. Vol. 13 is the only volume of the series where Malipiero functions like a musicologist, comparing sources, determining what he considers to be the better reading, and annotating

son io held in Verona, Venice, and Mantua in December 2005. I am grateful to Professor Carter for sharing a copy of his paper with me prior to publication.

carefully his interventions, though he does not make corrections in the Naples manuscript excerpts.

The last three volumes of the original series comprise Monteverdi's sacred prints, published in chronological order. In the Latin-texted works, Malipiero avoids any dynamic markings, tacitly assuming that the kinds of expression he suggested for the madrigals and operas (including the five spiritual madrigals at the beginning of the *Selva morale et spirituale*) were not appropriate for sacred music. Vol. 14, again in two parts, contains Monteverdi's youthful *Sacrae cantiunculae* of 1582 and the 1610 *Missa In illo tempore* and *Vespro della Beata Vergine*. Although facsimiles of the title pages and dedications of both prints are provided, there is no indication that the title page of the Bassus Generalis part-book for the 1610 print used for the facsimile differs in some important particulars from that of the vocal part-books. In the *Sacrae cantiunculae*, Malipiero sometimes changes ₵ mensurations to C, without any indication of his having done so, and ignores Monteverdi's black notation, therefore sometimes misinterpreting it, leading to note values and barring that distort Monteverdi's meaning.[16]

The *Vespro della Beata Vergine* presents a new editorial issue, since the Bassus Generalis part-book includes upper parts for the four motets and *Sonata sopra Sancta Maria* as well as for virtuoso passages in the psalms and Magnificats as a guide to the continuo player(s). These upper parts differ in details from the vocal part-books and are reproduced faithfully in the score of *Pulchra es* and *Duo Seraphim* as well as the *Sonata*, giving the reader the opportunity to see the differences and decide which version might take priority. In the *Sonata* the upper parts are simplifications of the ornamented lines in the instruments. Unaccountably, Malipiero leaves these upper parts of the Bassus Generalis out of his transcription of *Nigra sum*, *Audi coelum* and the *Deposuit* of the Magnificat *a 7*, perhaps because the differences of detail between the Bassus Generalis and vocal versions are frequent and would have required editorial intervention and commentary. On the other hand, Malipiero does include the upper parts of the Bassus Generalis in the *Deposuit* of the Magnificat *a 6*. As with *L'Orfeo*, Monteverdi's mensurations in the *Vespro* are varied and, in the 1610 print, inconsistent. Once again, Malipiero maintains the original mensurations and note values except in the hymn *Ave maris stella*, where Monteverdi notates the Bassus Generalis in ₵ and the voices in C, whether the meter is duple or triple (₵ or ₵ $\frac{3}{2}$), as well as in some verses of the two Magnificats. Unlike Monteverdi, who is consistent in confining ₵ to

---

[16]   See *O magnum pietatis* and its second part, *Eli clamans*.

XII

the Bassus Generalis in the hymn and Magnificats, Malipiero is inconsistent, sometimes extending the Bassus Generalis mensuration to the voices, other times reproducing the vocal mensuration in the Bassus Generalis, but always without comment.[17]

The engraving plates of the last two volumes of Malipiero's original series, the first devoted to the *Selva morale et spirituale* of 1641 and the second to the posthumous *Messa a quattro voci e salmi* published by Alessandro Vincenti in 1650 (each Malipiero volume published in multiple parts) were lost during World War II. In 1967 and 1968 Universal Edition reprinted these volumes, edited by Denis Arnold, by recopying one of Malipiero's own private copies. According to Arnold's notes, the original versions, published in 1941 and 1942 under conditions of war, were badly corrected, contained many errors, and the quality of the printing was poor. Arnold emended errors in Monteverdi's original prints as well as in the first versions of Malipiero's edition, with more extensive annotations than Malipiero. Arnold also standardized orthography, which in the 17th century was typically inconsistent, and restored the original rubrics that Malipiero had omitted. On the other hand, he corrected only minor details of Malipiero's basso continuo. According to Arnold, "the edition remains the work of G.F. Malipiero and the pupils to whom he refers in his original preface."

In Vol. 15 Malipiero had reproduced in facsimile the original 1640 title page of the *Selva morale*, which exists only in the Bologna copy, and not the final 1641 title page also present in the Bologna copy and all others, leading to frequent references in the scholarly literature to the *Selva* with the wrong publication date.[18] The table of contents is transcribed in modern print and omits the sectional divisions indicated in Monteverdi's original. In Vols 15 and 16 the edition distinguishes for the first time Monteverdi's original phrase markings from those that are editorial. Malipiero closed the final volume of his series with an "Abschied" in which he excoriated those performers and musicologists who added accidentals to Monteverdi's music and deplored arrangements, performances, publications and recordings which altered Monteverdi's original text in order to popularize the music. Someone had

---

[17] Monteverdi notates the *Missa In illo tempore* in ₵ throughout in all parts. Malipiero adopts this mensuration in all parts as well except for the four-voice *Crucifixus*, where he unaccountably uses a C mensuration.

[18] Furthering the confusion was Malipiero's inclusion of the facsimile of the dedication, dated May 1, 1641. The dedication date was ignored by many scholars, who relied solely on the original, but obviously superseded, title page of 1640 without consulting other copies of the print, where only the 1641 title page is found.

XII

12 *Collected Works of Claudio Monteverdi:*

also brought to Malipiero's attention his misunderstanding of Monteverdi's rhythmic and mensural notation in the *Sacrae cantiunculae,* for Malipiero defended himself with the bizarre and disdainful declaration:

> If we are occasionally supposed to have read various conventional markings wrongly, as apparently happened in the "sacrae cantiuncolae" [sic], we are not convinced that we have erred; since Monteverdi did not warn us, this would indicate that he perhaps prefers our seemingly faulty interpretation to that of false scholars.[19]

Malipiero's edition generated a great deal of commentary from Hans F. Redlich, a pioneering Monteverdi scholar, and others, beginning only two years after the appearance of the first volume. While Redlich initially praised Malipiero's synthesis between musicological and pragmatic methods, Redlich's response grew more critical as the volumes were released, finding fault with Malipiero's editorial judgment and noting mistakes in his transcriptions. Ultimately, after the series was completed, Redlich called for a complete revision of Malipiero's edition.[20]

Malipiero published Vol. 17, the supplementary volume, in 1966, long after completing the original series. This volume contains a series of *canzonette, arie,* motets and other short secular pieces from four different anthologies and a manuscript, as well as facsimiles of the aforementioned bass part of the *Madrigali spirituali* of 1583, the title page of one of the anthologies (RISM

---

[19] *Tutte le opere,* XVI/2, p. 527.

[20] See Hans F. Redlich, *Monteverdi-Gesamtausgabe,* in: *Musikblätter des Anbruch* 10 (1928), pp. 207–11; idem, *Neue Monteverdiana,* in: *Musikblätter des Anbruch* 13 (1931), pp. 127–8; idem, *Sull'edizione moderna delle opere di Claudio Monteverdi,* in: *Rassegna musicale* 8 (1935), pp. 23–41; idem, *Zur Bearbeitung von Monteverdis ‚Orfeo',* in: *Schweizerische Musikzeitung* 76 (1936), pp. 37–42; idem, *Monteverdi's Religious Music,* in: *Music & Letters* 27 (1946), pp. 208–15; idem, *Aufgaben und Ziele der Monteverdi-Forschung,* in: *Die Musikforschung* 4 (1951), pp. 318–22; idem, *Notes to a New Edition of Monteverdi's Mass of 1651,* in: *Monthly Musical Record* 83 (May 1953), pp. 95–9; idem, *Claudio Monteverdi,* in: *Die Musik in Geschichte und Gegenwart,* XVI (Kassel: Bärenreiter-Verlag, 1960), columns 511–32; idem, *Problemi monteverdiani,* in: *Rivista italiana di musicologia* 2/2 (1967), pp. 328–31; idem, *Claudio Monteverdi (1567–1643): Some Editorial Problems of 1967,* in: *The Consort* 24 (1967), pp. 224–32. Others who critiqued Malipiero's edition are Giacomo Benvenuti, *Il manoscritto veneziano della ‚Incoronazione di Poppea',* in: *Rivista musicale italiana* 41 (1937), pp. 176–84; Bernard Jacobson, *Murder at Aix,* in: *Music and Musicians* 13 (October 1964), pp. 34–5; Henry Prunières, *Le couronnement de Poppée,* in: *Revue musicale* 19 (1938), pp. 135–6; Guglielmo Barblan, *Nota bibliografica monteverdiana,* in: *Rivista italiana di musicologia* 2/2 (1967), pp. 387–9; Jack A. Westrup, *Review of Claudio Monteverdi: L'Orfeo edited by Denis Stevens,* in: *Music & Letters* 48 (1967), pp. 400–402; idem, *Review of 'Tutte le opere di Claudio Monteverdi',* Vols 12, 13, 14, pt. i & 14, pt. ii," in: *Music & Letters* 48 (1967), pp. 171–8.

SD1629[5]) represented in the volume, the first piece of the volume (*Io ardo sì*), a page from the libretto of Giulio Strozzi's *Proserpina rapita*, composed by Monteverdi but lost, and an excerpt from an essay by Matteo Caberloti in praise of Monteverdi from Giovanni Battista Marinoni's *Fiori poetici*, published in Venice as a memorial in 1644, a few months after Monteverdi's death. In this last volume, Malipiero abandoned his editorial performance markings, whether tempo suggestions, dynamics or phrasing in favor of a more simple, pristine transcription. However, he also abandoned his adherence to Monteverdi's original mensurations and note values in triple time, changing the meter signatures and reducing the note values by half. In *Venite et videte*, for example, the opening ₵ with three minims per triple unit becomes $\frac{3}{4}$ with quarter notes. Later in the piece, the mensuration 3 with three semibreves per unit becomes $\frac{3}{2}$ with three minims comprising a triple unit. Thus, in the supplementary volume, one of the chief advantages of Malipiero's edition – the retention of original mensurations and note values – is lost.

Claudio Monteverdi: Opera Omnia, published under the auspices of the Fondazione Claudio Monteverdi of Cremona

In 1970 the Fondazione Claudio Monteverdi of Cremona began a new critical edition of the complete works of Monteverdi to supplant the Malipiero edition with all its critical weaknesses. The first volume was edited by Raffaello Monterosso, general editor of the series, at that time Director of the Fondazione and Professor at the Scuola di Paleografia e Filologia Musicale of the University of Pavia, located in Cremona and the seat of the Foundation. The goal of the edition was to provide a modern, fully critical edition of use to both scholars and performers.

The edition is conceived in twenty volumes; each volume has its own editor, although some have edited, or will edit, more than one volume.[21] To

---

[21]   Editors and co-editors of the volumes already issued and announced are as follows: Raffaello Monterosso (*Madrigali Libro* I), Anna Maria Monterosso Vacchelli (*Madrigali Libro* II, VIII, IX, *Scherzi musicali* 1632, *L'Orfeo* and *Lamento di Arianna*), Maria Teresa Rosa Barezzani (*Madrigali Libro* III), Elena Ferrari Barassi (*Madrigali Libro* IV), Maria Caraci (*Madrigali Libro* V), Mariella Sala (*Messa a quattro voci et Salmi* of 1651), Denis Stevens (*Selva morale et spirituale*), Frank Dobbins (*Scherzi musicali* of 1607 and 1632, Anthology of secular compositions), Antonio Delfino (*Madrigali Libro* VI; *Missa in illo tempore* and *Vespro della Beata Vergine* of 1610, Anthology of sacred compositions), Anna Maria De Chiara (*Madrigali Libro* VII), Lawrence Cummings (*L'Incoronazione di Poppea*), Emily Corswarem (Anthology of secular compositions), Anthony Pryer (*Sacrae cantiunculae, Madrigali spirituali a quattro voci, Canzonette a tre voci*). The only edition for which an editor has not yet been announced is *Il Ritorno d'Ulisse*. My own editions of the *Missa*

date, sixteen of the projected twenty volumes have appeared, including all of the madrigal books, the two books of *Scherzi musicali*, the three juvenile prints, comprising the *Sacrae cantiunculae*, the surviving bass part of the *Madrigali spirituali* and the *Canzonette a tre*, all three of the major volumes of sacred music, and an anthology of miscellaneous sacred compositions. Volumes announced for publication soon are an anthology of secular compositions, *L'Orfeo* and the *Lamento di Arianna*, and *L'Incoronazione di Poppea*. Once these appear, only *Il Ritorno d'Ulisse* will remain to be published. Four of the volumes so far issued, the First, Second and Sixth Books of Madrigals and the *Messa a quattro voci et salmi* of 1650, are accompanied by complete compact disc recordings.

As with Malipiero's edition, the criteria of the Foundation's series are established in the first volume containing the *Primo libro de madrigali*. In keeping with modern standards for critical editions, each volume begins with a substantial introduction. Typically, the introduction includes a transcription of the dedication and other prefatory material; a comparison of the various editions of each publication; an analytical discussion of the pieces contained in the print, focusing on particularly relevant compositional features; a discussion of performance issues, especially Monteverdi's varied and often confusing mensurations; a complete critical apparatus based on all the surviving editions; a critical edition of the texts of all the compositions; and, unique to the best of my knowledge of critical editions, a complete facsimile of the principal source or sources used for the modern edition.[22] The presentation of the facsimiles, however, is not uniform from volume to volume: some reproduce each piece in all its parts on a single or facing pages, while others present each complete part-book in succession. The former method is much more convenient for the user, since the transcription of any composition can readily be checked against the facsimile, whereas the latter arrangement requires the reader to browse successively through each part-

---

in illo tempore, published by Carus-Verlag in 1994 and of the *Vespro della Beata Vergine* of 1610, published in 1999 by Oxford University Press, were originally prepared in 1974 for the Cremona edition. However, I was uncomfortable with Prof. Monterosso's policy that Monteverdi's triple-meter notations be reduced, and that difference of opinion, combined with the absence of funding at the time to pay for the publication, led to my withdrawal from the series by mutual, friendly agreement with Prof. Monterosso.

[22] The introduction to the Fifth Book of Madrigals also contains a discussion of the Note to Readers in this print and historical commentary on the Prima & Seconda Pratica mentioned in that note.

book to find the individual voices or instruments of a composition. Most of the volumes contain a bibliography and a discography as well.[23]

The notational criteria for this edition include the use of modern clefs, barring through the staff, the realization of the abbreviation *ij* by means of italic text, the indication of ligatures in the original by brackets over the notes, and similarly, the indication of coloration in the original by broken brackets over the notes. The edition repeats accidentals within a measure as many times as they appear in the original print, but some accidentals on the staff are editorial additions deemed necessary (such as the repetition of an accidental after a modern barline). Editorial accidentals are printed above the staff: those judged indispensable are without brackets; those regarded as uncertain are in square brackets; those considered as reminders, but in essence superfluous, are in parentheses. Monteverdi's basso continuo parts as well as those added to the Fourth and Fifth Books of madrigals in the 1615 and subsequent reprints by the Antwerp publisher Pierre Phalèse are included and realized in a simple and appropriate 17th-century style with a small note font as in the Malipiero edition. The editors of all the volumes reject high clefs (G_2, C_2, C_3, and C_4 or F_3) as a sign of transposition – a position no longer tenable.

Monterosso, as editor of the first volume, *Il primo libro de madrigali*, is critical in his introduction of Malipiero's standardized barring in duple time, because of its implication of 18th and 19th-century accentuation on the first and third beats of each measure. In compensation, Monterosso offers practical advice regarding the interpretation and performance of the tactus, contrasting the meaning of the *battuta* with modern metric accentuation. Despite the flexibility in Monteverdi's metric accentuation, Monterosso nevertheless elects to bar everything in semibreves, including passages in *sesquialtera*, just as Malipiero had done. Thus, the barring is identical between the two editions in *Il primo libro*. Monterosso's concern over musicians misunderstanding Monteverdi's accentuation might well have been exaggerated, though performers were less aware of these issues, when the first volume was published in 1970 than they are today. Monterosso could have chosen to use *Mensurstriche*, as in so many modern critical editions of Renaissance music, thereby allowing Monteverdi's original notation to illustrate better his accentuation of the text rather than breaking phrases up by barlines through the staff and tying notes over barlines. Unfortunately, Monterosso's decision to use barlines through the

---

[23]   Volumes lacking a bibliography are *Il quinto libro de madrigali, Concerto settimo libro* and the *Madrigali guerrieri et amorosi*. Volumes lacking a discography are *Il secondo libro de madrigali, Concerto settimo libro*, the Anthology of sacred compositions and the *Selva morale et spirituale*. I have not yet seen the recently issued volume of juvenile prints.

staff throughout the series led him to a number of other editorial decisions regarding mensurations and note values that this writer finds confusing and distorting.

With the few exceptions noted above, Malipiero had preserved Monteverdi's original mensurations and note values, so that the reader has an accurate picture of Monteverdi's method of notating both meters and the rhythms that comprise them. That is still true in the first volume of Monteverdi's madrigals in the Cremona edition because of Monteverdi's own uncomplicated notation, but not in subsequent volumes where the editors, attempting on the one hand to notate Monteverdi's accentuation and on the other to use modern forms of triple notation, alter note values and meter signatures at will. The argument is that Monteverdi's original notation can be seen in the facsimiles that accompany each volume, but the transcriptions give an inaccurate and often misleading picture of that notation. In *Il secondo libro de madrigali*, the third piece, *Bevea Fillide mia*, opens with a mensuration of $\mathbb{C}\frac{3}{2}$, notated by Monteverdi principally in semibreves and minims, which alternates with a $\mathbb{C}$ mensuration. The editor, however, treats the opening meter as a diminution, cutting the note values by half and obscuring the fundamentally triple meter by using a modern C signature and grouping the semibreves (now minims) in triplets. When the mensuration in Monteverdi's print shifts to $\mathbb{C}$, the original mensuration and note values are retained, obscuring the original notational relationship between the triple and duple meter and enforcing a proportional relationship between the two that Monteverdi may or may not have intended. In some madrigals, a shift from triple to duple meter at a cadence requires a proportional tempo relationship in order to effect the intended ritardando, but this is not the case in *Bevea Fillide mia*; yet the editor's notation leaves no choice regarding a proportional relationship between the two meters. Moreover, one cannot discern what Monteverdi's original notation was from the transcription and must refer to the facsimile to become aware of the discrepancy in the modern edition. This is most unfortunate, because it does not allow the reader to work with Monteverdi's own notation and determine the temporal relationships between triple and duple sections on that basis. Moreover, such a transcription obscures the function of mensuration signs as tempo indications in addition to their role as the organizing basis of the rhythm and meter. In contrast, the editor of *Il quinto libro* retains Monteverdi's original $\mathbb{C}\frac{3}{2}$ mensuration in the *sinfonia* of *Questi vaghi concenti* and bars the passage with three semibreves per tactus (*tripla*). The introduction to *Il quinto libro* takes the position that no proportional relationship is necessary or desirable between the *tripla* and the duple meter of the vocal sections, in opposition to the implicit requirement of a proportional relationship in the transcription of *Bevea Fillide mia* of *Il secondo libro*.[24]

In *Il terzo libro*, the one madrigal notated by Monteverdi in **₵**, *O dolce anima mia*, is transcribed in **C**, once again masking the tempo implication of the original *alla breve* mensuration sign. In *Il sesto libro* an unusual example of *tripla* in *Zefiro torna*, notated by Monteverdi in groups of three minims with a mensuration **C3**, alternates with the mensuration **C**. The **C3** is transcribed and barred as $\frac{3}{2}$, maintaining the original minim note values and groupings, but this mensuration and barring suggest *sesquialtera* between the triple- and duple-meter sections, so the editor is forced to contradict the *sesquialtera* and indicate the *tripla* proportional relationship by means of a note equivalency annotation above the staff.

Concerto settimo libro de madrigali is notated entirely in **C**[25] with the exception of four pieces containing short passages in triple meter: *Tempro la cetra*, *Dice la mia bellissima Licori*, *Non vedrò mai le stelle*, and *Perche fuggi* as well as the *ballo Tirsi e Clori*, which alternates between **C** and a triple meter notated by Monteverdi sometimes with ₵ $\frac{3}{2}$ and sometimes merely $\frac{3}{2}$. In the Cremona edition of *Tirsi e Clori*, reductions of groups of three semibreves by 4:1 to semiminim triplets under both $\frac{2}{2}$ and $\frac{3}{2}$ meters creates a complex and confusing visual image to the reader, even if the original mensuration sign is given above the staff. Moreover this notation results in what I believe to be an erroneous proportional relationship between triple-meter passages and their concluding cadences in **C**, wherein the cadence emerges twice too slow in relation to the triple time. It is not clear whether in this piece Monteverdi is accurately using old-fashioned, even outdated, meanings of mensuration signs, or they have lost their proportional significance with regard to note values and are simply indications of an even or uneven tactus. Ironically, the practical result of either interpretation is the same in this instance. The three aspects of Monteverdi's triple notation are the ₵, which originally indicated a 2:1 diminution; the $\frac{3}{2}$, which was a sign of *sesquialtera*; and groupings of three semibreves, which were the typical notation of *tripla* – a 3:1 proportional relationship. If the ₵ is taken as a sign of diminution, then the semibreves should be read as minims, and the *tripla* becomes *sesquialtera* as indicated by the $\frac{3}{2}$ meter. Understood as *sesquialtera*, the temporal relationship between notes in triple time and the cadences in duple time is three minims = two minims. This is exactly

---

[24] Wolfgang Osthoff had warned in 1962 against altering the note values in editions of Monteverdi as distorting the music: *Per la notazione originale nelle pubblicazioni di musiche antiche e specialmente nella nuova edizione Monteverdi*, in: *Acta musicologica* 34 (1962), pp. 101–27.

[25] *Con che soavità* is erroneously notated in **₵** in four of the five surviving editions.

the same result as considering triple and duple mensuration signs, whatever versions and at whatever note levels they may be notated, as simply signs for an uneven or even tactus, though at times possibly with faster or slower tempo implications. Under this interpretation, the groups of Monteverdi's three semibreves are beat with an uneven tactus, whereas the shift to **C** for the cadence means that the tactus, which is of an unchanging duration, now evenly subdivides the semibreve, resulting in the same *sesquialtera* note proportions as the older interpretation of the mensuration signs. I am inclined to believe, as I've argued elsewhere, that by this period, the mensuration symbols have largely lost their earlier proportional significance and are now thought of as indications of even and uneven tactus, which may or may not remain the same in its duration, depending on the musical circumstances.[26] Triple meter concluding with a duple-time cadence is one circumstance suggesting an unchanging tactus duration to obtain the appropriate retarding effect of the close. This emphasis on the tactus as the meaning and role of mensuration signs by the second decade of the century, and perhaps earlier among some composers, is to me the only reasonable explanation for the remarkable variety and inconsistency of mensural signs, especially triple-meter signs, in this period.[27]

It is just this confusion in relation to earlier mensural theory that should warn us that proportional note relationships are no longer the object of the notation, but simply indications of how to subdivide the tactus. In *Tirsi e Clori*, by whatever route we reach our conclusion, the notation of the Cremona edition emerges as erroneous in its tempo relationship.

That Monteverdi himself is sometimes inconsistent in his own metric notation of triple meters is suggested by the mensuration in *Tempro la cetra* where one of the instrumental interludes near the end of the piece is in **C**$\frac{3}{2}$. According to sixteenth-century theories of proportions, such a signature would ordinarily indicate *sesquialtera* with a notation in groups of three minims. Monteverdi's notation, however, as shown in the basso continuo part, is in groupings of three semibreves, typical of *tripla* proportion. The upper parts, however, move more quickly and are notated in blackened minims, three per

---

[26]   Jeffrey Kurtzman, *The Monteverdi Vespers of 1610: Music, Context, Performance* (Oxford: Oxford University Press, 1999), pp. 437–54.

[27]   Uwe Wolf, who has most thoroughly studied mensurations in this period, repeatedly finds inconsistency and confusion in the use of triple signatures and their relationship to duple time, even within a single print. See Wolf, *Notation und Aufführungspraxis: Studien zum Wandel von Notenschrift und Notenbild in italienischen Musikdrucken der Jahre 1571–1630*, 2 vols, Berlin and Kassel: Merseburger, 1992.

semibreve. The tempo relationship between this section and the preceding and following ones in duple meter is unproblematic, since the preceding section and the triple-meter section both come to full cadences and there is flexibility for any musically reasonable relationship. Nevertheless, a steady tactus, alternating between even and uneven, is feasible, resulting in a very lively tempo for the triple-meter passage.

Preserving Monteverdi's notation in this case is somewhat awkward in modern terms: maintaining the perfect semibreves in the bass would require notating the upper parts in triplets of minims. Converting the perfect semibreves to modern dotted semibreves would not require triplets in the upper parts, but would obscure the blackened notation. Both the Cremona and Malipiero editions choose to notate the bass in dotted minims and maintain the black notation in the upper parts, in essence, creating a 2:1 diminution of Monteverdi's notation. However, only the Cremona edition indicates that the upper parts are actually blackened minims by means of the standard open brackets. Malipiero's edition makes them appear as semiminims.

The Cremona edition, while indicating the original mensuration above the staff, bars this passage in $\frac{6}{4}$. As a consequence, the regularly occurring cadences all fall in the middle of the bar. For an edition whose premise is that modern barring often implies accents in the wrong place, this is a peculiar choice. Malipiero's barring in $\frac{3}{2}$ brings some of the cadences at the beginning of a bar, but suggests shifts of accent that belie the regularity of the phrase structure. The barring problem results from Monteverdi's phrases being in regular units of four semibreves. The $\frac{6}{4}$ barring of the Cremona edition preserves the regularity of the phrase structure, but displaces the cadences. What would be required to locate them in the proper position in relation to the barring is to begin the passage with a half bar, resulting in all the cadences falling on a "downbeat."

Dice la bellissima Licori, *Non vedrò mai le stelle*, and *Perche fuggi* each have brief passages in triple meter indicated, as in *Tirsi e Clori*, by ₵ $\frac{3}{2}$ with note groupings in units of three semibreves. The Cremona edition reduces both continuo and voices by a 4:1 ratio and employs a $\frac{2}{2}$ meter for these passages with the semiminims of the voices in triplets. The triple meter of *Dice la bellissima* begins by completing a cadence but closes with a retarding cadence in C, suggesting a proportional relationship between the two meters. Moreover, the triple-meter sections repeat the text of the preceding duple-meter passages and convert their principal melodic motive from duple to triple time. If a proportion is maintained, the Cremona edition's transcription generates twice the speed for the triple meter in relation to the surrounding duple time than a simple change from a steady even-to-uneven tactus would. For the performer, however, freedom and flexibility of tempo do not necessarily require a proportional relationship even in this passage.

In *Non vedrò*, the triple-meter section both begins and ends with a cadence, so that no inherent proportional relationship is implied between it and the surrounding duple-meter passages. In *Perche fuggi* the triple-meter passages are preceded by a cadence, but themselves continue uninterruptedly into duple meter, suggesting a proportional relationship between the two, though even more than *Dice la mia bellissima*, the tempo throughout this piece can vary substantially according to the contrasting affects of the text. A proportional relationship can be created, as suggested above, by a largely unchanging tactus duration from triple meter to duple. The Cremona edition's reduction of the triple meter, however, results in the duple meter being twice as slow in relation to the triple as a steady tactus would. The matter is further confused by the duple meter being notated at first in two bars of $\frac{3}{2}$, in order to make the first syllable of the word *morto* fall at the beginning of the bar.

The insertion of $\frac{3}{2}$ bars in a duple-meter context is common throughout the Cremona *Concerto* edition in order to accommodate bar lines to word and musical phrase accents. In addition, even pieces in **C** with an even metrical accent throughout are notated superfluously with a modern $\frac{2}{2}$ meter signature. The editor is always careful to indicate the original mensuration sign above the staff, but the insertion of $\frac{3}{2}$ bars is often distracting and unhelpful. For example, in *A quest'olmo*, at the text *acque amiche sponde il mio passato ben quasi presente Amor . . .*, the editor has mixed several $\frac{3}{2}$ bars among the underlying $\frac{2}{2}$ because of harmonic and melodic syncopations or in order to make accented syllables fall at the beginning of a bar. But the $\frac{3}{2}$ barring tends to obscure the syncopations as well as the cross-accents Monteverdi typically creates between accented melodic notes and text syllables on the one hand and the underlying duple meter on the other. It is just such cross accents that give Monteverdi's music much of its lively rhythmic character. The shifting meters created by the editor result near the end of the madrigal in the succession $\frac{3}{2}$, $\frac{2}{2}$, $\frac{3}{2}$, $\frac{4}{2}$, $\frac{2}{2}$, $\frac{3}{2}$, $\frac{2}{2}$, $\frac{3}{2}$, $\frac{2}{2}$ in the space of only 12 bars. Such a visually bewildering sequence assumes that performers are so rigid and uncomprehending in their accentuation of the bar lines in **C** that they can't possibly perceive Monteverdi's cross accents without the metrical reorganization of the editor. Malipiero's evenly barred **C** is far easier to negotiate, especially since the texture is entirely homophonic, with the word accents occurring in the same metric position in all voices. Fortunately, *A quest'olmo* is the worst example, and most others are limited in the quantity and proximity of their changes – distracting and perhaps annoying, but at least not confounding the reader.

However, it is in the *Madrigali guerrieri et amorosi* and the *Madrigali e Canzonette* of 1638 and 1651 respectively, that the decision to alter Monteverdi's mensuration signatures, whether to indicate phrasing or triple time, has the most confusing, sometimes bizarre results. In the *Madrigali guerrieri*, but not in the *Madrigali e Canzonette*, Monteverdi's original mensurations are printed over the first appearance of the editor's meter signature, at least giving the reader a reference point to the original print. However, triple meters are again rendered as duple-time triplets in the transcription, with note values reduced, distorting Monteverdi's original notation. In duple time, barring is according to what the editor views as the natural melodic groupings of notes, which, however, results in irregular measures, juxtaposing such oddities as $\frac{2}{2}$ and $\frac{4}{2}$, with and without triplets, and **C** followed by triplets representing $\mathbf{C}\frac{6}{4}$. In *Hor che'l ciel e la terra*, the editor attempts to notate the prosodic accentuation by shifting back and forth between $\frac{2}{2}$ and $\frac{3}{2}$ bars in passages where Monteverdi simply notates **C**, suggesting triple meter where Monteverdi subsumes everything under duple meter. In another passage the editor shifts from **C** to $\frac{3}{4}$ to $\frac{2}{2}$ to $\frac{5}{4}$ to $\frac{2}{2}$ in the space of 7 measures. Similar notational anomalies occur in one madrigal after another, misrepresenting in the modern transcription the original metric notation and often engendering more confusion than clarity. In piece after piece, the reader is hard-pressed to discern what Monteverdi's original notation must have been, and must consult the facsimile to know. Modern performers are more familiar with 17th-century notational practices than a generation ago, and would have been better served by Monteverdi's original notation, while the scholar is not served at all by the transcription.[28]

The metric and rhythmic notation is even more anomalous and confusing in the *Madrigali e Canzonette*. The introduction discusses extensively the variety of Monteverdi's metric signatures as well as the natural prosody of texts and music that contradict Monteverdi's mensuration signs; it is this prosody that is the justification for altering the changing mensurations, and employing triplets and even duplets. But the results are problematic; in *Si si ch'io v'amo*, a $\frac{6}{4}$ meter is followed by $\frac{9}{4}$ with duplets, while another madrigal notates duplets in $\frac{2}{2}$ meter, which is particularly baffling. The editor also employs $\frac{3}{2}$ for both duple meter and *sesquialtera* in contradiction to Monteverdi's use

---

[28]   In the introduction to *Il primo libro de madrigali*, p. 20, Monterosso himself had criticized the continual alternation of polymeters employed by Hugo Leichtentritt in his undated Leipzig edition of *12 fünfstimmige Madrigale von Claudio Monteverdi* as "in practice more cumbersome than useful" ("all'atto pratico, più ingombrante che utile").

of $\frac{3}{2}$ as *sesquialtera* or *tripla* only. Since the editor of this volume doesn't give the original mensuration signs in the score, the result is further confused. The notation of some pieces is a forest of triplets and triplet group marks; in *Bel pastor*, because the triplet groups are at different rhythmic levels, the relationship between notes is practically indecipherable. *Quando dentro al tuo seno* begins in $\frac{6}{8}$ and then proceeds with $\frac{4}{4}$, $\frac{5}{4}$, $\frac{3}{4}$, $\frac{5}{4}$, and $\frac{4}{4}$, but the editor at least publishes a second version entirely in duple time ($\frac{2}{2}$). Since the editor's intent is to map out metrically and rhythmically the scansion of the text, the editor becomes the interpreter of the musical text, changing it to suit the editor's understanding of the poetry and its prosodic relationship to the music, arguing that "it is precisely every editor's responsibility consciously to attempt to reconstruct … the most authentic meaning of the music of the past."[29] One cannot disagree with this principle, but the user is forced to rely on the editor's judgment regarding scansion, and the modern notation doesn't make it possible to decipher easily what Monteverdi's original notation was (nor sometimes, to decipher the modern notation itself). Yet in some instances, delineated in the introduction, the editor does avoid such interference. Ultimately, the attempt to render Monteverdi's complex text scansion and metric variety through the editor's own meter signatures and barring flounders in a sea of mind-boggling notational complexity. As with the *Madrigali guerrieri et amorosi*, the user of the edition would again have been better served by maintaining Monteverdi's original mensurations and note values, possibly with editorial note equivalencies indicated above the staff, and with explanations of temporal relationships and a discussion of particular points of scansion in the introduction. The notational complexity of this volume is enough to drive the reader back to the Malipiero edition where Monteverdi's original notation is mostly clear. Similar issues are encountered in the two volumes of *Scherzi musicali* (1607 and 1632), whose editor similarly alters Monteverdi's metric notation to indicate the prosody of the text and flexibility of musical phrases. However, as in some of the other volumes, there is no indication in the score of Monteverdi's original mensurations.

The same criteria, procedures and problems seen in the nine books of madrigals and *Scherzi musicali* are also evident in the four volumes of sacred music published to date. The organ part for the *Missa In illo tempore* and the *Vespro della Beata Vergine* of 1610 is in places unaccountably in a small type font, making it unclear what is in Monteverdi's Bassus Generalis part-book

---

[29]   *Madrigali Libro Nono*, p. 25: "…. è compito preciso di ogni editore consapevole tentare di ricostruire … il significato più autentico delle musiche del passato."

and what is editorial. Monteverdi's Bassus Generalis includes upper parts for several compositions as well as a short score for a number of passages. Since these upper parts sometimes differ, especially rhythmically, from the vocal part-books, it would have been useful to include them in the transcription of the Bassus Generalis so that the user could choose the more desirable reading. The editor makes such choices himself, sometimes using the upper parts from the Bassus Generalis as better readings than the comparable passages in the vocal part-books, but this can only be determined by consulting the critical notes or comparing the score with the facsimile rather than from the transcription itself. In the *Sonata sopra Sancta Maria*, it is this writer's view that the editor has misinterpreted Monteverdi's black notation. Once again, high clefs are ignored as signs of transposition, despite the evidence of a manuscript partitura of the Mass with all parts transposed down a fourth and Padre Giambattista Martini's example of the first *Agnus Dei* of the Mass transposed down a fourth in his counterpoint treatise of 1776.[30]

The introduction to the *Selva morale et spirituale* (whose facsimile is missing its cover title) is especially problematic in its historical account of the music of the print. Unfortunately, too much of it is simply the fantasy of the editor, Denis Stevens, and has little or no evidentiary basis at all. A number of useful passages from Monteverdi's letters and other documents regarding performance issues are quoted in the introduction, but the significance of high clefs is once again denied. All rubrics in the part-books are included in the transcription and the missing Altus I and Bassus I parts in the *Magnificat a 8* are restored. On the other hand, the editor omits in this piece a rubric in the basso continuo calling for two violins at bar 213 and doesn't supply missing parts; nor is any note made of this rubric in the Critical Commentary. For the first time in the Cremona series, the editor adds slurs in the transcription, which are clearly missing from the original print.

The introduction to the *Messa a quattro voci et Salmi* of 1651 does acknowledge numerous authorities and treatises dealing with transposition of high clefs. However, the editor doesn't distinguish between transposition for vocal convenience and transposition because of high clefs, and he ultimately concludes lamely and unconvincingly that Monteverdi's high clefs may simply have been a bow to tradition in the notation of the *stile antico*. Because the copy of this print in the University Library in Wroclaw, Poland, has a significant number of hand-written accidentals added to the parts, the editor includes

---

[30] Giambattista Martini, *Esemplare o sia Saggio fondamentale pratico di contrappunto fugato* … *parte seconda* (Bologna: Lelio della Volpe, 1776), pp. 242–50. The transcription is notated in the natural clefs with a one-sharp key signature.

these in his edition above the affected notes in angled brackets (< >). Also for the first time, the introduction includes a bibliography of modern editions of the music of this print.

A bibliography of modern editions, facsimiles and secondary sources is also included in one of the most recent volumes of the Cremona edition, comprising a series of sacred compositions found in manuscript or originally published in anthologies and not already appearing in one of the other sacred music volumes. Each piece is preceded by its facsimile, which is much more convenient than having all the facsimiles printed at the end of the introduction according to the model of the other volumes. Because the sources are so diverse, the process of transcription is more complicated. Once again, triple meters are rendered in reduced note values, sometimes by 2:1, other times by 4:1, with new meters (original mensurations are printed above the staff), while duple time is transcribed in *integer valor*. This approach is applied both within individual pieces, as well as to successive pieces from the same source. Most of these pieces are not so complicated metrically as to be seriously problematic in their transcriptions with note reductions and modern meter signatures, but sometimes, as in *Venite et videte*, the reduction of triple meters and the note equivalency given by the editor results in a duple meter tempo twice too slow for the preceding triple meter. Once again, both the scholar and the performer would have been better served by preserving Monteverdi's original notation.

Since this volume appeared, two settings of the Marian antiphon *Salve Regina* and one of *Regina caeli laetare* have been newly attributed to Monteverdi in a print missing its title pages and with no indication of date, but likely by Alessandro Vincenti from between 1662 and 1667. The print consists only of three *Salve Regina*s and the *Regina caeli*, but the first *Salve Regina* is clearly identified as Monteverdi's and is a reprint of the version first published in an anthology by Lorenzo Calvi in 1629[31] and later reissued in the *Selva morale et spirituali*. It is probable that in the (Vincenti?) print of the 1660s the following two settings of the antiphon as well as *Regina caeli*, though not directly attributed to Monteverdi, are also by him. All four antiphons have recently been published in both a critical edition and complete facsimile of the part-books.[32]

---

[31] *Quarta racolta de sacri canti a una, due, tre, et quattro voci …. fatta da don Lorenzo Calvi* (Venice: Alessandro Vincenti, 1629). RISM B/I: 1629⁵.

[32] Luigi Collarile, ed., *Salve Regine del Sig. Claudio Monteverde* (Bologna: Arnaldo Forni Editore, 2011).

The Cremona edition of Monteverdi's complete works is a vast improvement over Malipiero's edition in every respect except for its metric and rhythmic notation and its failure to consider the meaning of high clefs in terms of actual sounding pitch. The editorial policy of altering Monteverdi's mensurations and note values in an effort to notate Monteverdi's prosody, phrasing and metric relationships results in confusion regarding the notation of triple meter and its relationship to duple meter, which is sometimes erroneous in its representation. Modern notational schemes can be at least as problematic when applied to this music as Monteverdi's original notation was, though in different ways, and the attempt to improve on Monteverdi's notation fails in too many respects, including simple readability. Even though a complete facsimile is published in each volume to facilitate comparison with the original source(s), the process is too cumbersome to be very useful, especially when the facsimile presents each part-book in succession rather than assembling the parts for a single piece on the same page or facing pages. The Malipiero edition is superior to the Cremona edition in usually representing accurately Monteverdi's notation in its transcriptions. Modern scholars and performers are much more adept at understanding that notation than even a generation ago, and Malipiero's edition is not only a factor in their gaining that comprehension, it continues to be preferred to the Cremona edition by many early music performers because of its easier readability. The complexities of Monteverdi's prosody, phrasing and metric relationships are better handled through discussion and examples in the introduction to an edition rather than by altering the original notation so radically as the Cremona edition has done.[33]

These two editions represent two stages of historical musicology in Italy, less than fifty years apart, but separated by the Second World War. Malipiero's edition, while following in the footsteps of earlier Italian scholars, reflects the desire of many composers of his generation to break away from the dominance of 19th-century Italian opera in the musical life of the nation as well as Italian nationalism in its effort to escape foreign, especially Germanic, influence. Malipiero, unique among his compatriots, undertook to present Monteverdi's music in its original notation and form, but still felt it necessary to instruct performers on how that music should be performed on the basis of his own musical intuition. In the editorial process, Malipiero felt himself to

---

[33] The only published review of a volume of the Cremona edition known to me and to the Fondazione Claudio Monteverdi is Jeffrey G. Kurtzman, *Review of: Claudio Monteverdi: Madrigali à 5 voci, Libro Primo, edited by Raffaello Monterosso; and Claudio Monteverdi: Il Primo Libro di Madrigali a Cinque Voci, edited by Bernard Bailly de Surcy*, in: *Journal of the American Musicological Society* 27 (1974), pp. 343–8.

have an instinctive connection with Monteverdi which took precedence over historical knowledge and scientific methodology, which he disdained.

The Cremona edition emerged from quite different considerations. The post-war Scuola di Paleografia e Filologia Musicale of the University of Pavia is an institute based on modern musicological method, and the Cremona edition, published under the auspices of the attached Fondazione Claudio Monteverdi, is an effort to bring all the resources of musicological methodology to bear on the works of Monteverdi in conscious reaction to the problems and failings of the Malipiero edition. Again spearheaded by a single individual, Raffaello Monterosso, the demands of the project have required the services of many different editors who, while adhering to the general editorial principles first laid out by Monterosso, are not always consistent in their detailed application. But this edition has not itself solved all of the difficulties of translating Monteverdi's notation into a modern score. The flexibility of meter, tempo, phrasing, and rhythmic organization of Monteverdi's music, often not immediately discernible in Monteverdi's own notation, is not well served by the Cremona edition's methods, either. The latter appear more pedantic and confusing than helpful, whether to scholars or performers. Both the Malipiero and Cremona editions illustrate the fact that notation is not the piece itself, but only an approximation, insufficient and faulty in many respects, of the music as conceived and intended for performance. The purpose of a modern critical edition should be to clarify that notation as much as possible, while not distorting the original form, and to provide as much information as possible for the understanding of that notation and what it both represents and doesn't represent for the benefit of both performing musicians and scholars.

Claudio Monteverdi Editions

Malipiero and Fondazione Claudio Monteverdi Editions
Gian Francesco Malipiero, Tutte le opere di Claudio Monteverdi

Vols 1-2 cite Asola, Vols 3–16 "Nel Vittoriale degli Italiani," the villa of Gabriele D'Annunzio in Gardone Riviera, as the places of publication on their title pages. Vols 1–14 were printed in Bologna by Enrico Venturi, indicated on the penultimate page of each volume. The original, faulty and poorly produced editions of Vols 15 and 16 were printed in 1941 and 1942 during World War II (the original plates werre lost during the war). Denis Arnold's 1968 revised editions of these two volumes vastly improved the musical text.

In 1967, Universal Edition in Vienna reprinted Vols 1–14 and the subsequent Vols 15 and 16 in Arnold's edition. Vol. 17 was published by Malipiero in a private edition in 1966 and republished by Universal in 1968.

Vol. 1: *Il primo libro de madrigali* (Asolo, 1926)

Vol. 2: *Il secondo libro de madrigali* (Asolo, 1927)

Vol. 3: *Il terzo libro de madrigali* (Nel Vittoriale degli Italiani, 1927)

Vol. 4: *Il quarto libro de madrigali* (Nel Vittoriale degli Italiani, 1927)

Vol. 5: *Il quinto libro de madrigali* (Nel Vittoriale degli Italiani, 1927)

Vol. 6: *Il sesto libro de madrigali* (Nel Vittoriale degli Italiani, 1927)

Vol. 7: *Concerto. Settimo libro de madrigali* (Nel Vittoriale degli Italiani, 1928)

Vol. 8: *Madrigali guerrieri et amorosi. Ottavo Libro* (Nel Vittoriale degli Italiani, 1929)

Vol. 9: *Madrigali e Canzonette a due e tre voci. Nono Libro* (Nel Vittoriale degli Italiani, 1929)

Vol. 10: *Canzonette a tre voci, Scherzi Musicali a tre voci, Scherzi Musicali cioè Arie & Madrigali a 1 & 2 voci* (Nel Vittoriale degli Italiani, 1929)

Vol. 11: *Orfeo, Lamento d'Arianna, Musiche de Alcuni* (Nel Vittoriale degli Italiani, 1930)

Vol. 12: *Il Ritorno d'Ulisse in Patria* (Nel Vittoriale degli Italiani, 1930)

Vol. 13: *L'Incoronazione di Poppea* (Nel Vittoriale degli Italiani, 1931)

Vol. 14: *Sacrae Cantiunculae tribus vocibus, Sanctissimae Virgini Missa senis vocibus, Vespro della beata Vergine* (Nel Vittoriale degli Italiani, 1932)

Vol. 15: *Selva Morale e Spirituale* (Nel Vittoriale degli Italiani,1941; rev. ed. by Denis Arnold, Vienna: Universal Edition, 1968)

Vol. 16: *Messa a quattro voci et Salmi a 1.2.3.4.5.6.7. & 8 voci concertati, e Parte da Cappella & con le Letanie della B.V., Frammenti pubblicati in varie raccolte* (Nel Vittoriale degli Italiani,1942; rev. ed. by Denis Arnold, Vienna: Universal Edition, 1968)

Vol. 17, *Supplemento: Secular and sacred pieces from various anthologies, Villanella a 3 voci, Basso of Madrigali spirituali a 4 voci facsimile* (Venice: Fondazione Giorgio Cini, 1966 [private edition]; Vienna: Universal Edition, 1968)

Fondazione Claudio Monteverdi (Cremona)

Vol. 1: *Il Primo Libro dei Madrigali*, ed. Raffaello Monterosso (1970)

Vol. 2: *Il Secondo Libro dei Madrigali*, ed. Anna Maria Monterosso (1979)

Vol. 3: *Il Terzo Libro dei Madrigali*, ed. Maria Teresa Rosa Barezzani (1988)

XII

INDEX TO MONTEVERDI'S WORKS

INDEX OF NAMES AND PERSONAGES

INDEX OF SUBJECTS AND SOURCES